Hong Kong
Through the Looking Glass

Hae Won Shin

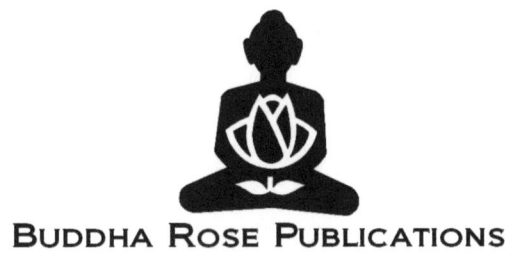

Buddha Rose Publications

Hong Kong Through the Looking Glass
Copyright © 2019 by Hae Won Shin
All Rights Reserved.

No part of this book may be reproduced in any manner without the expressed permission of the author or the publishing company.

First Edition 2019

ISBN 10: 1-949251-12-8
ISBN 13: 978-1-949251-12-8

10 9 8 7 6 5 4 3 2 1
Printed in the United States of America

HONG KONG
THROUGH THE LOOKING GLASS

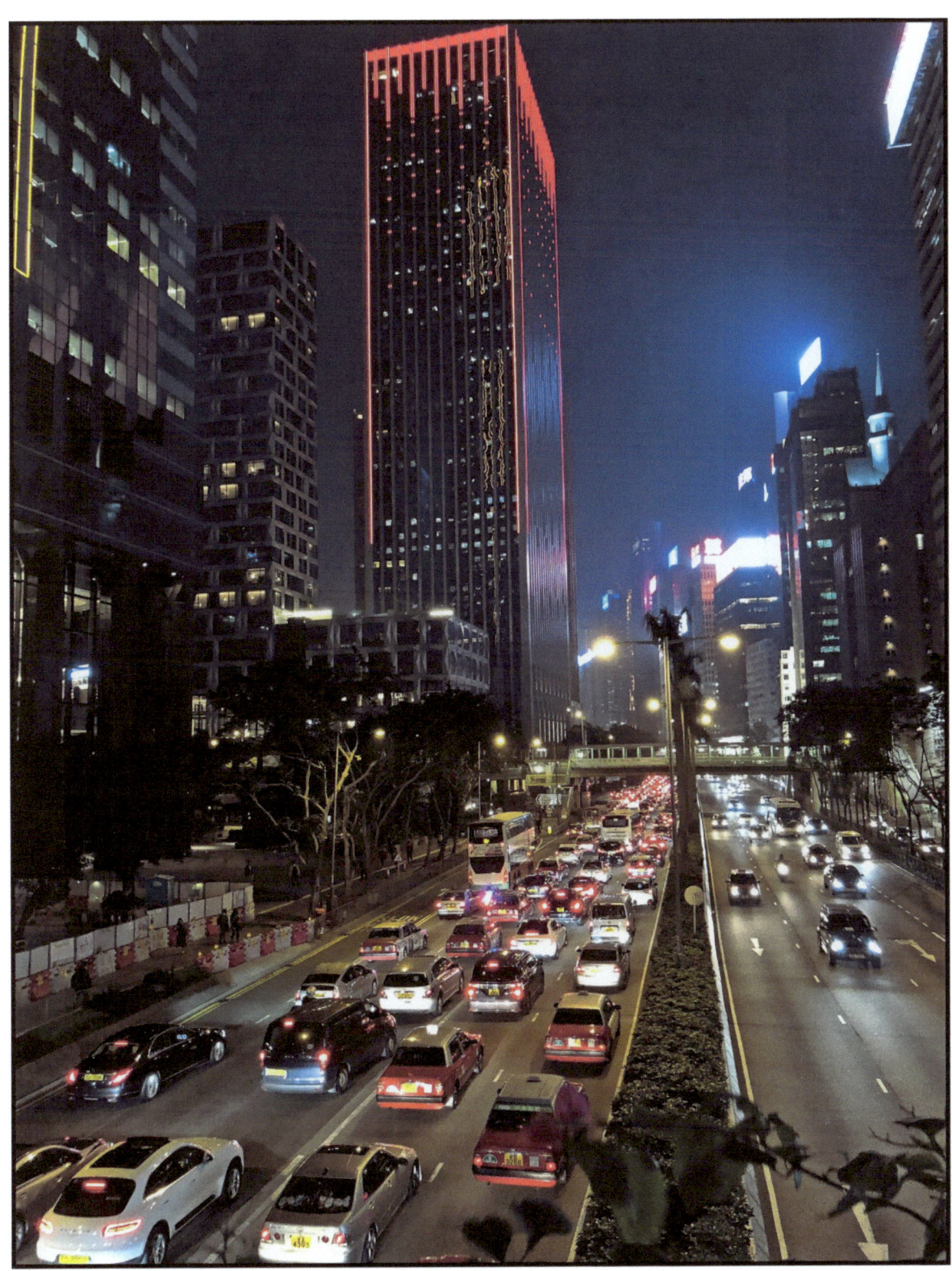

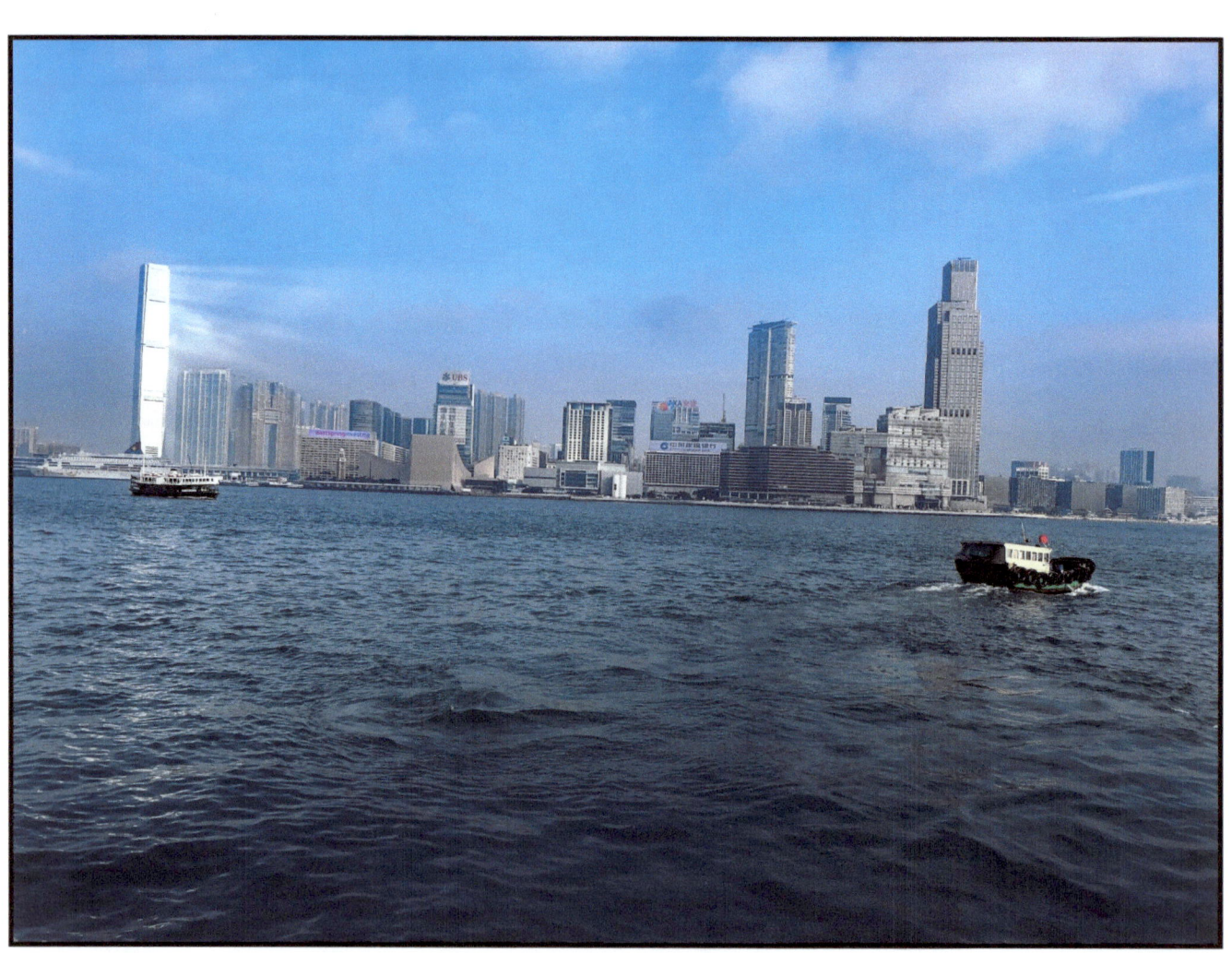

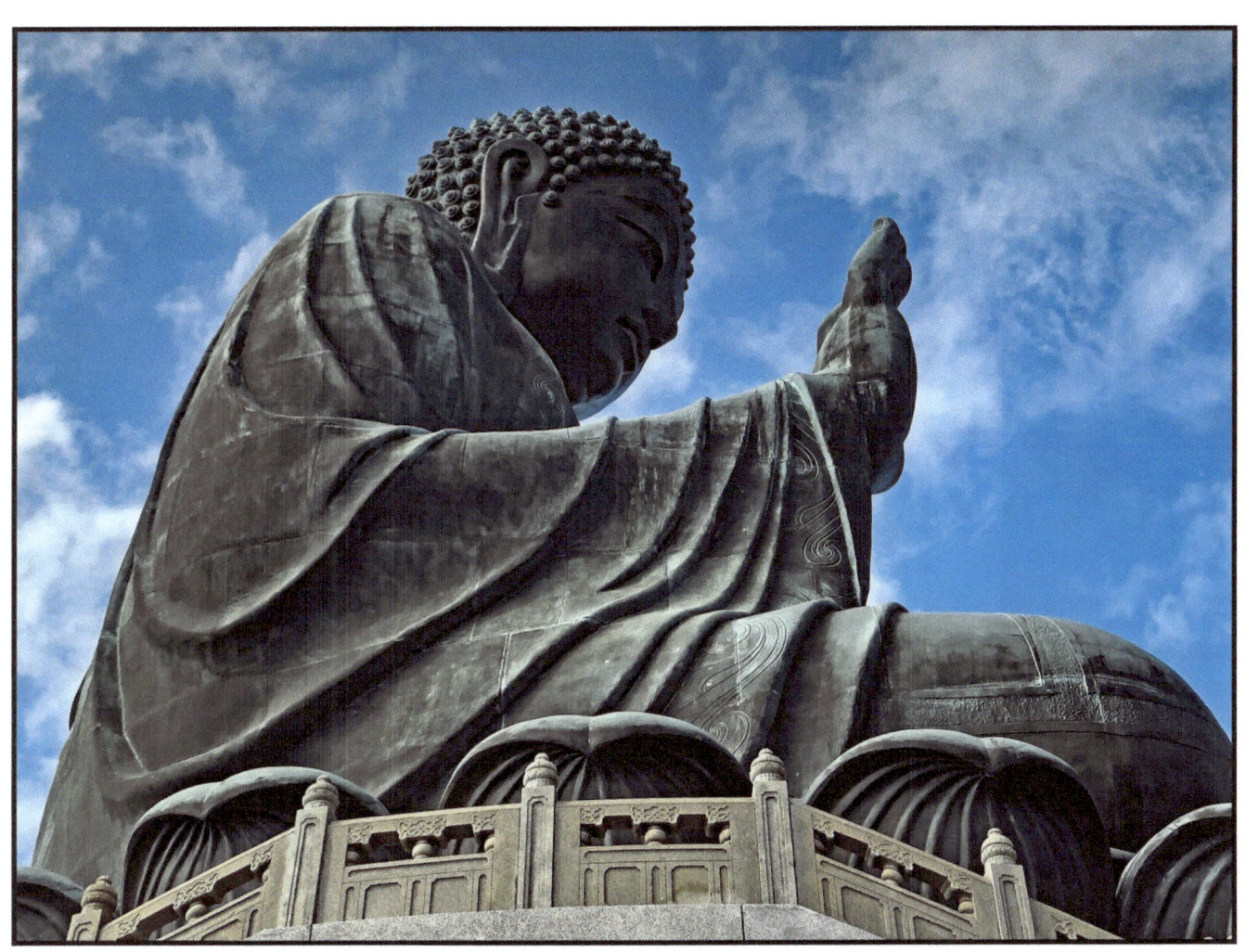

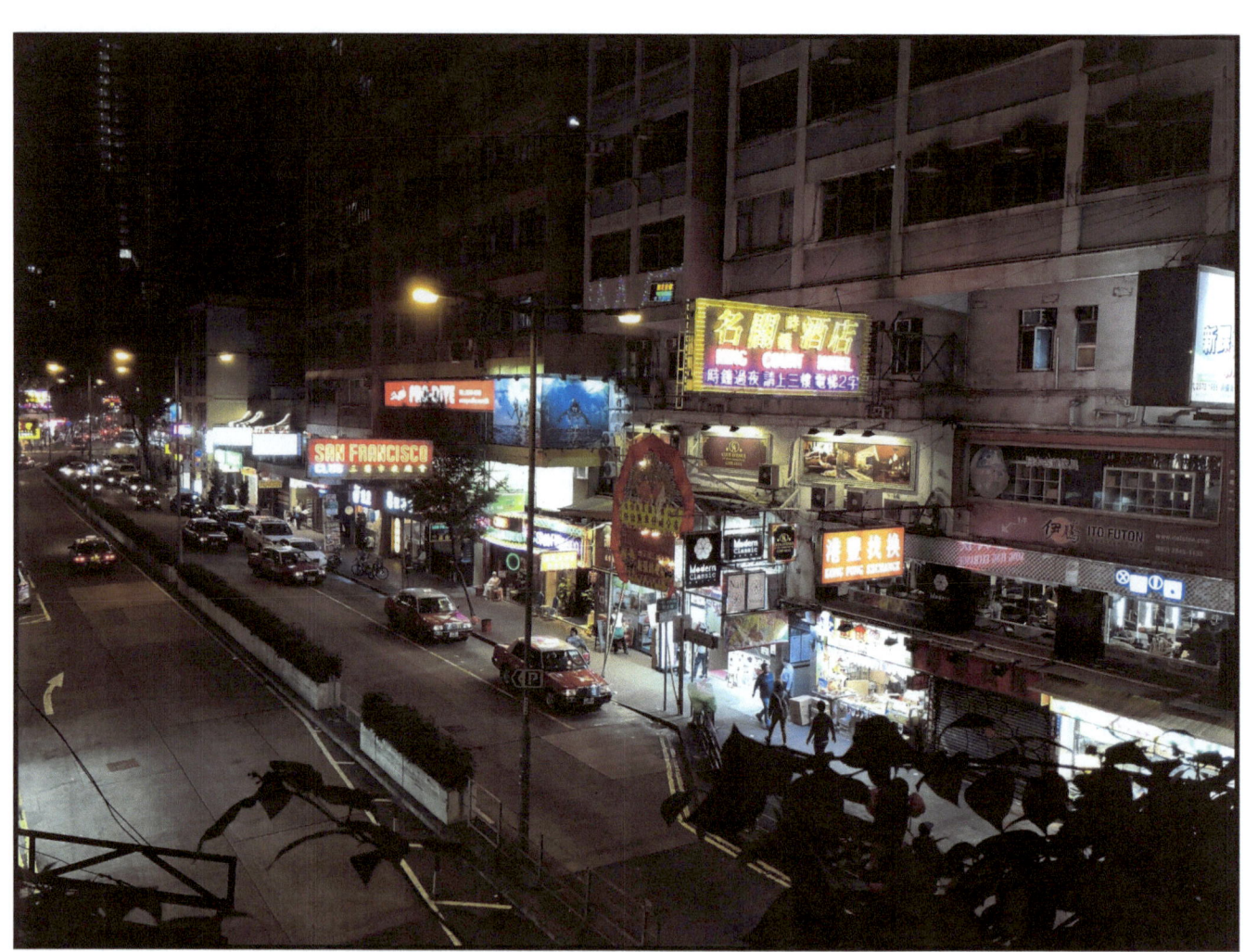

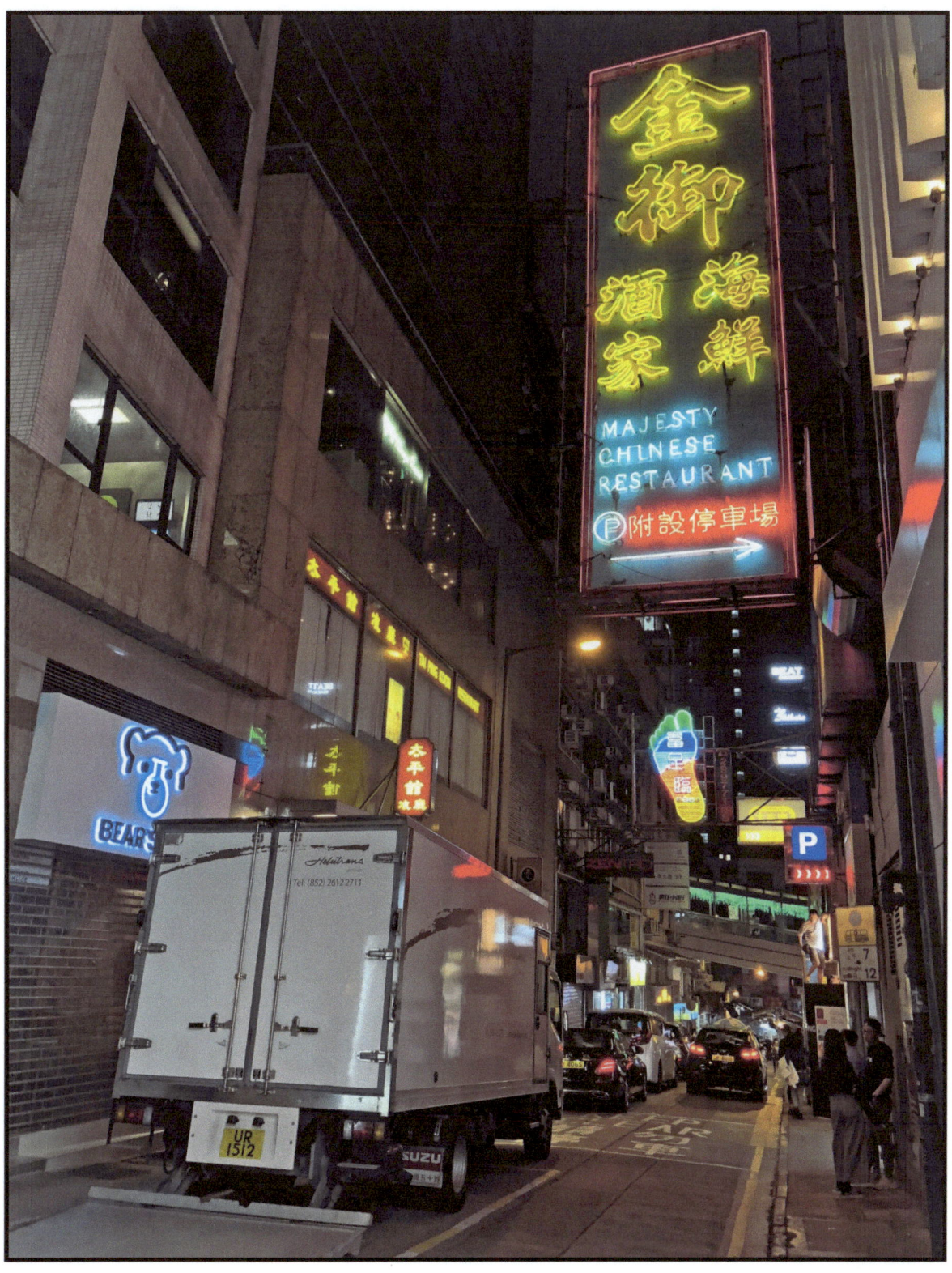

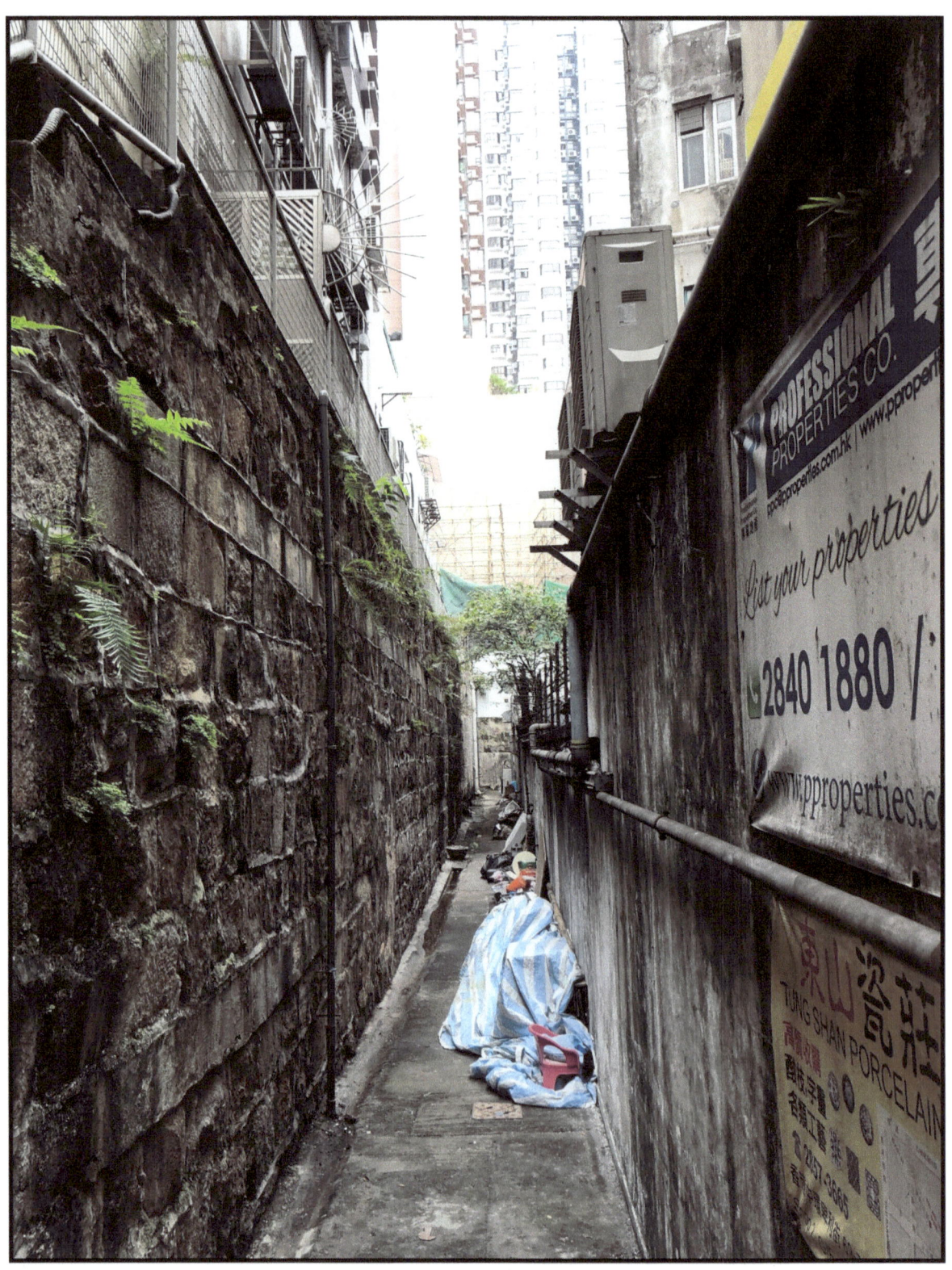

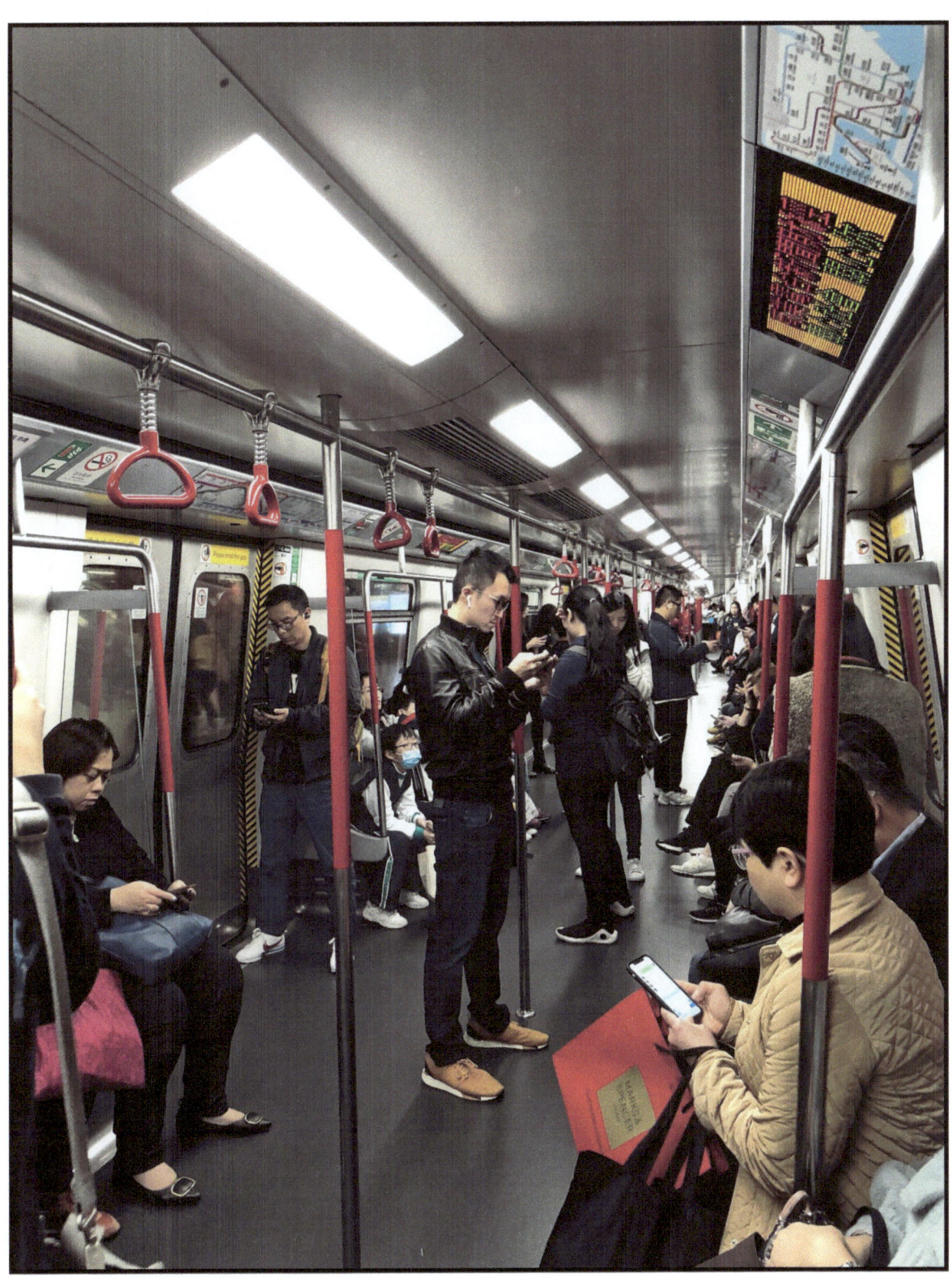

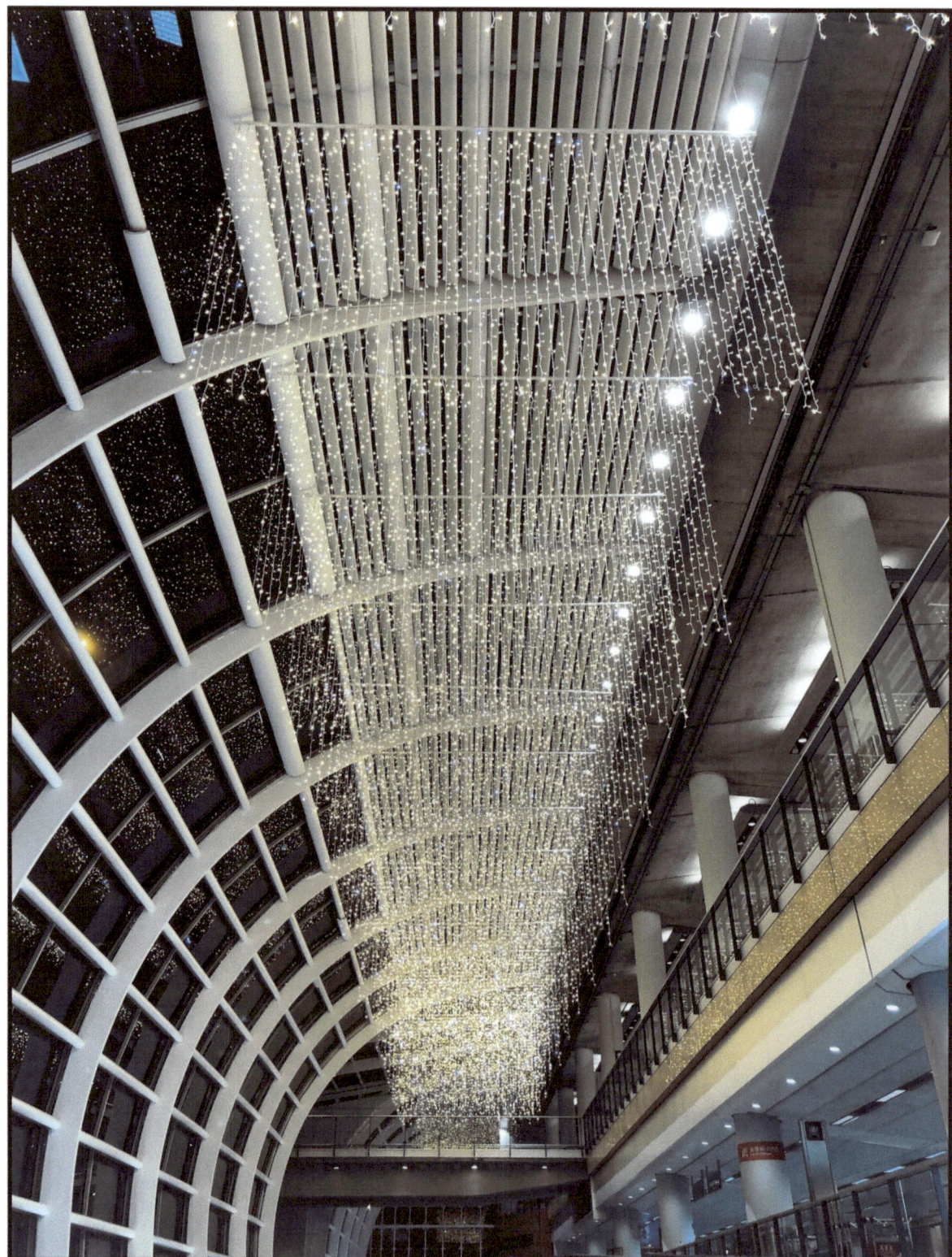

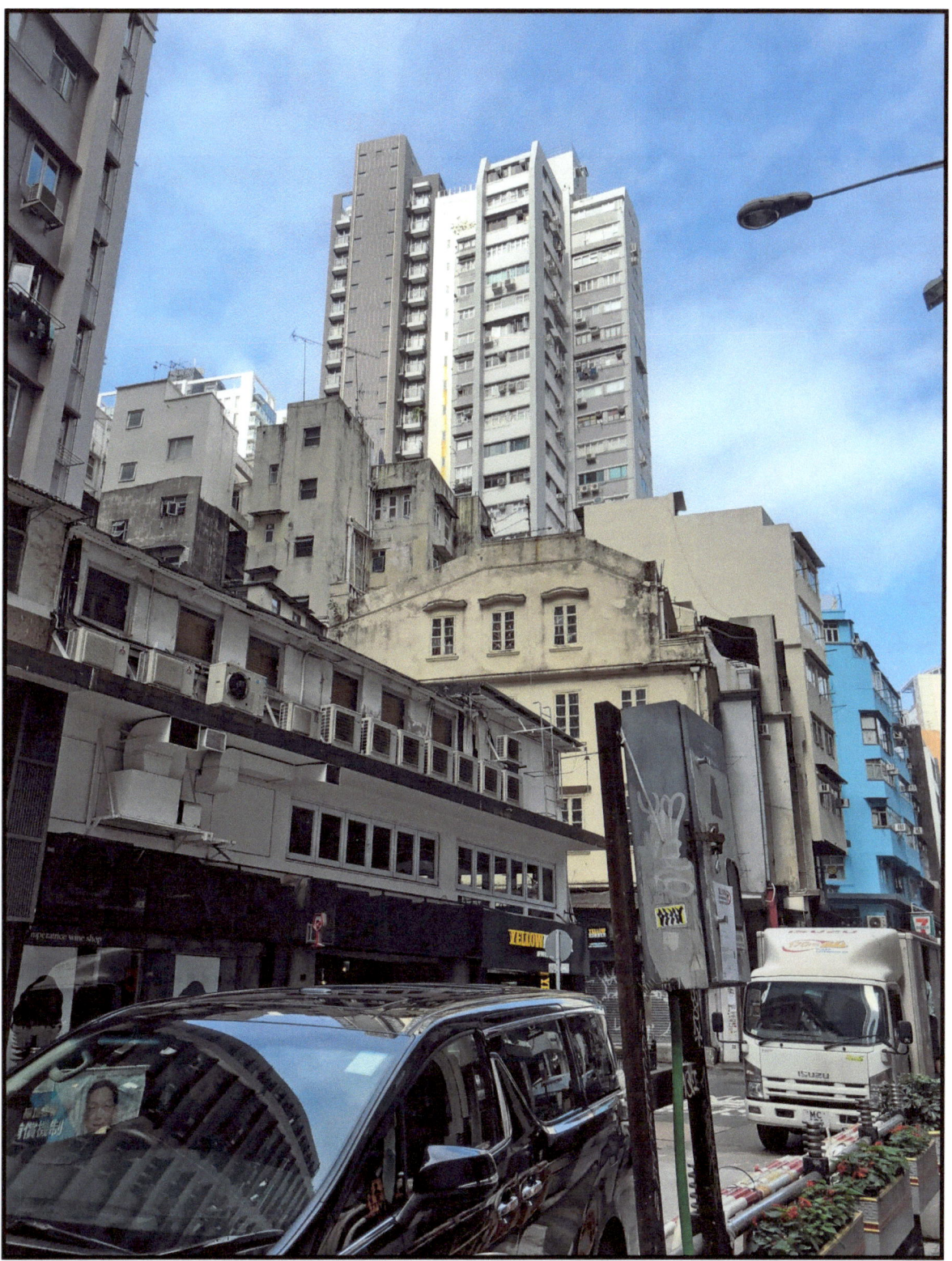

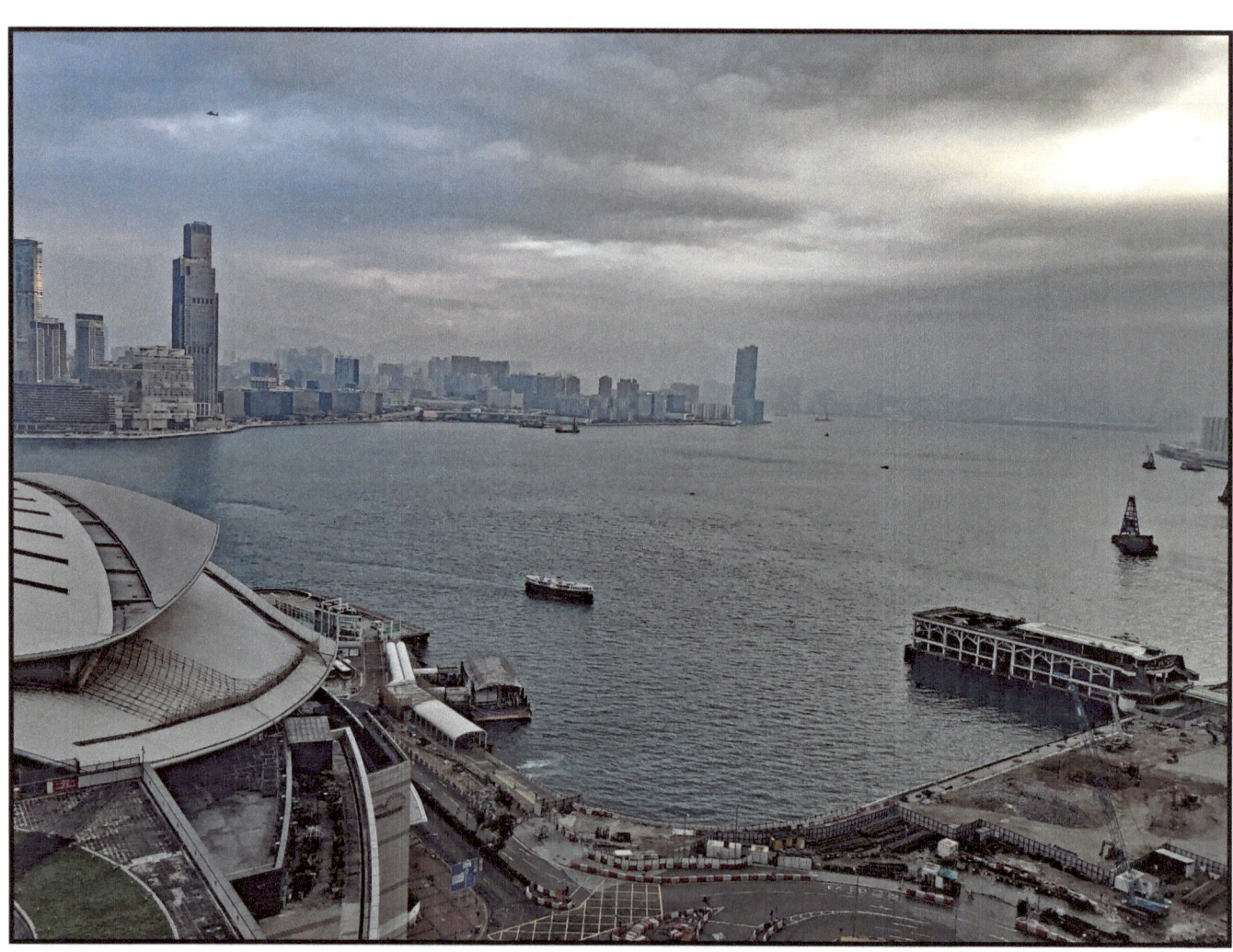

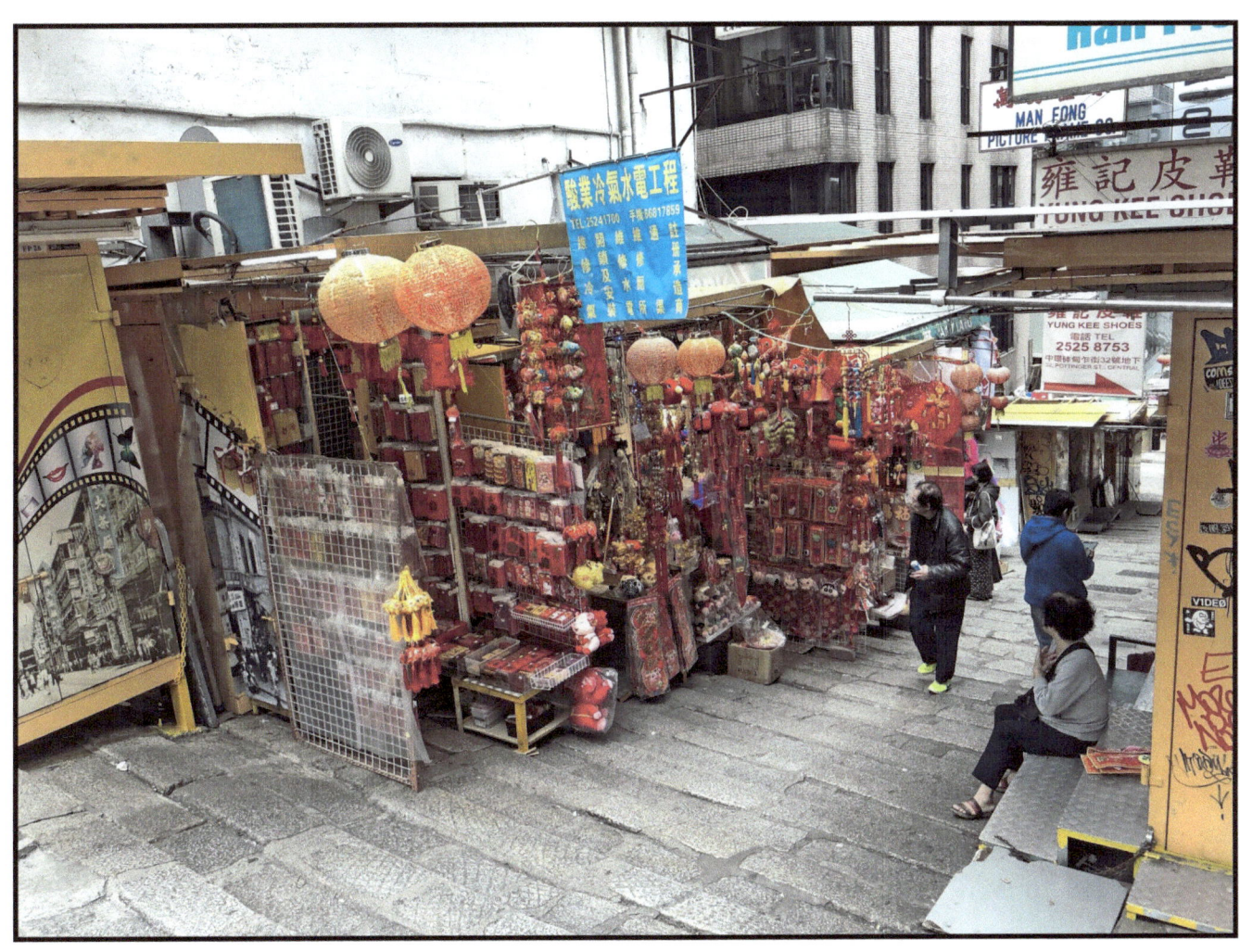

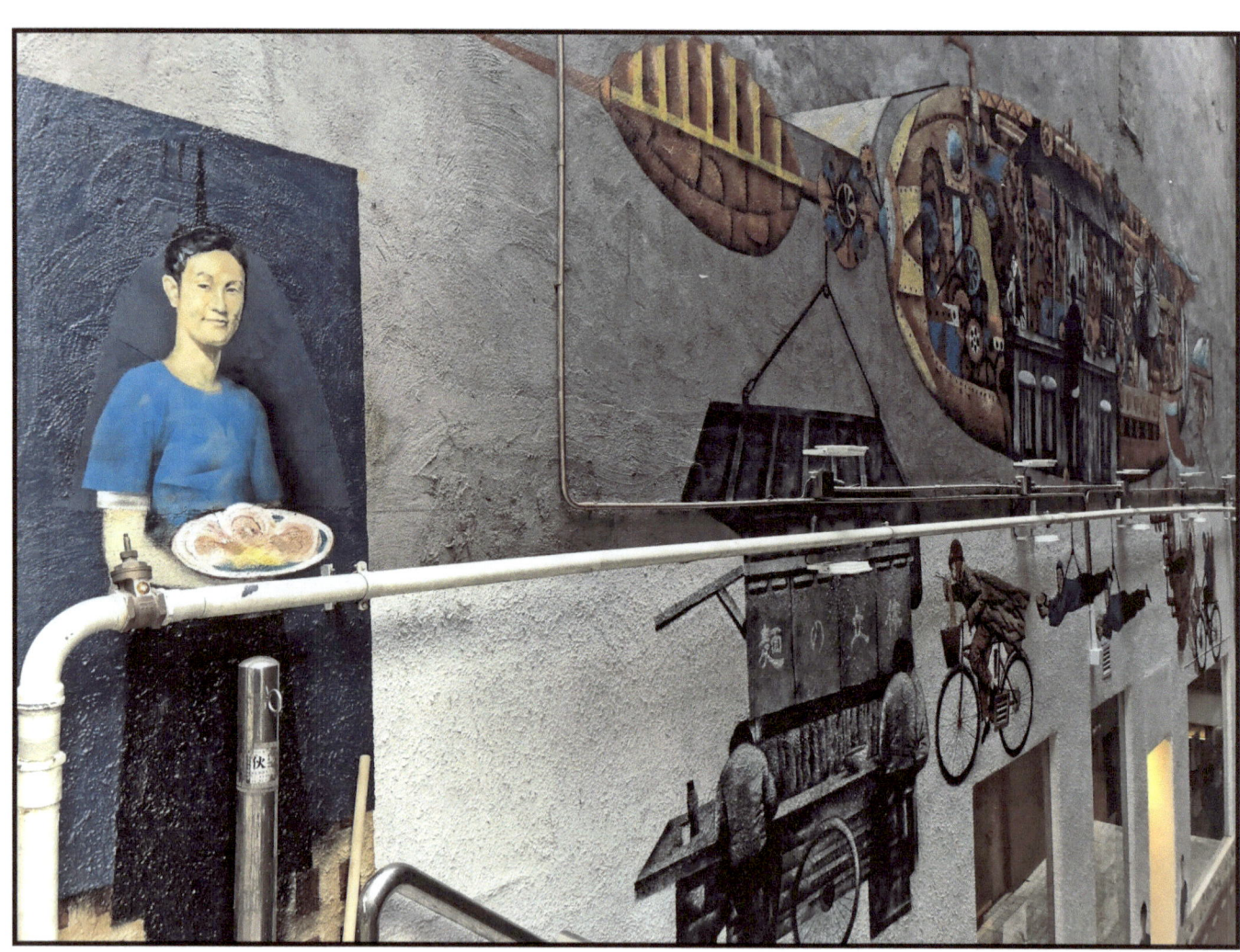

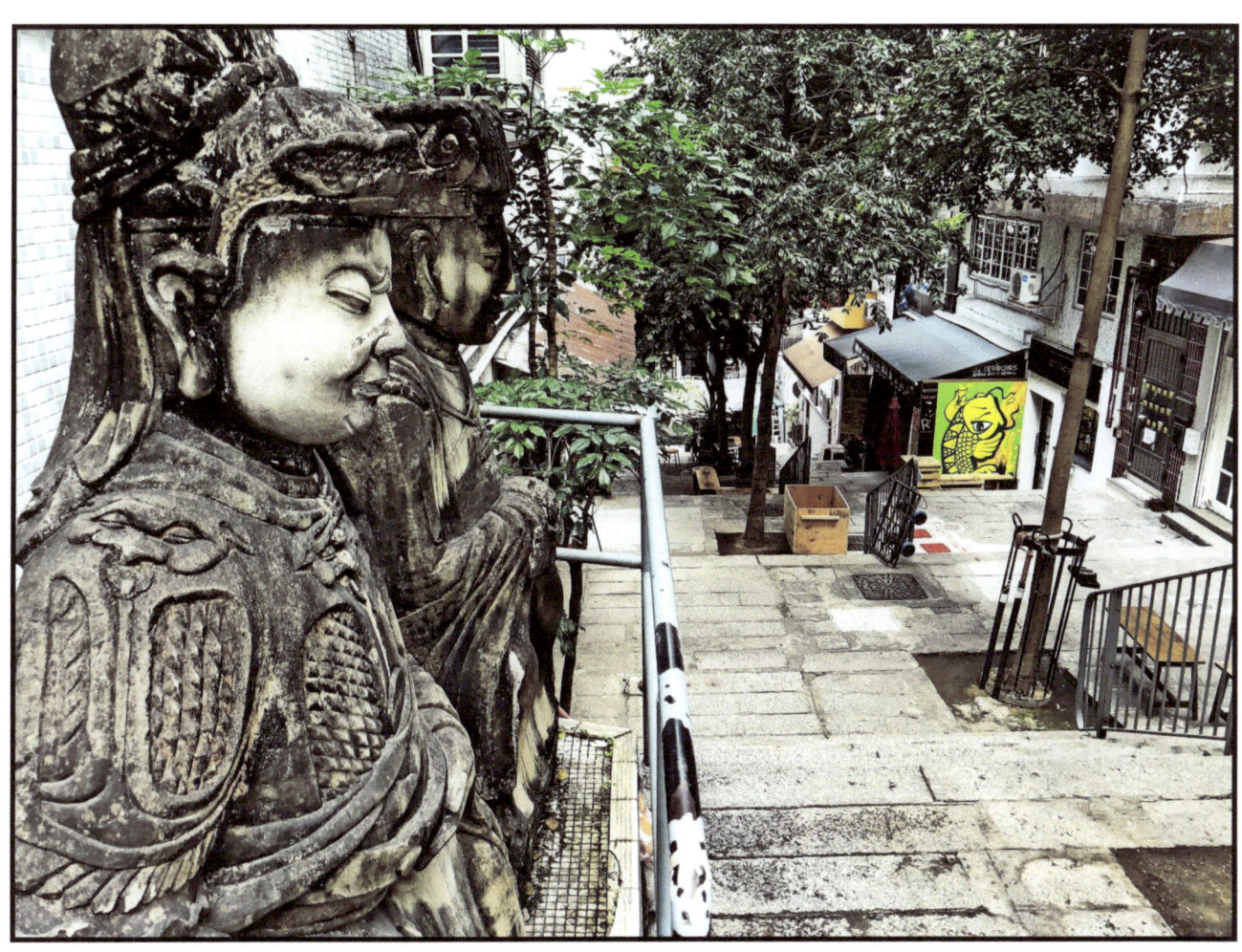

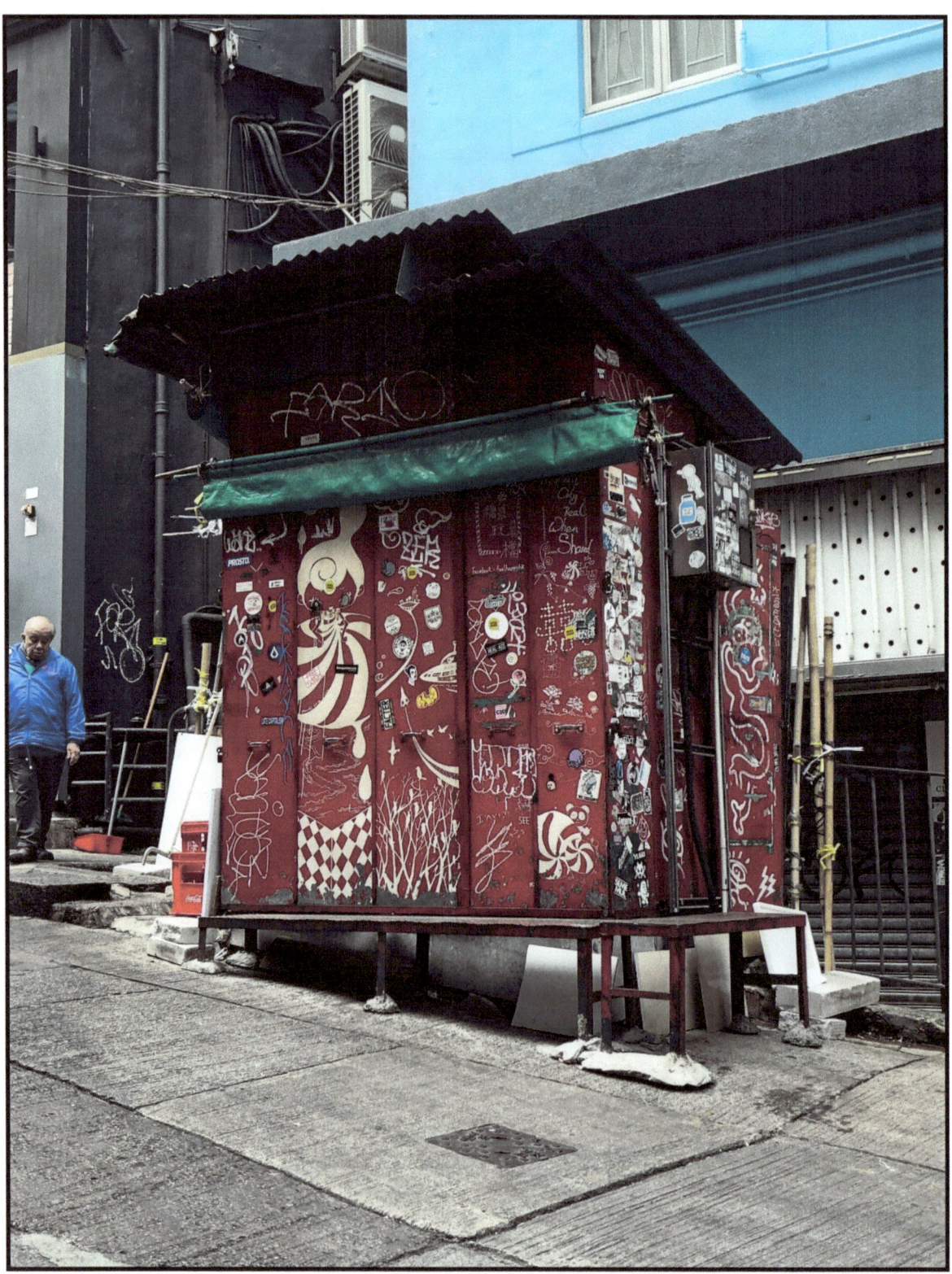

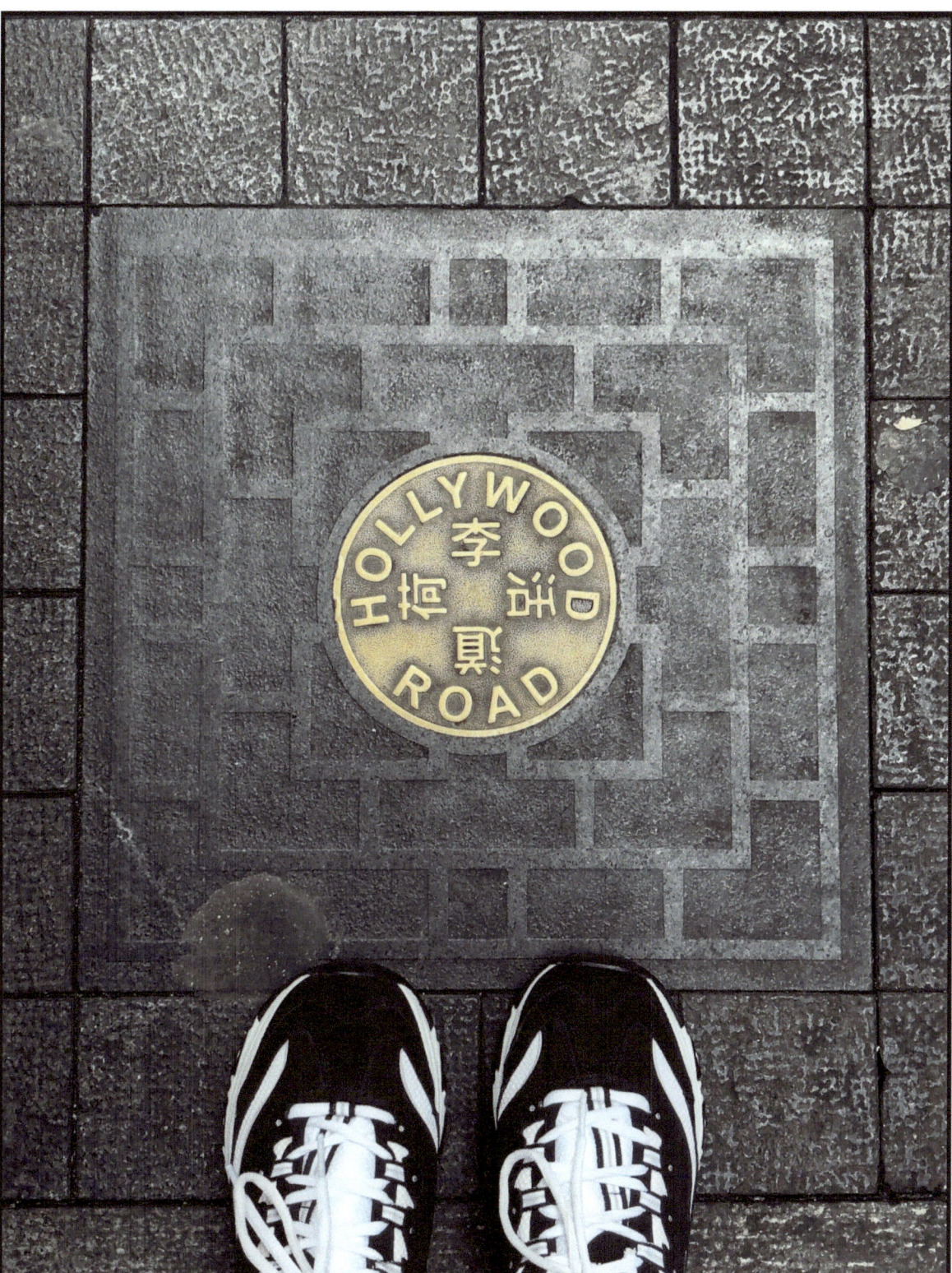

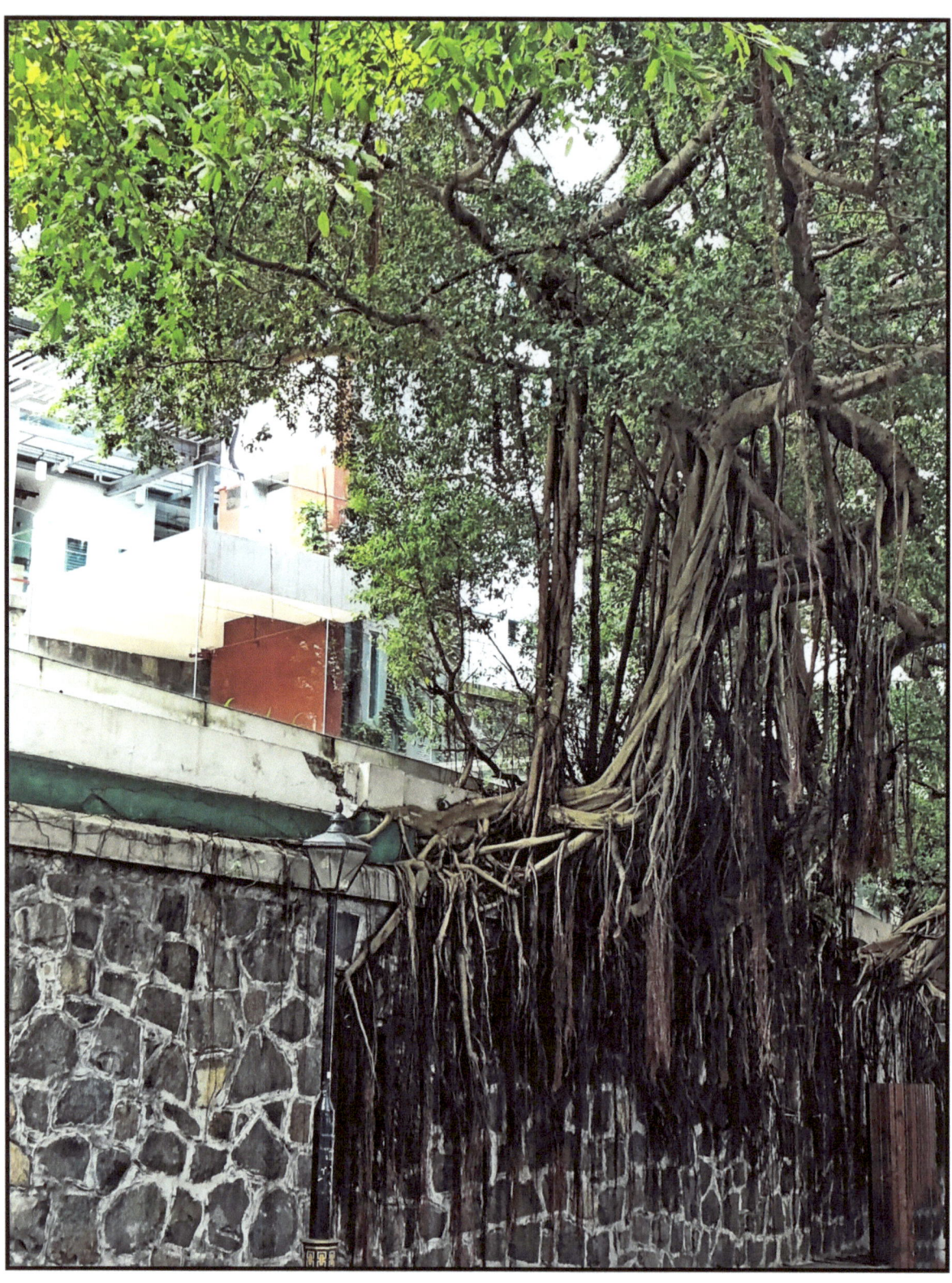

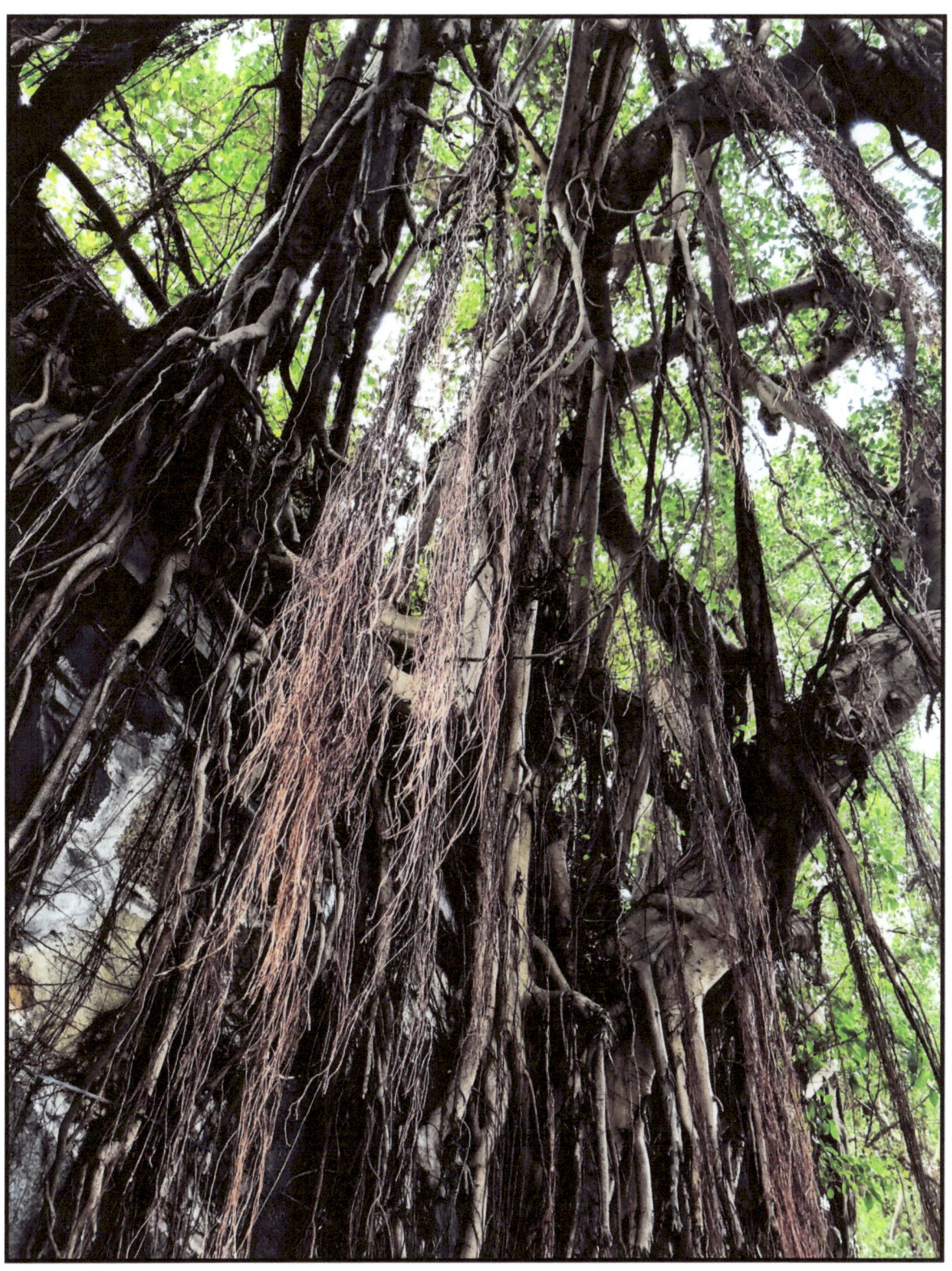

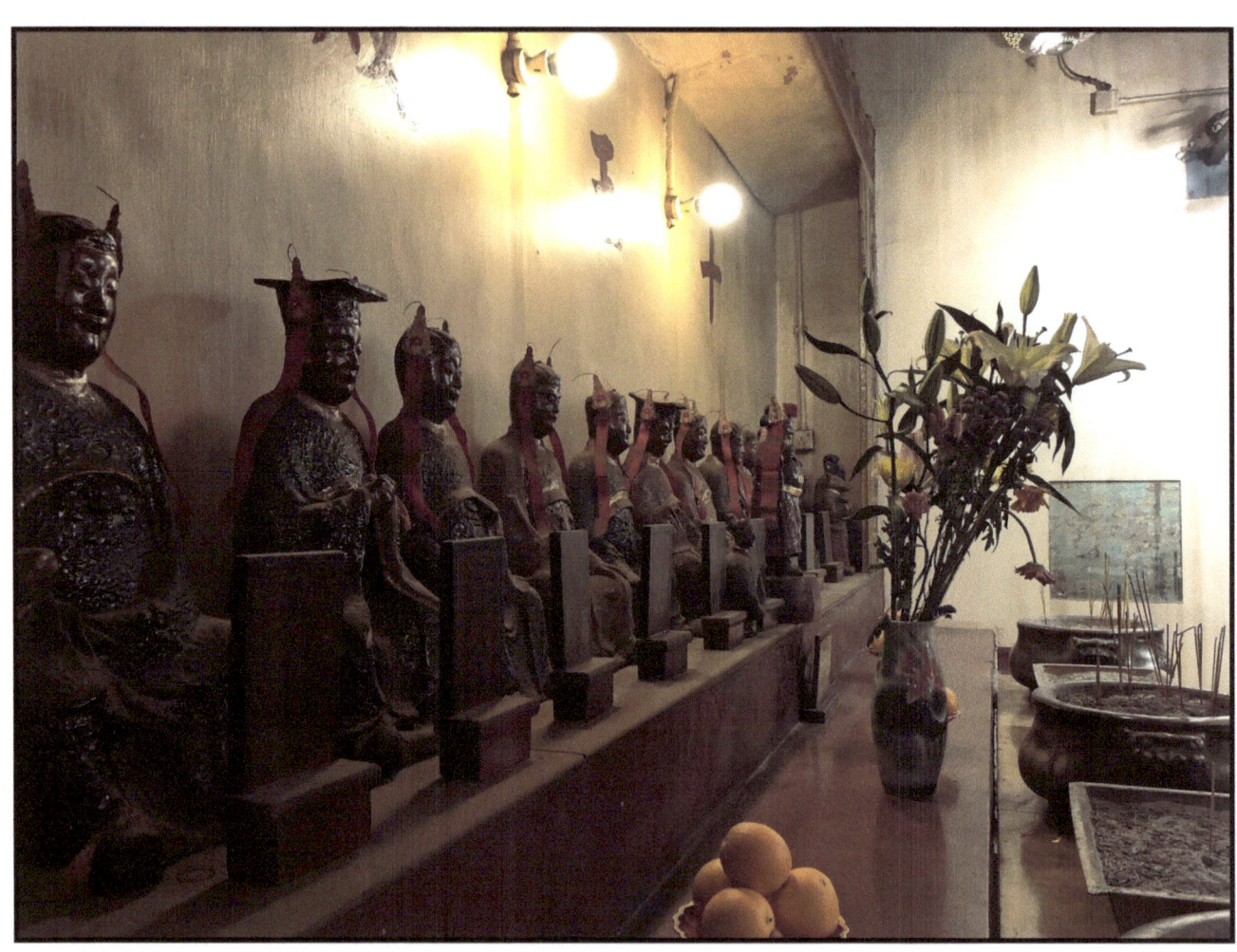

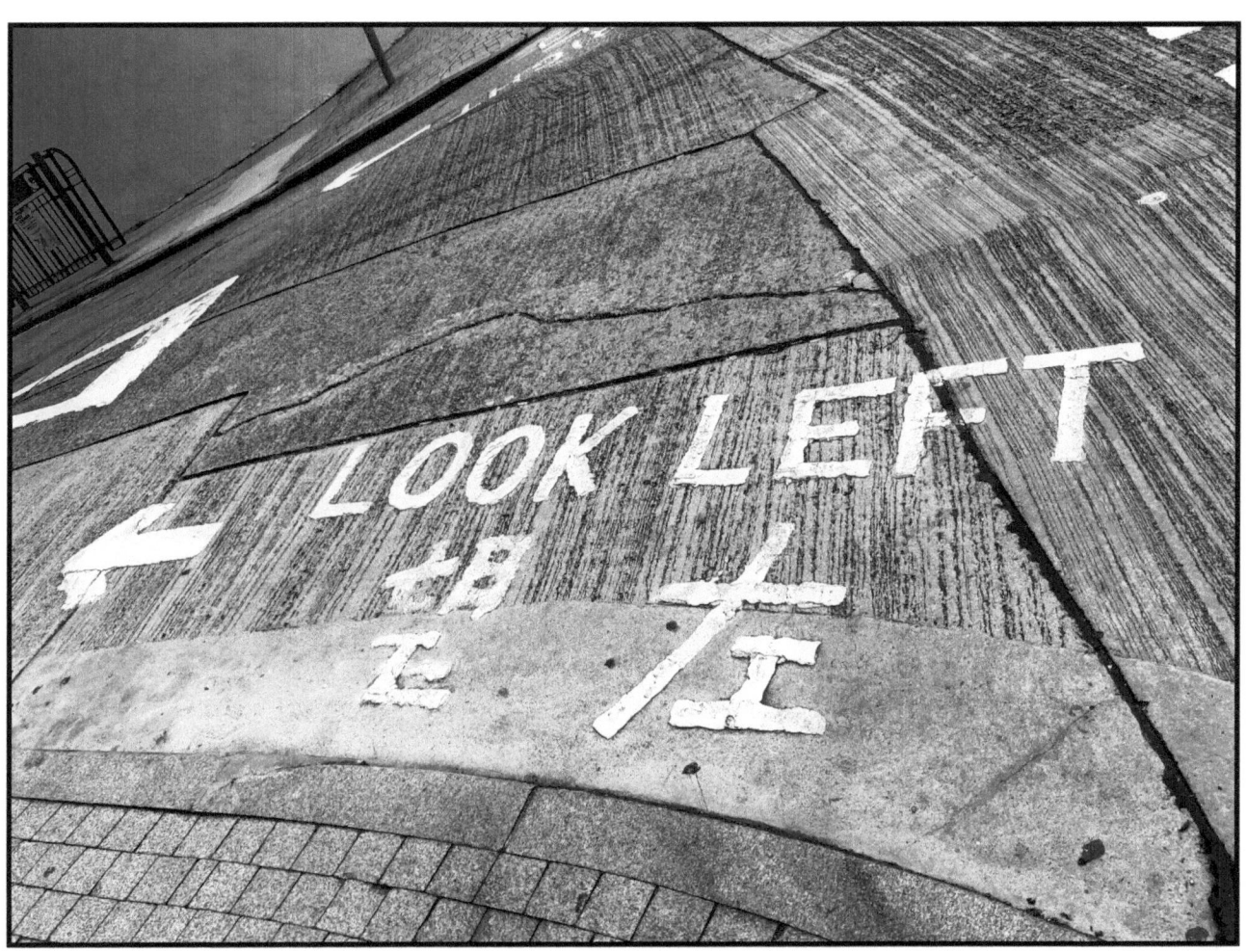

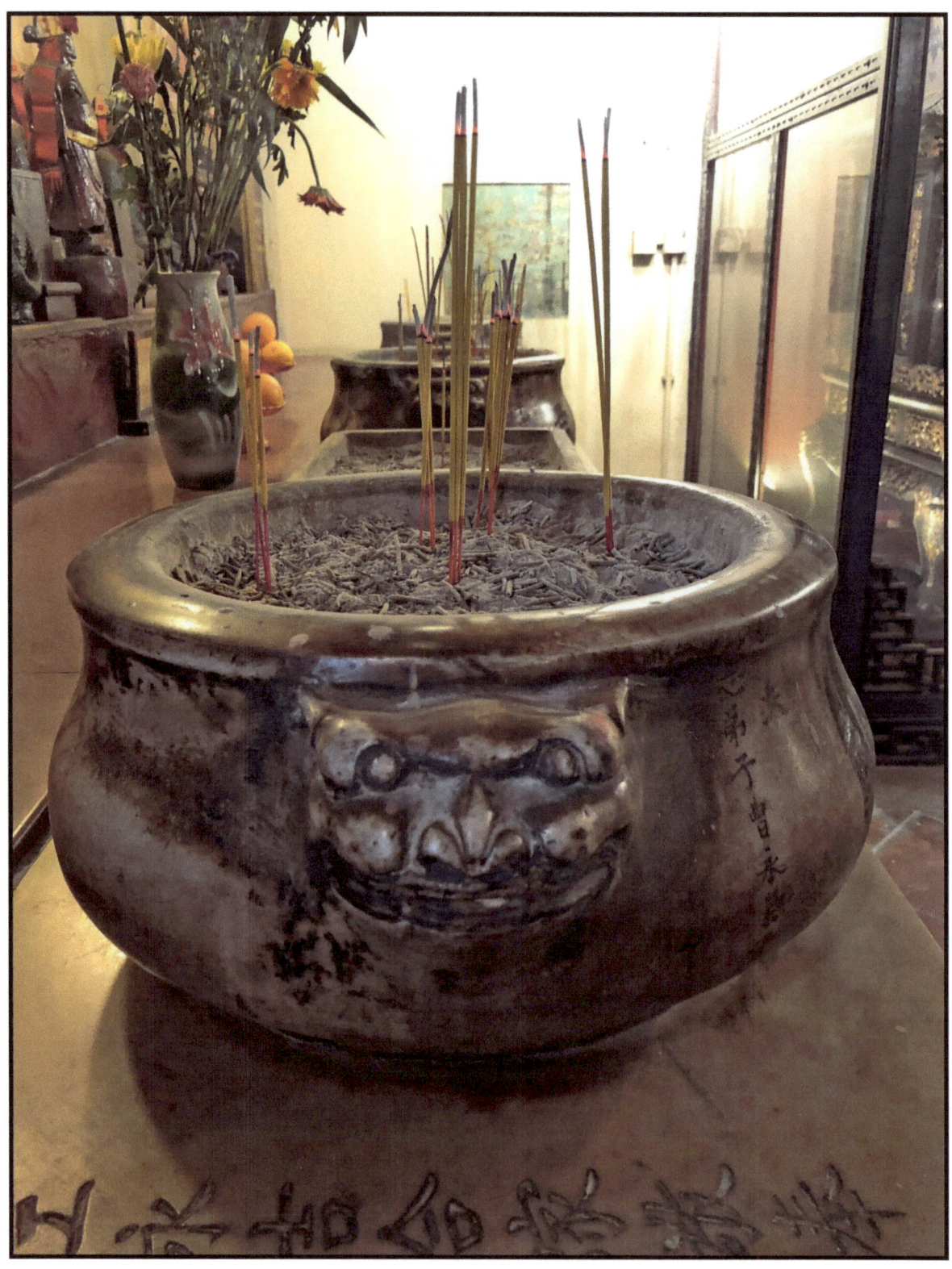

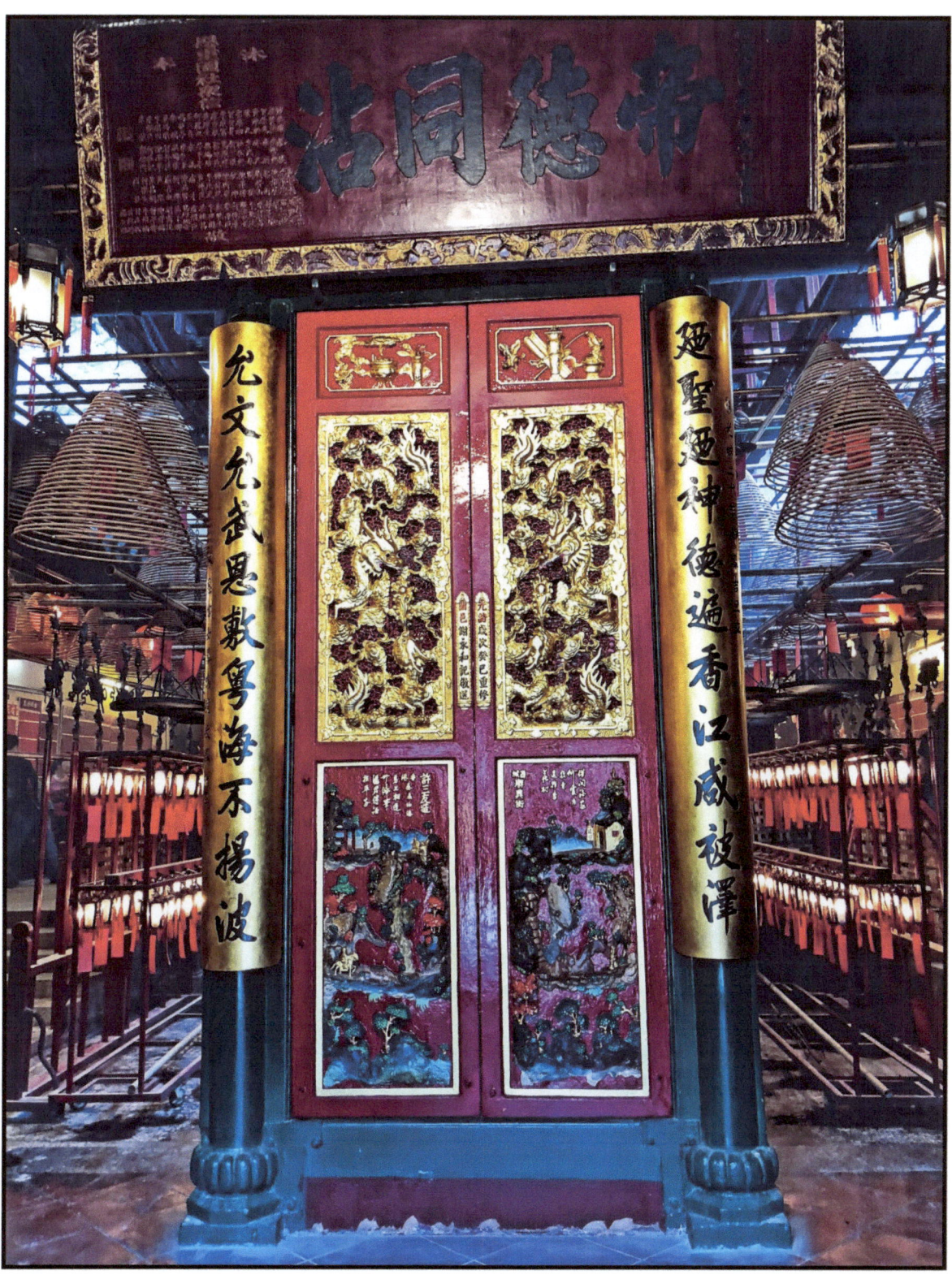

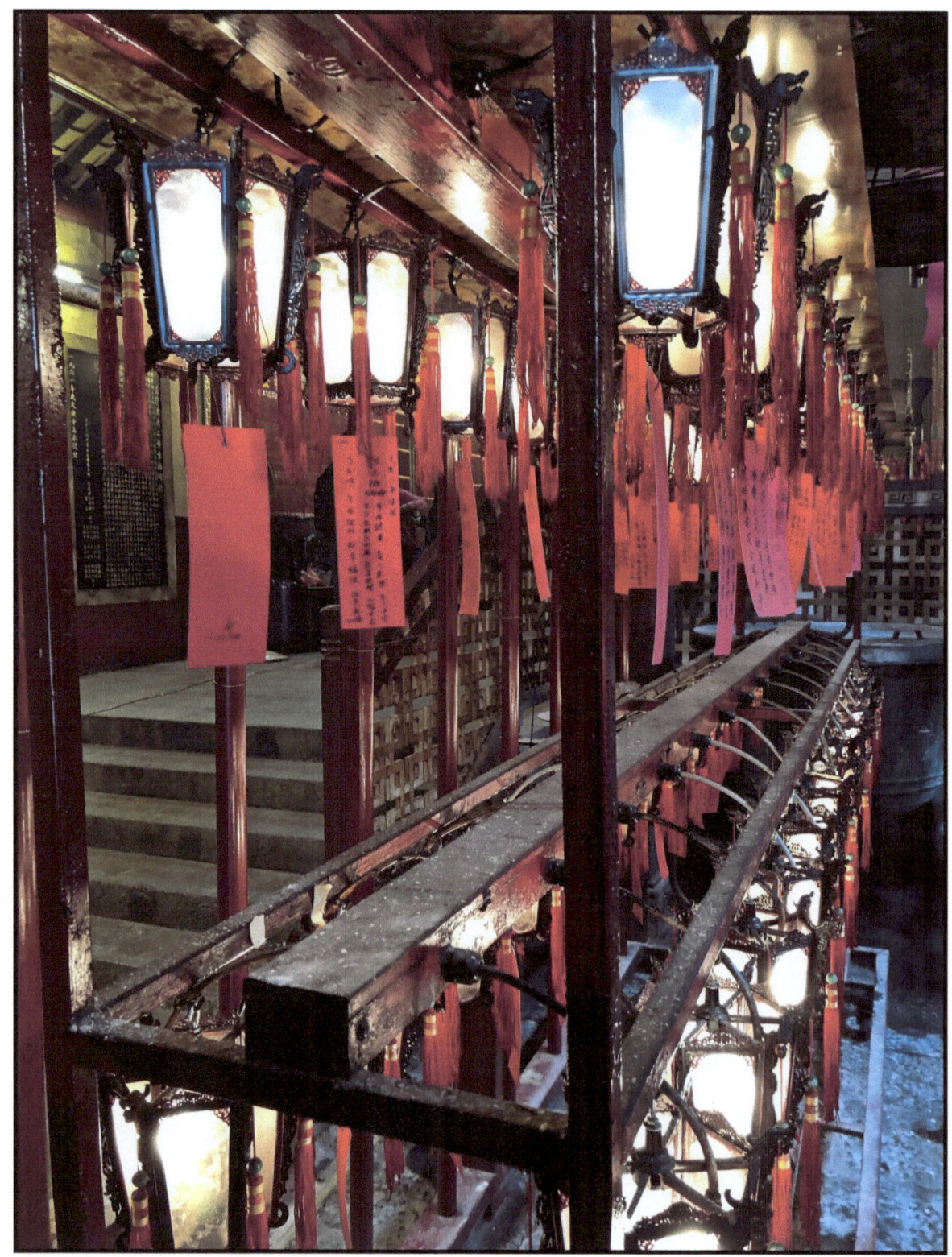

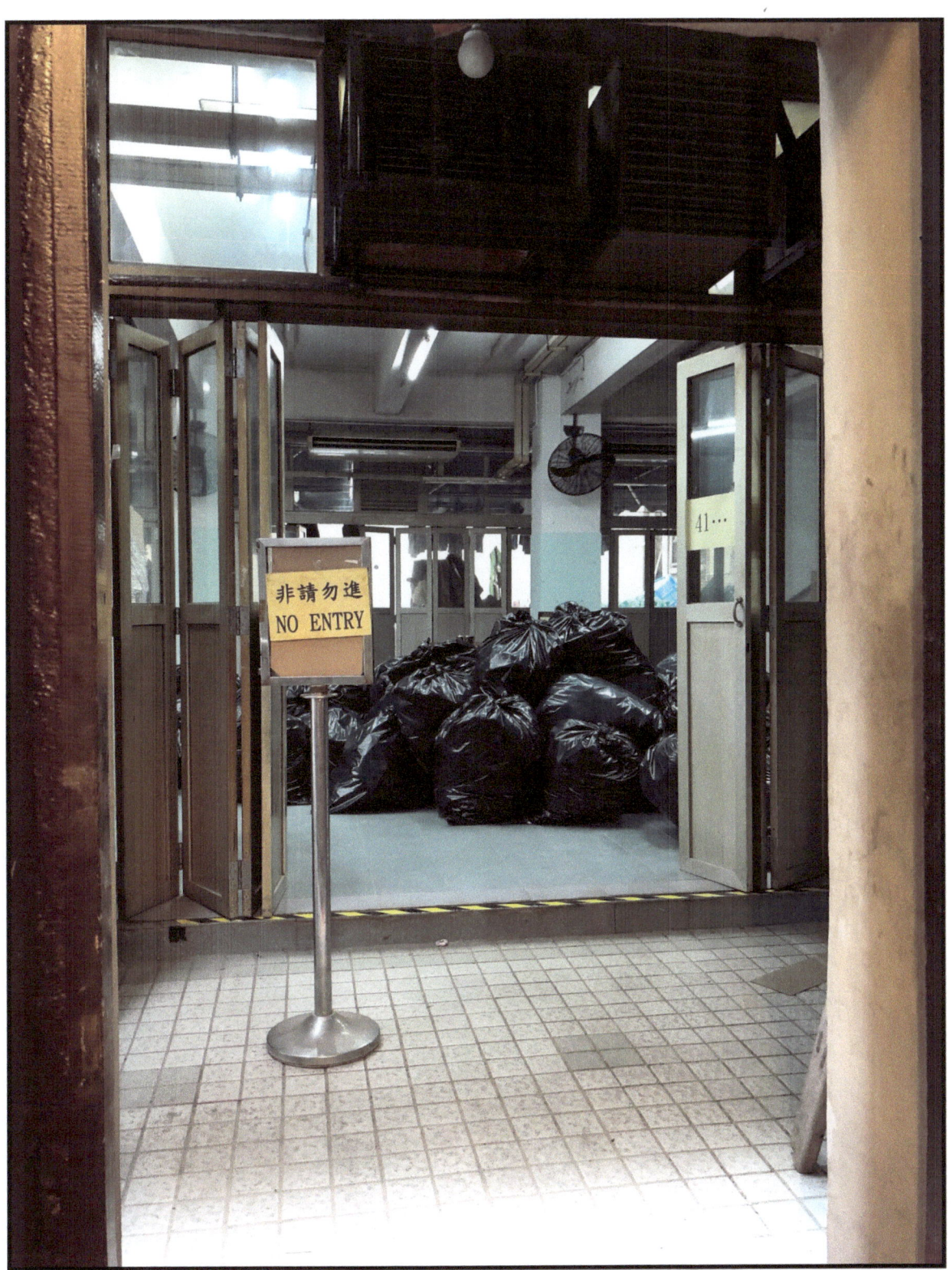

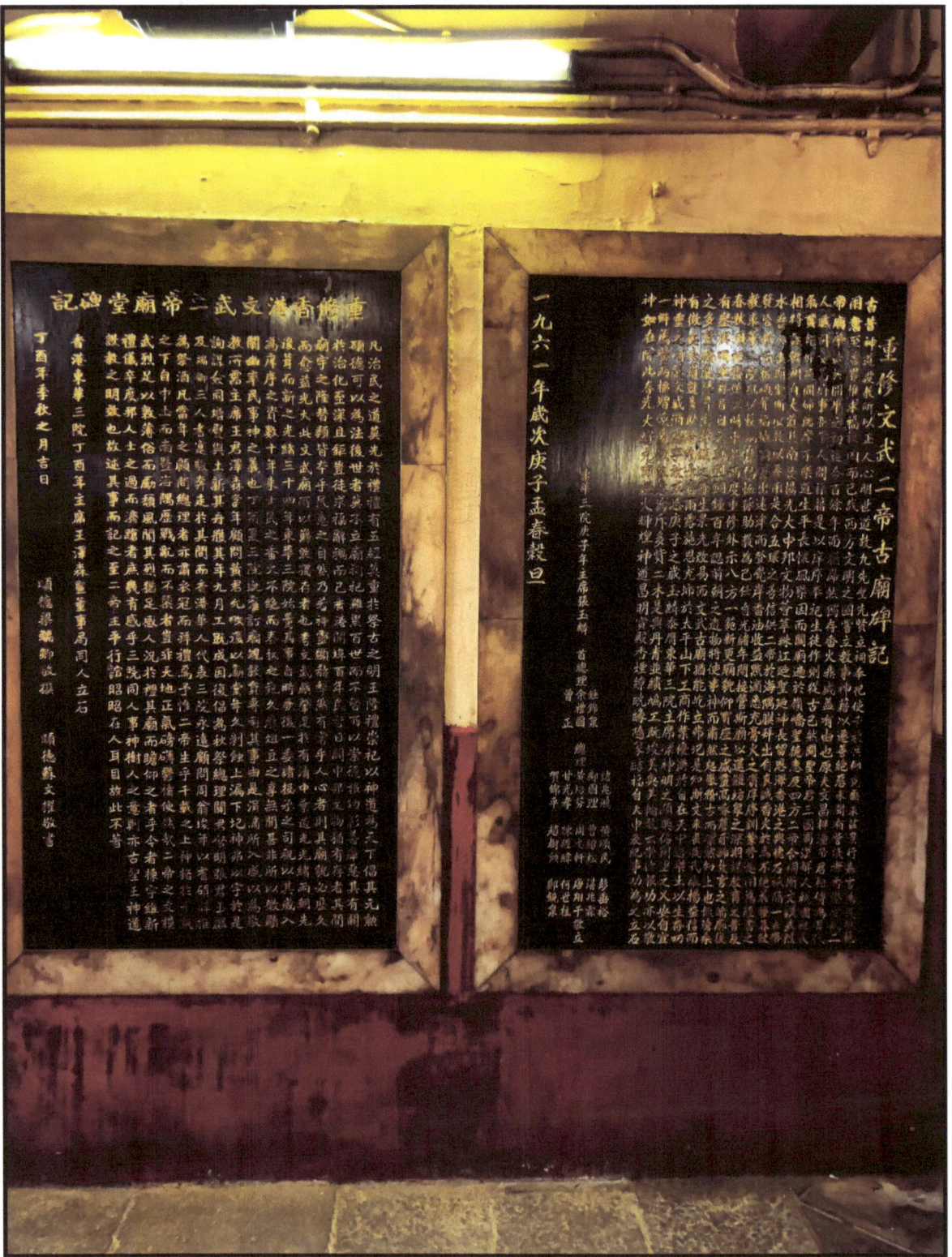

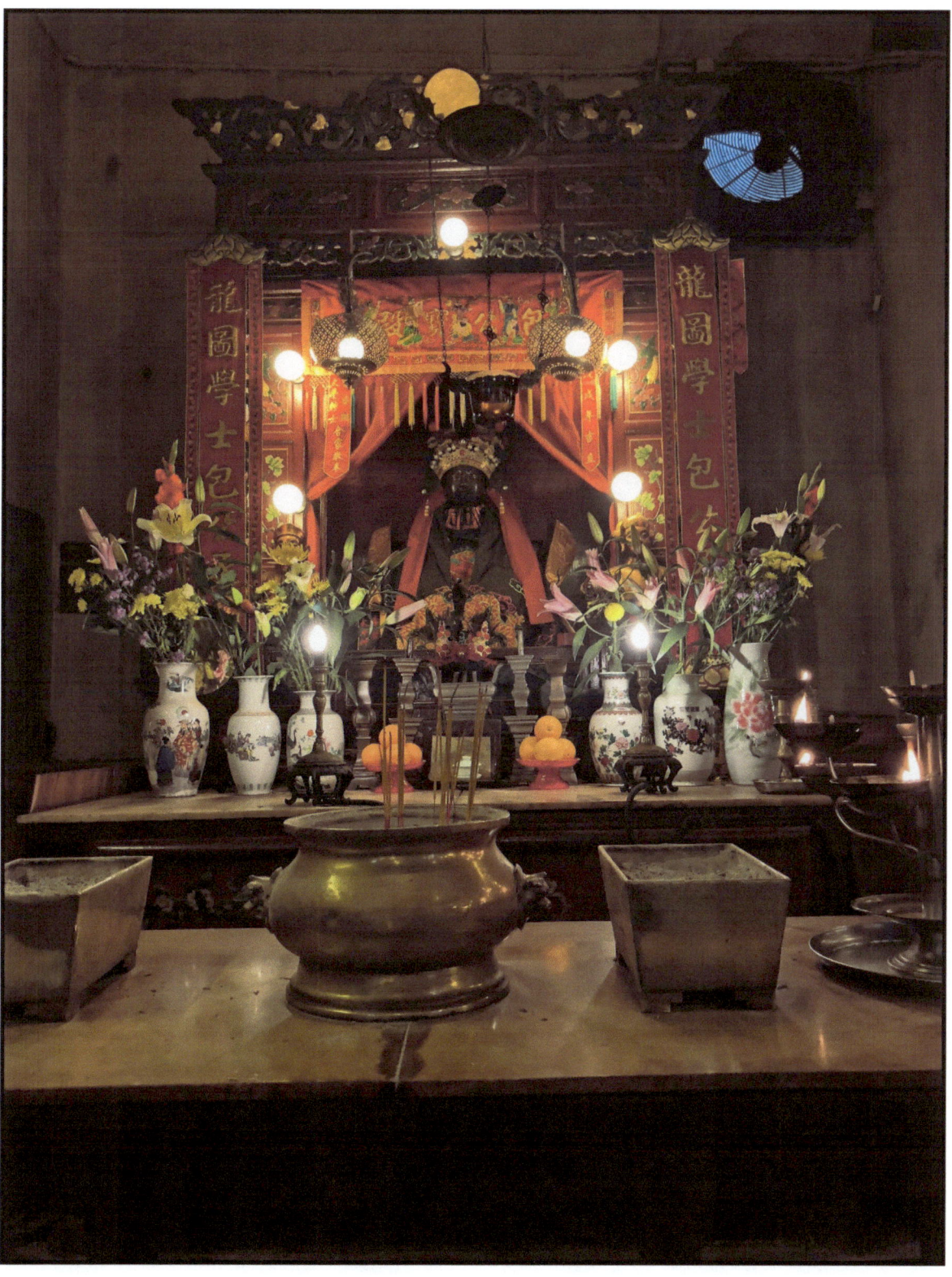

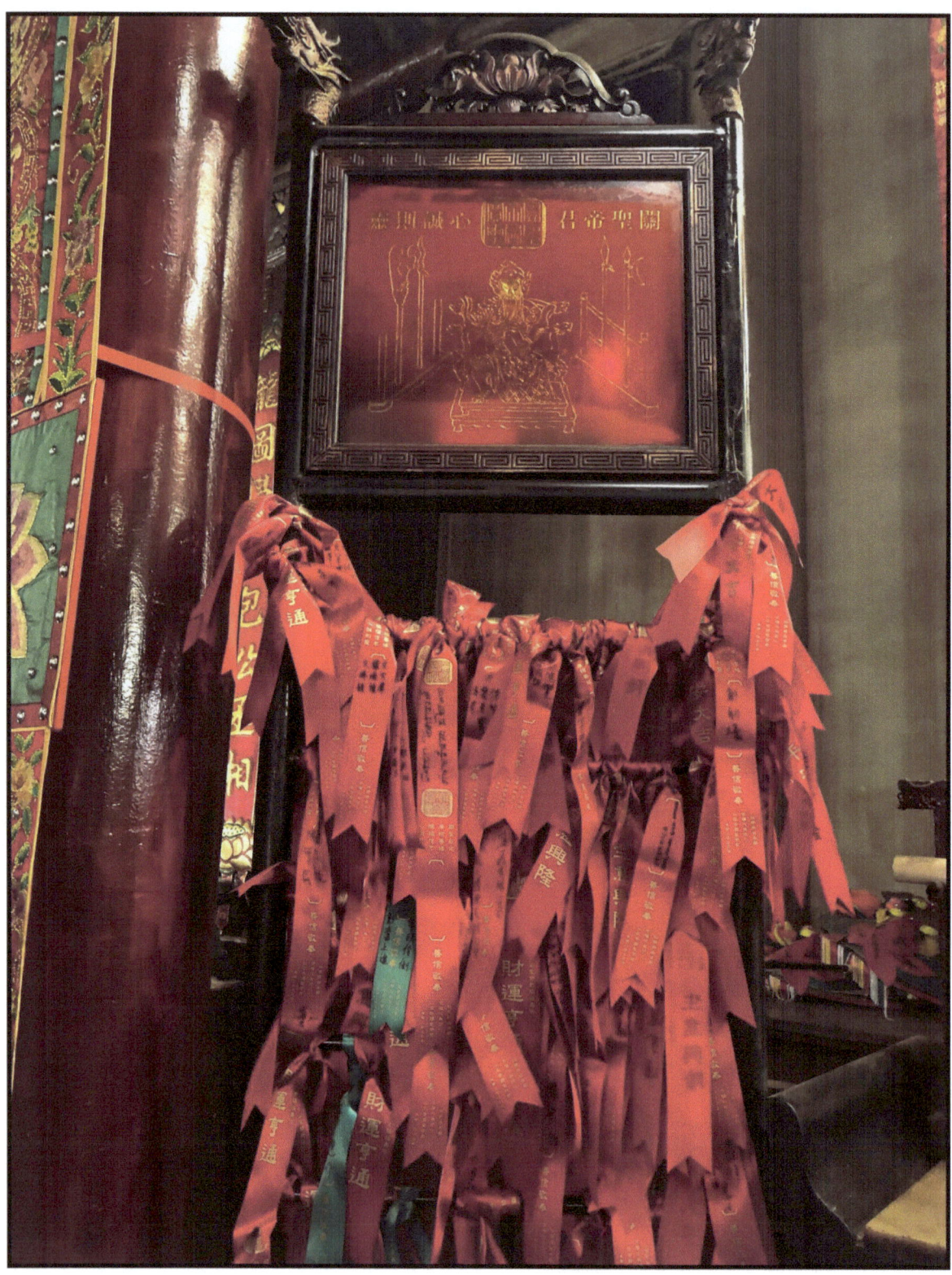

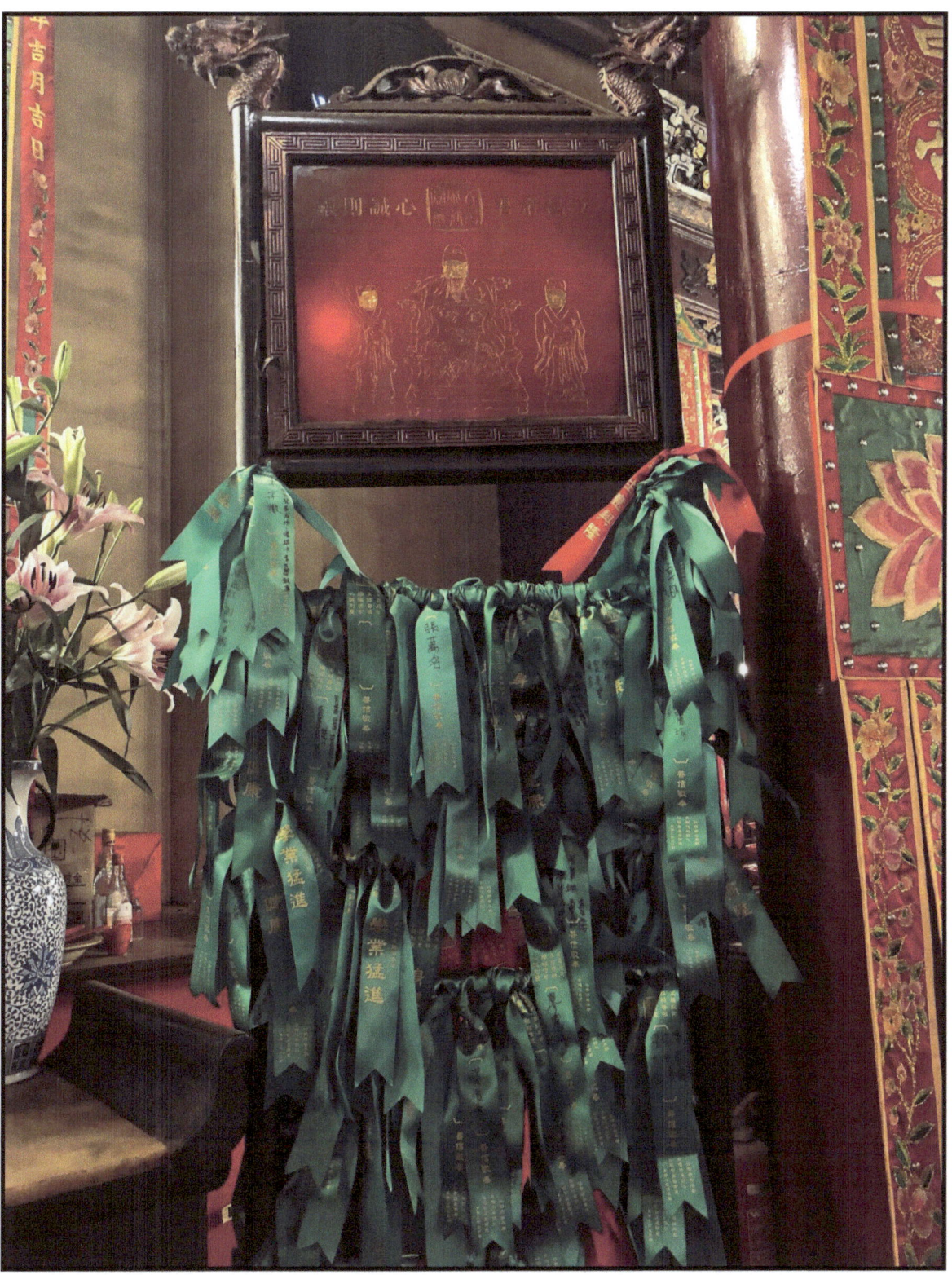

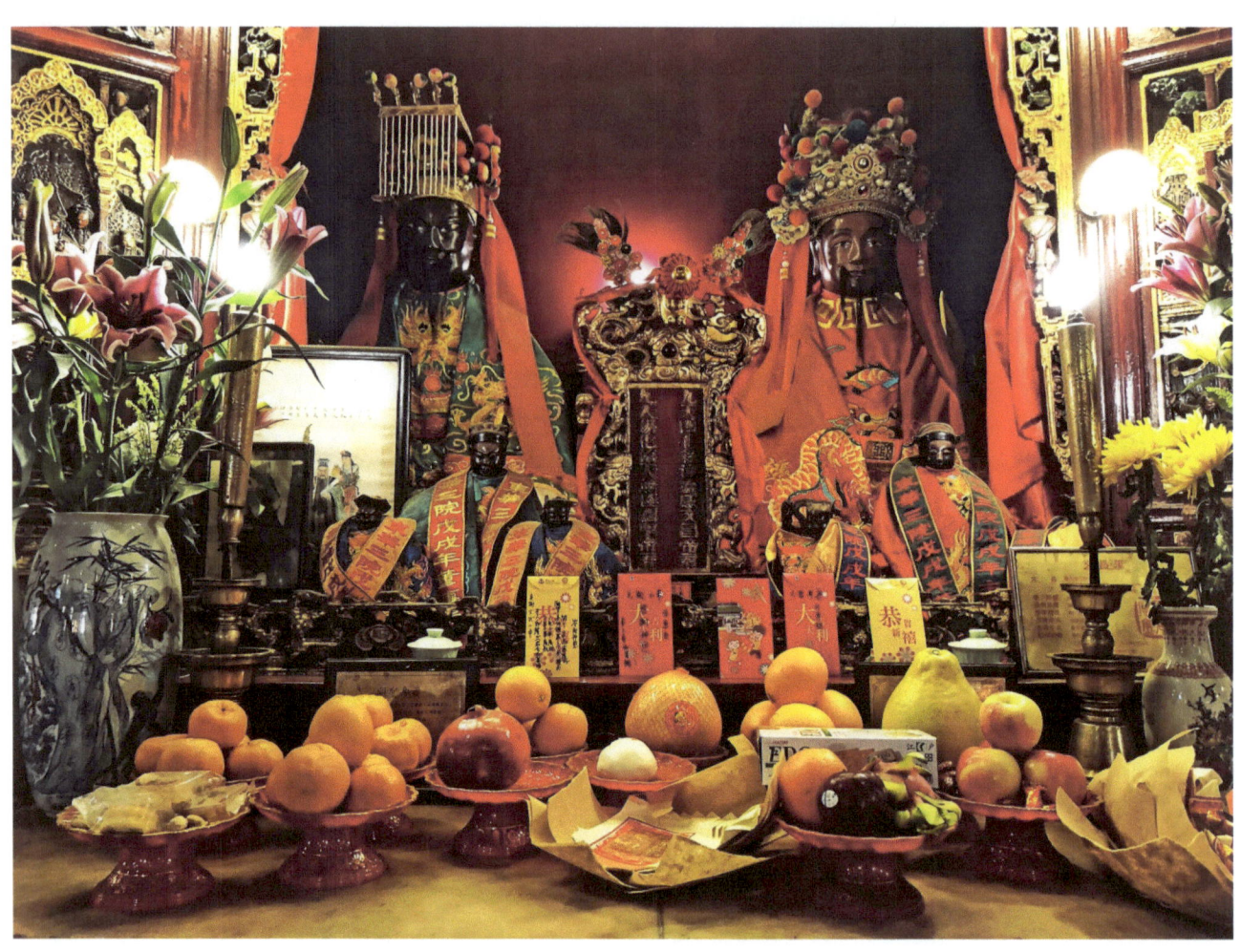

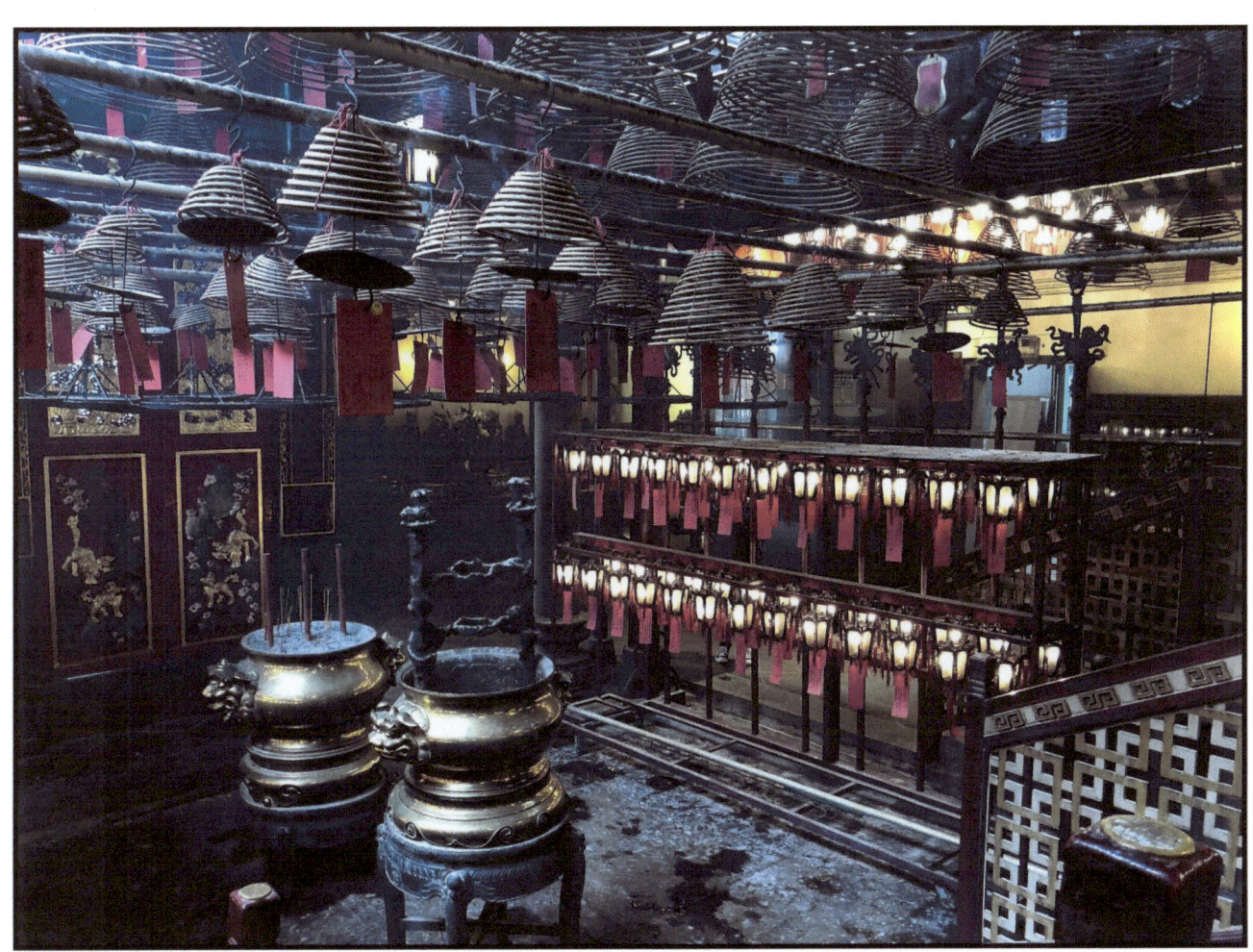

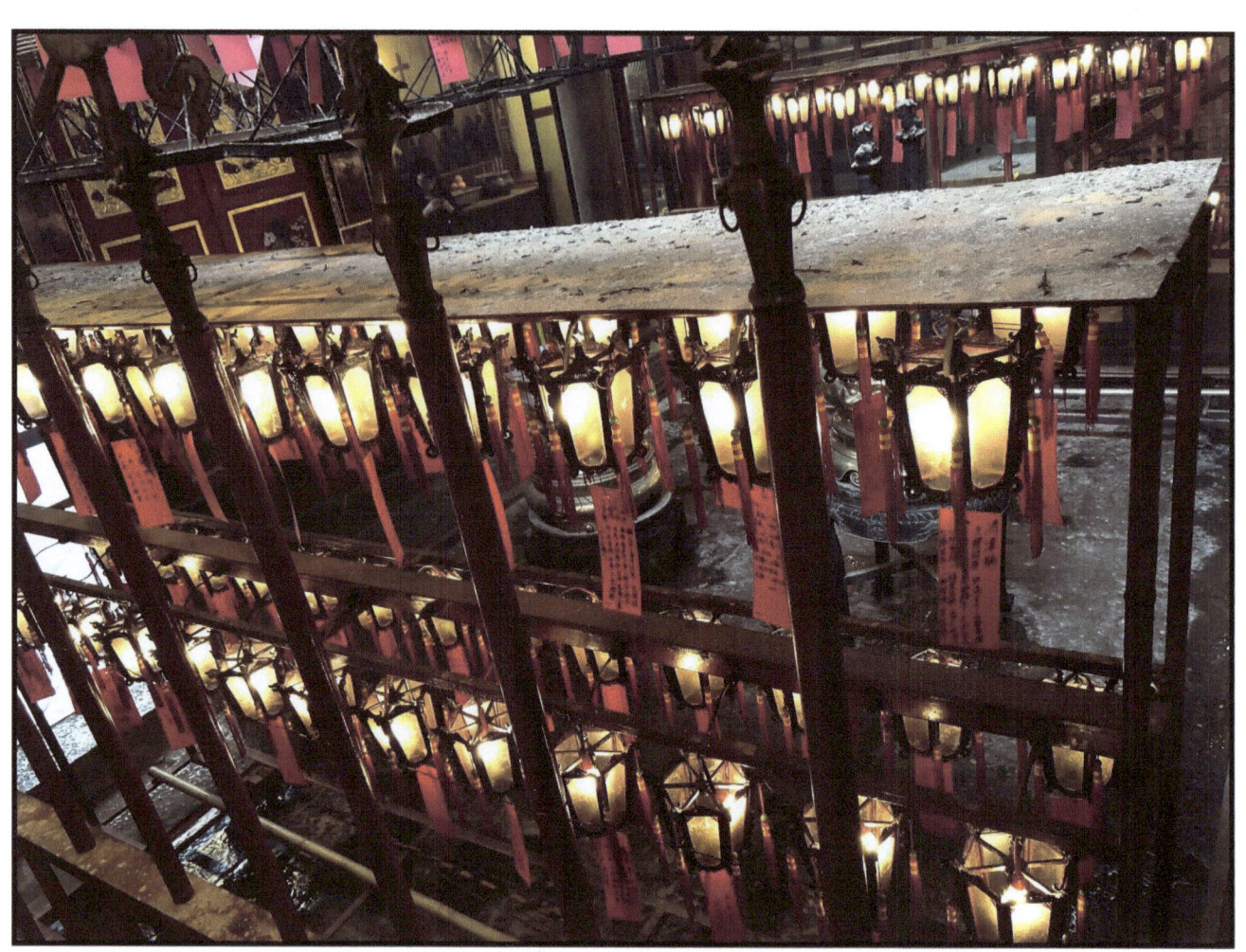

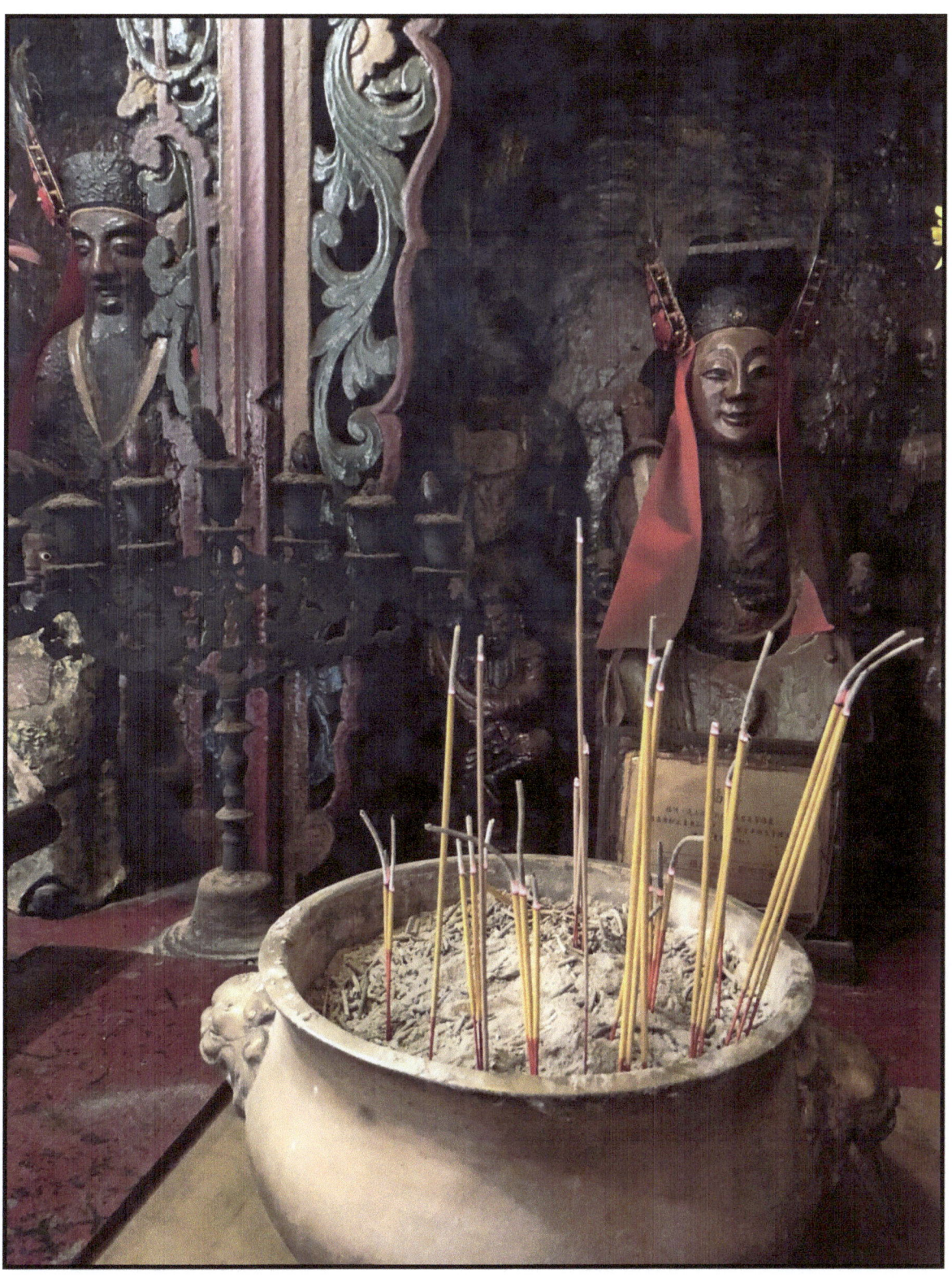

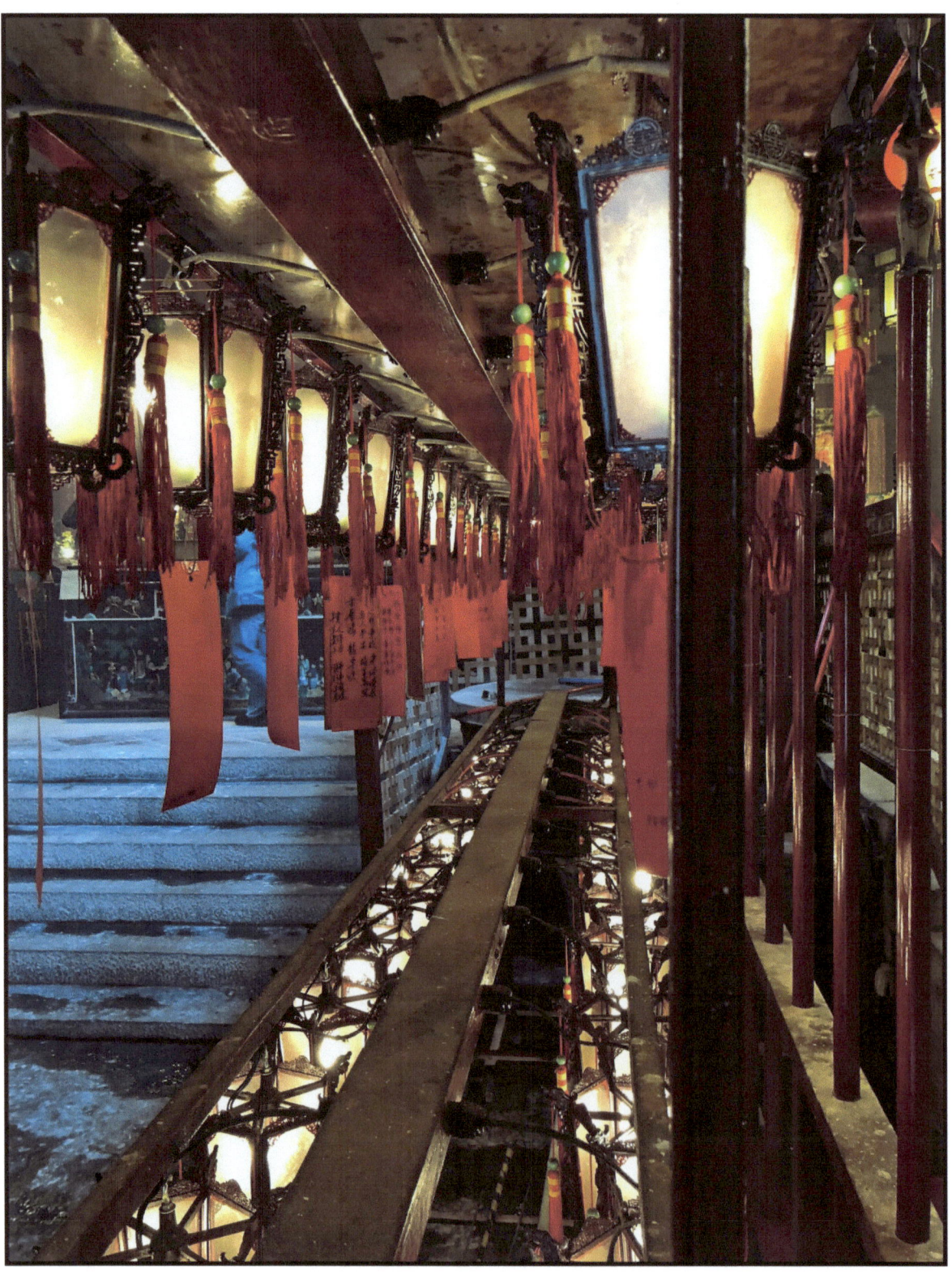

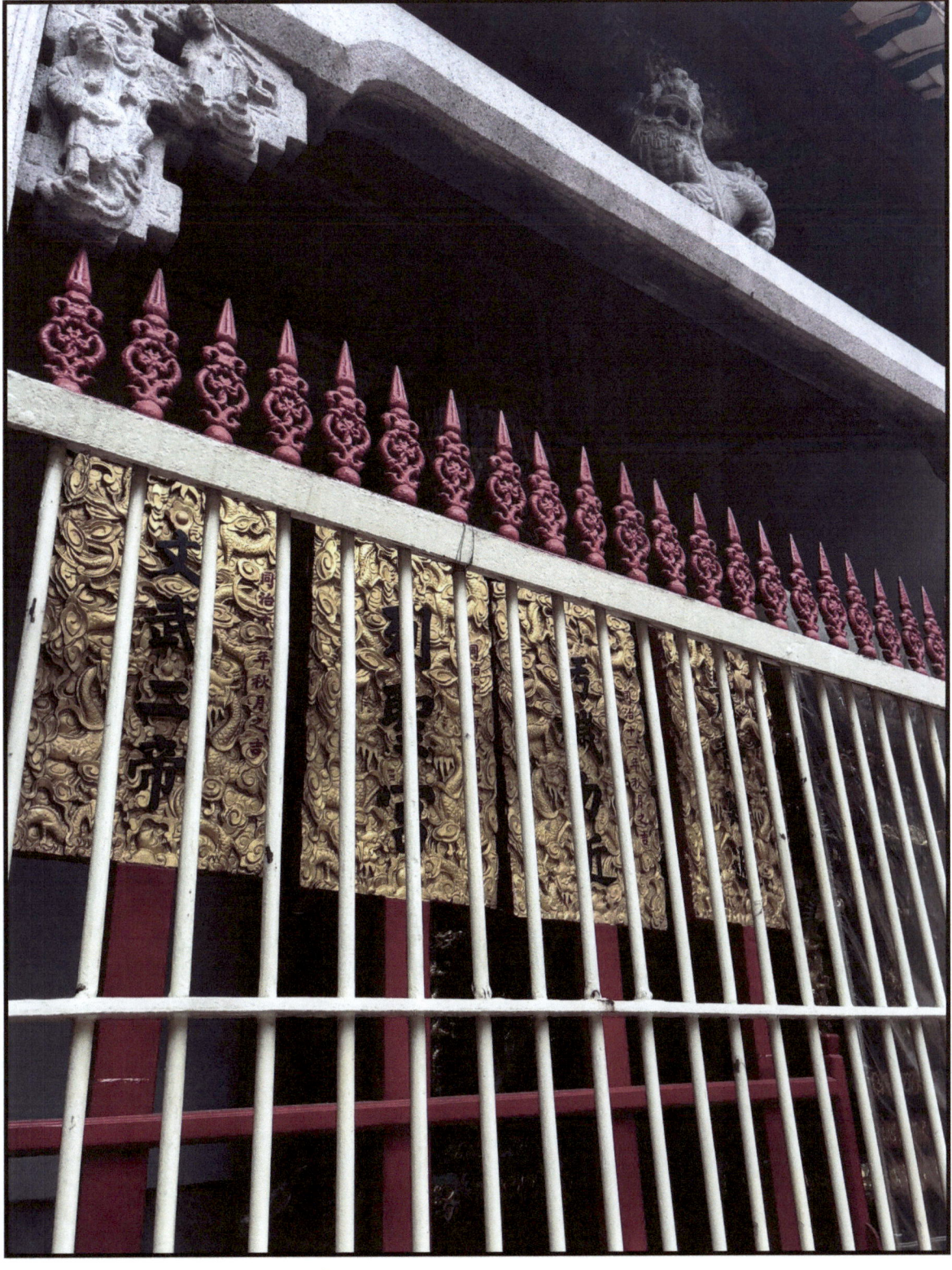

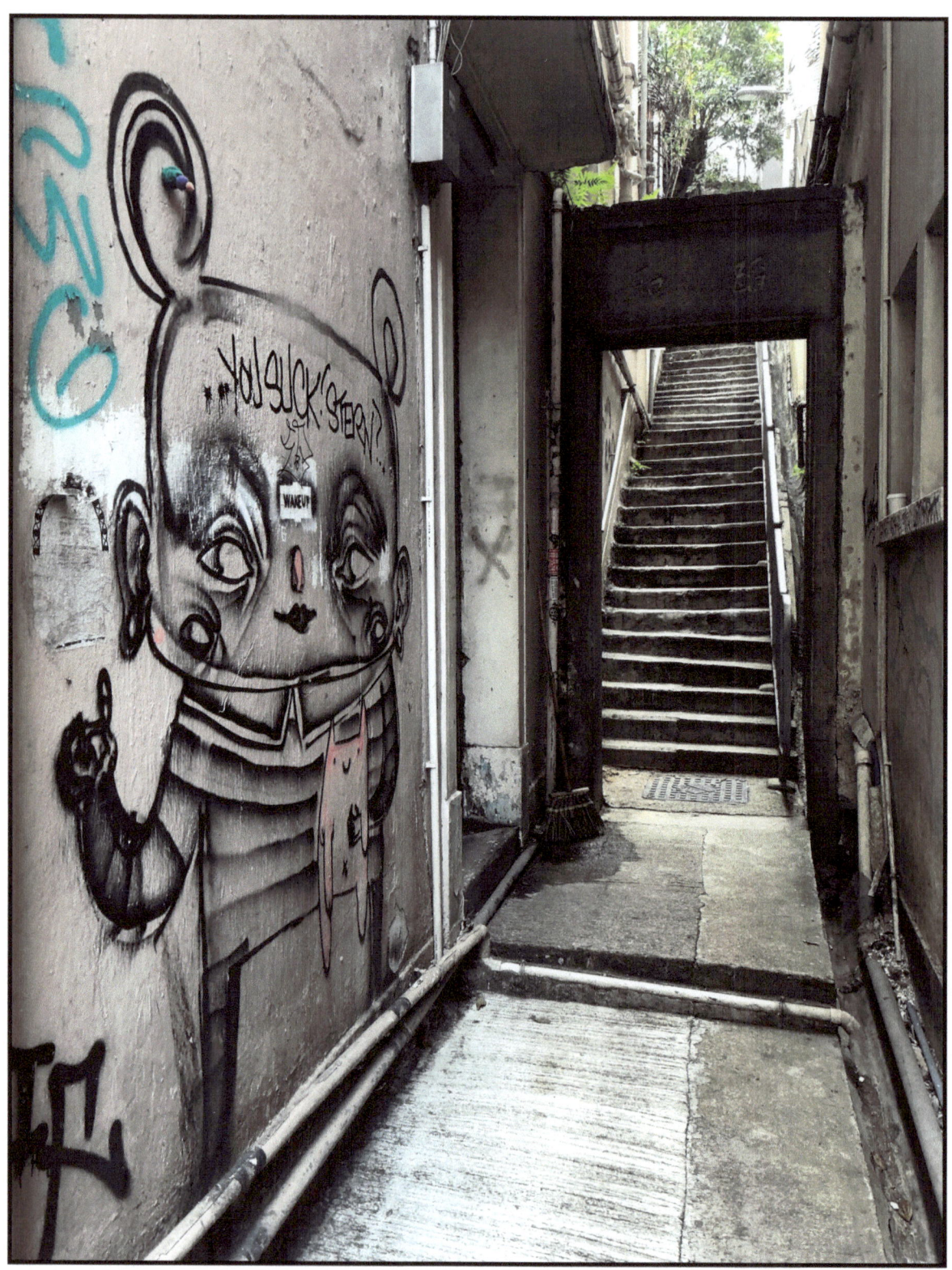

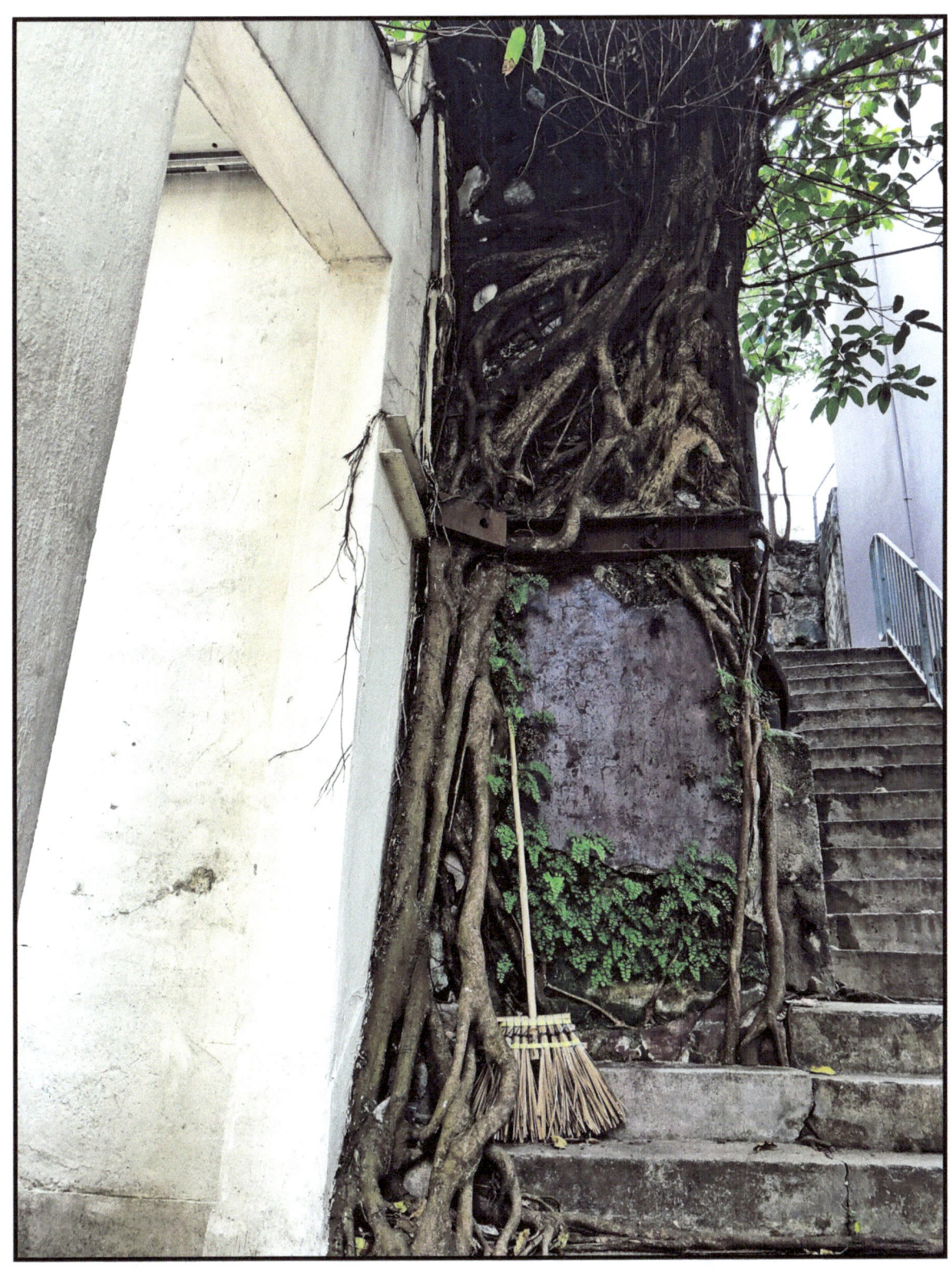

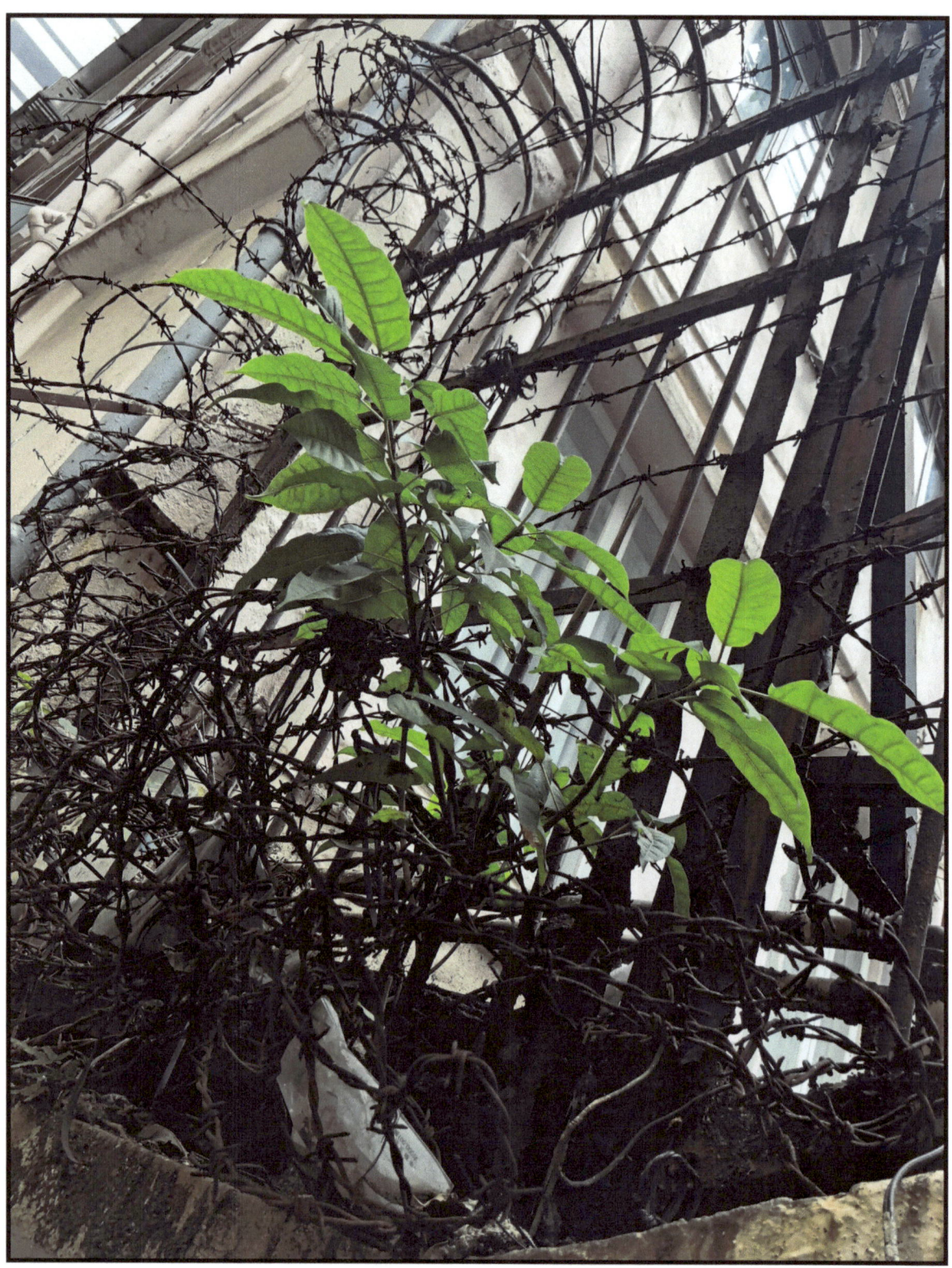

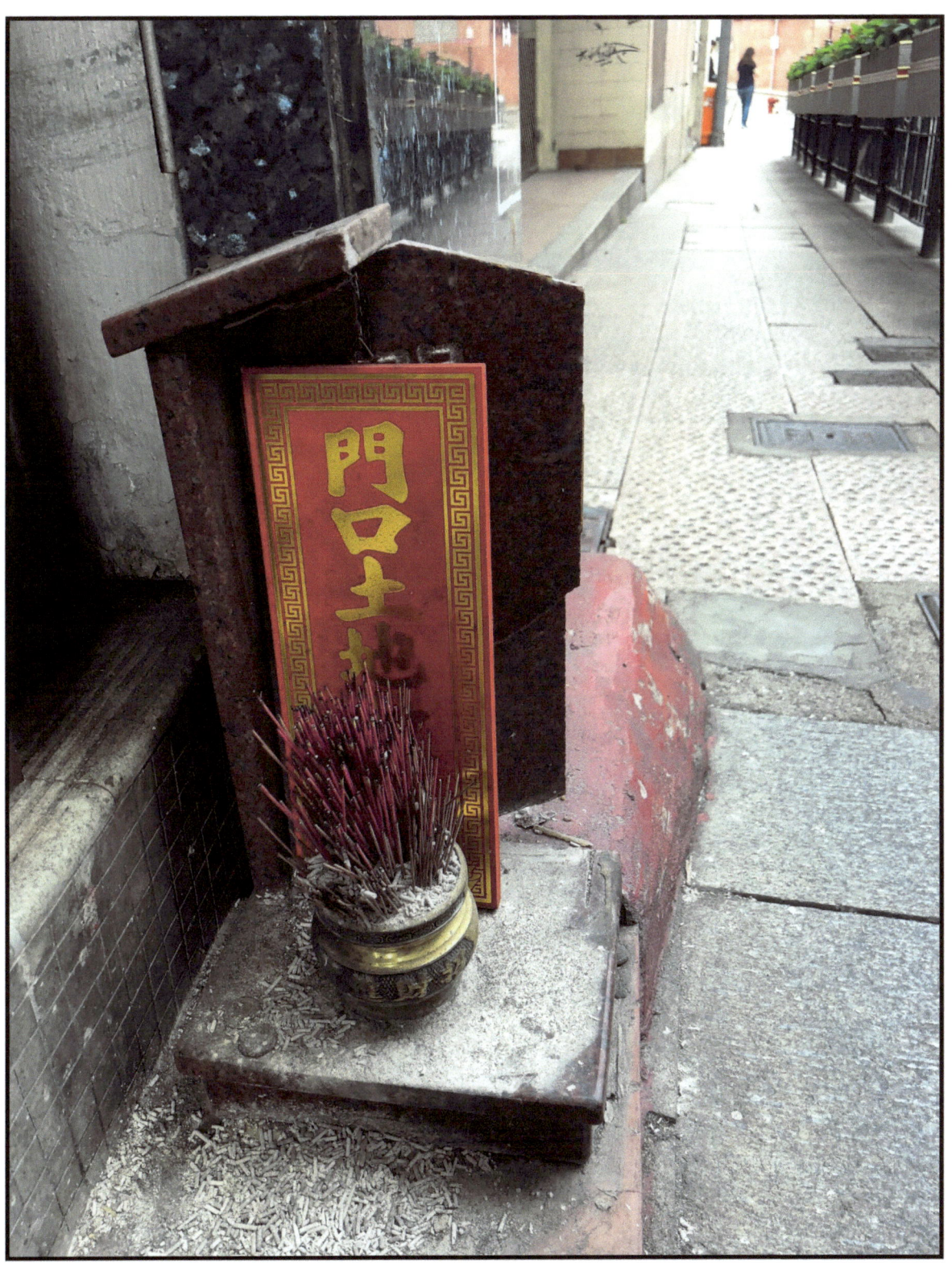

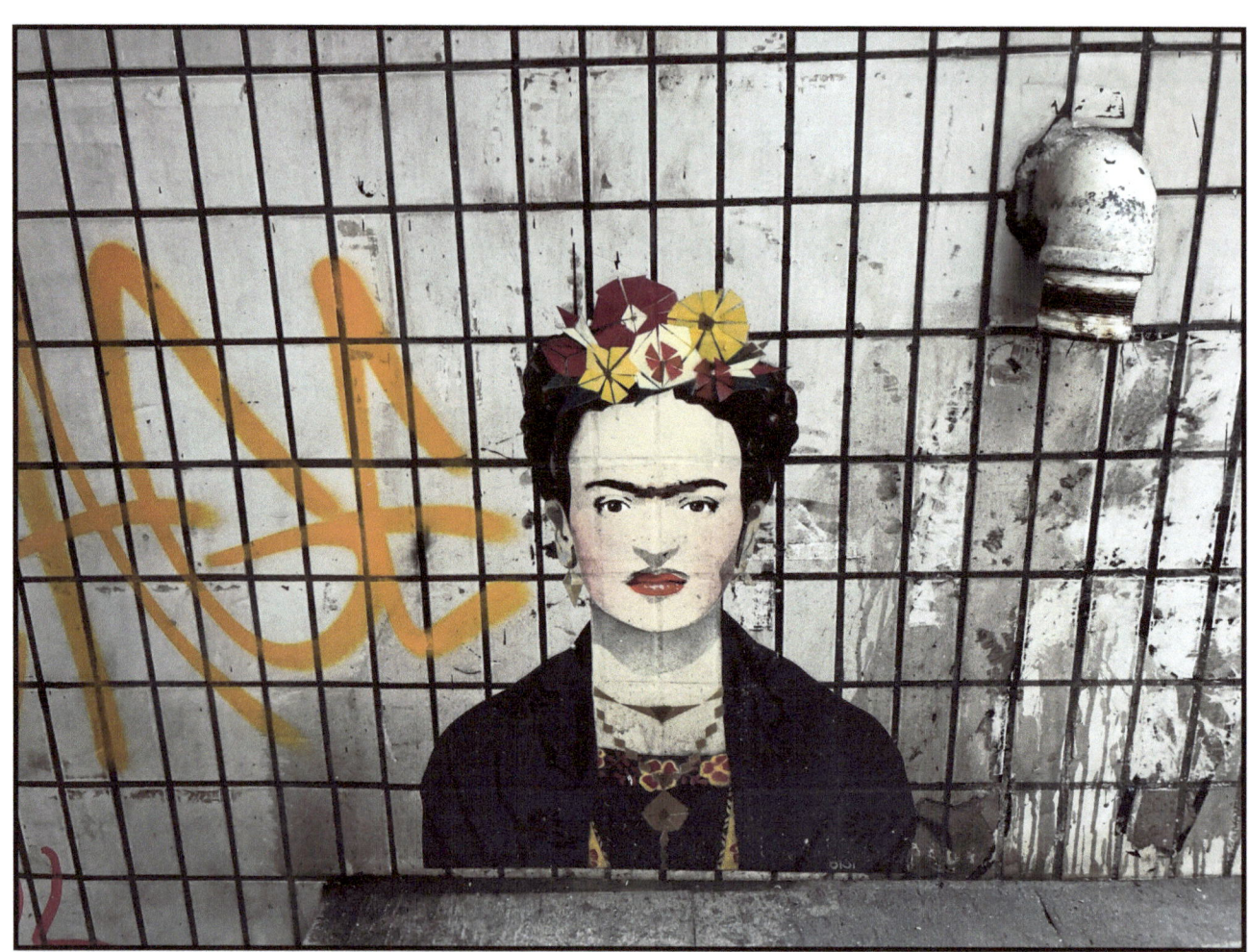

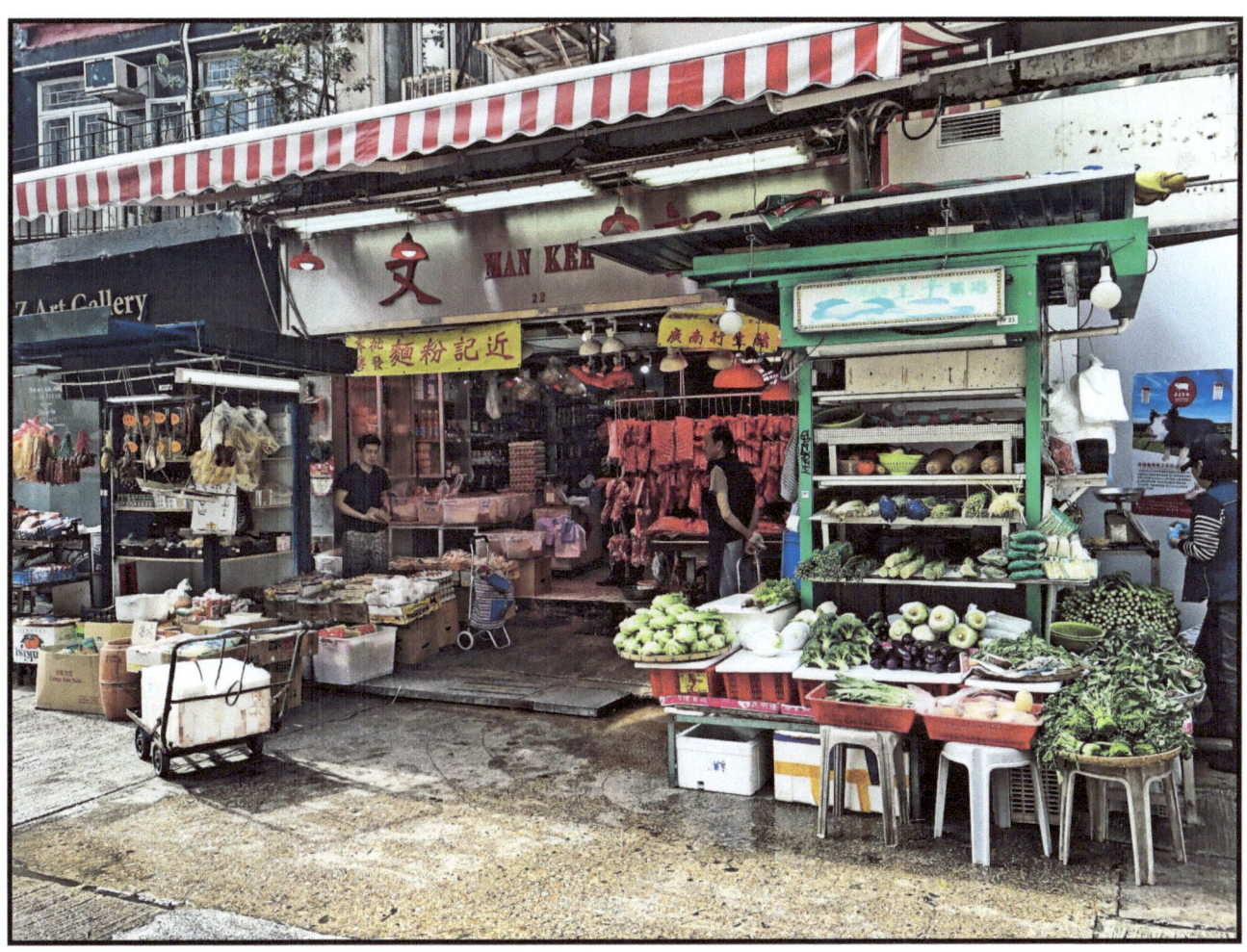

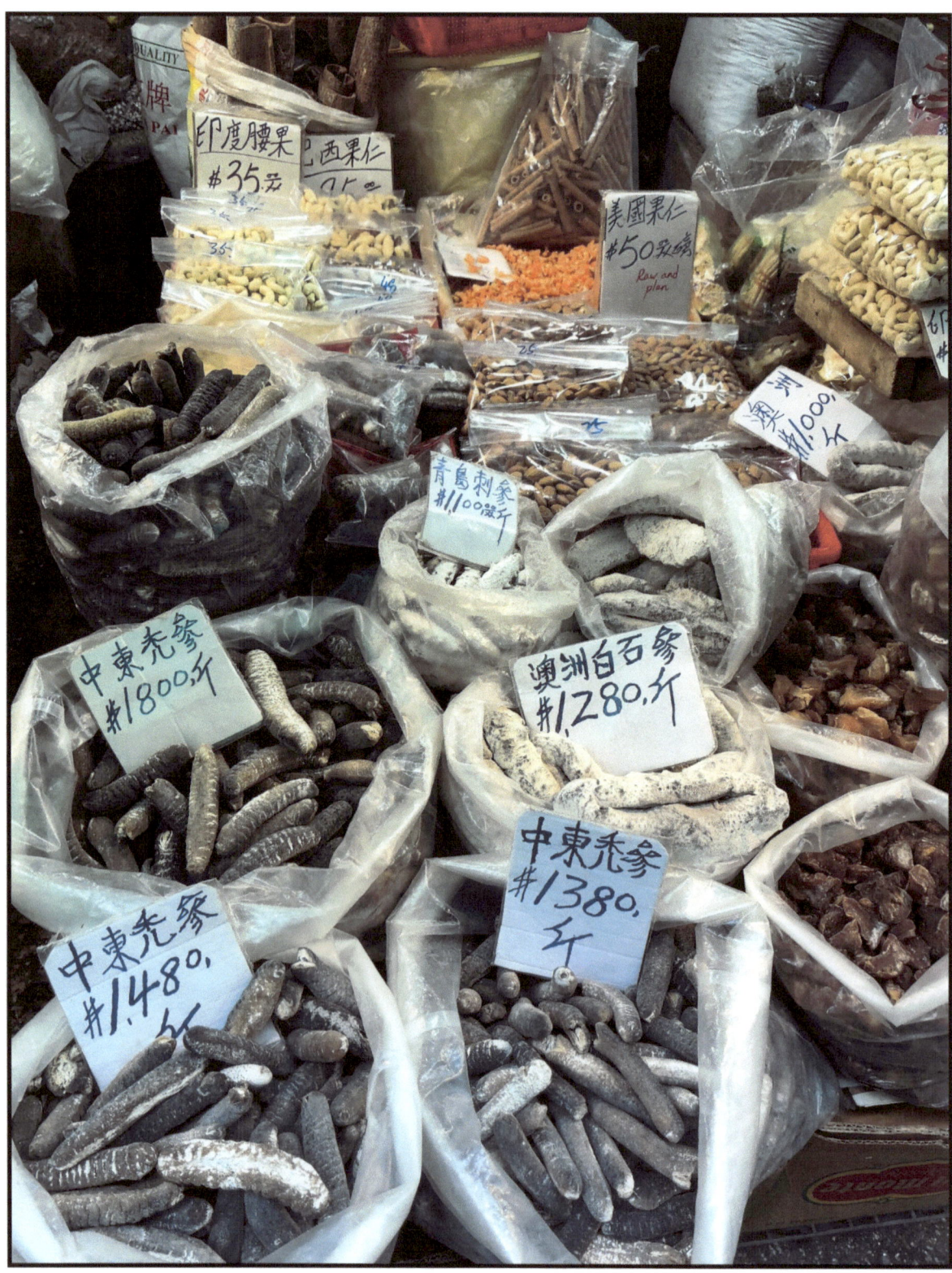

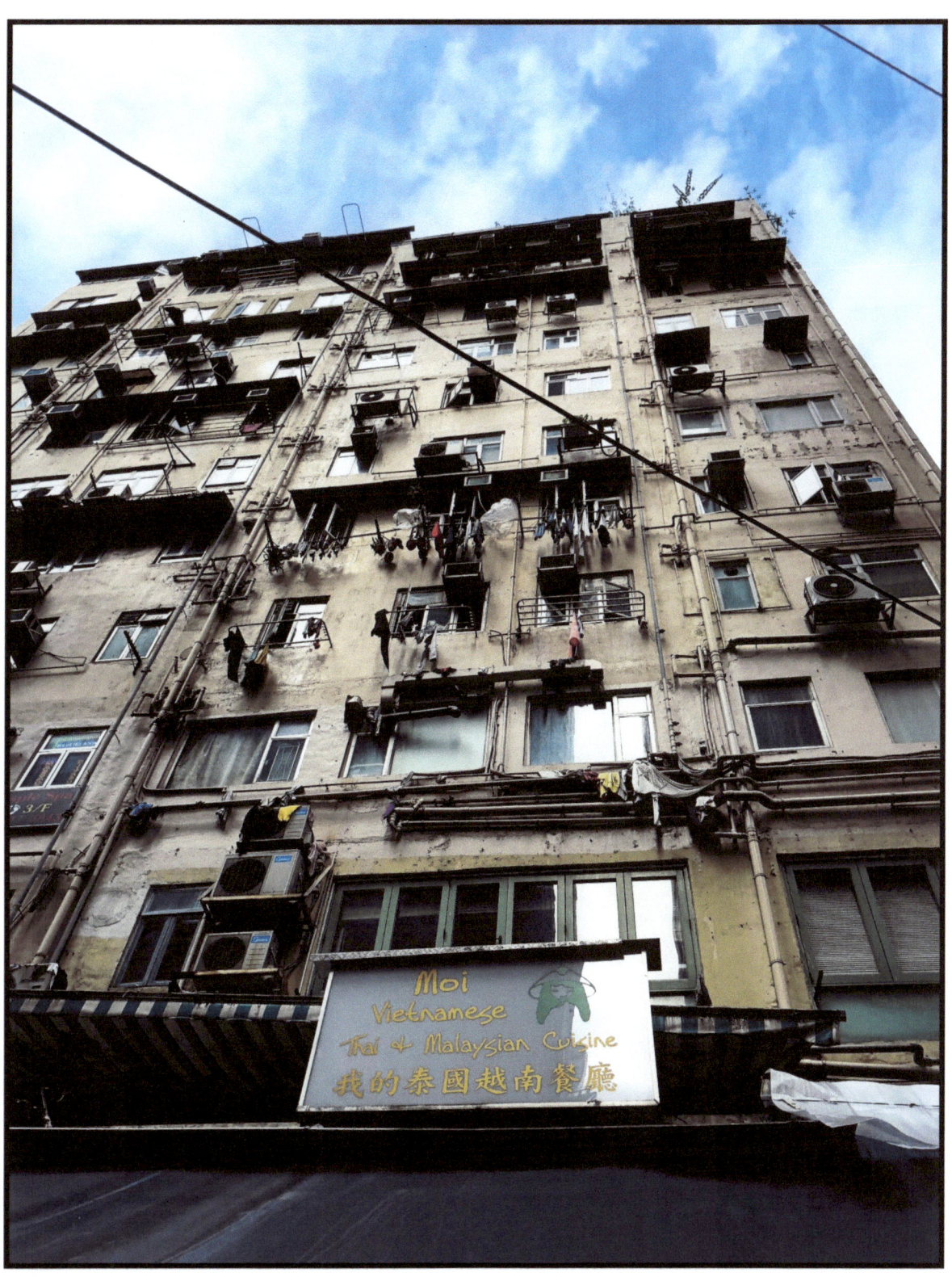

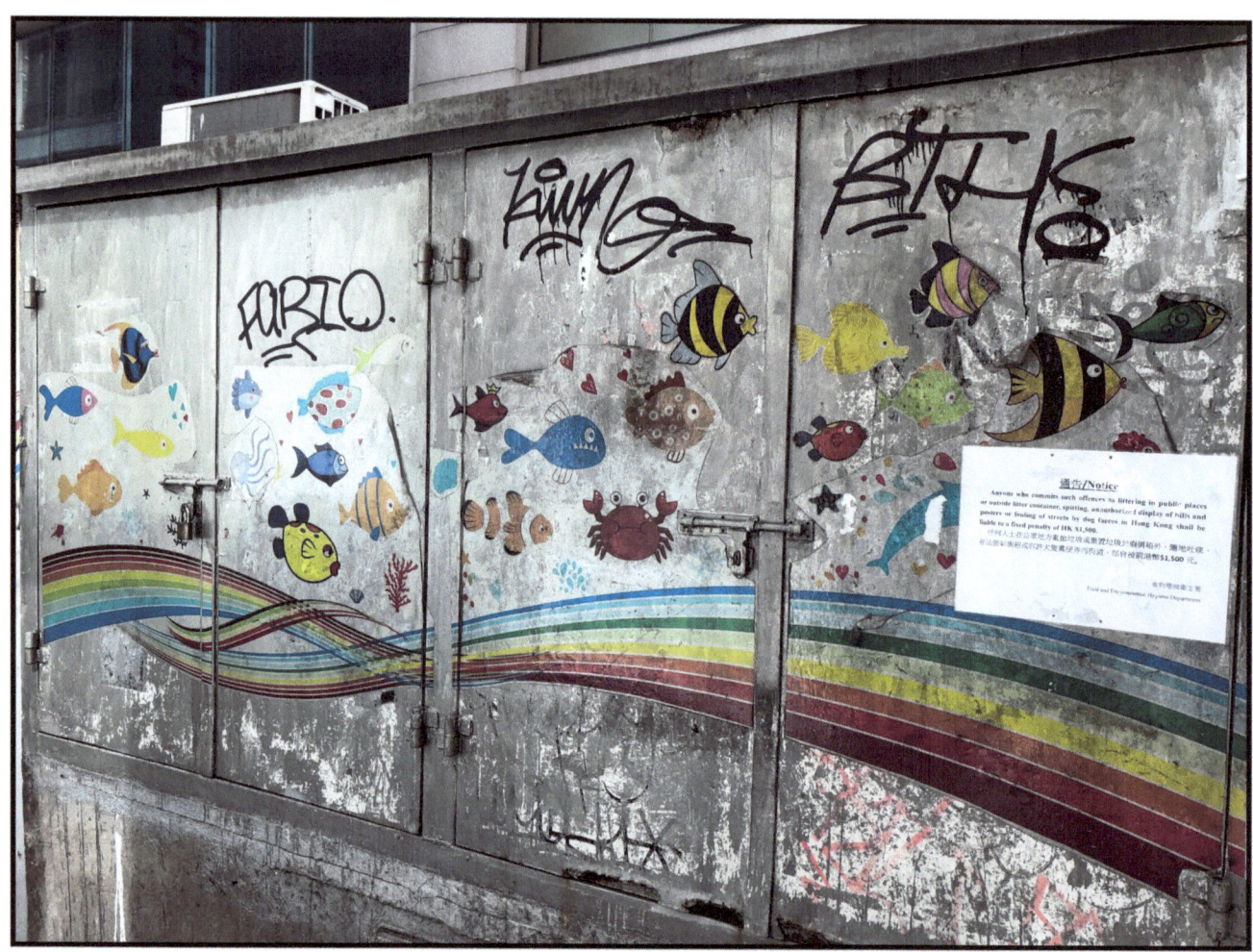

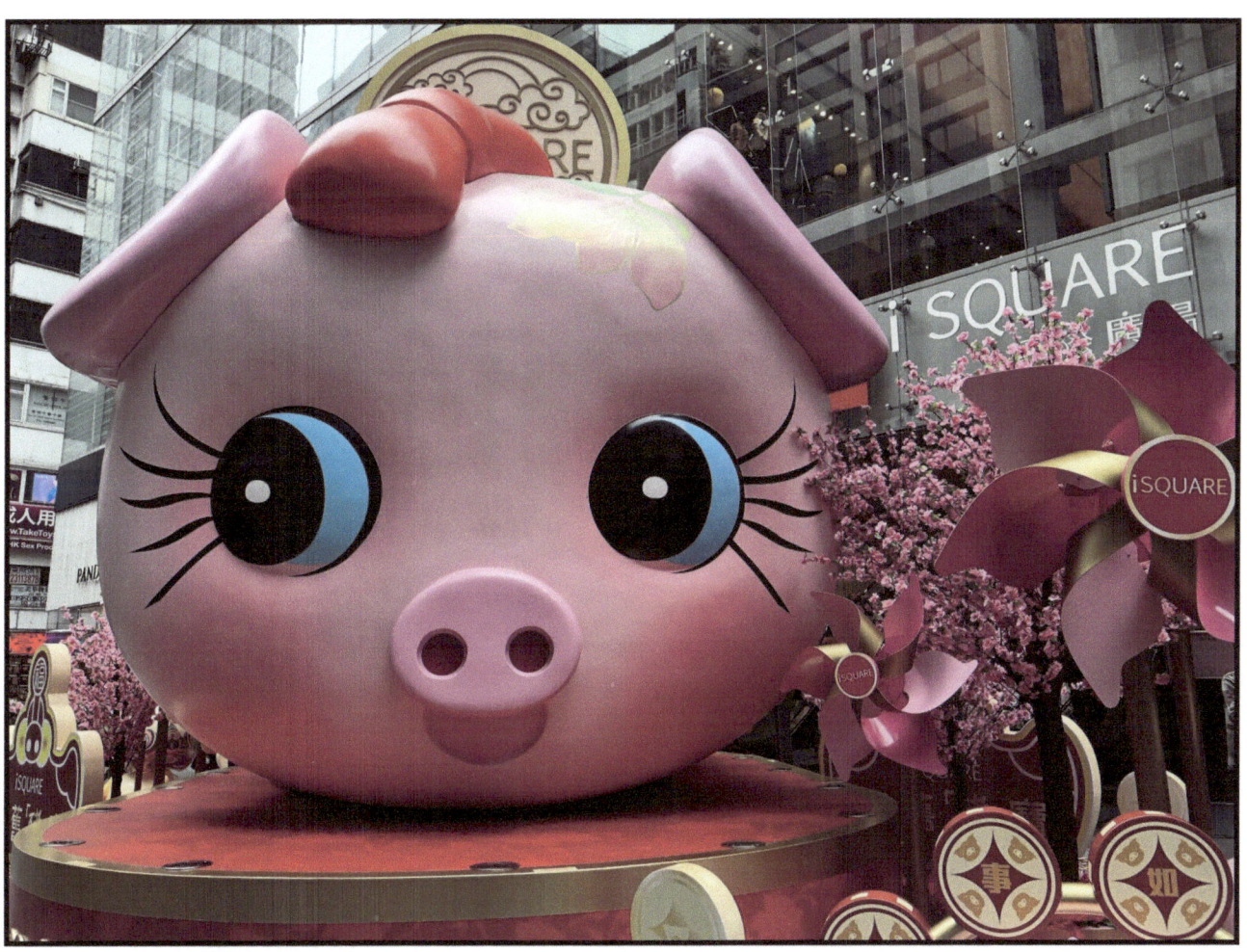

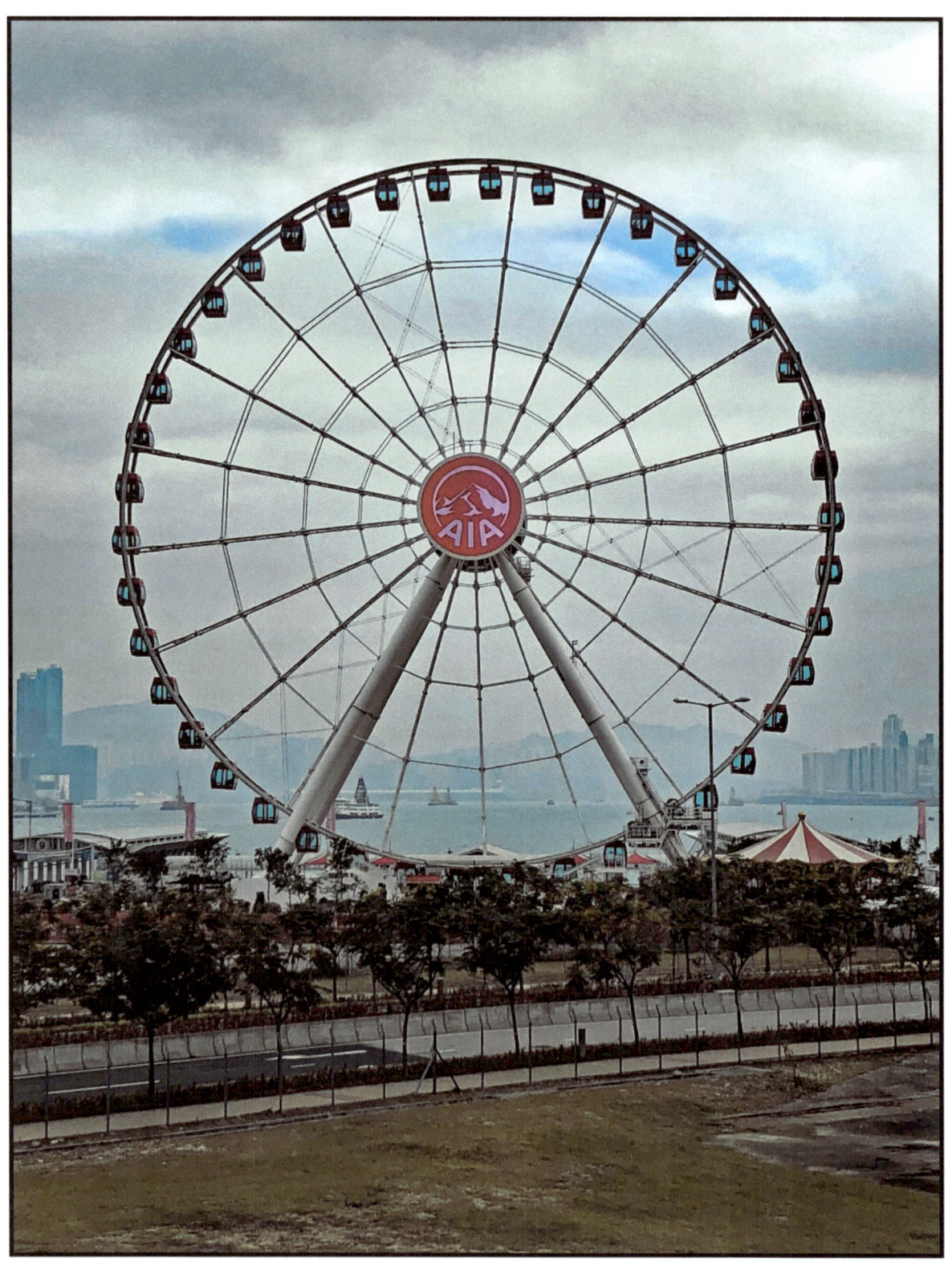

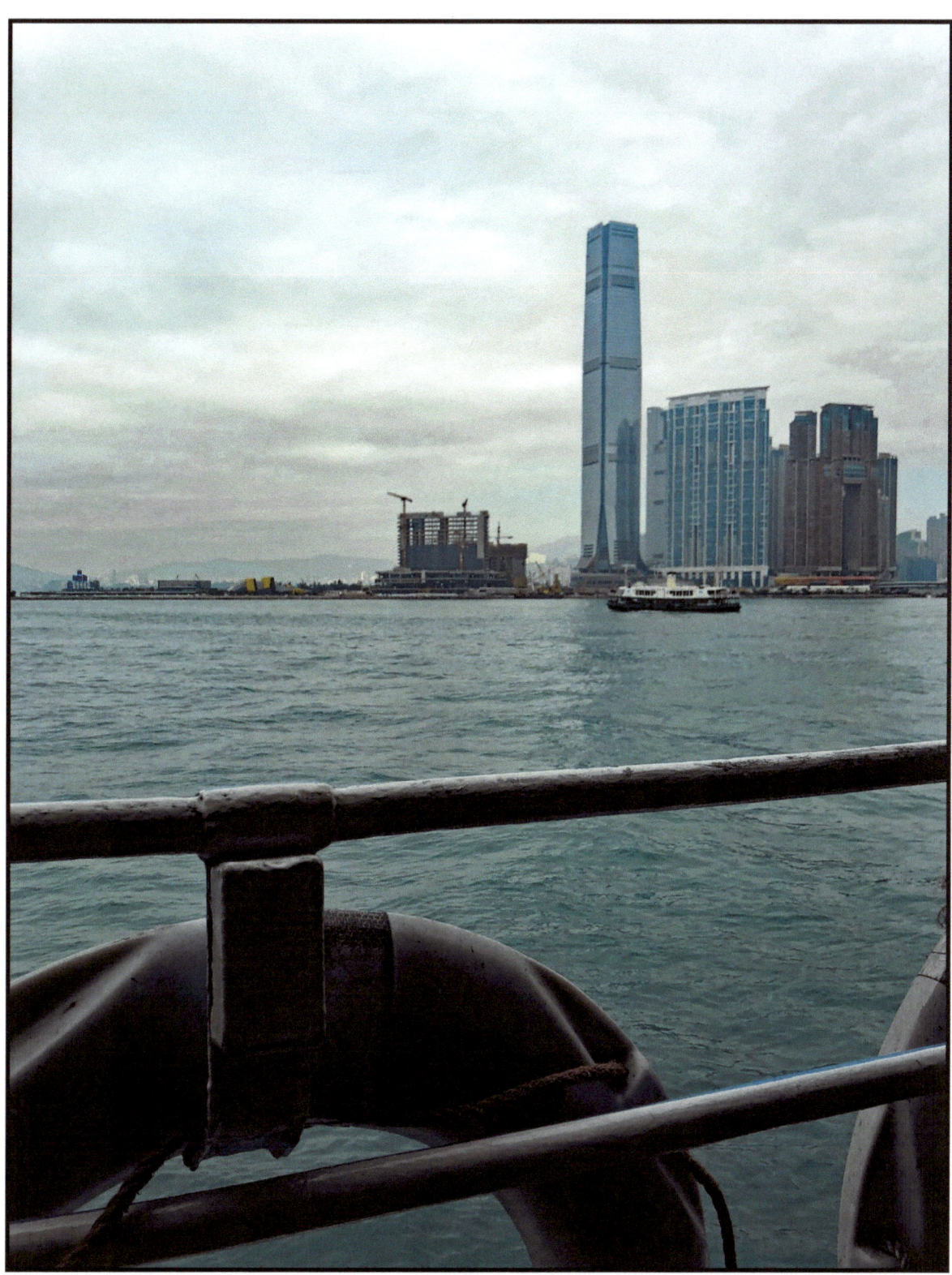

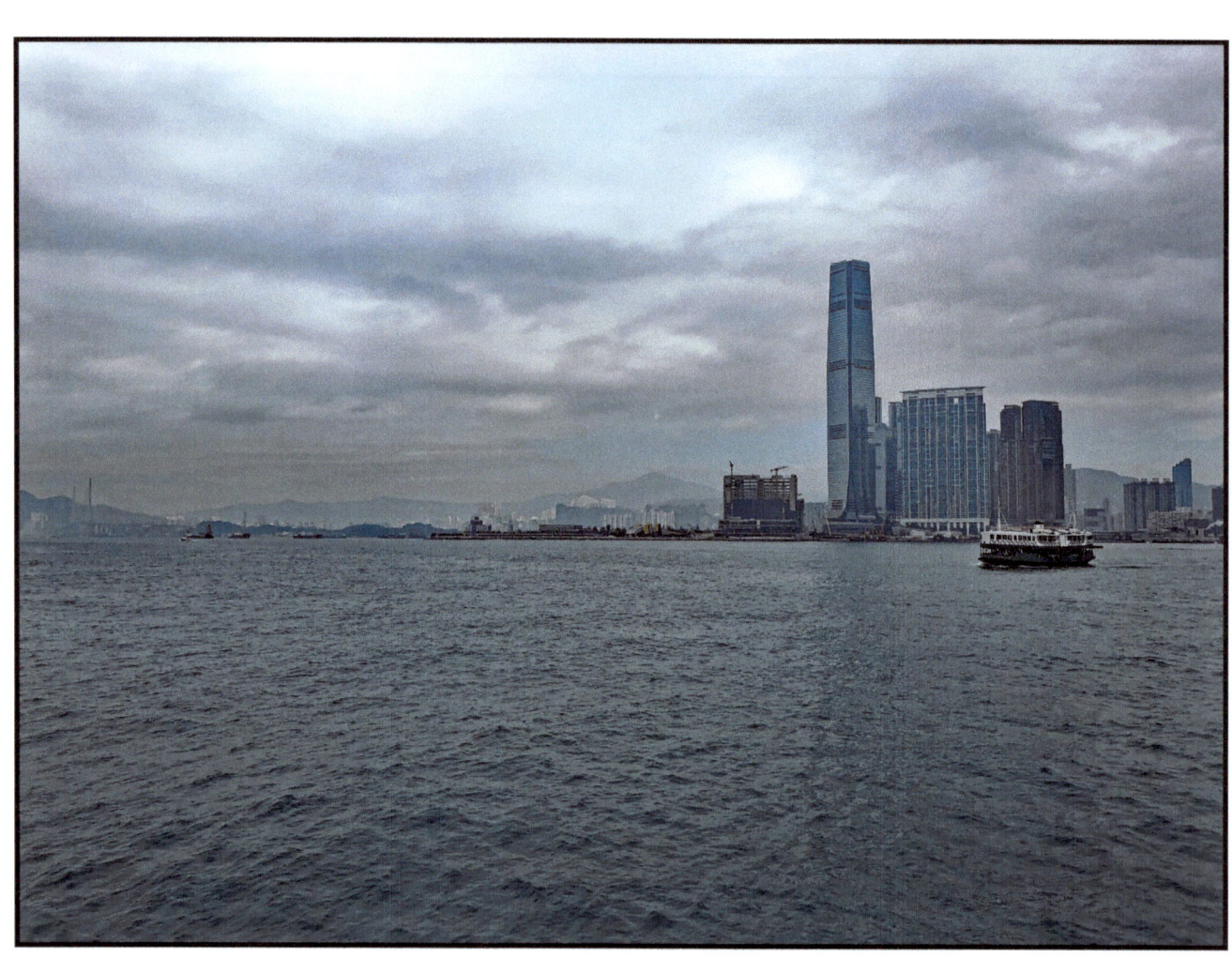

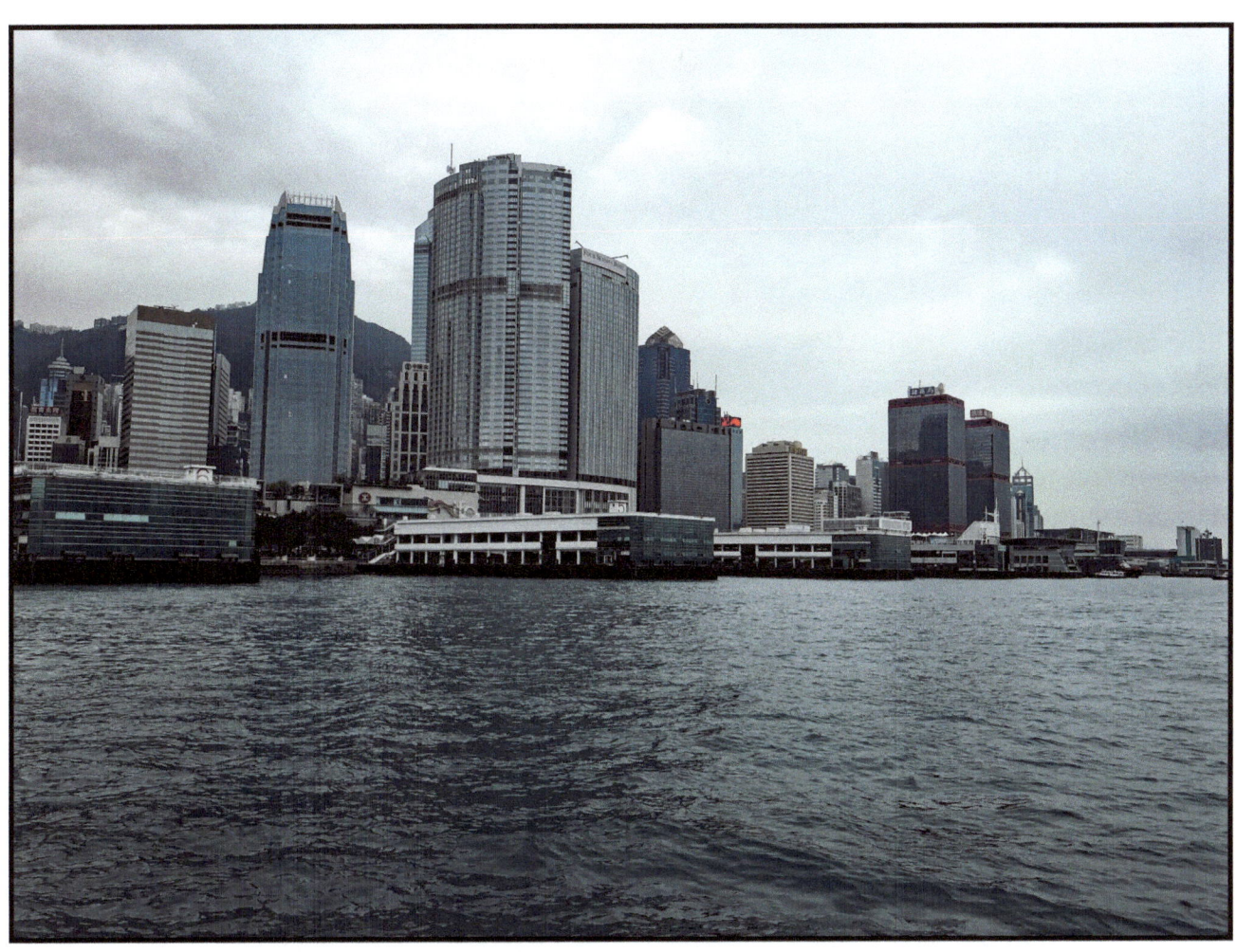

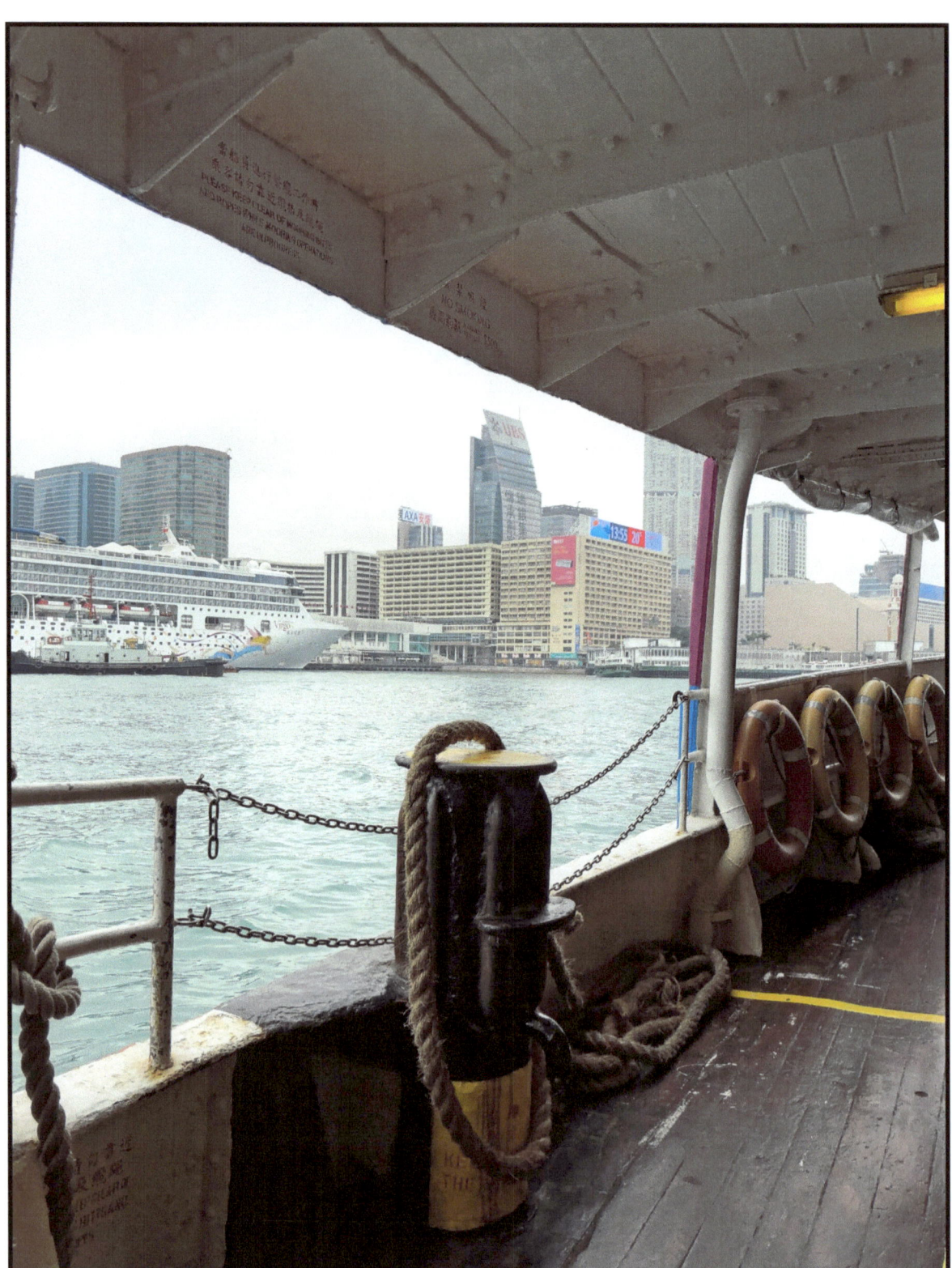

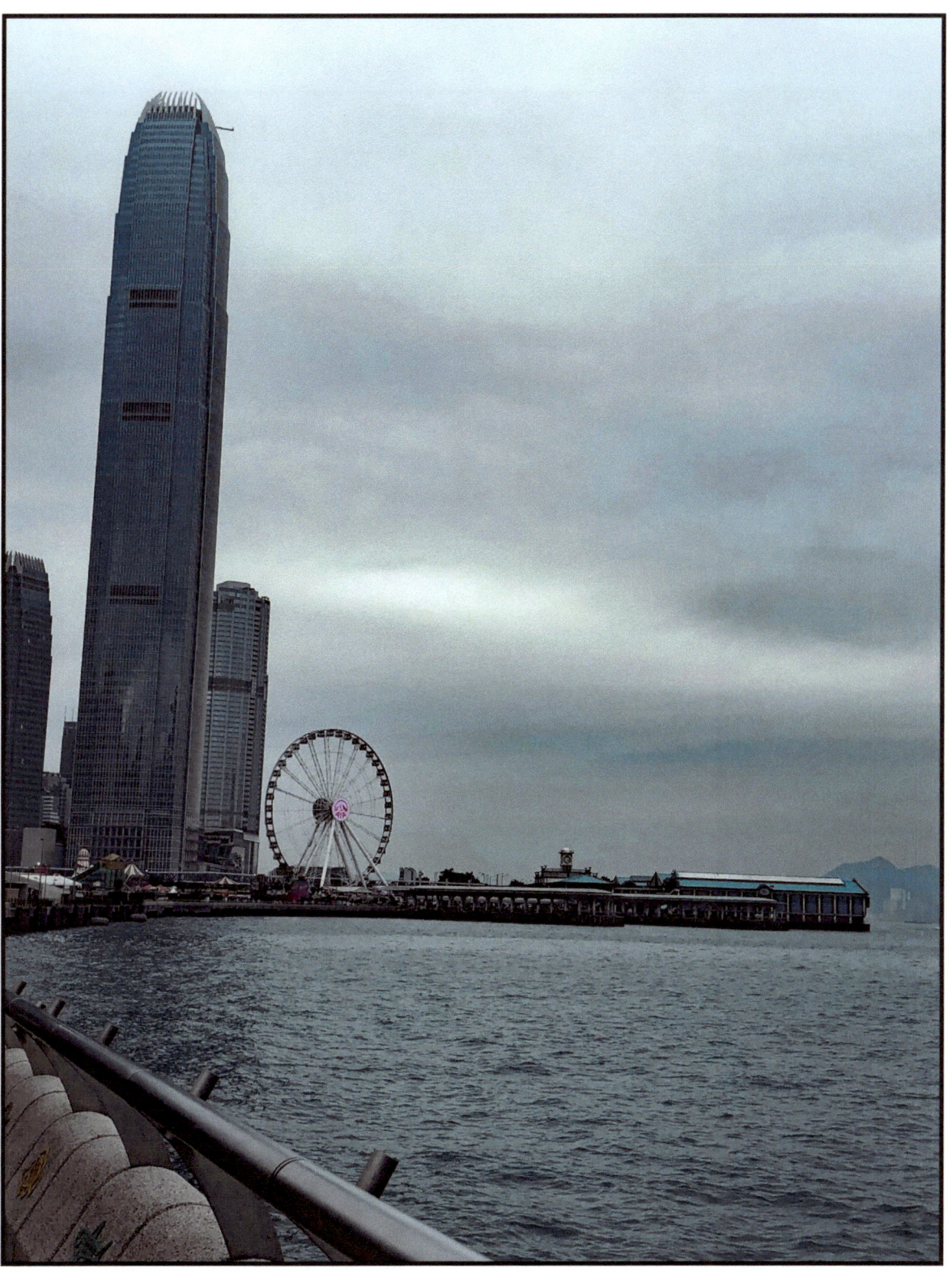

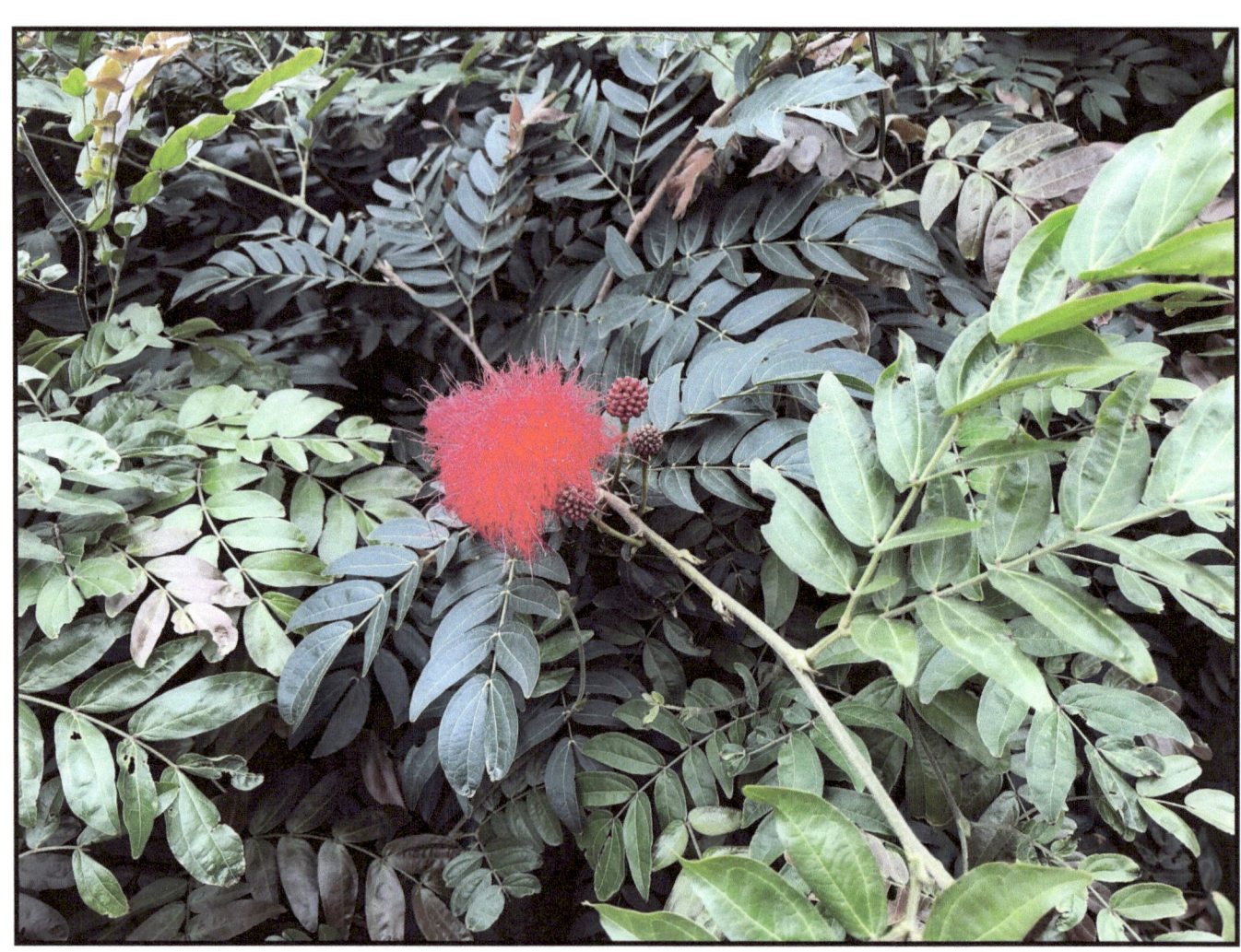

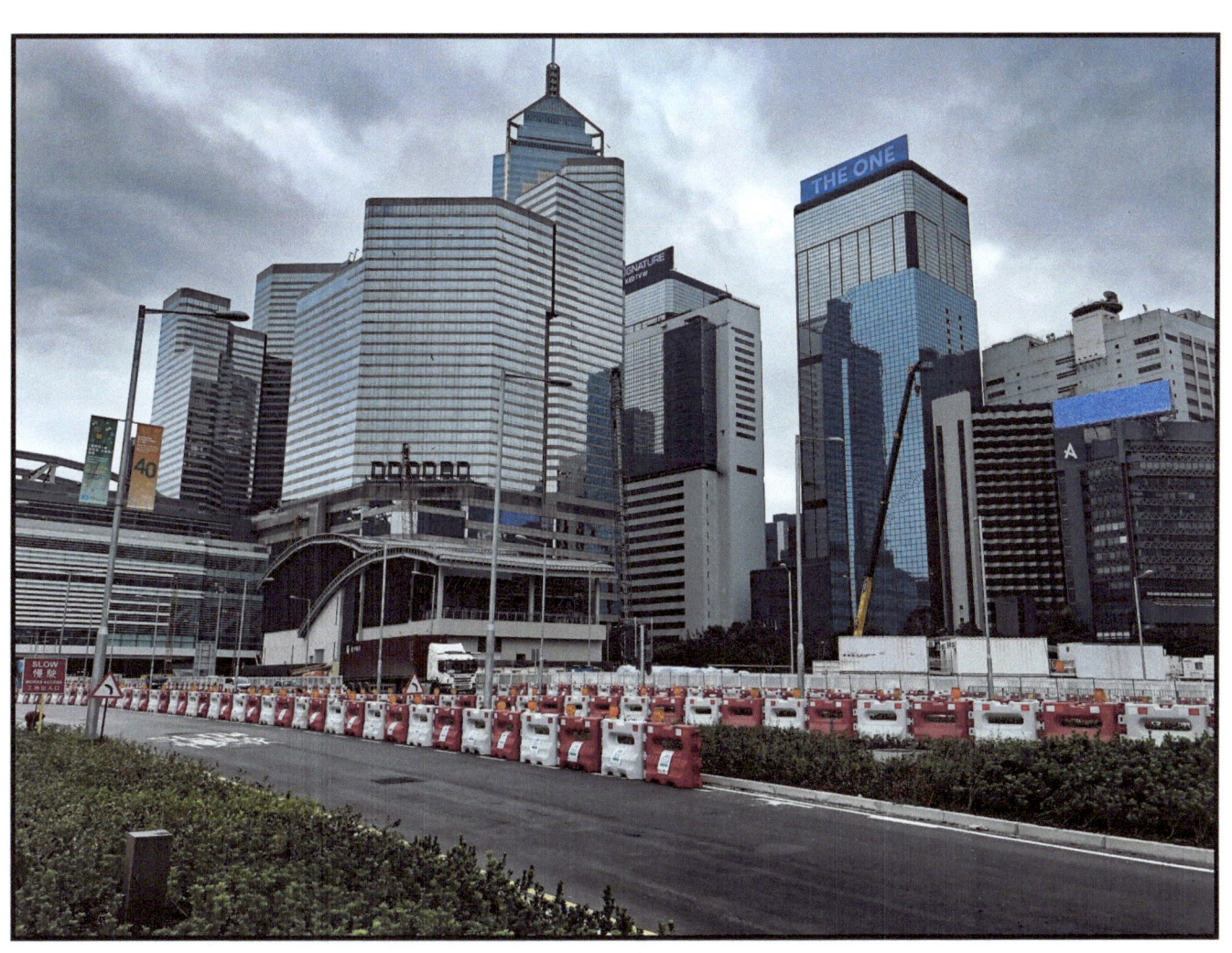

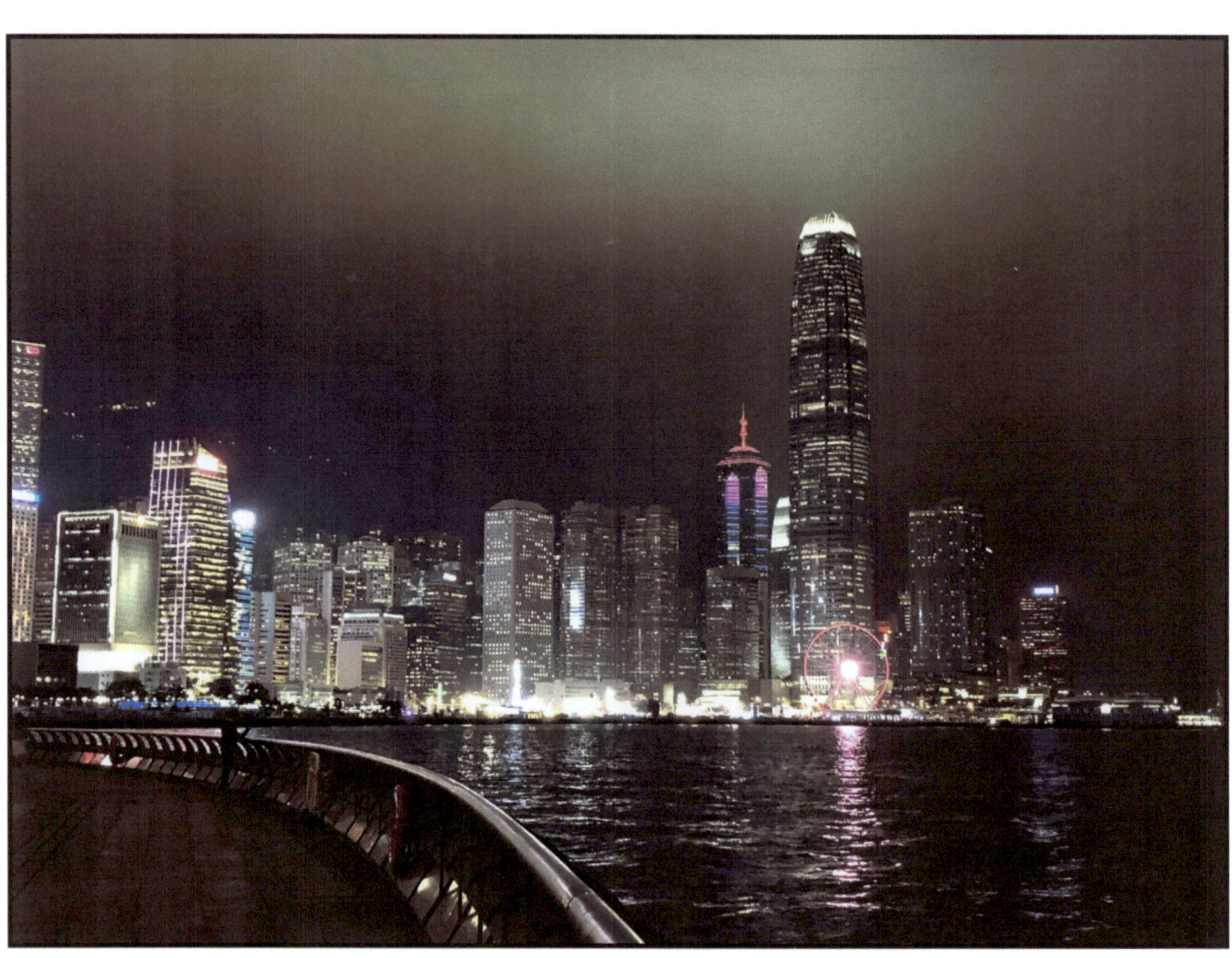

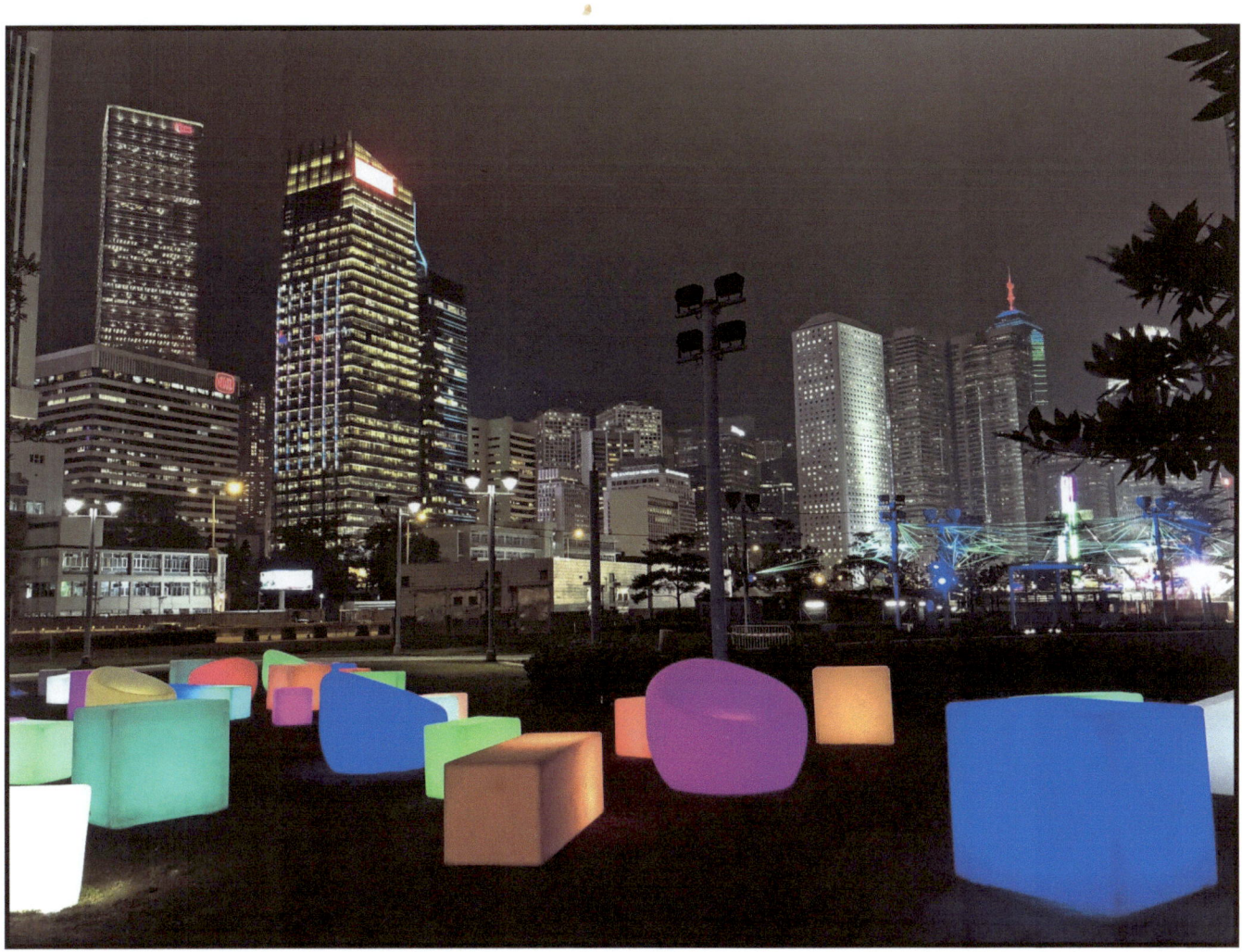

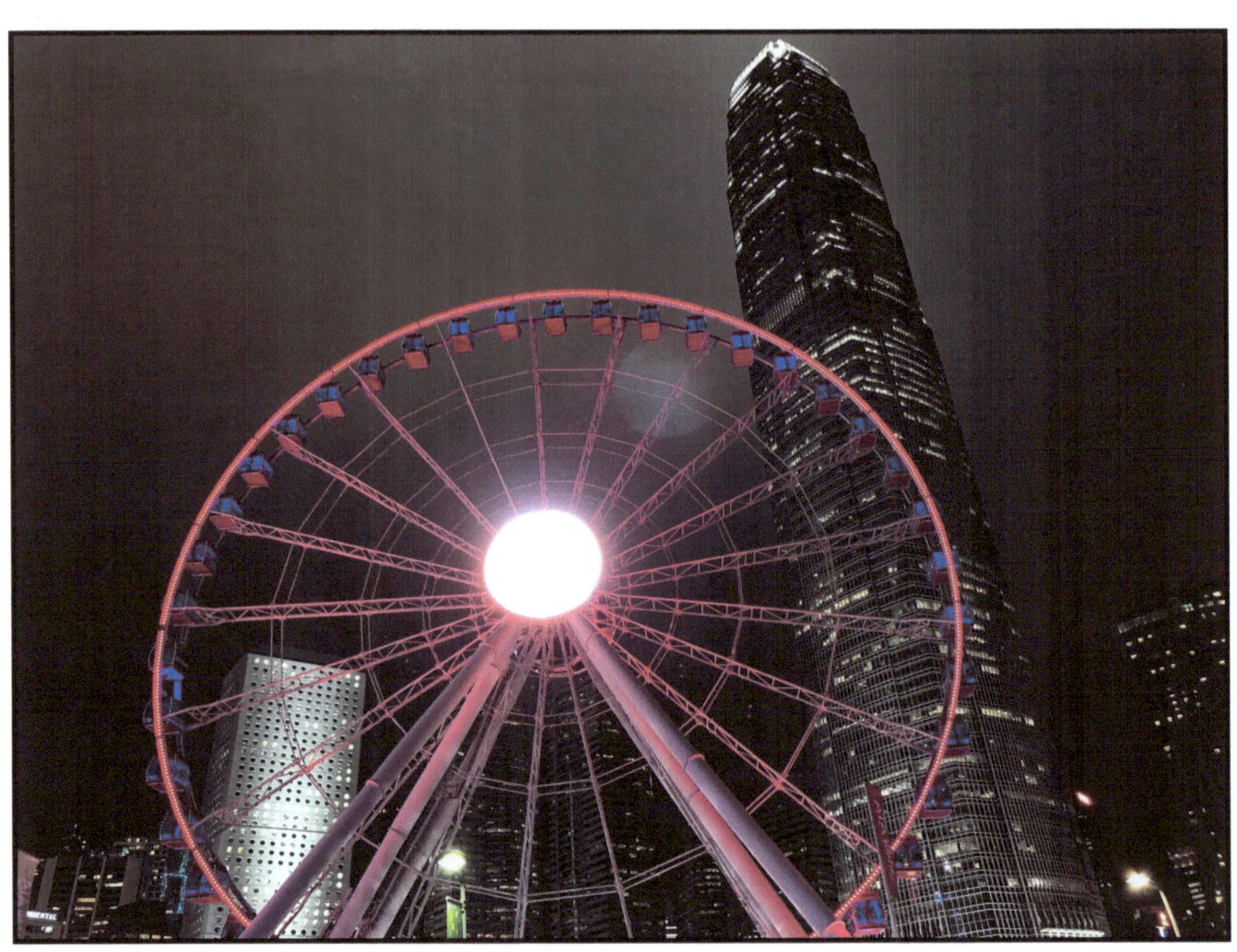

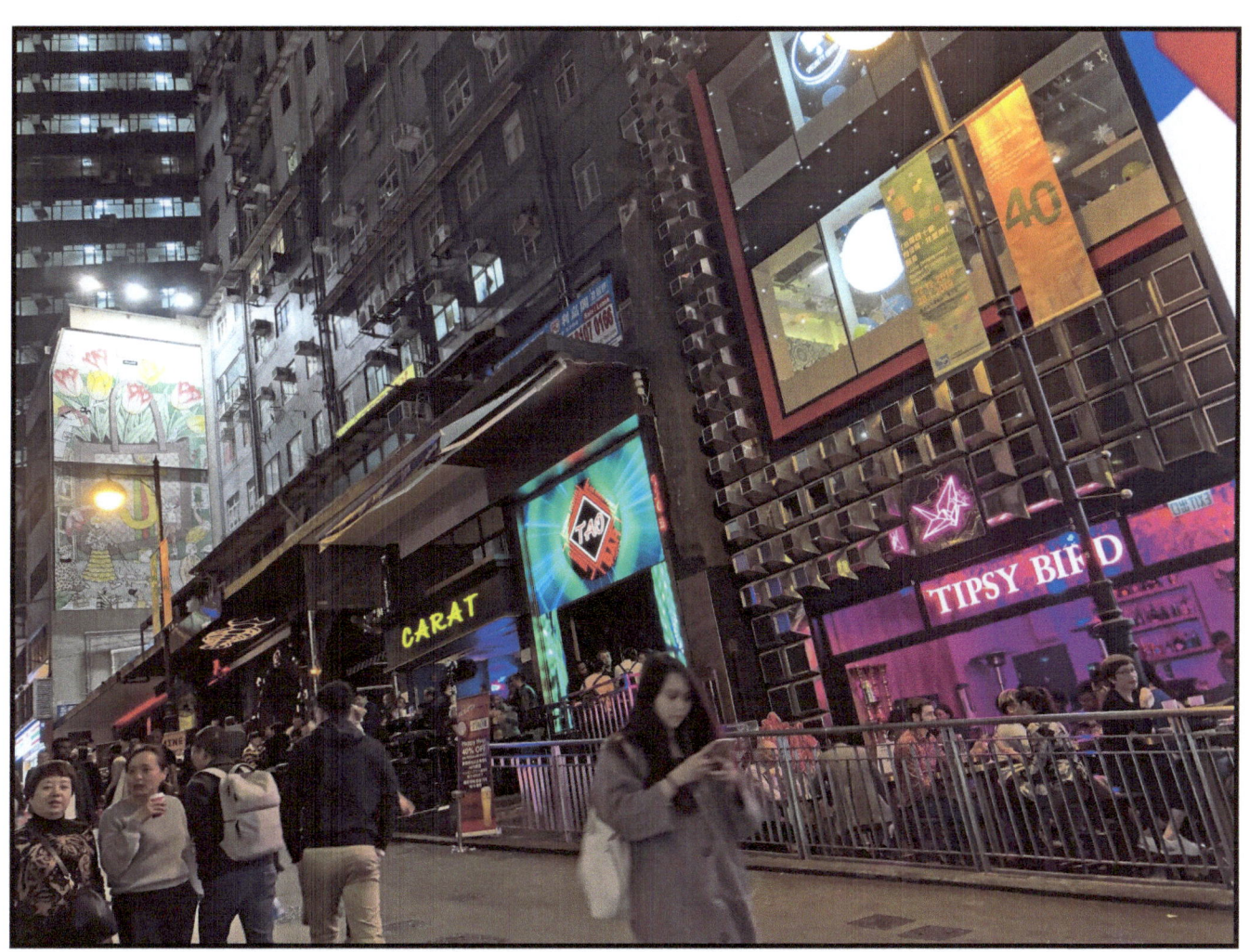

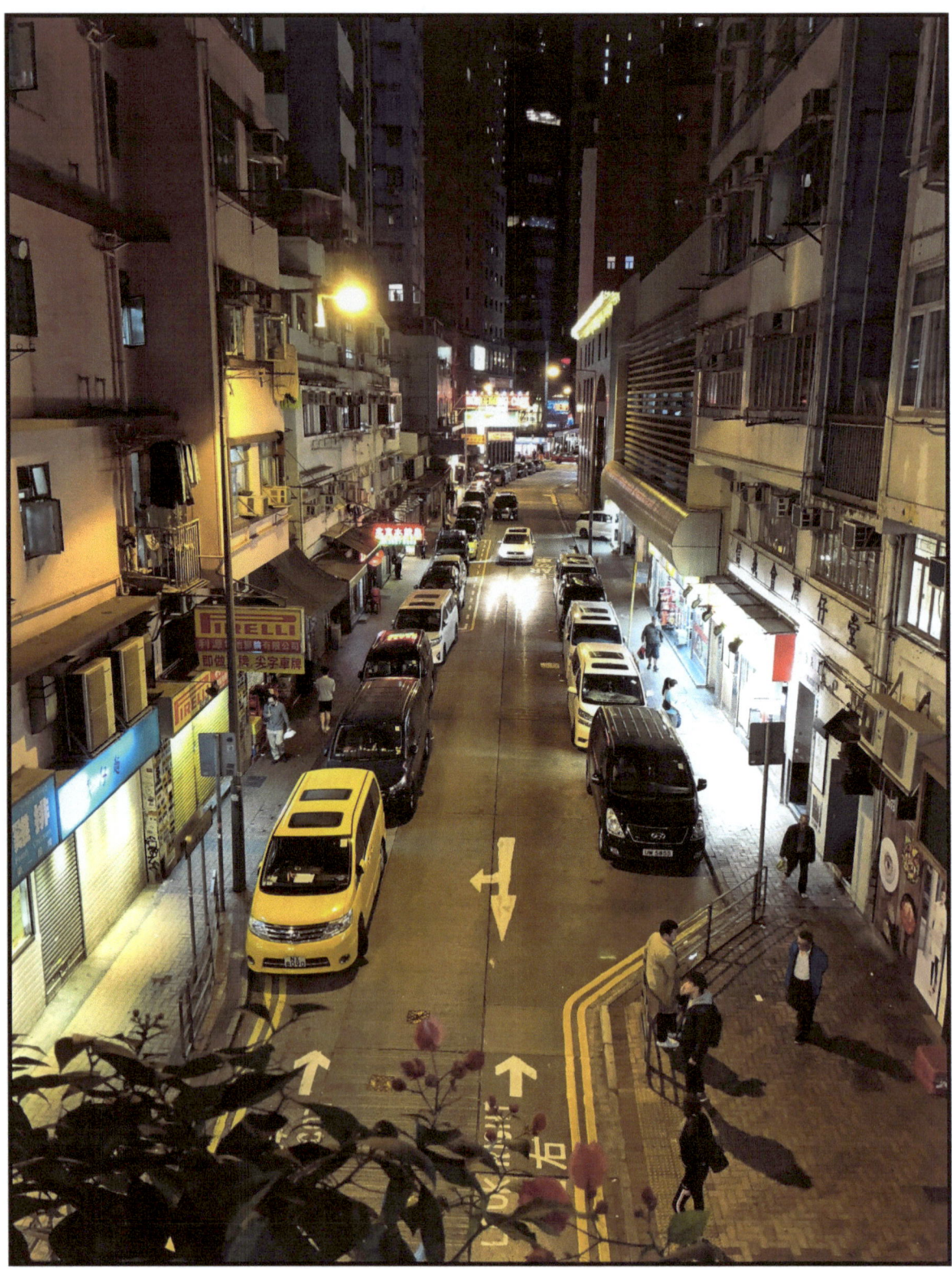

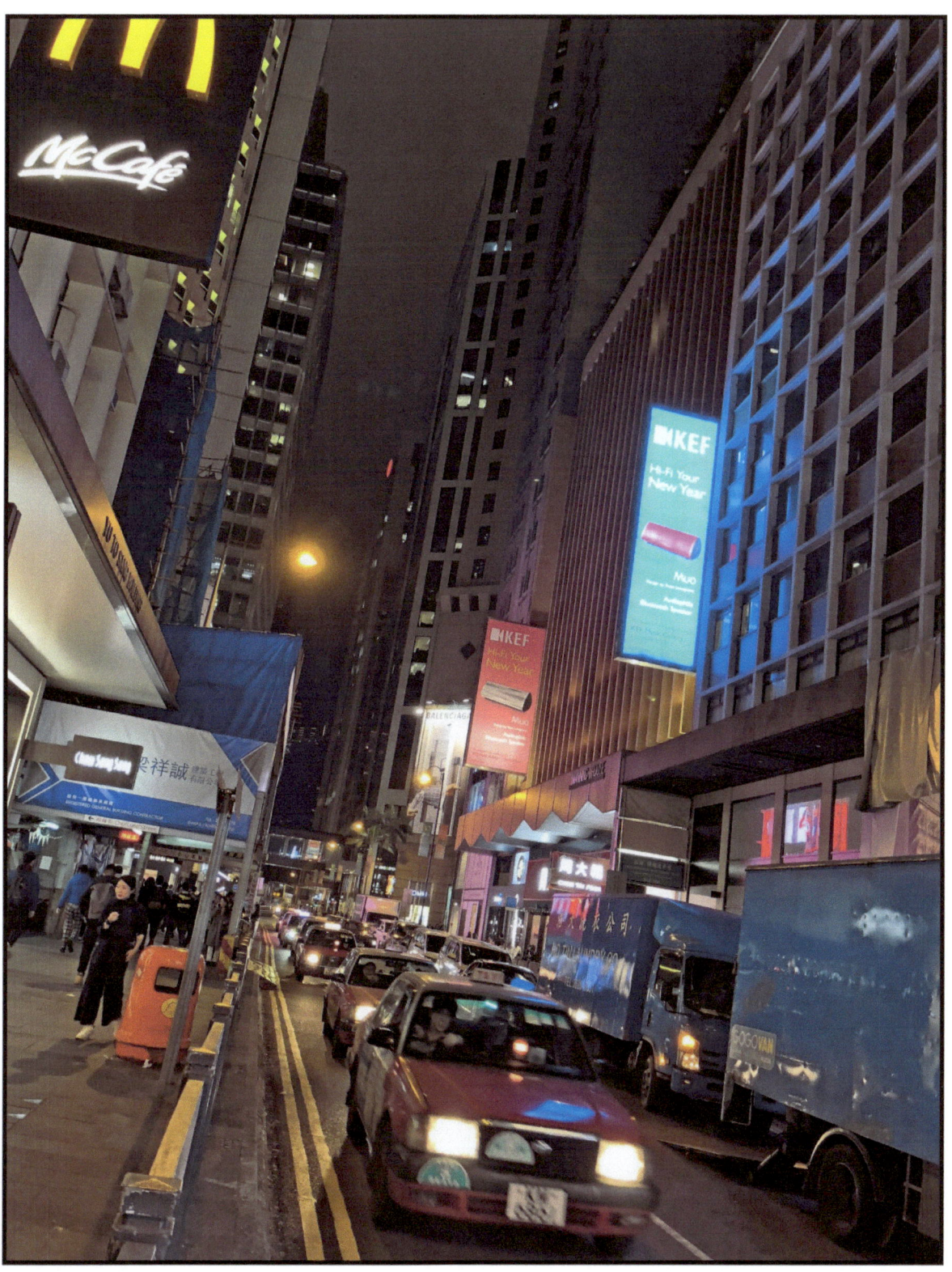

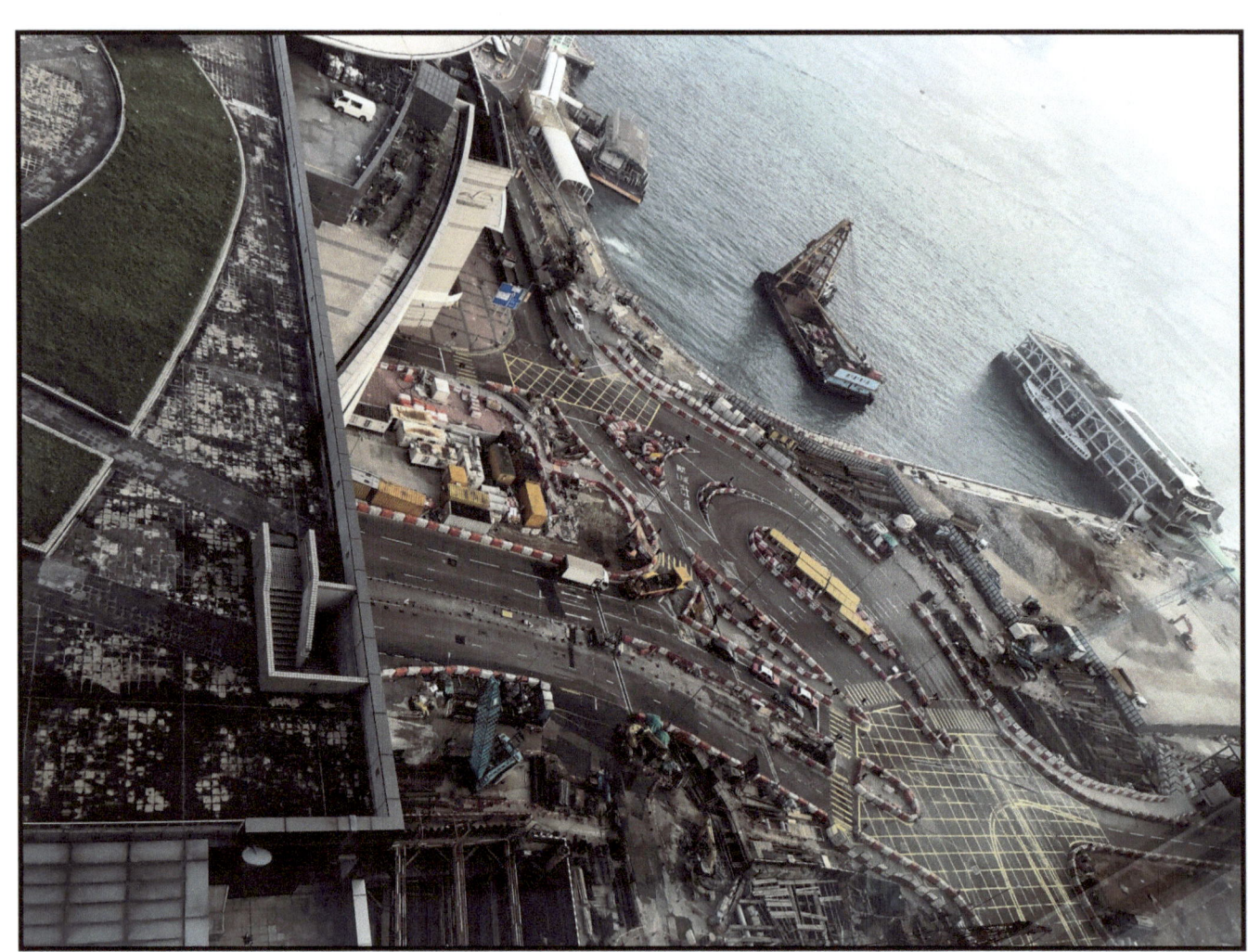

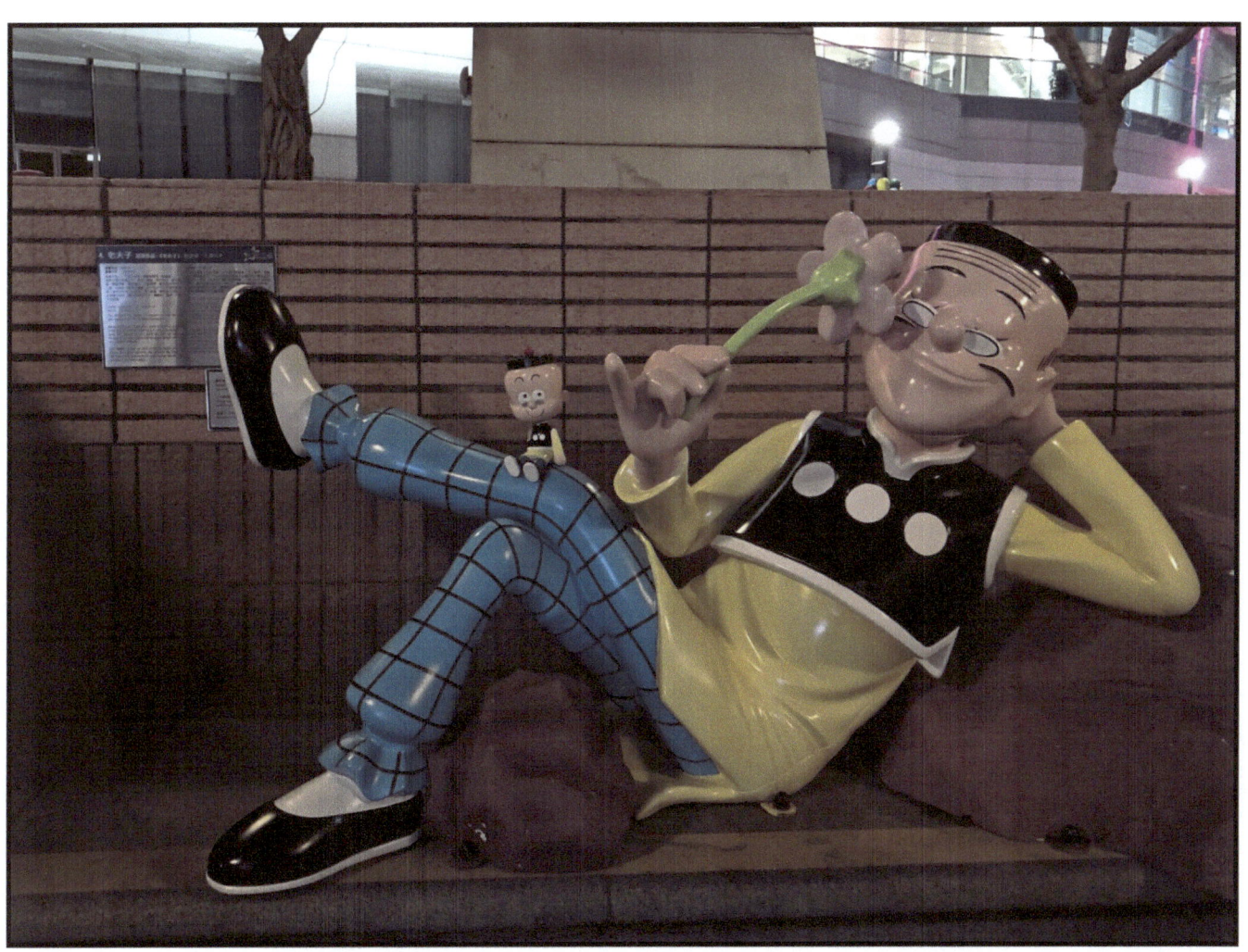

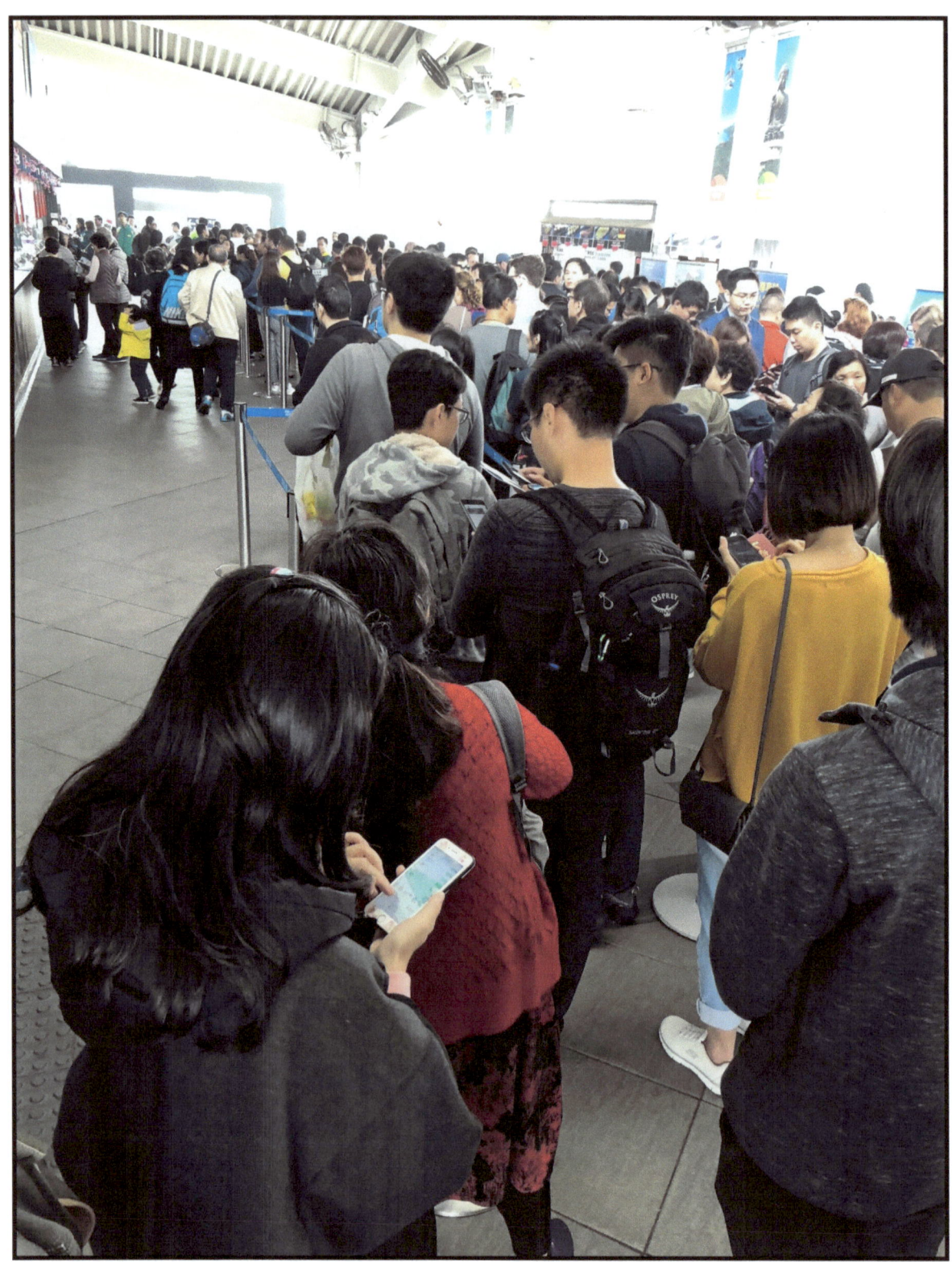

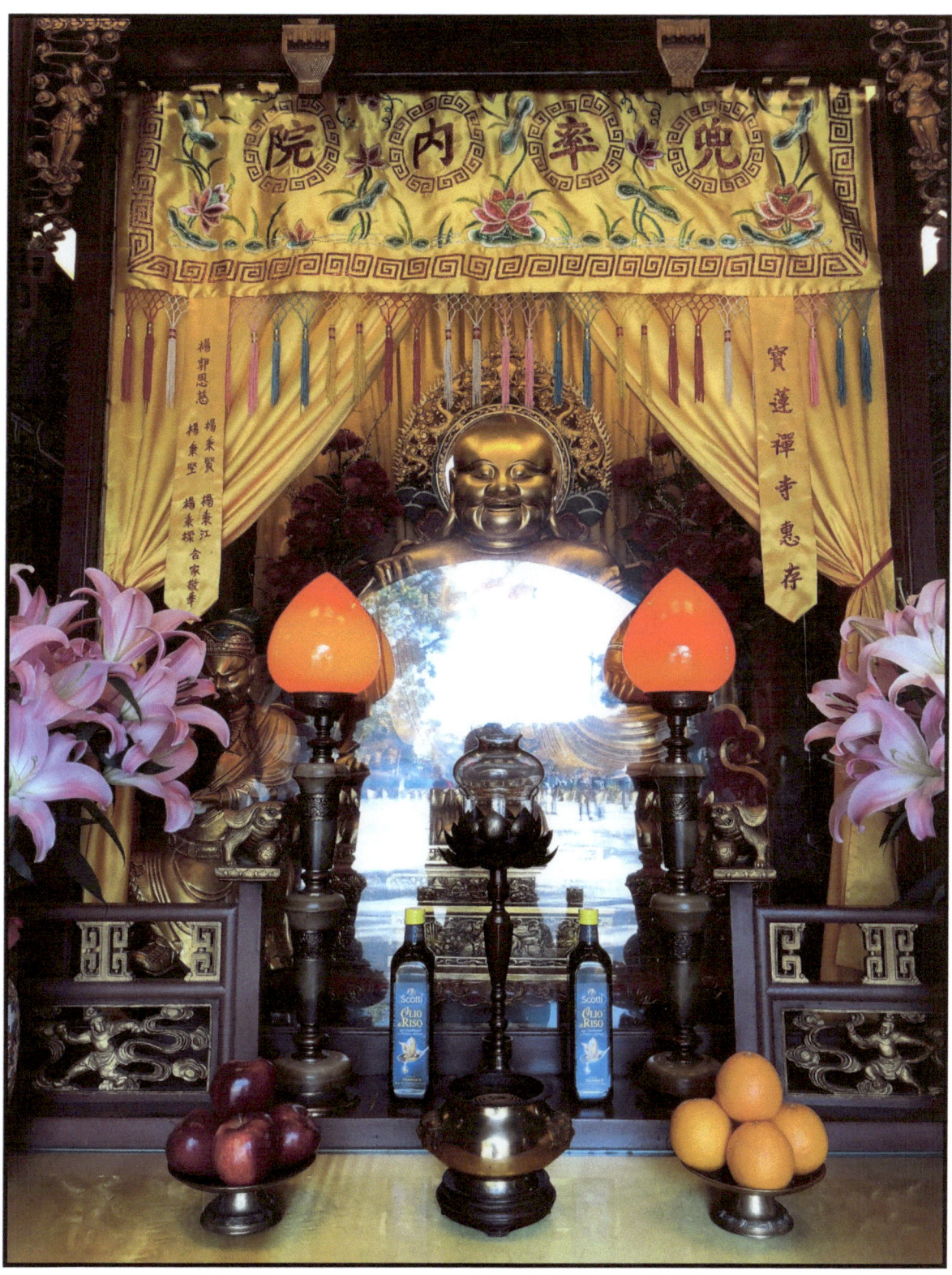

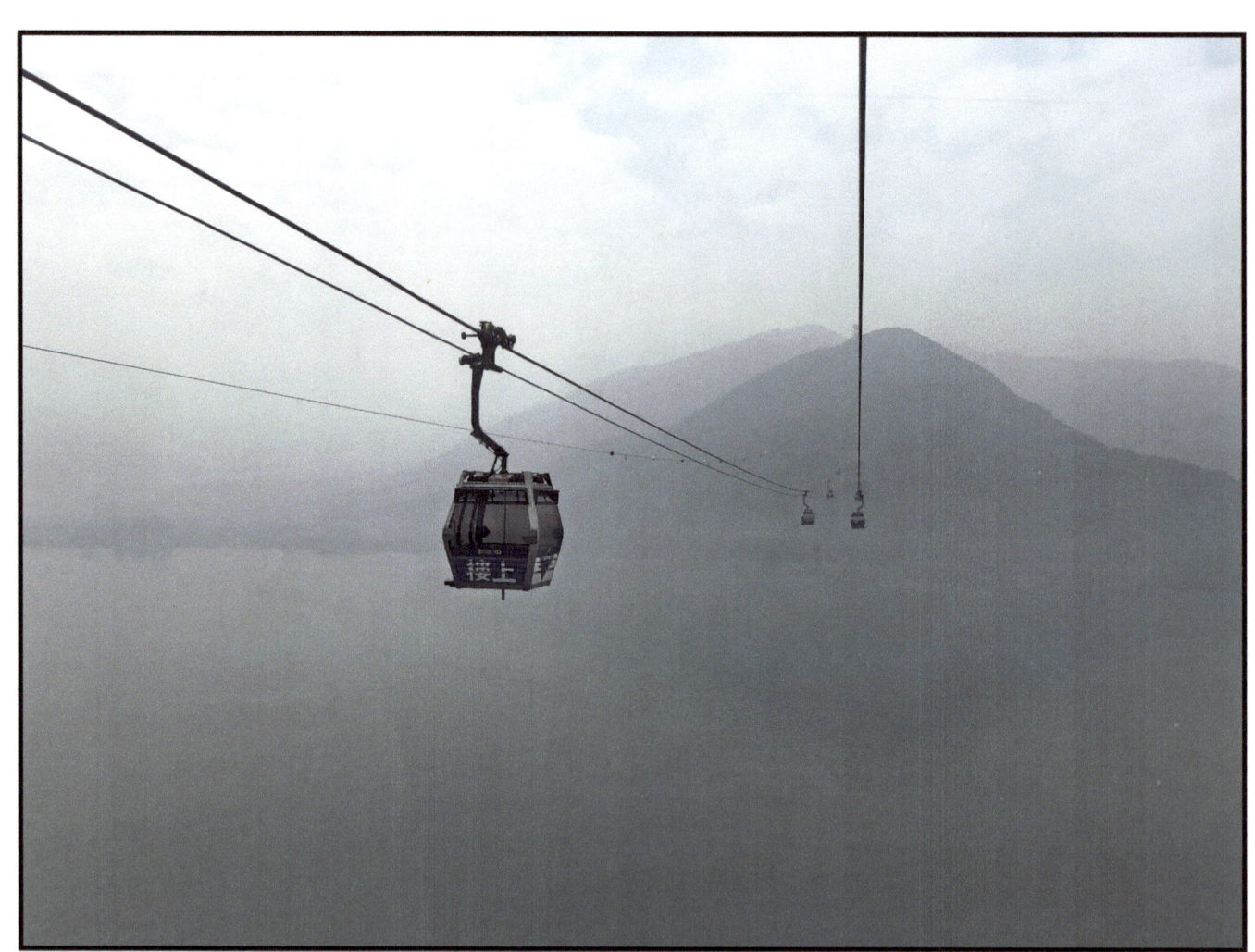

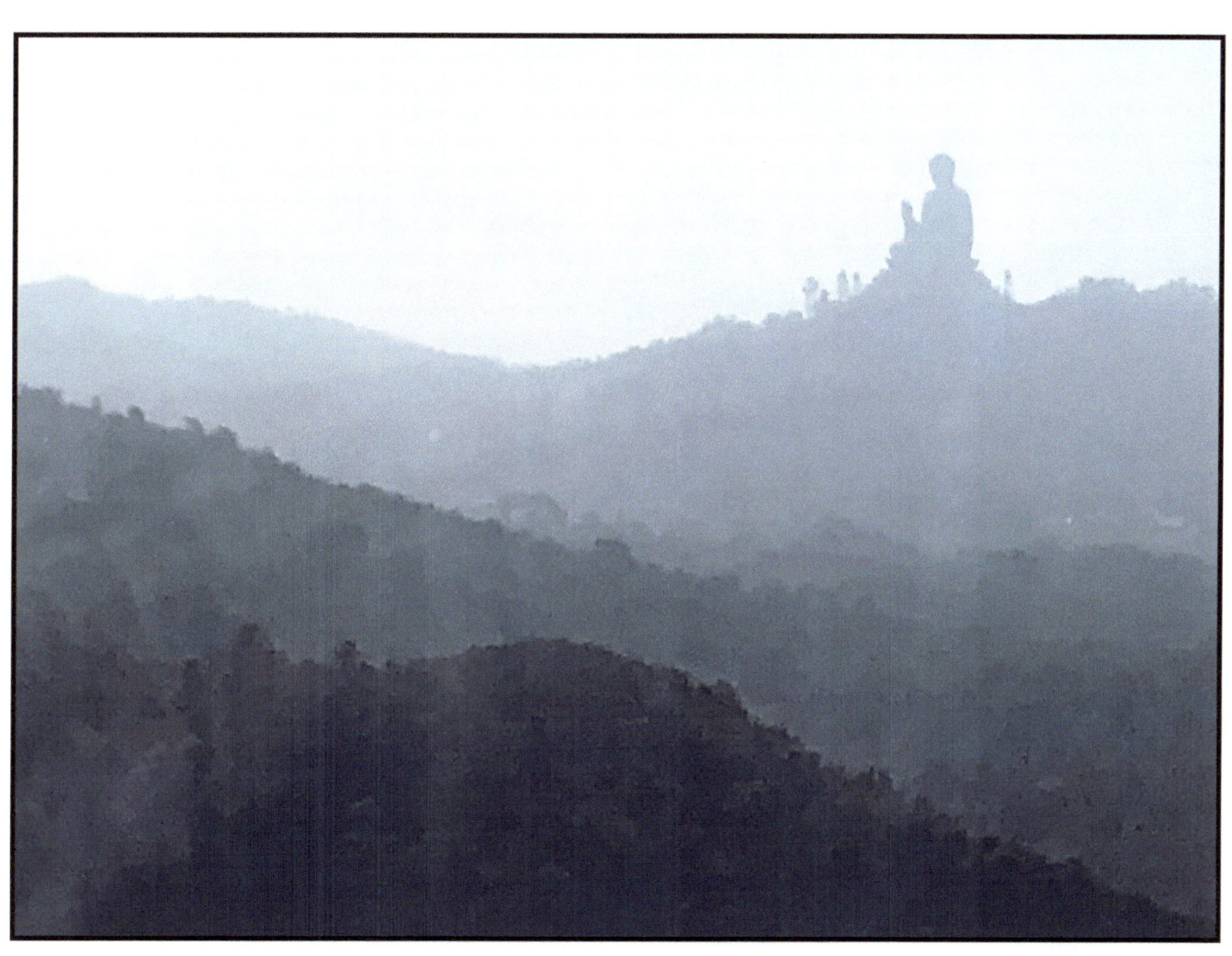

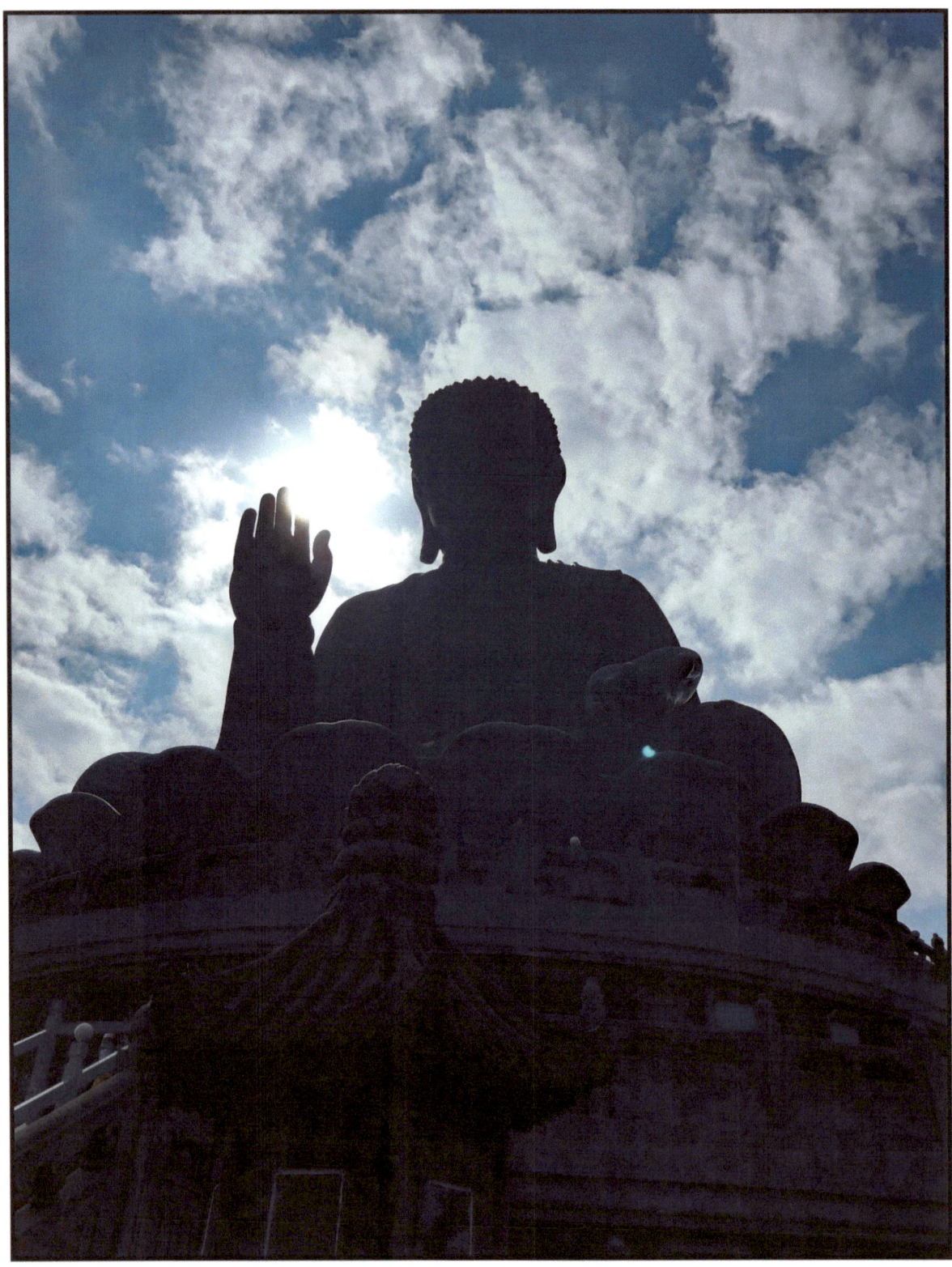

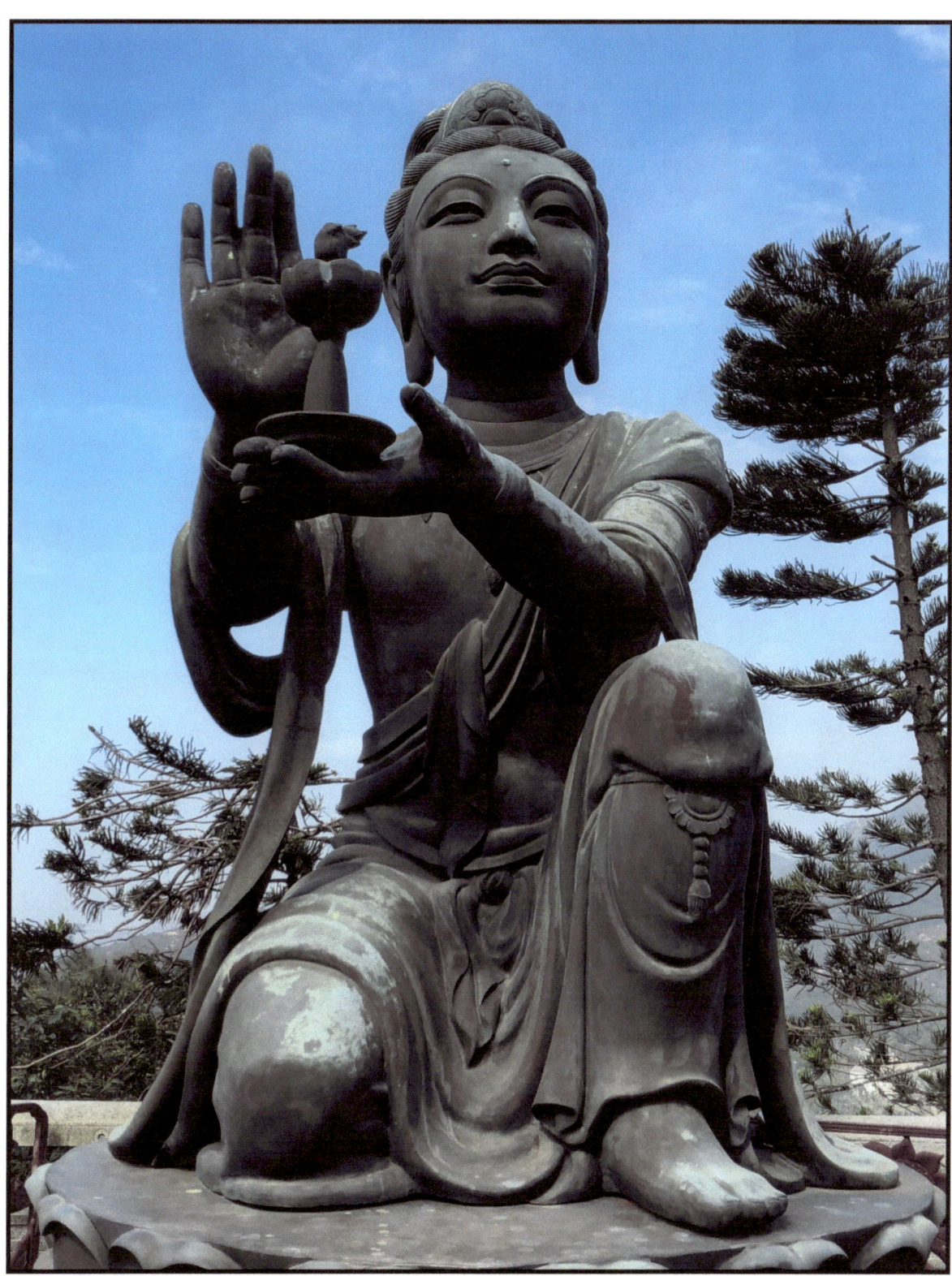

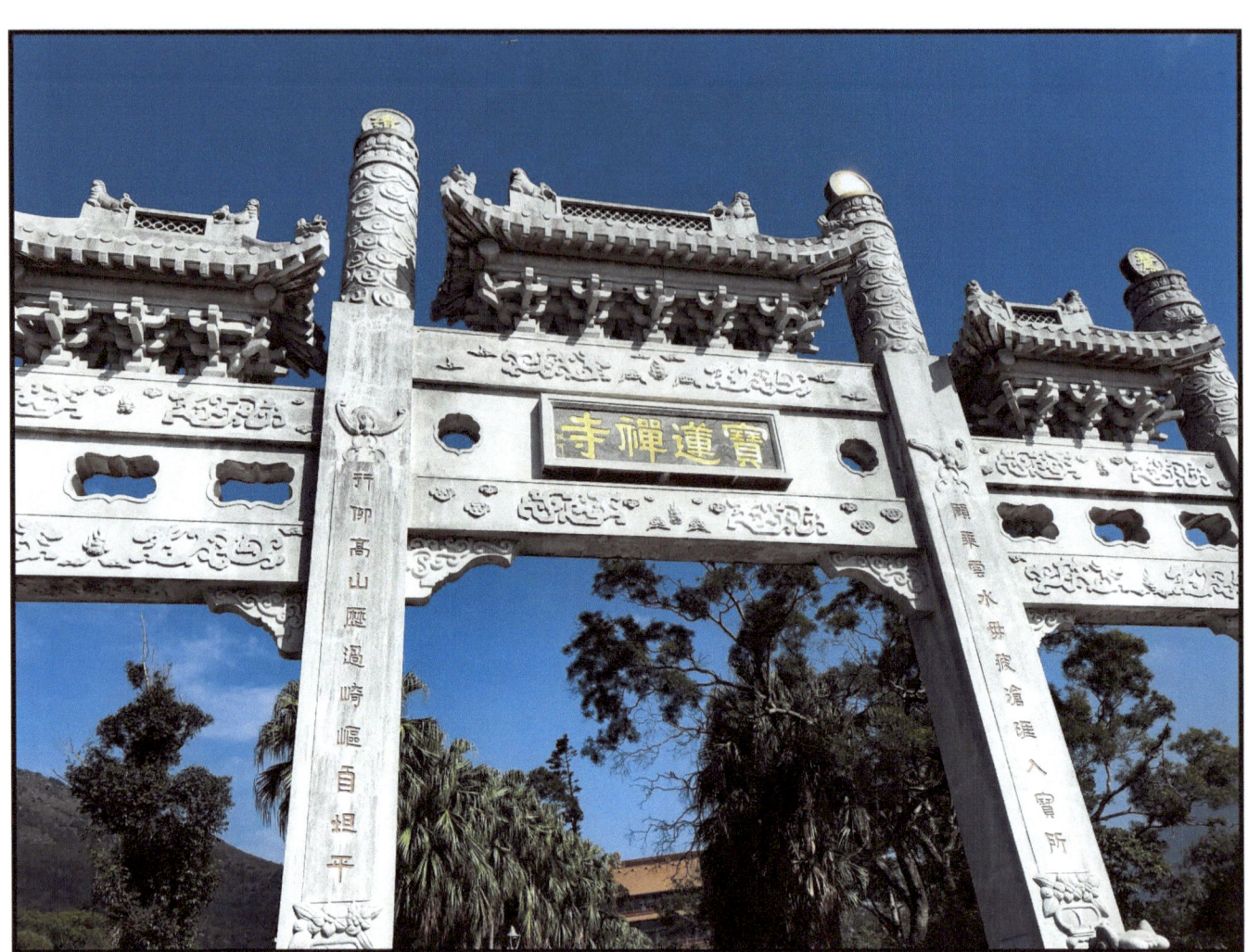

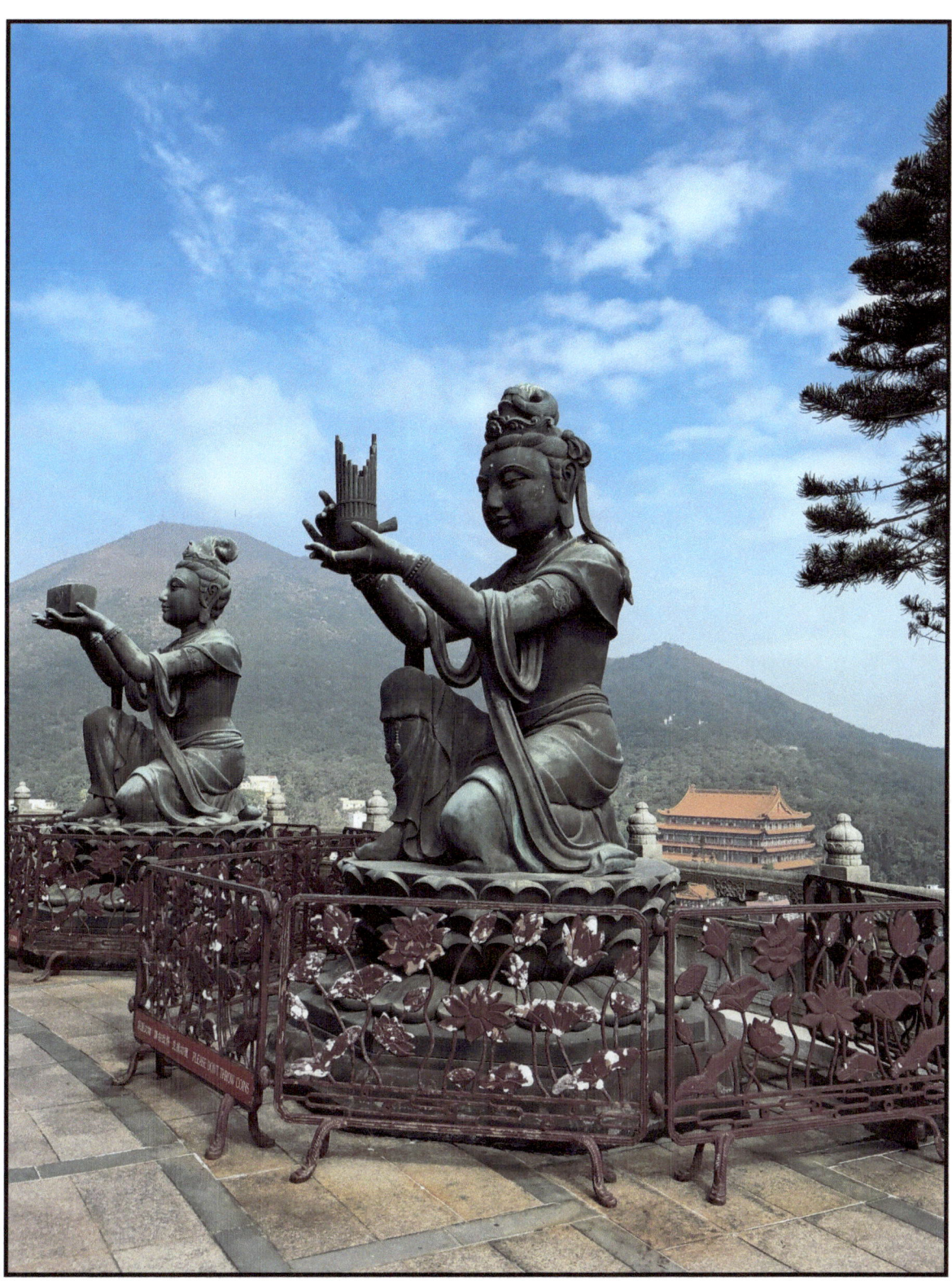

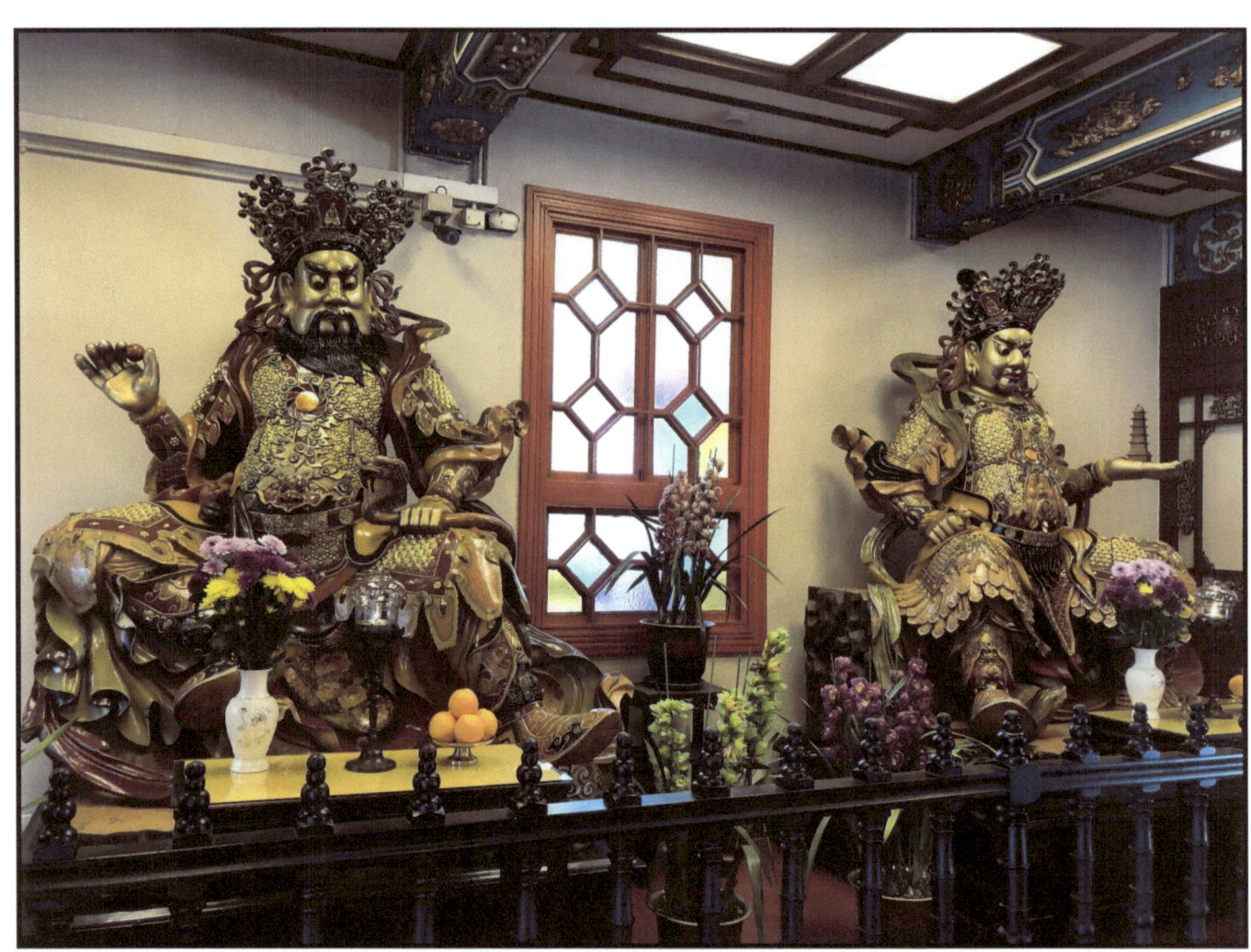

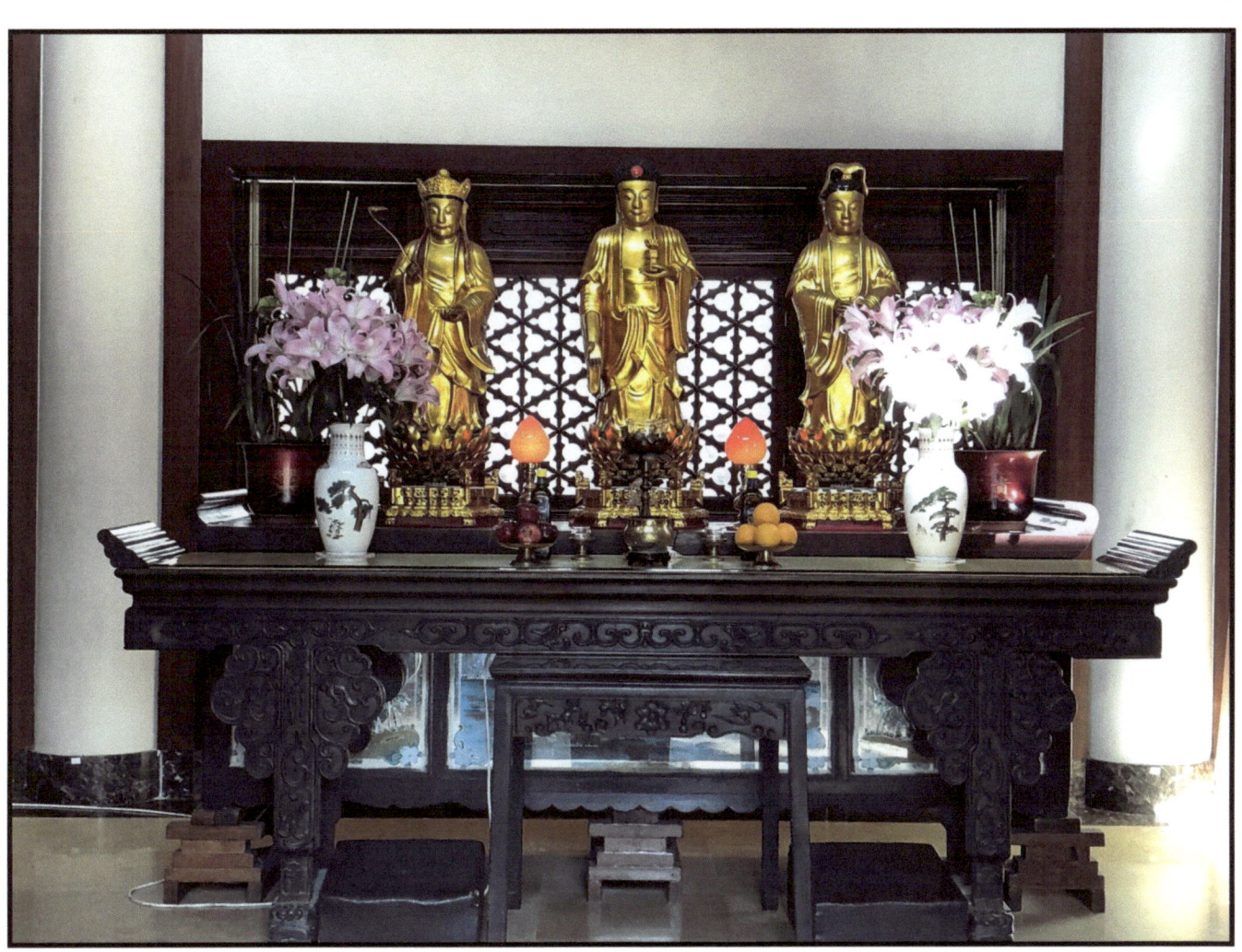

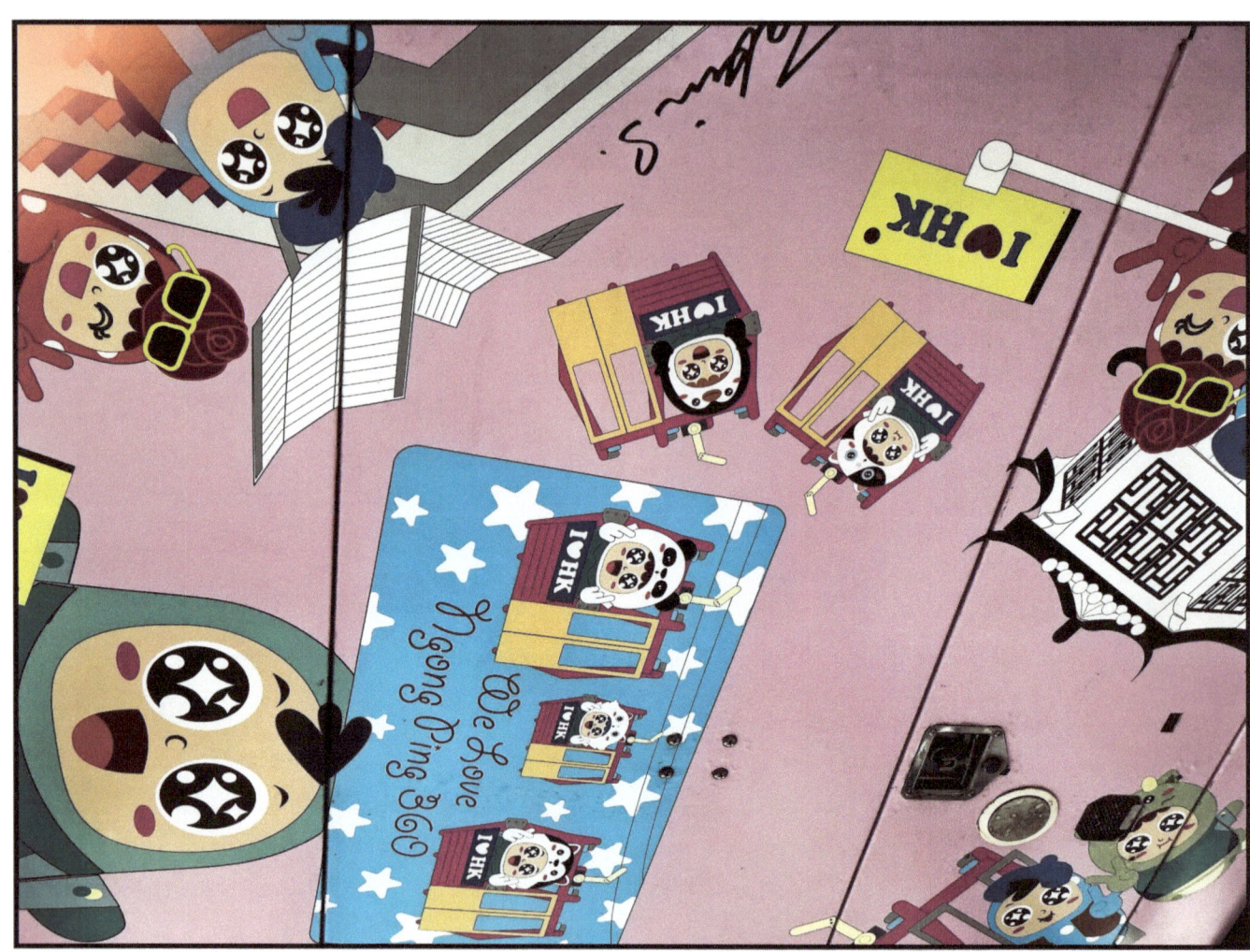

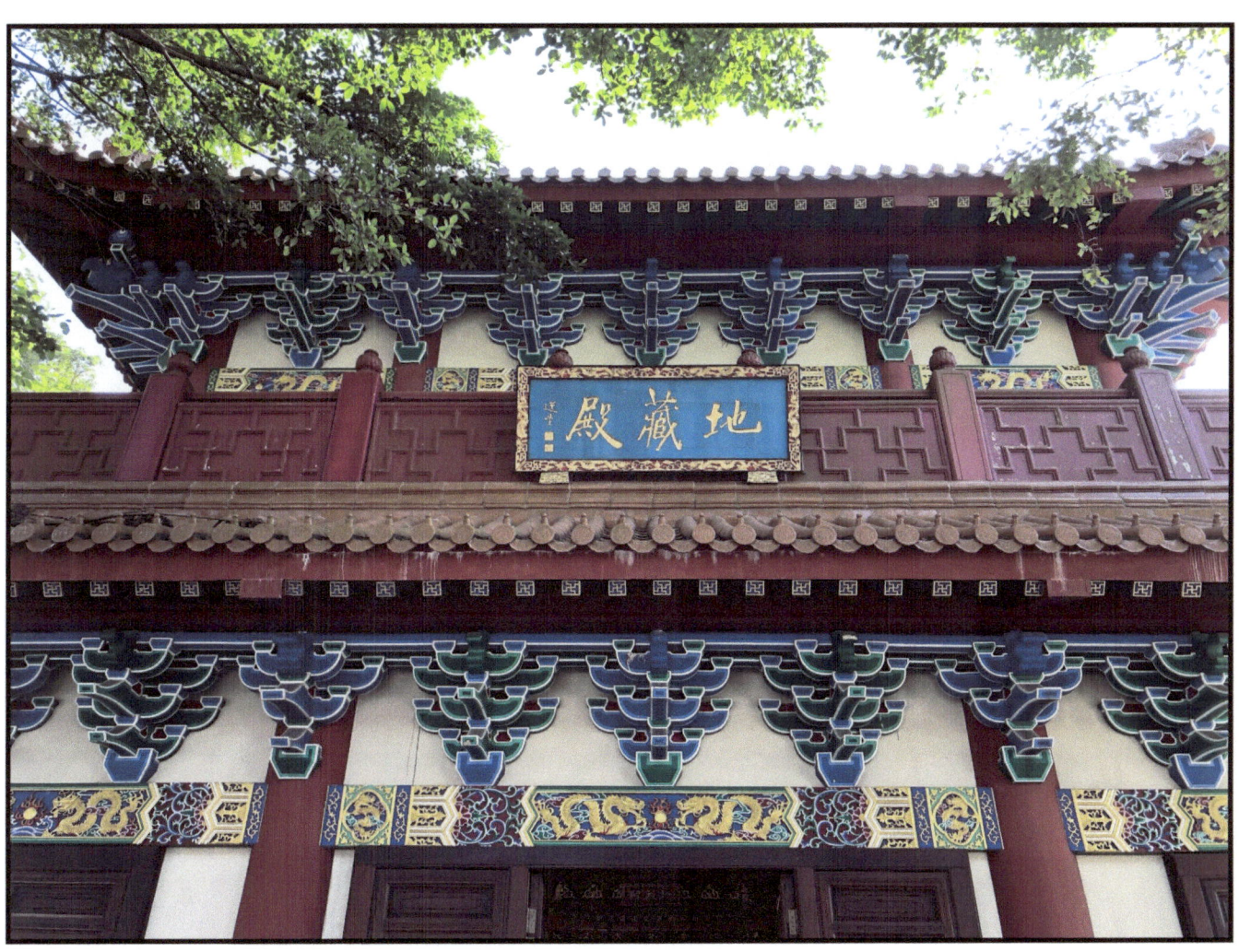

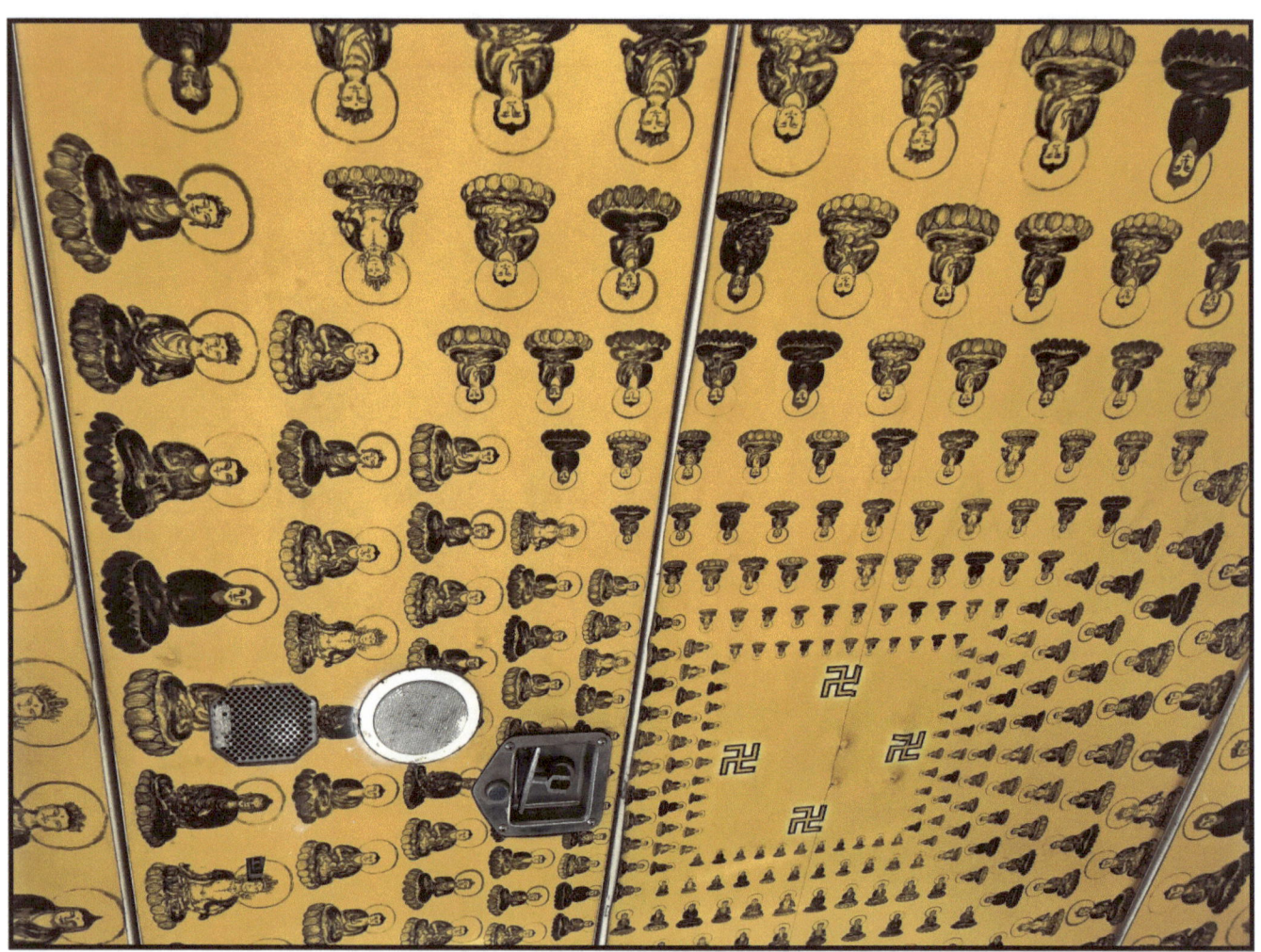

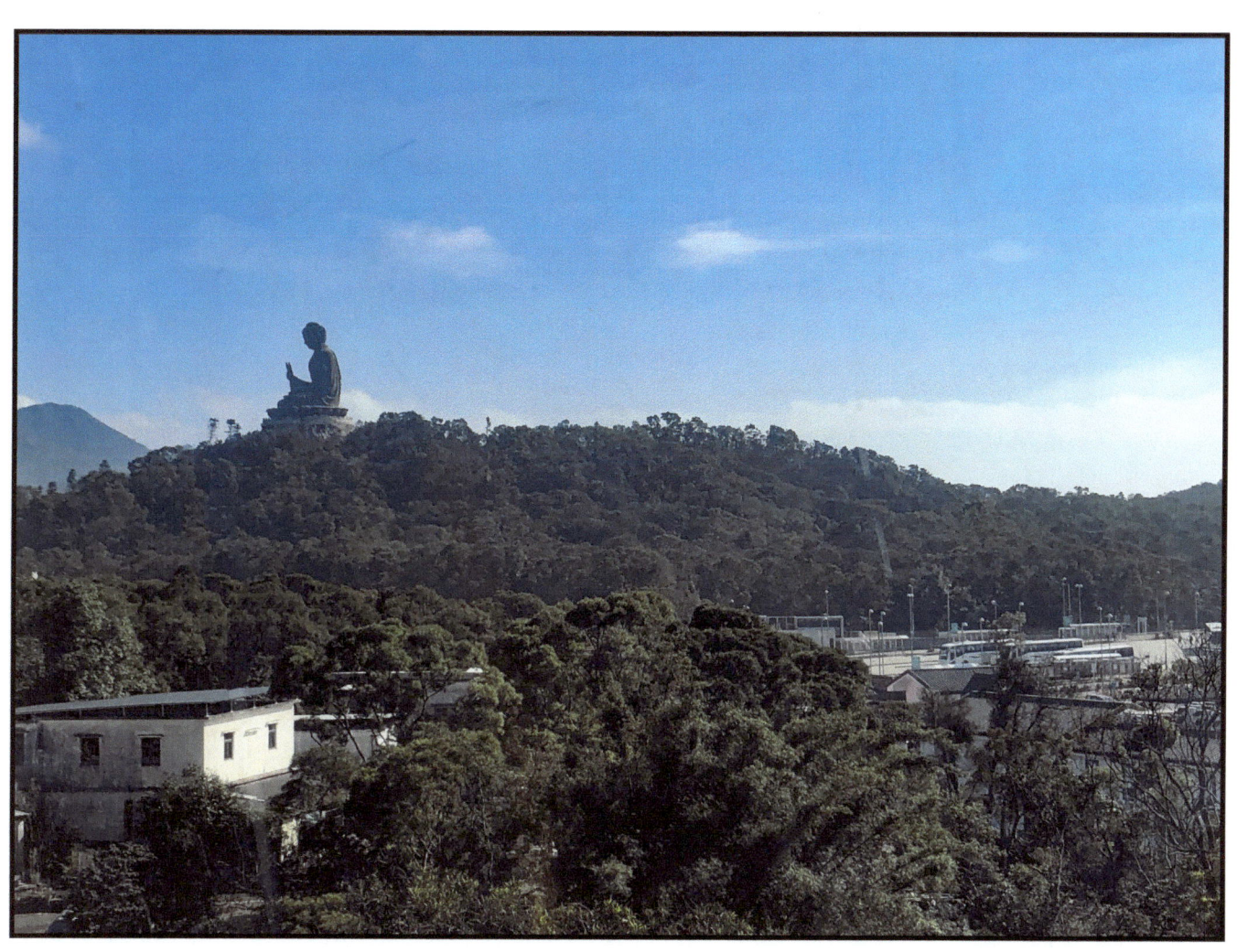

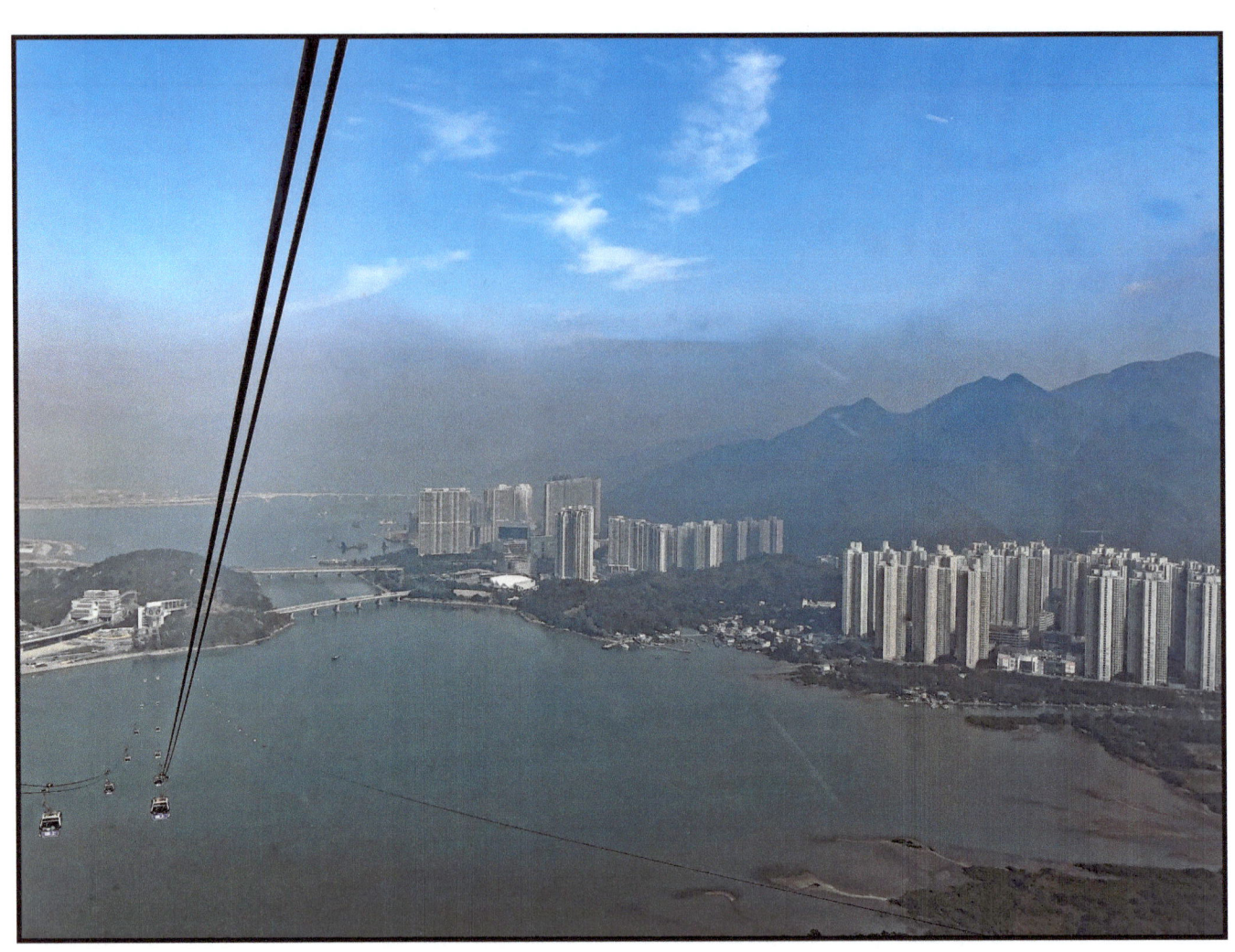

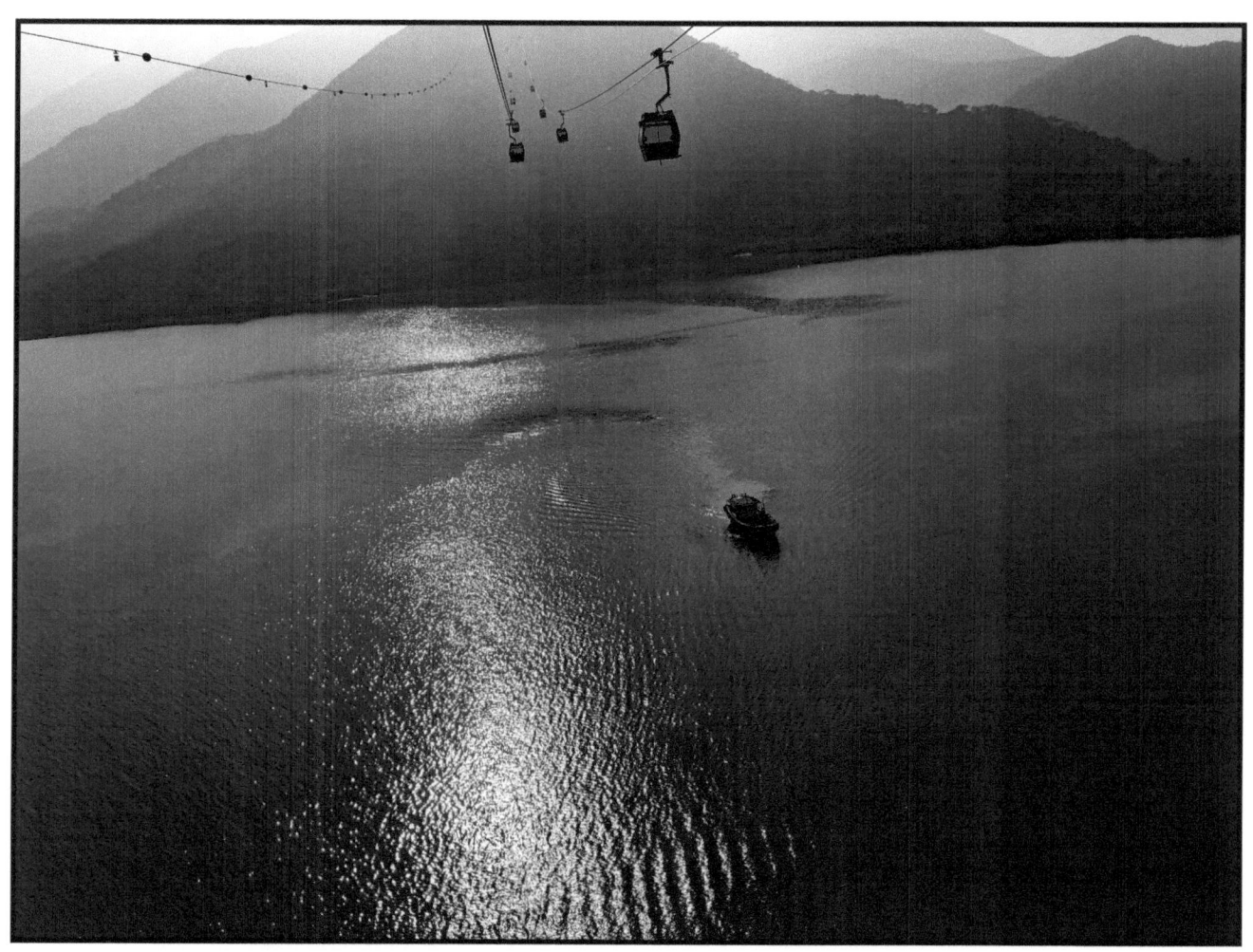

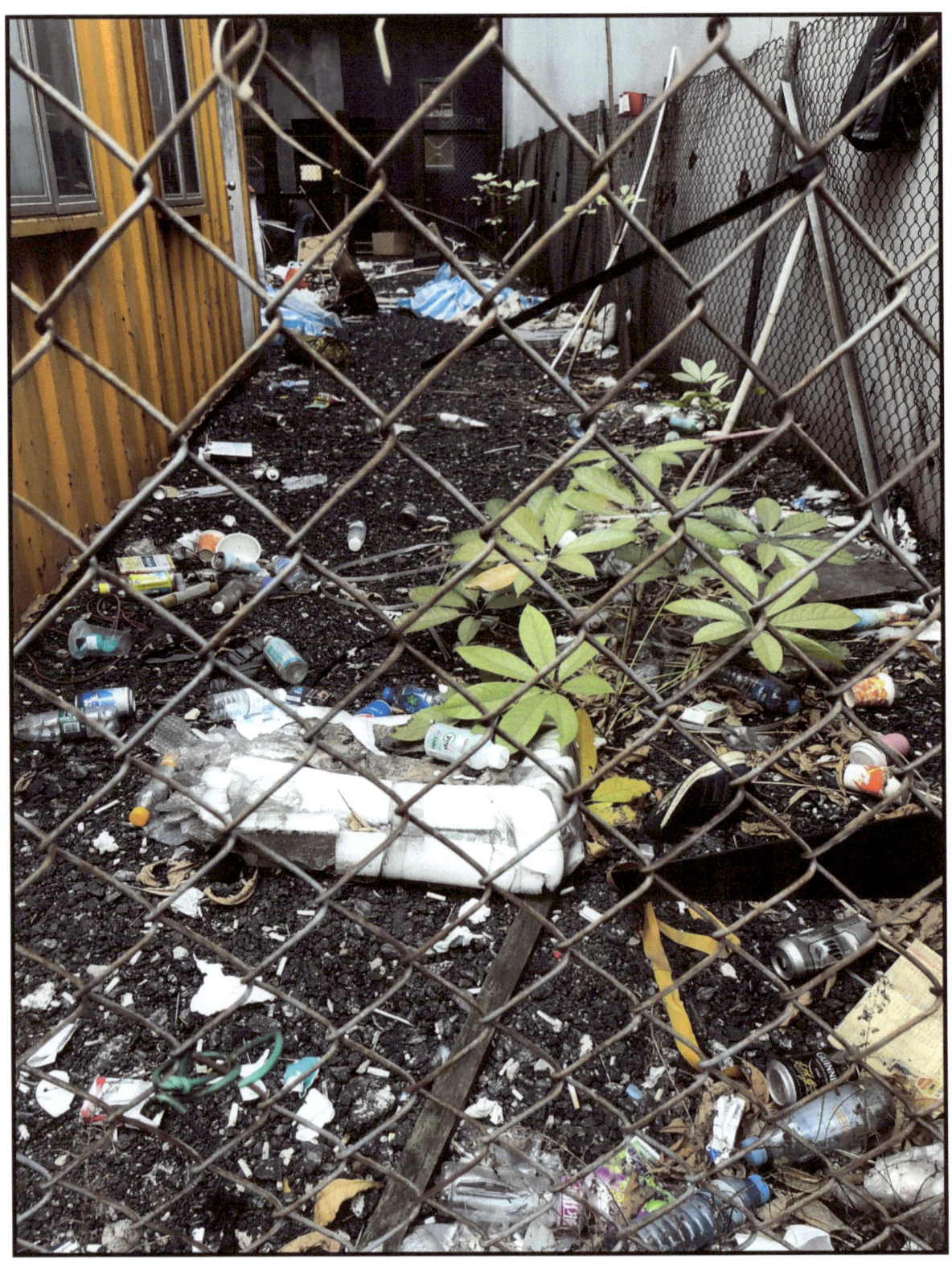

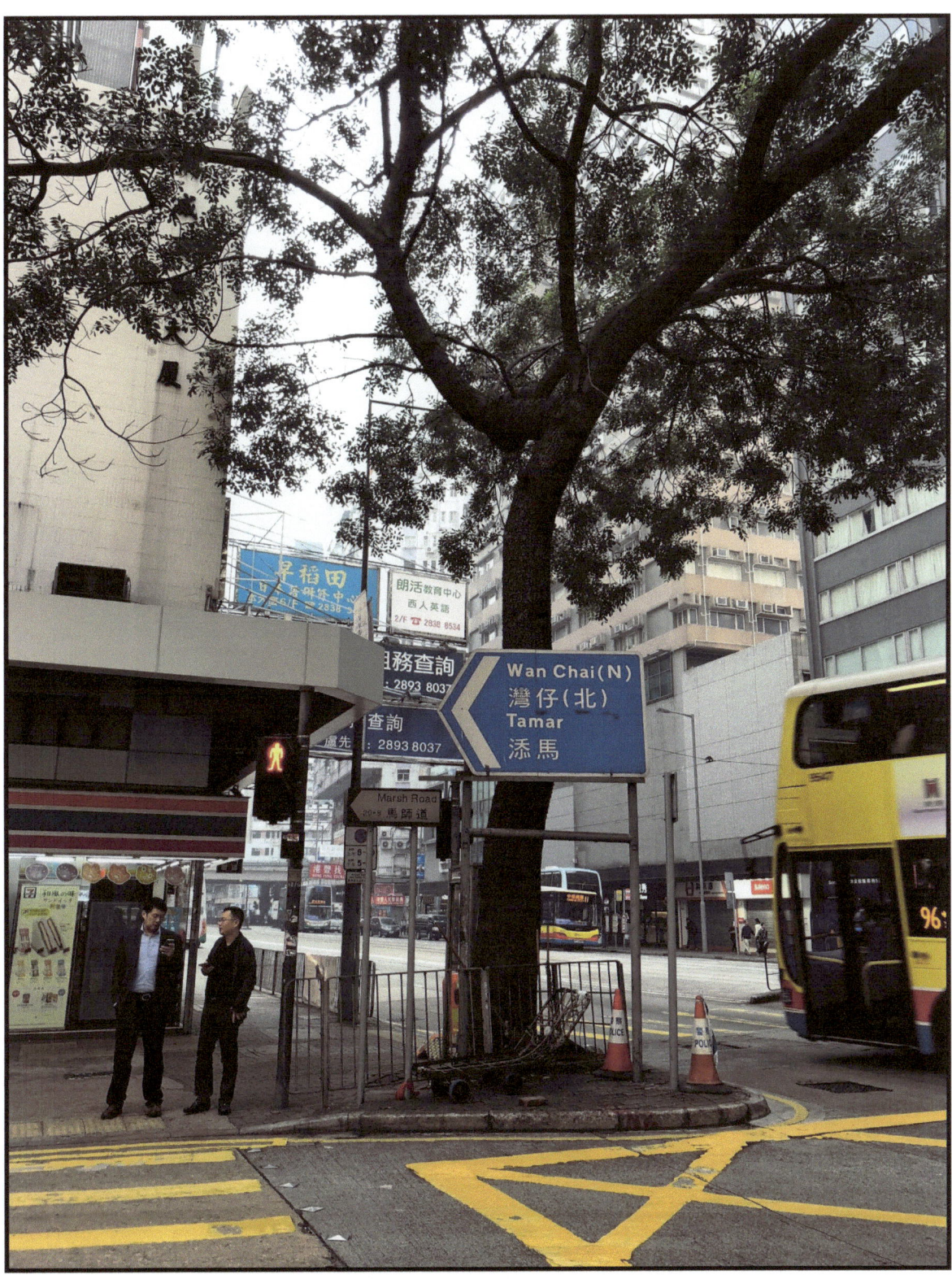

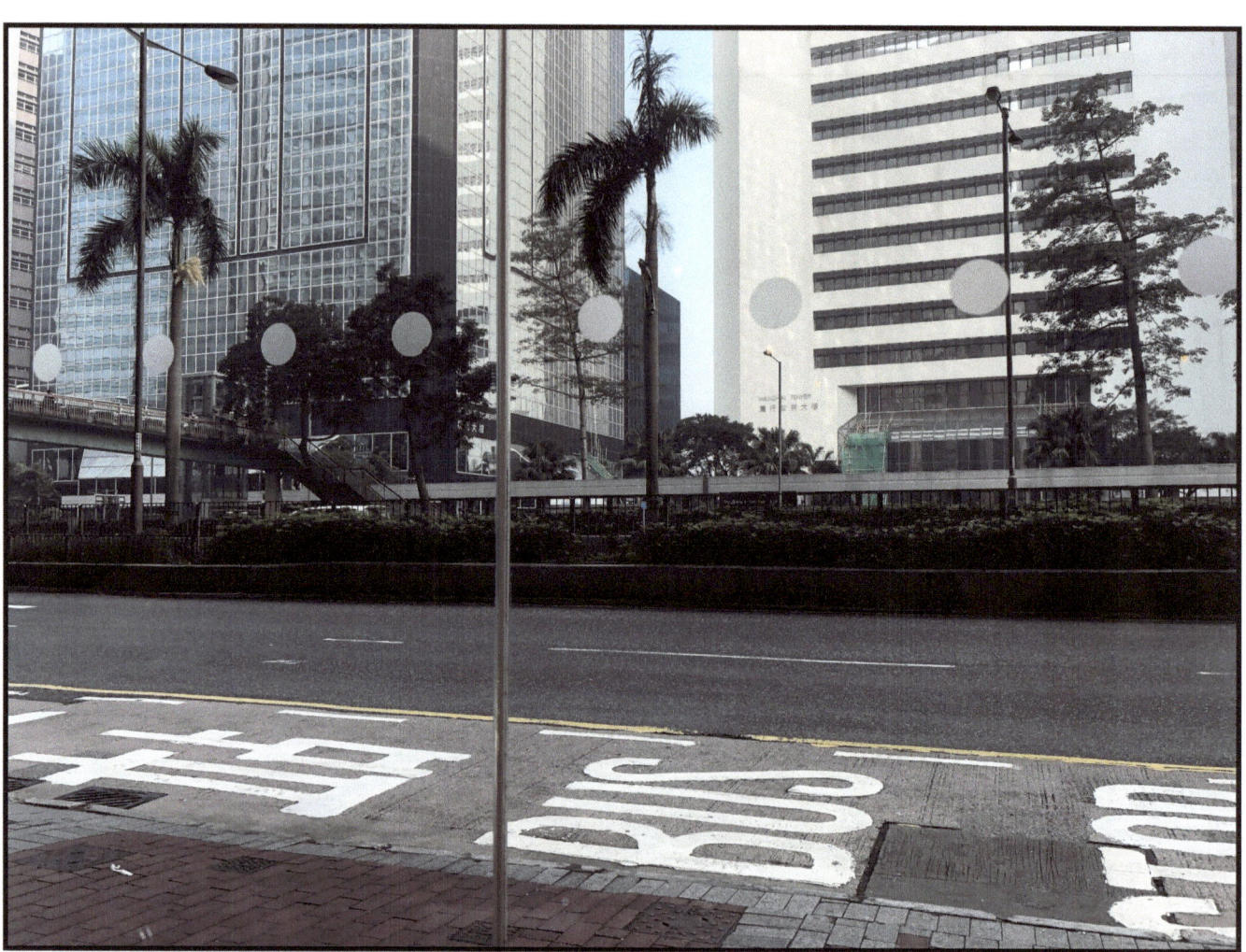

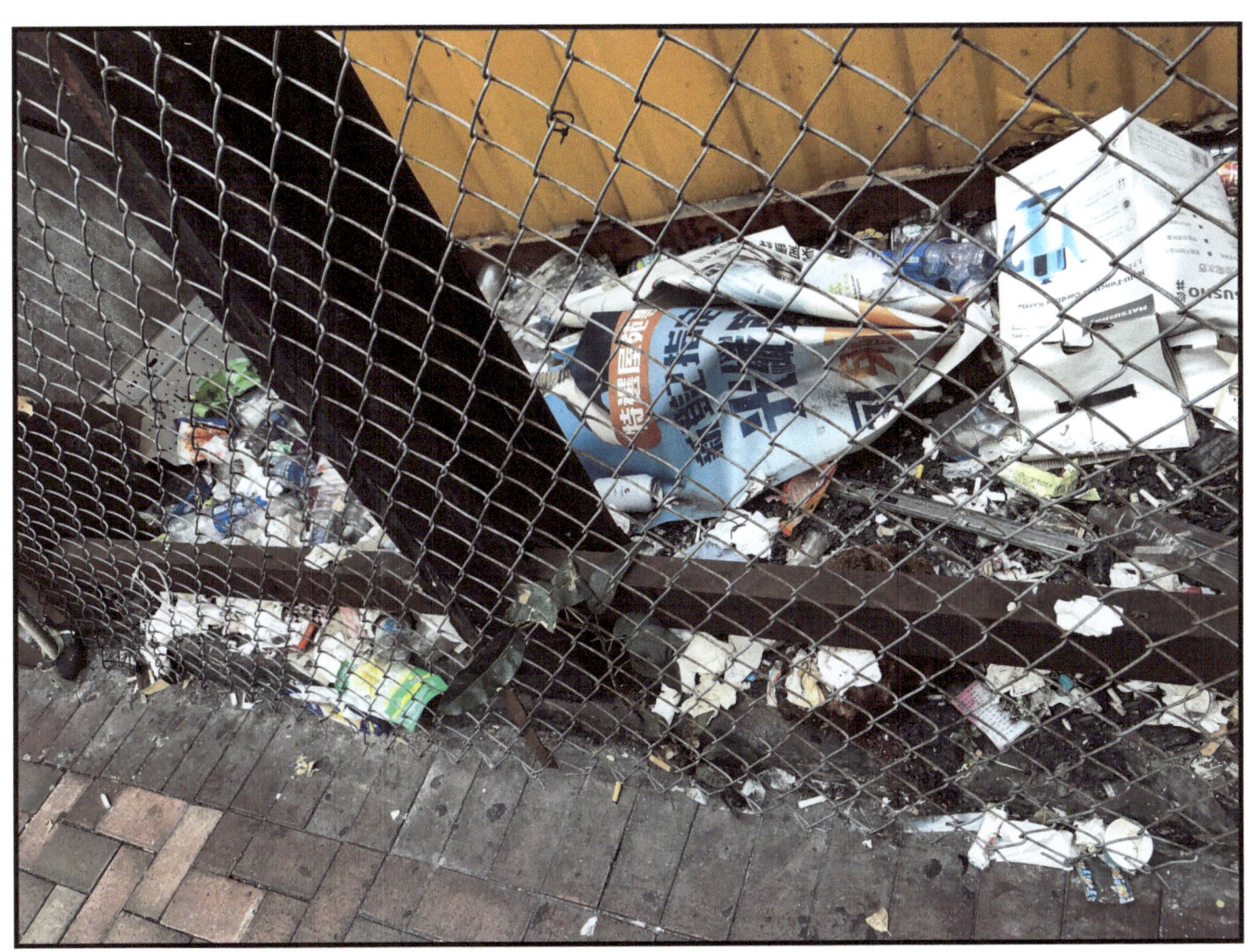

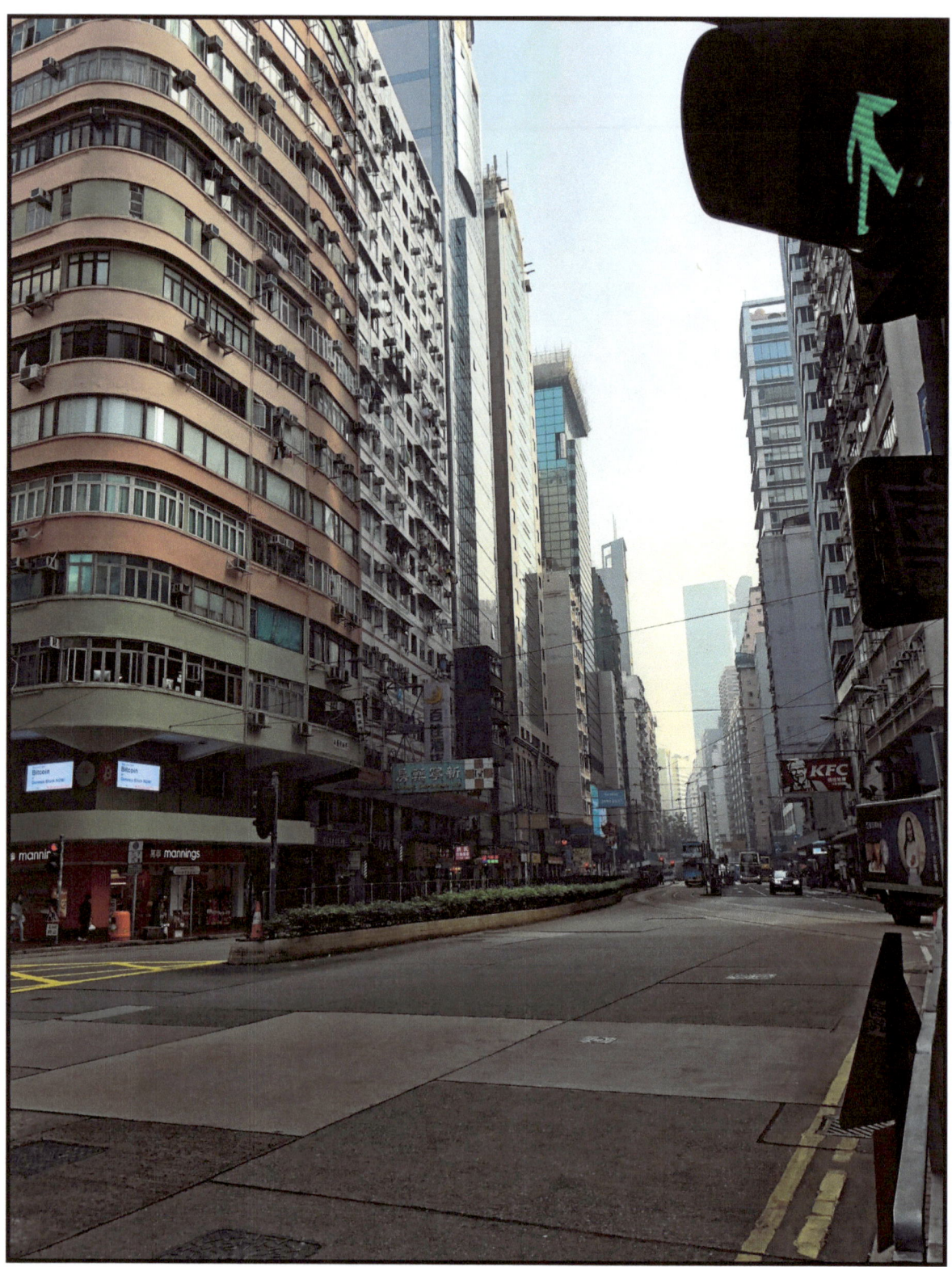

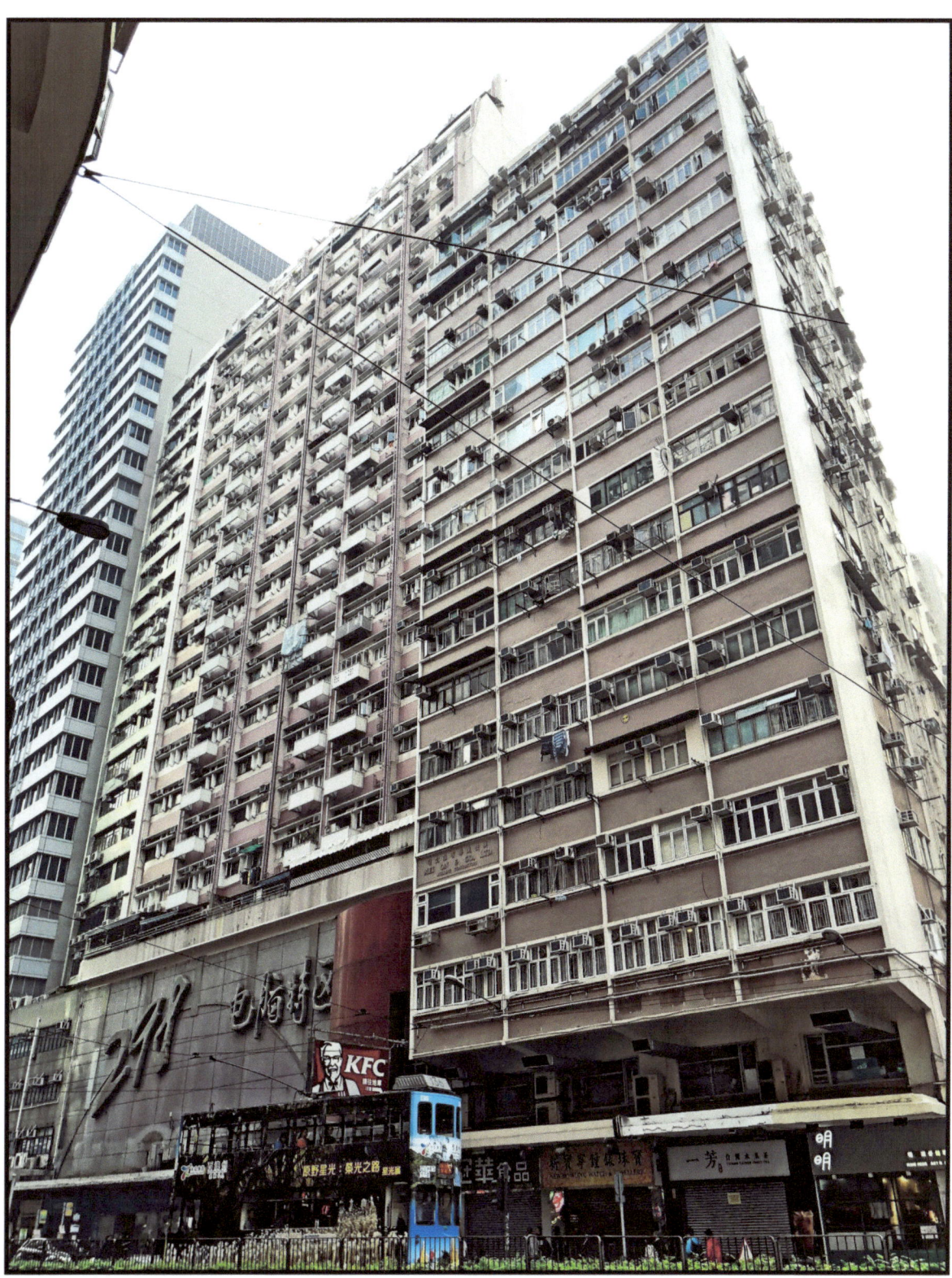

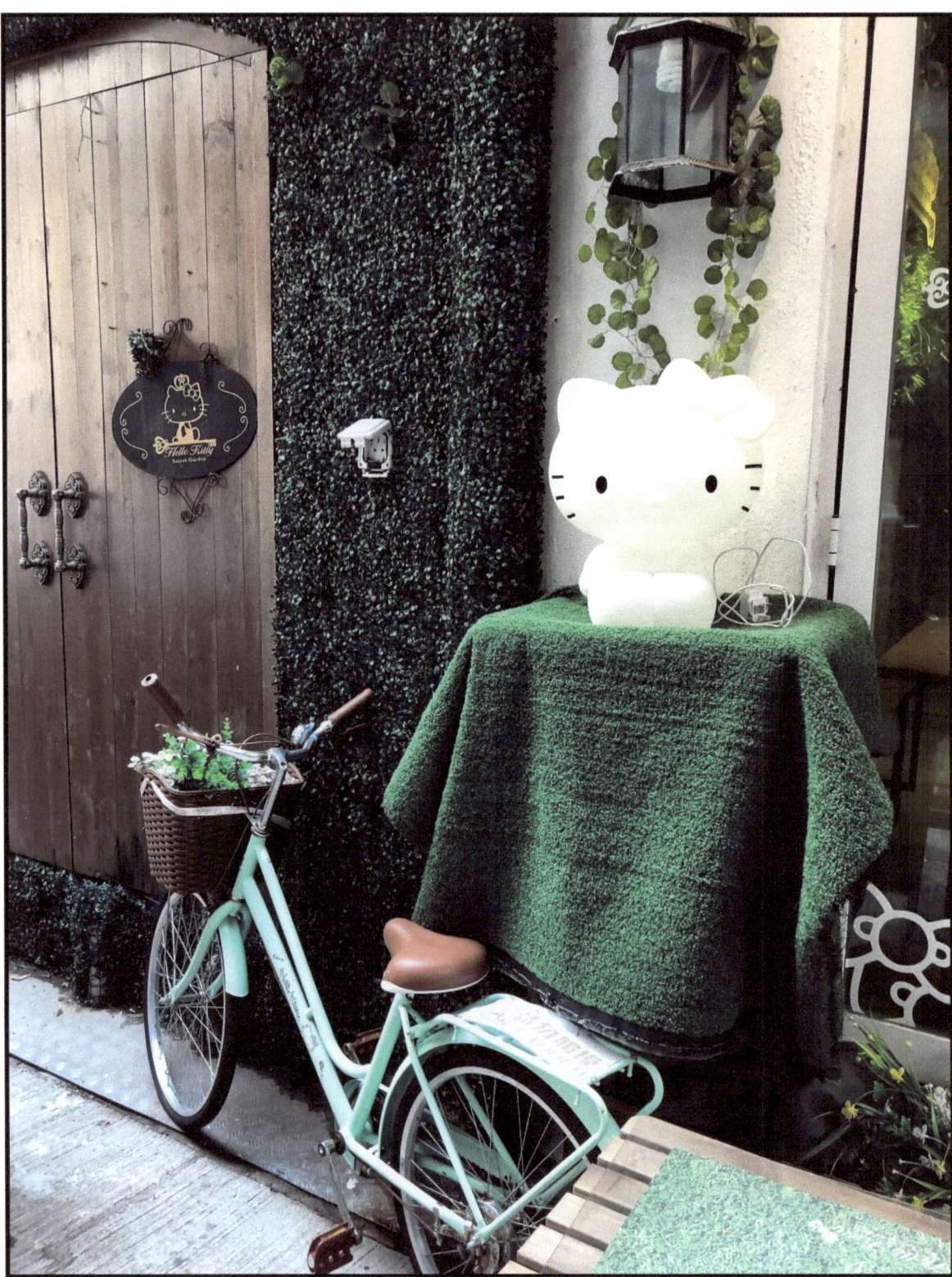

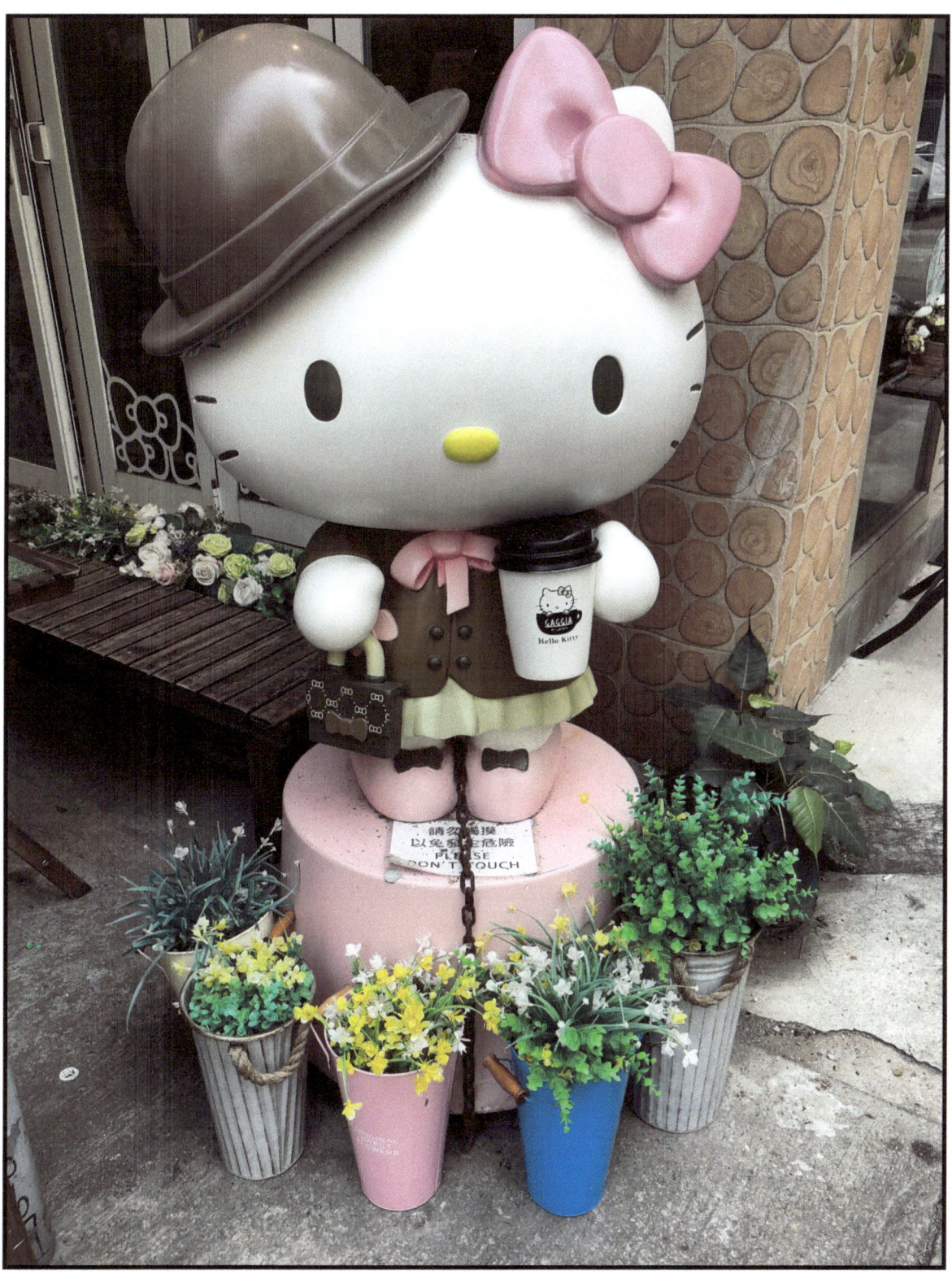

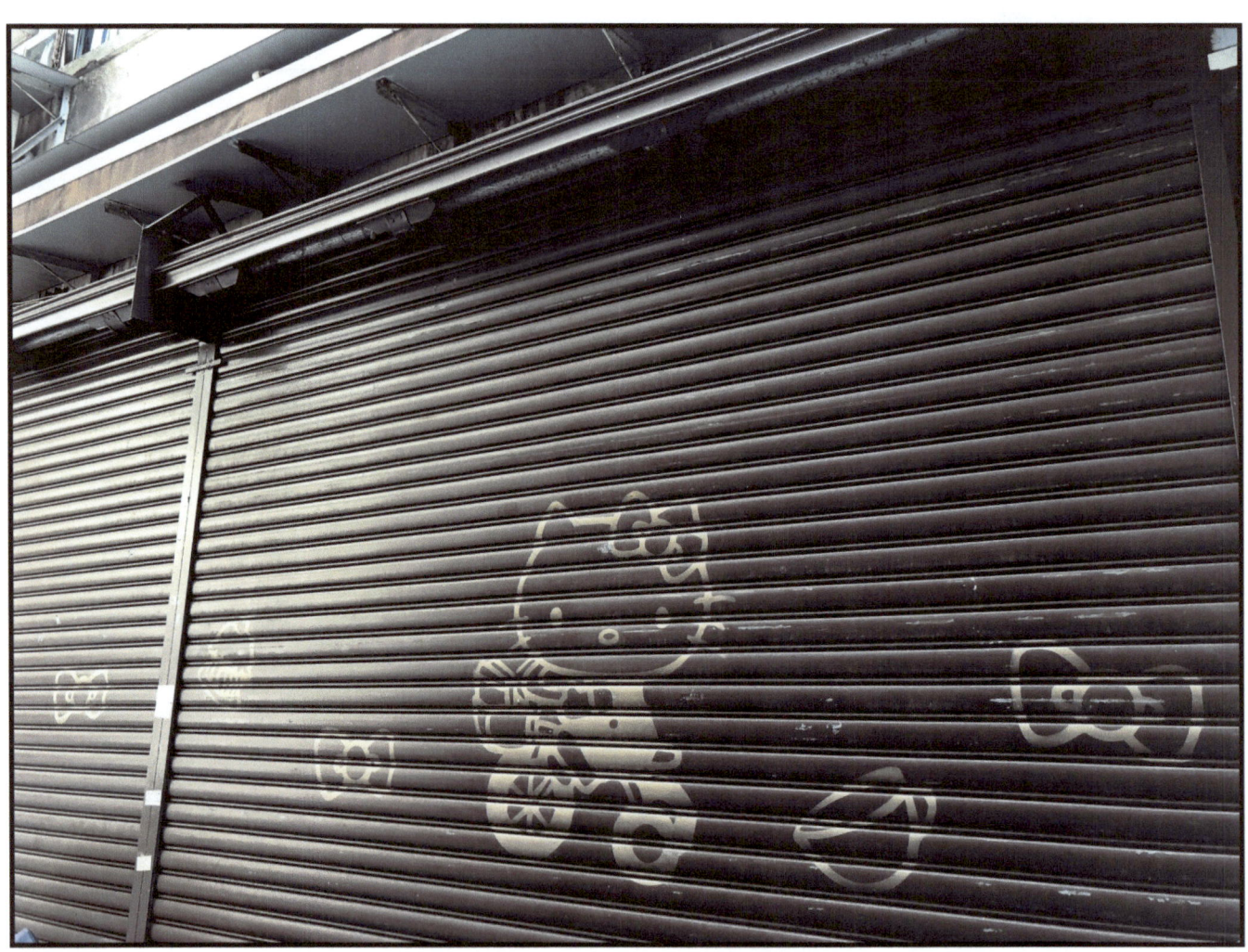

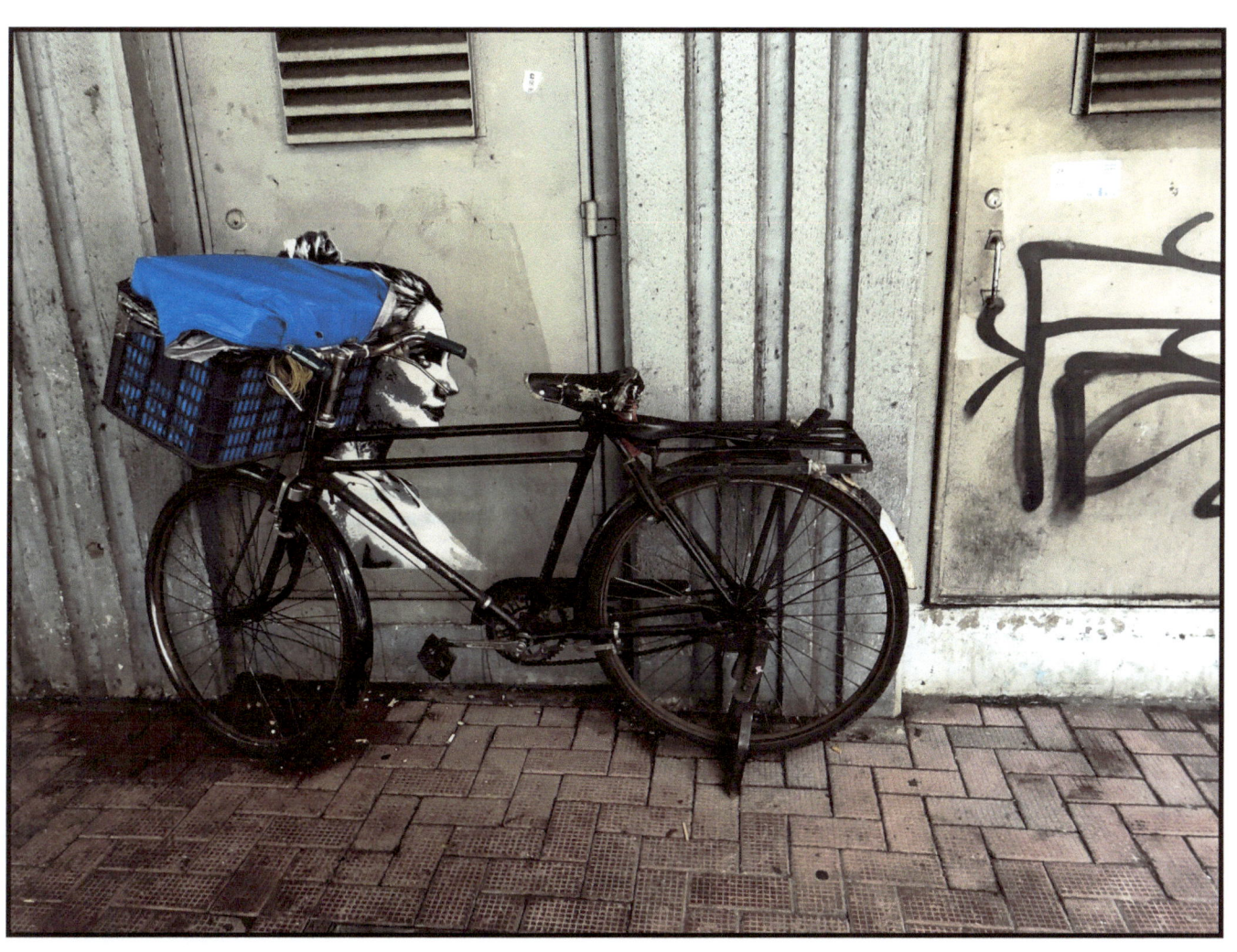

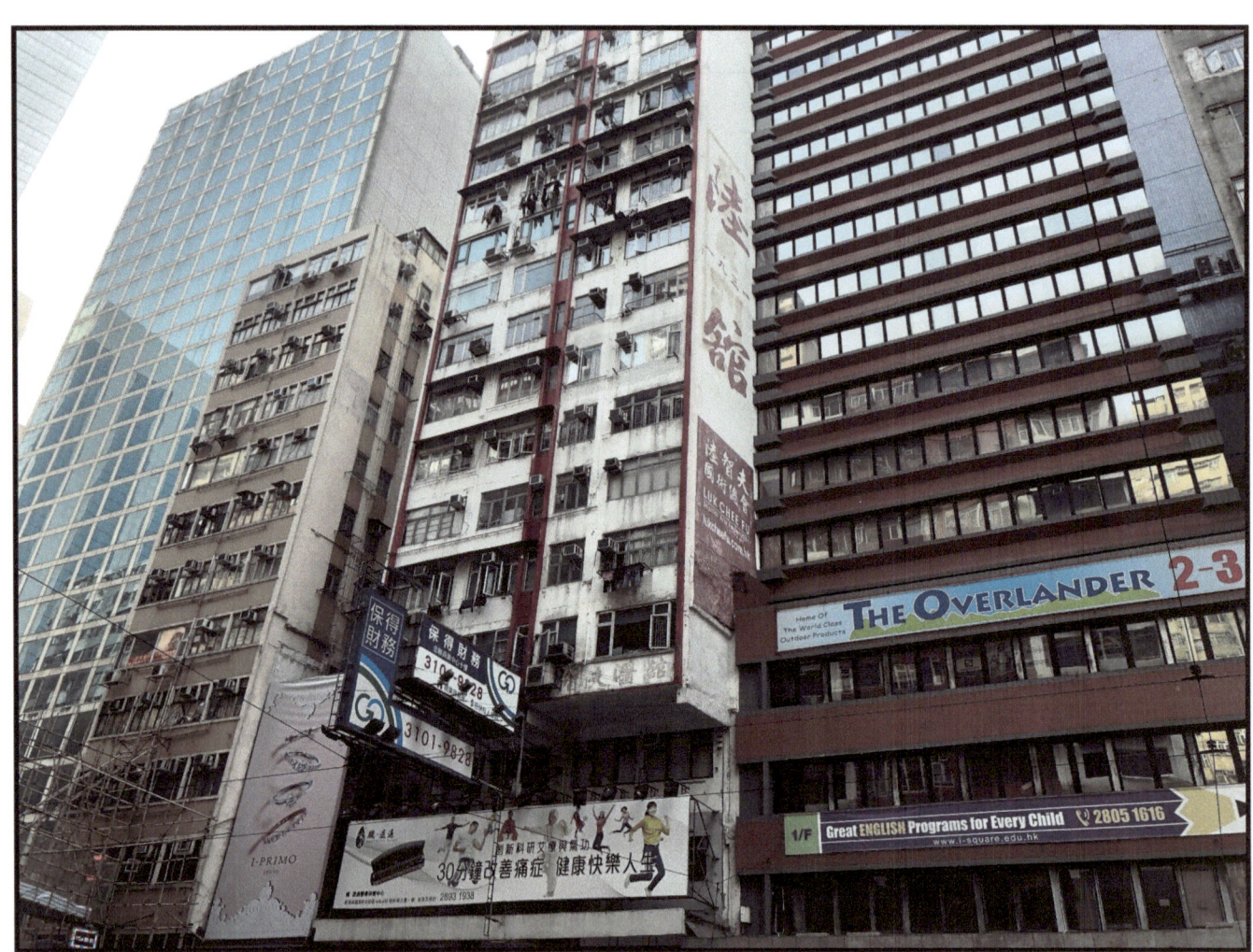

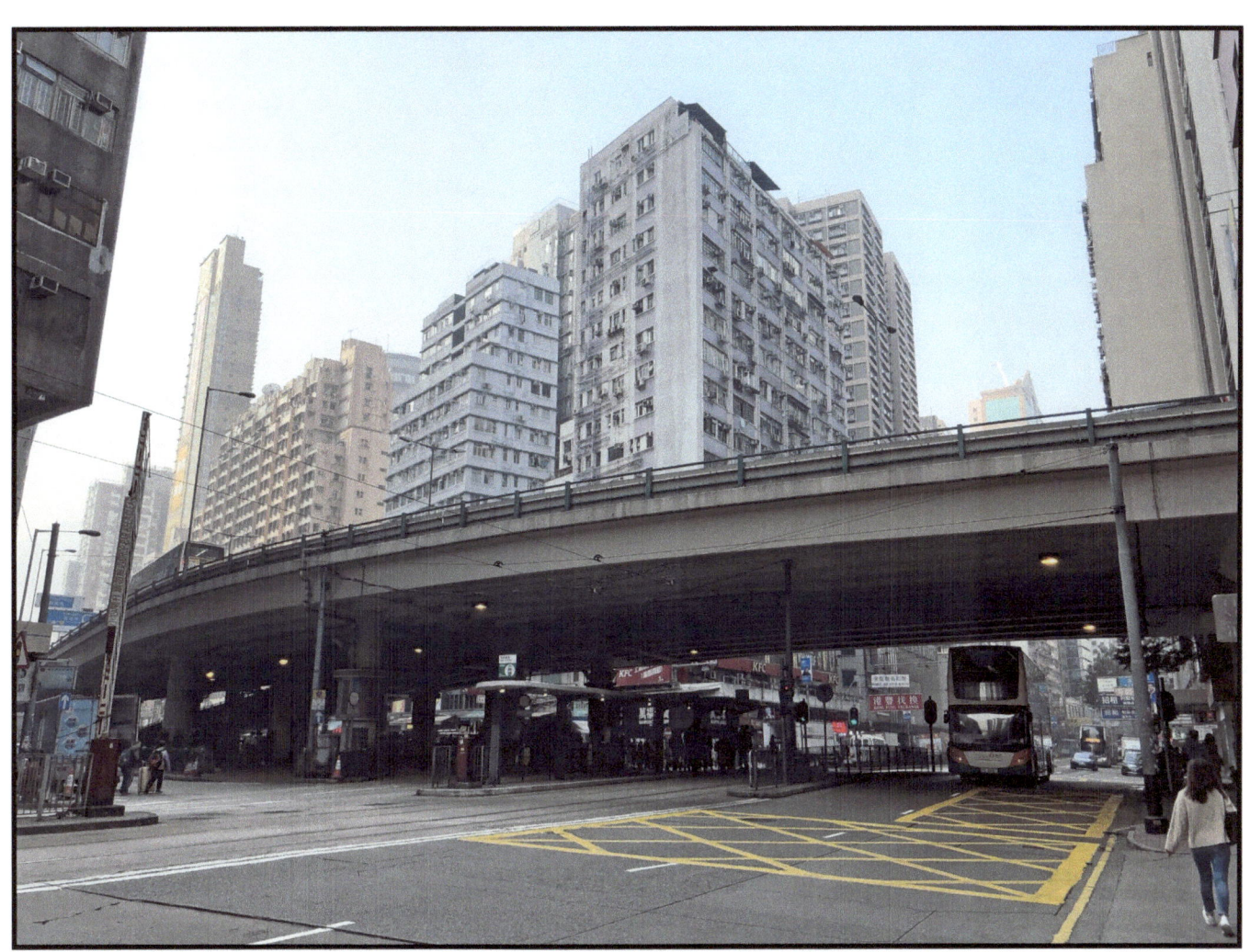

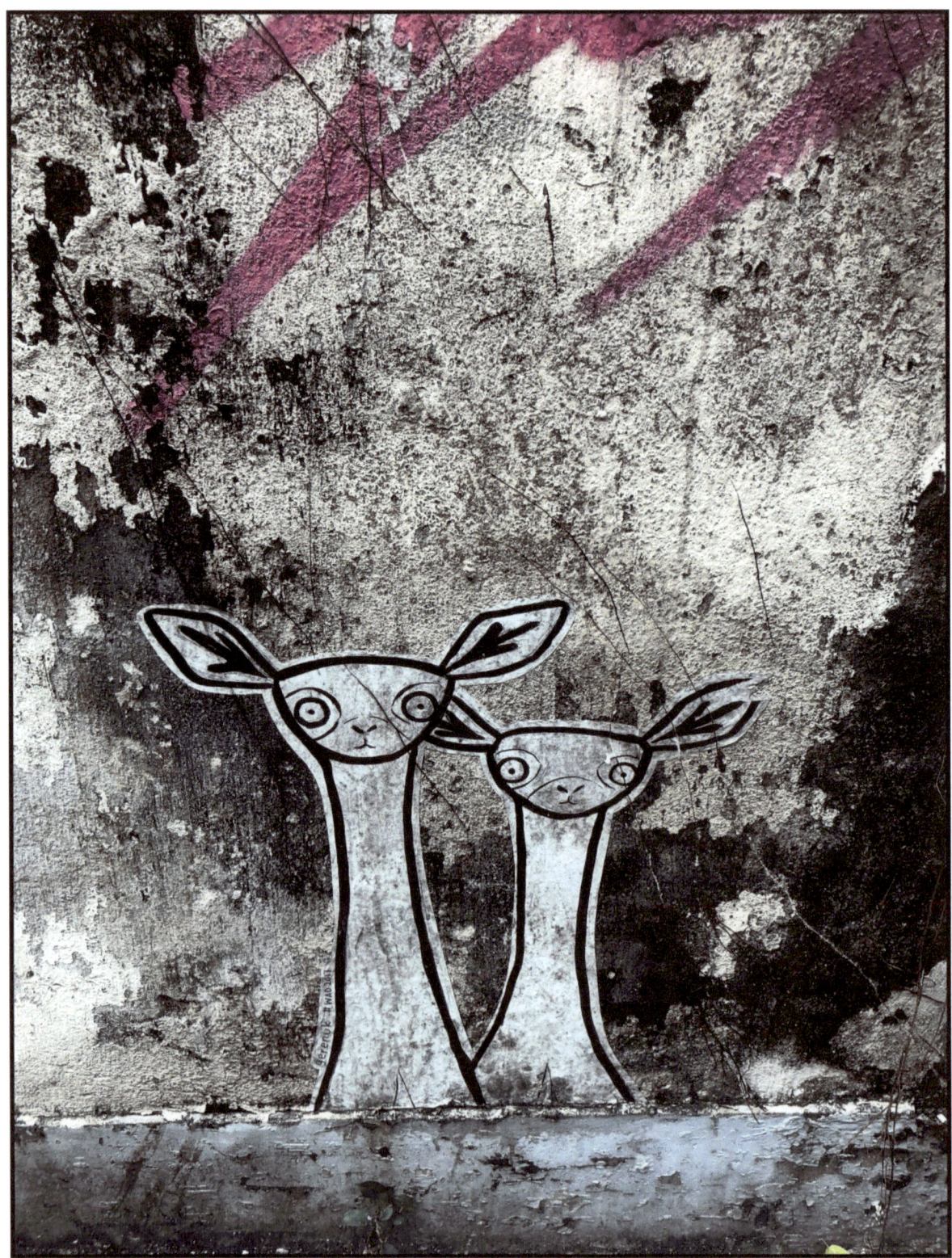

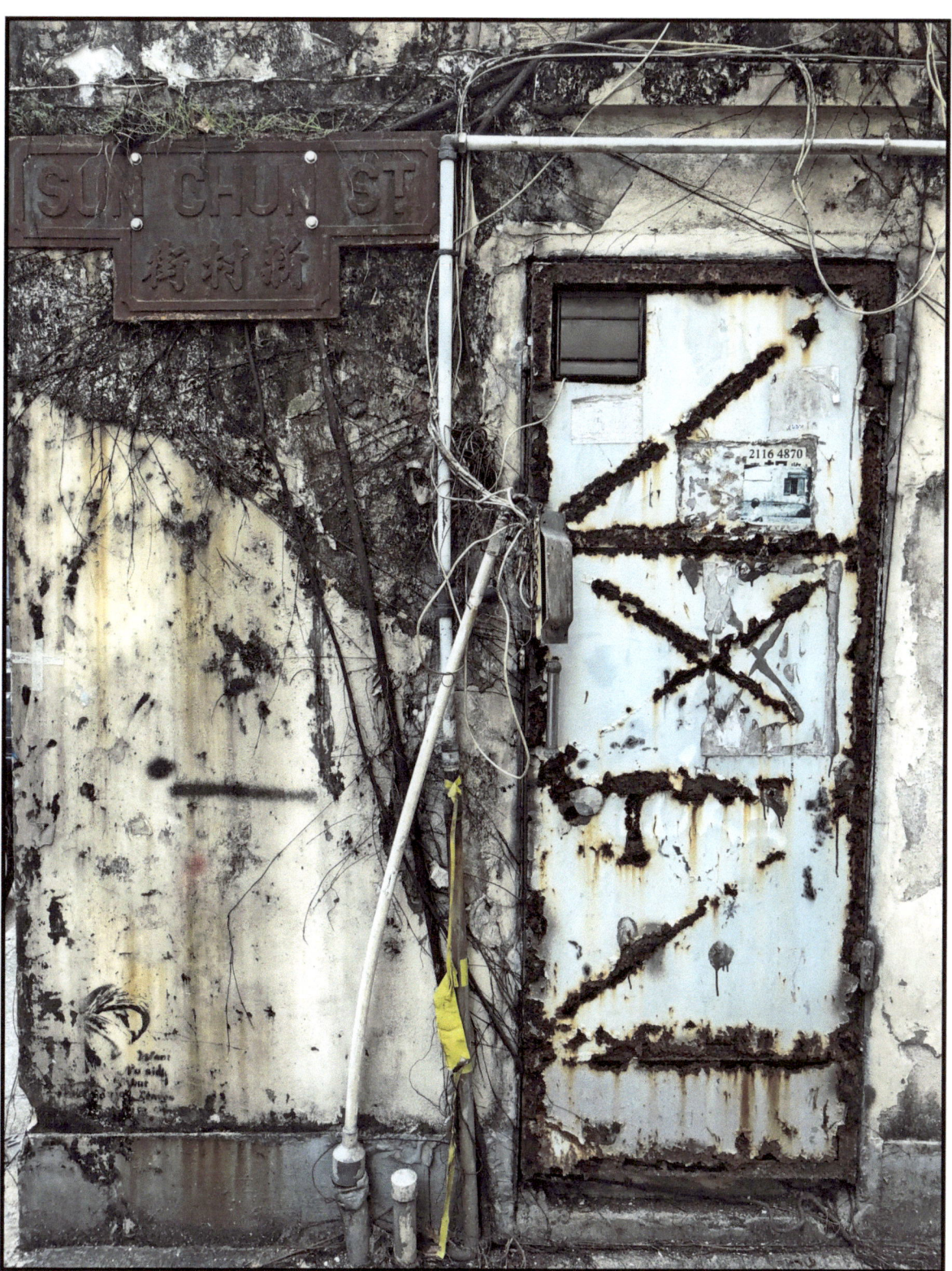

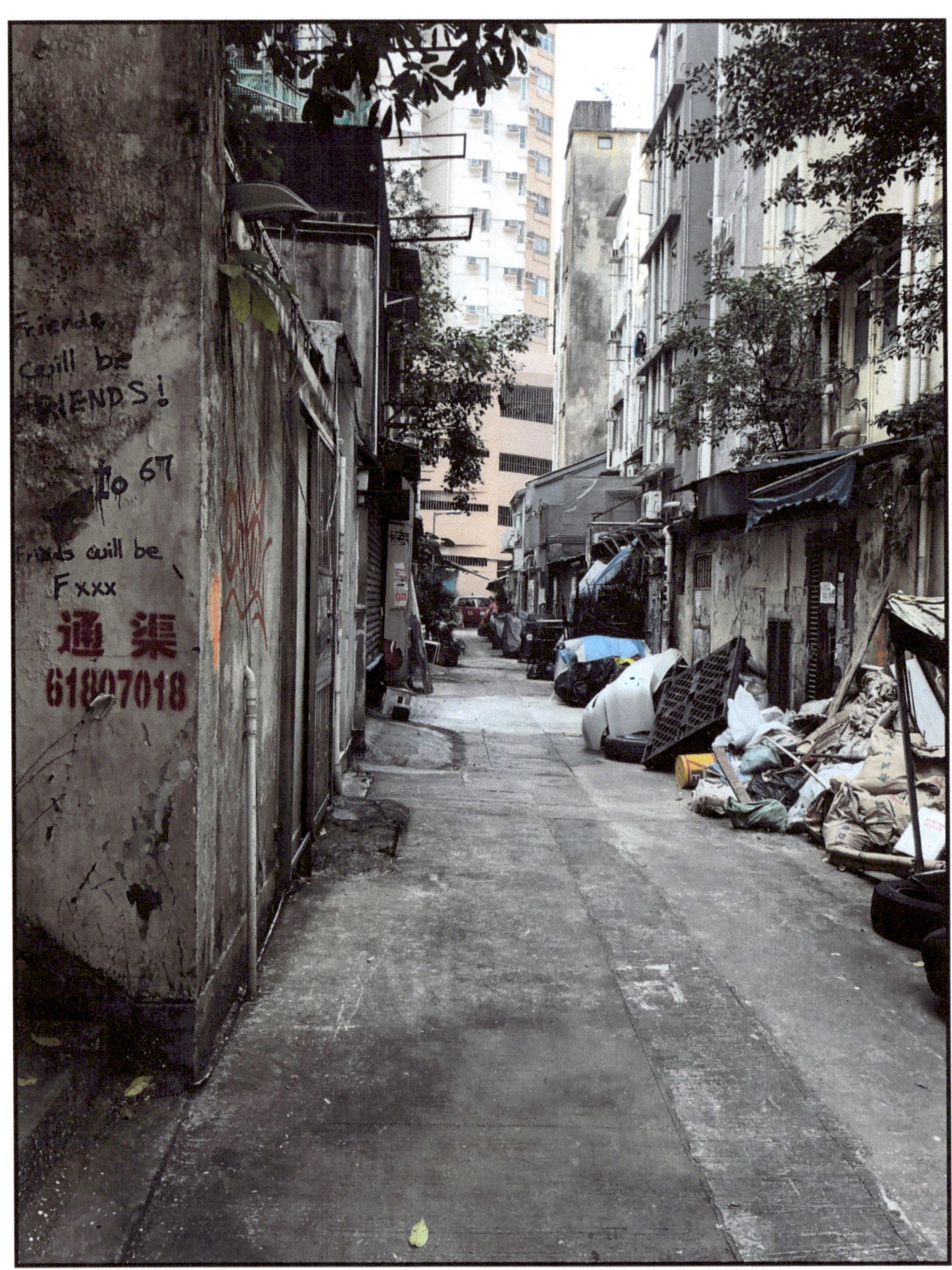

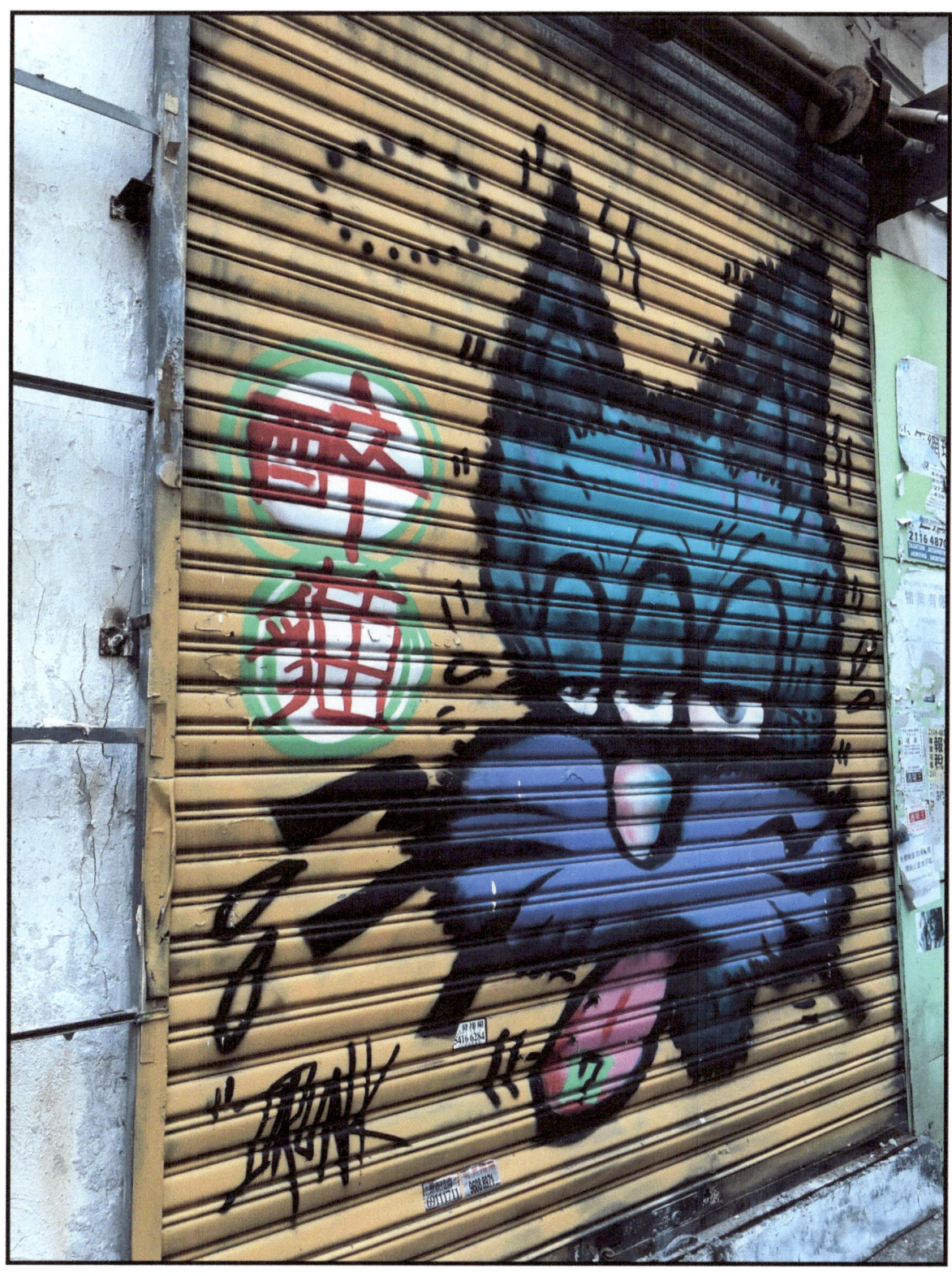

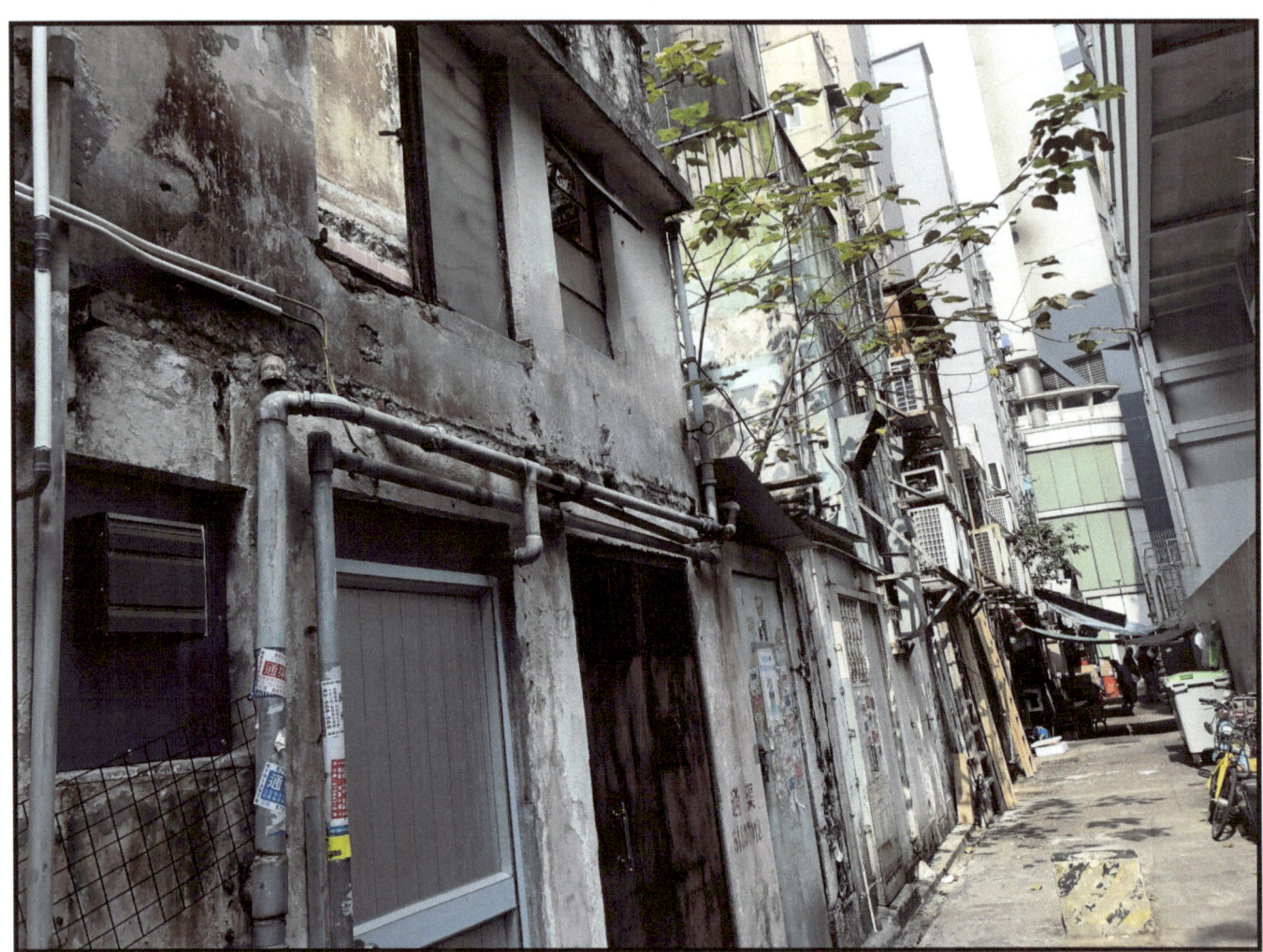

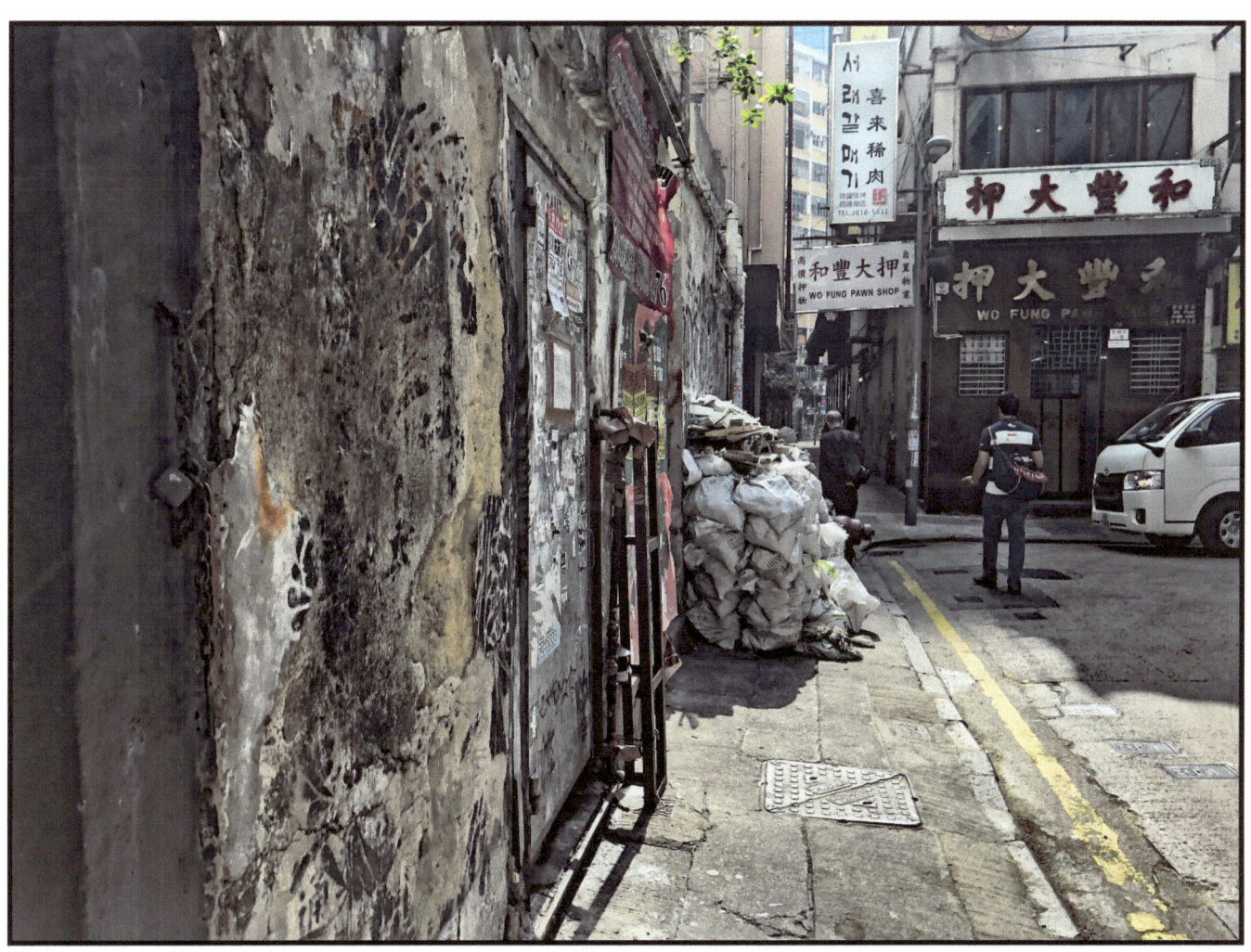

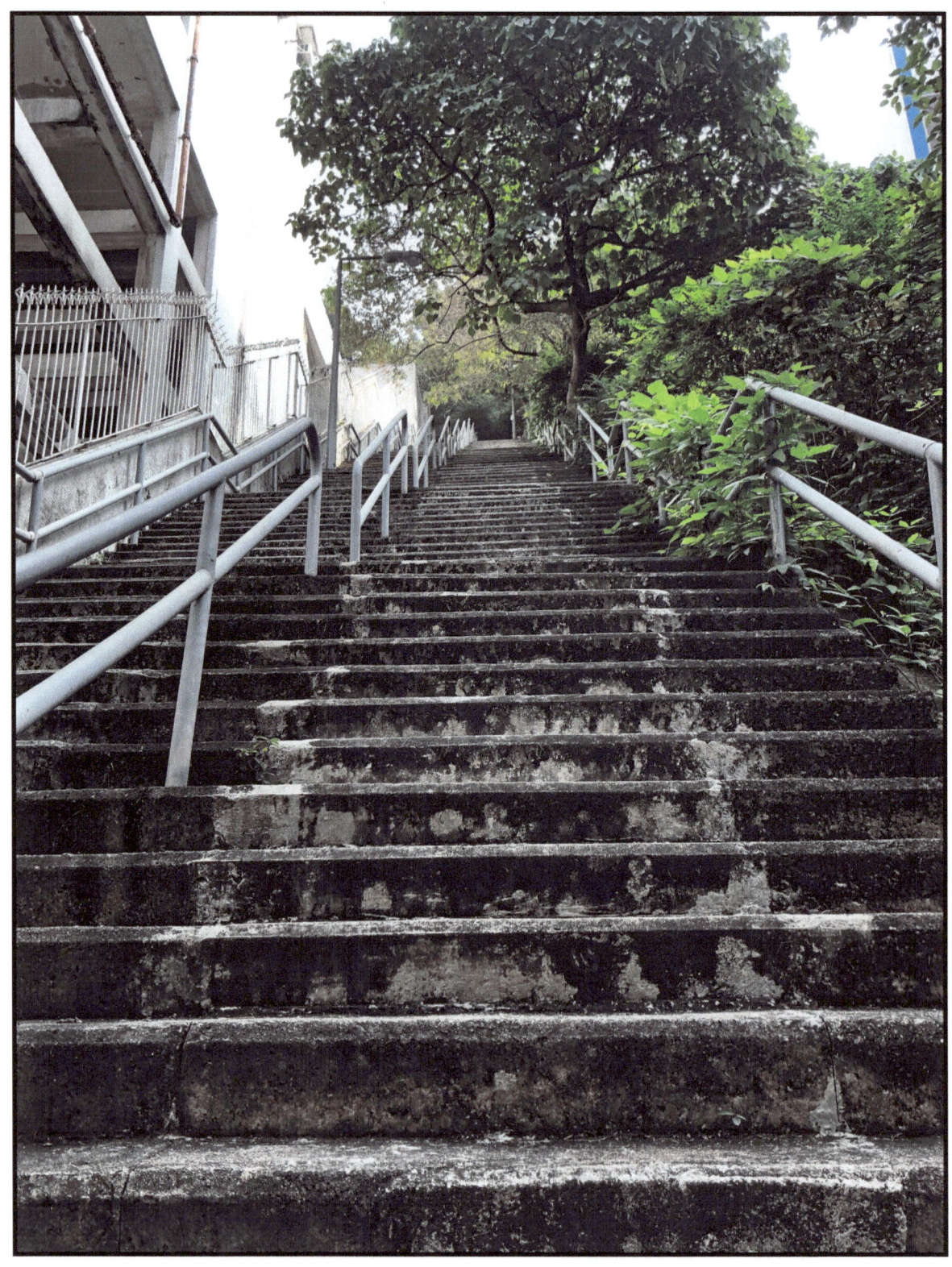

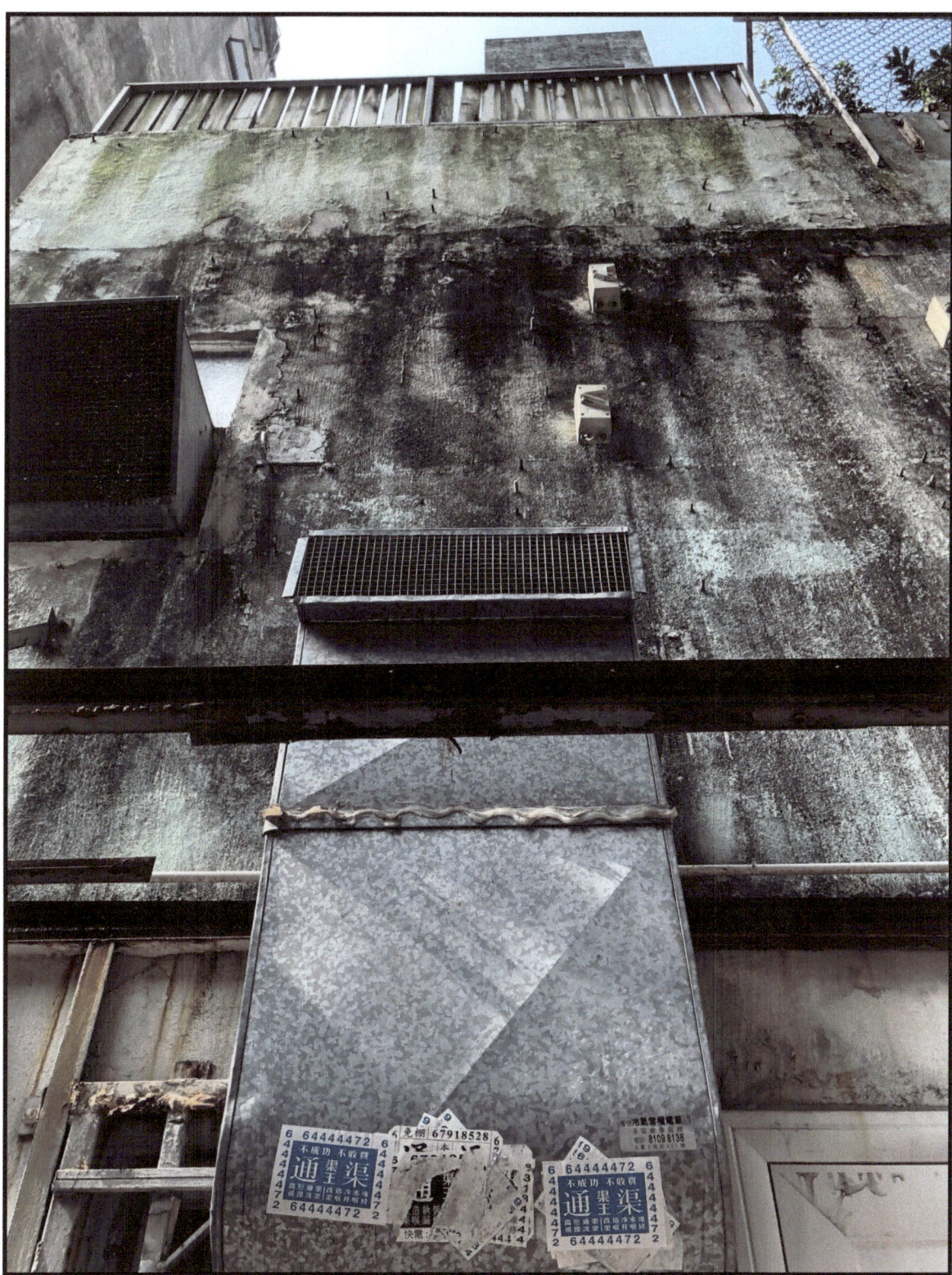

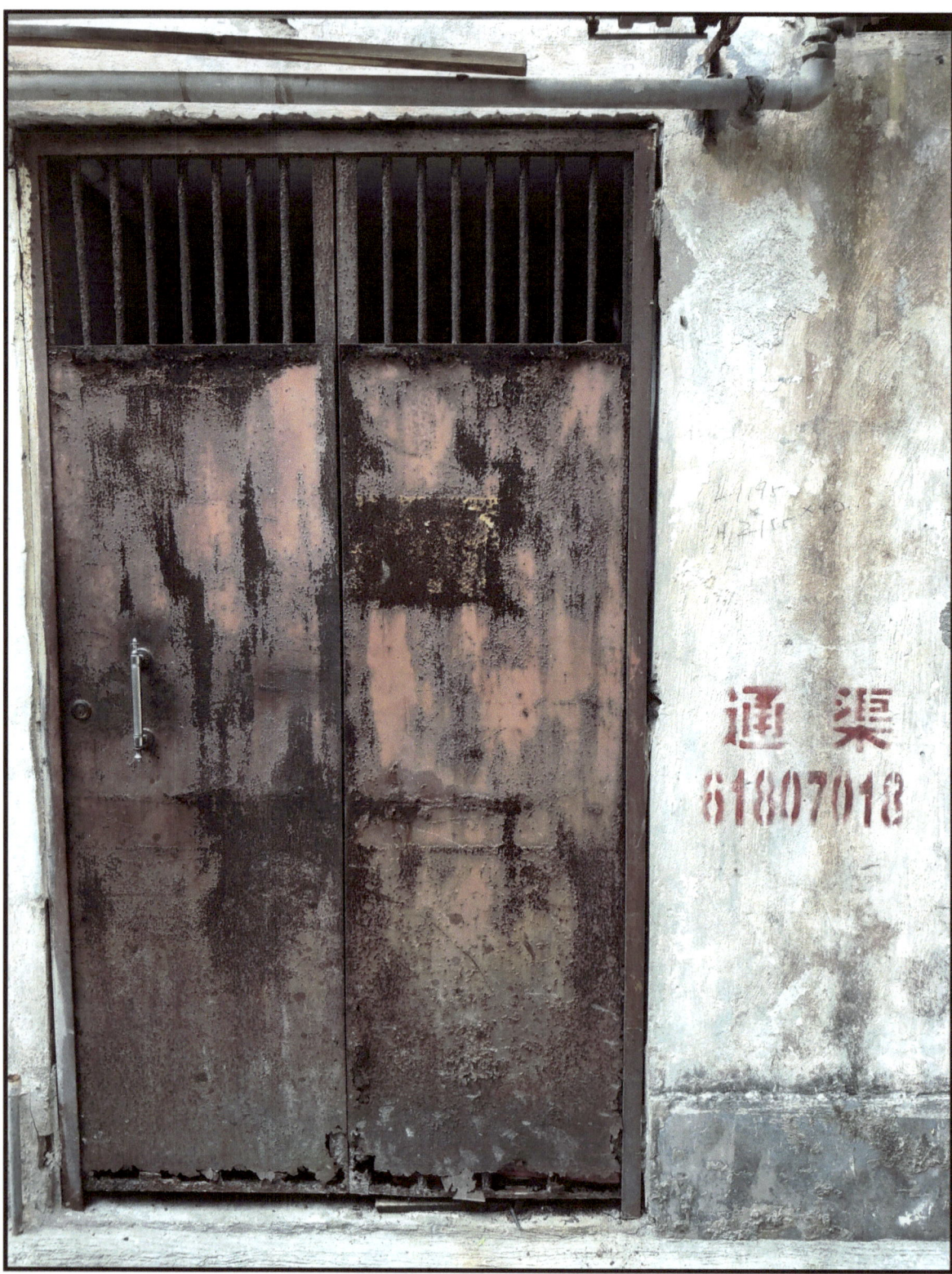

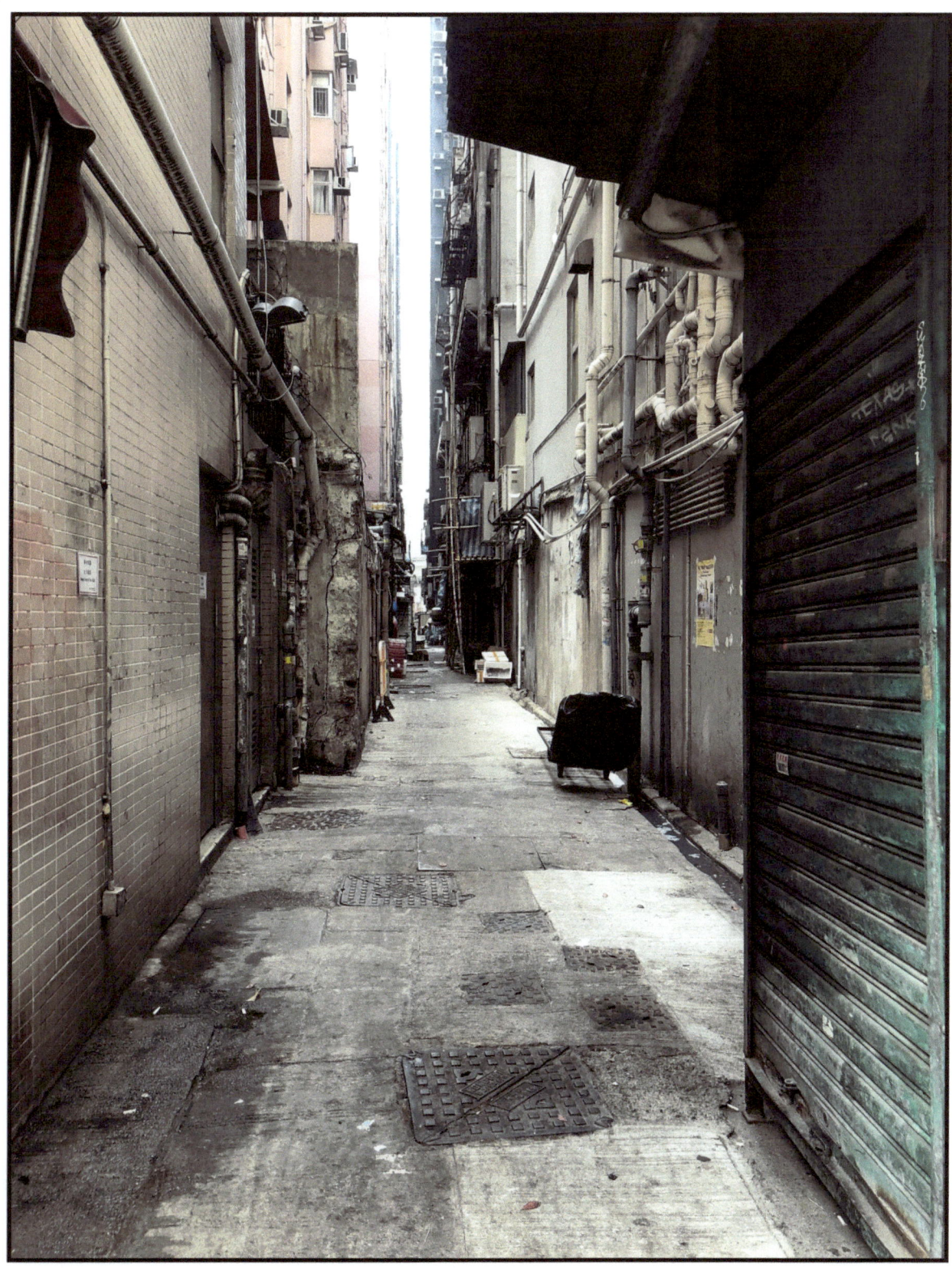

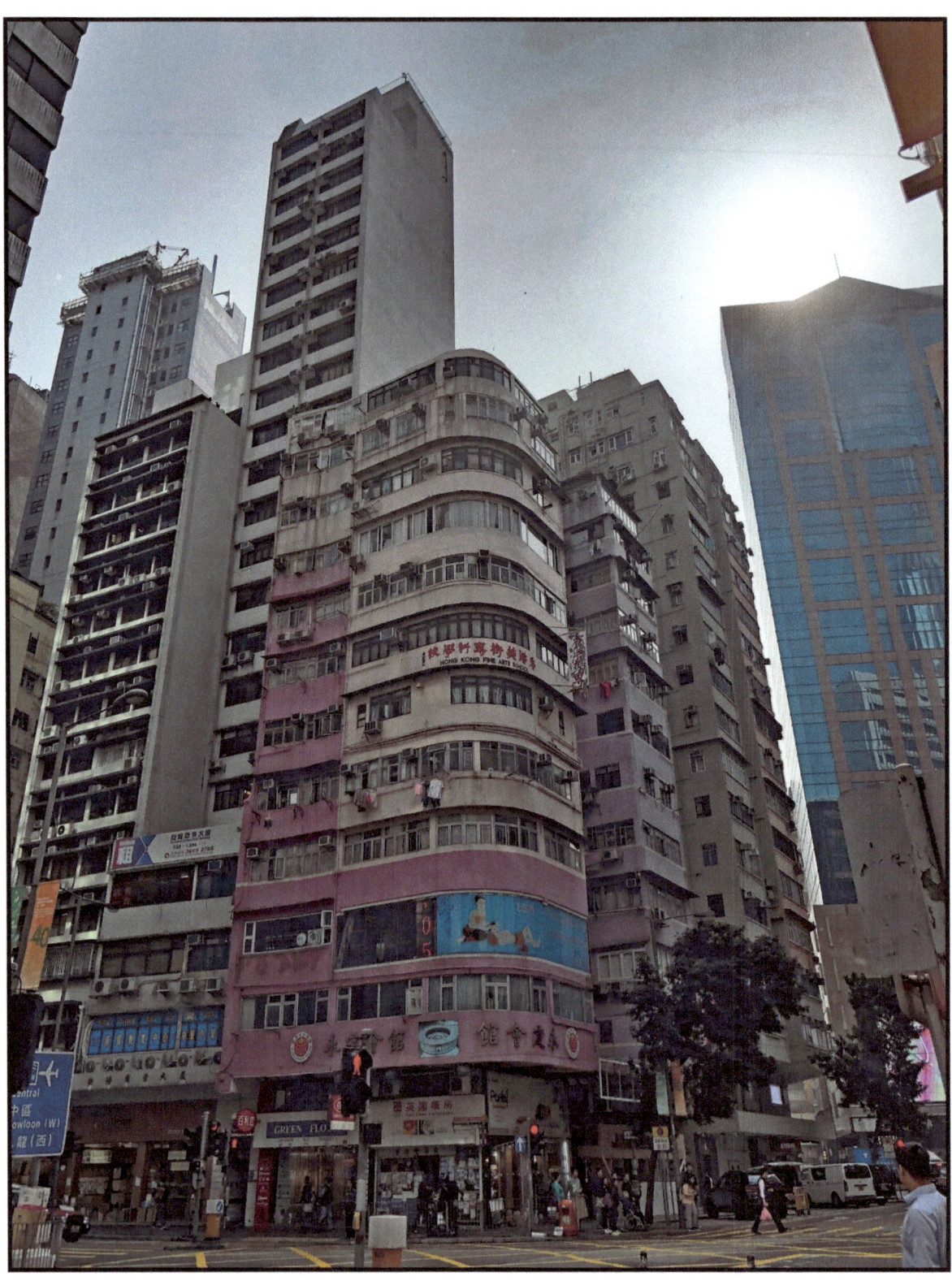

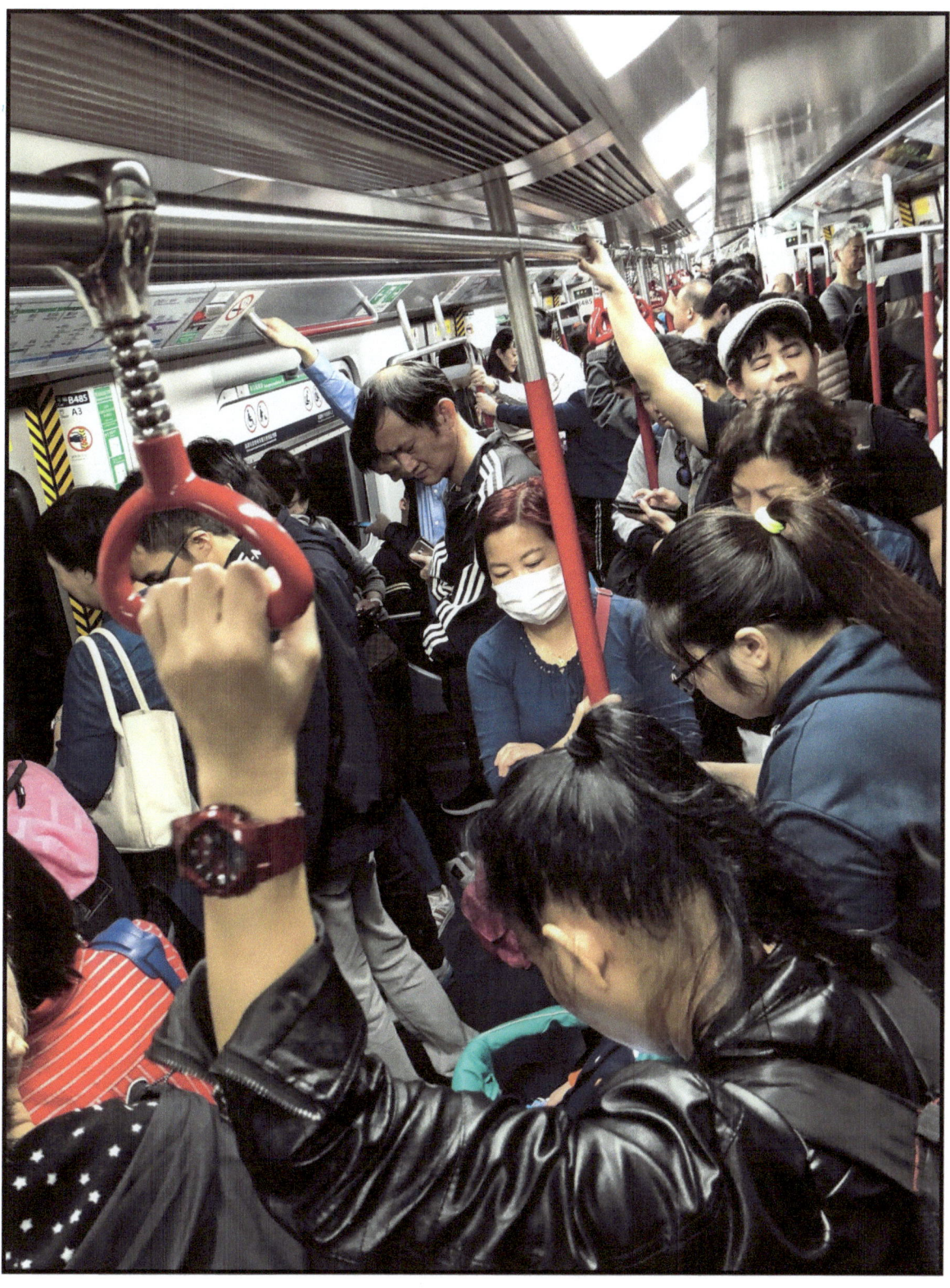

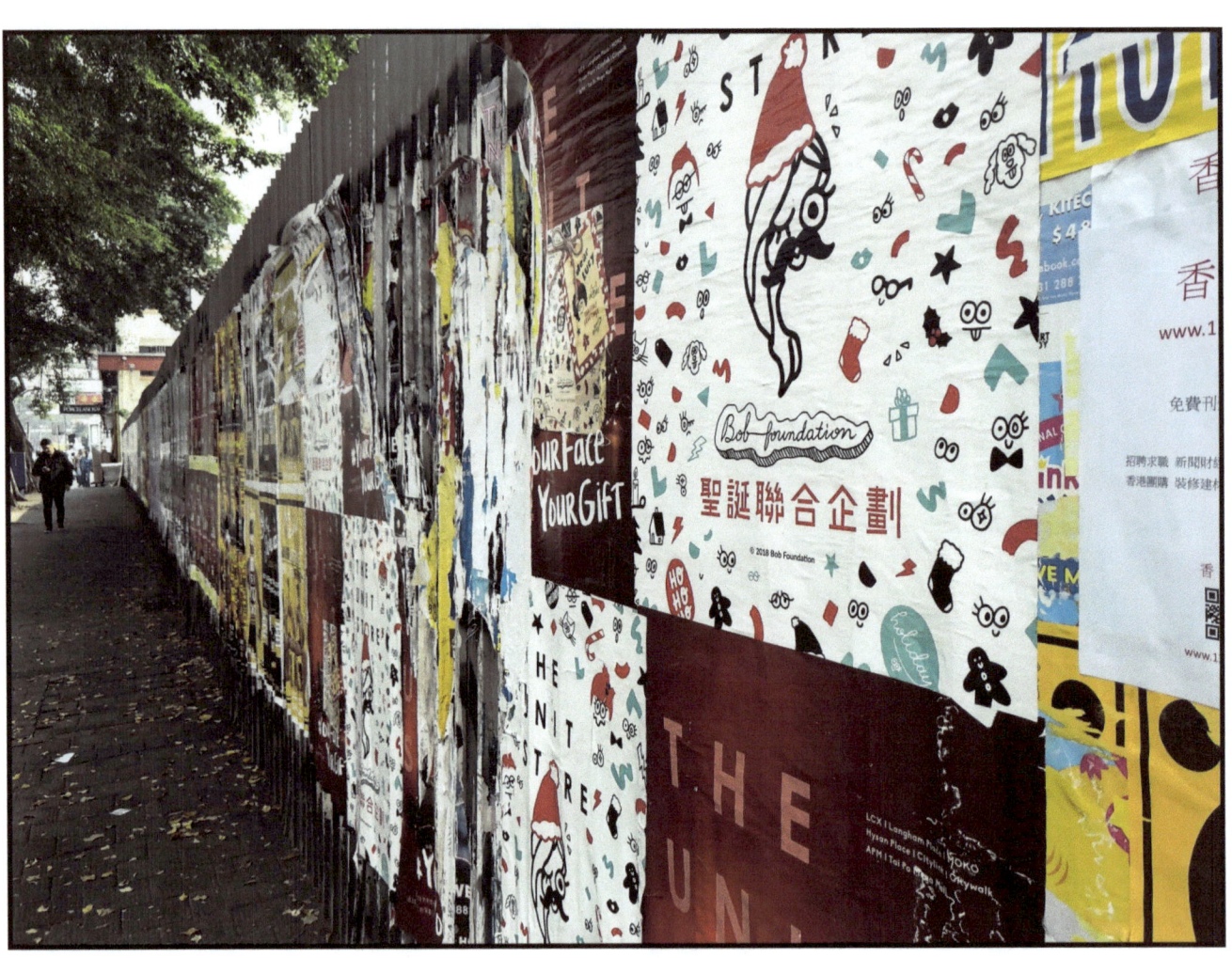

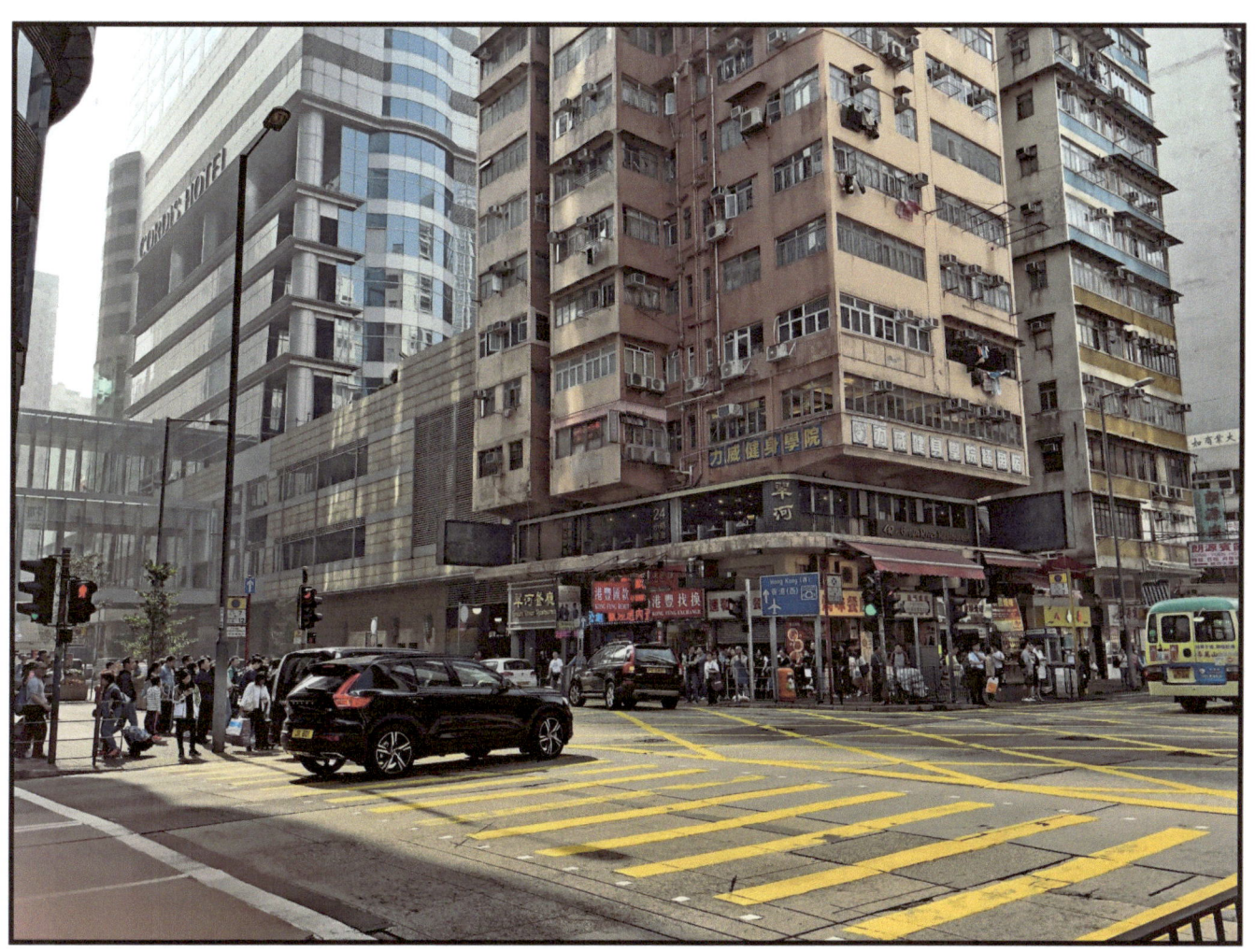

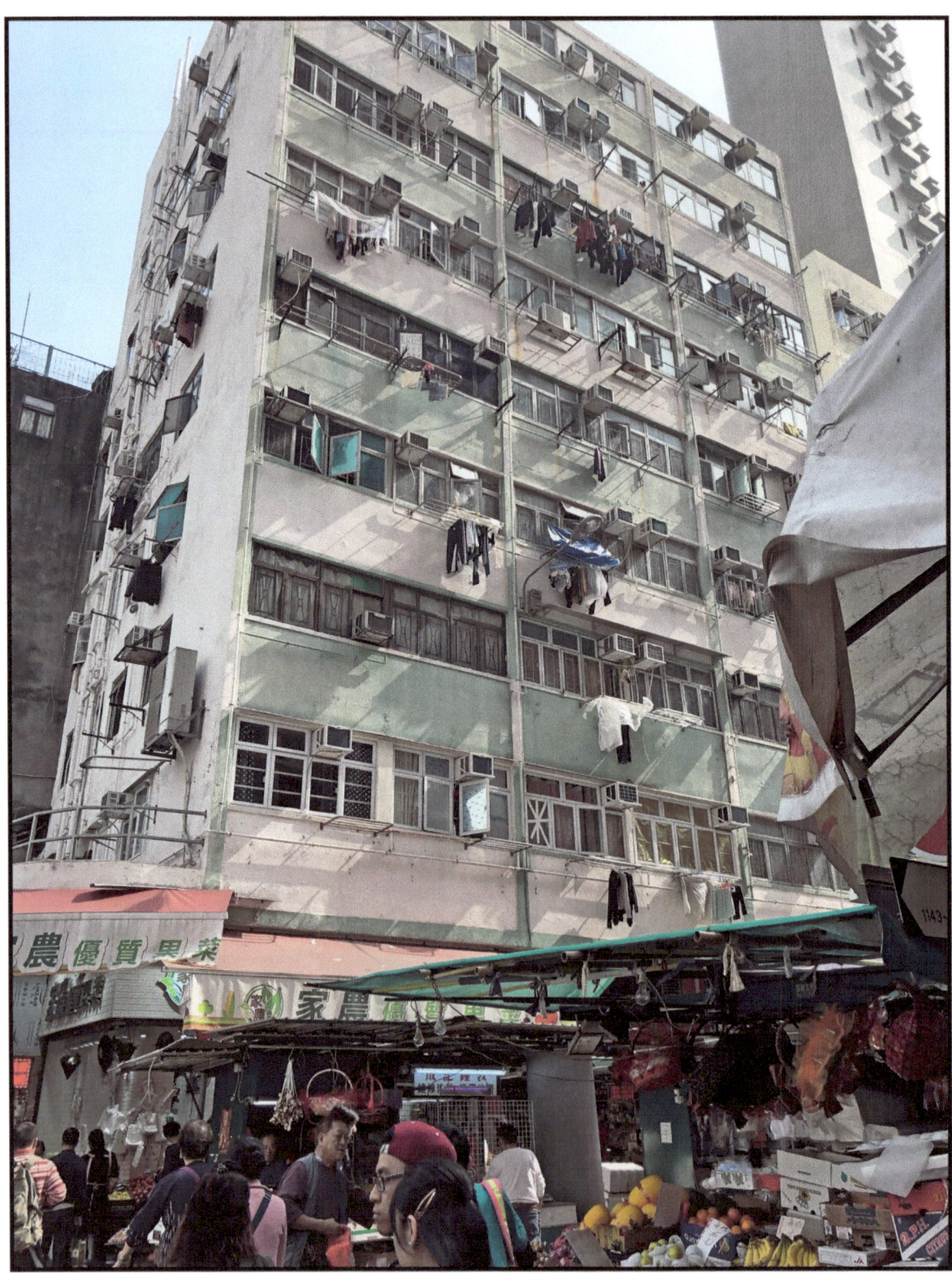

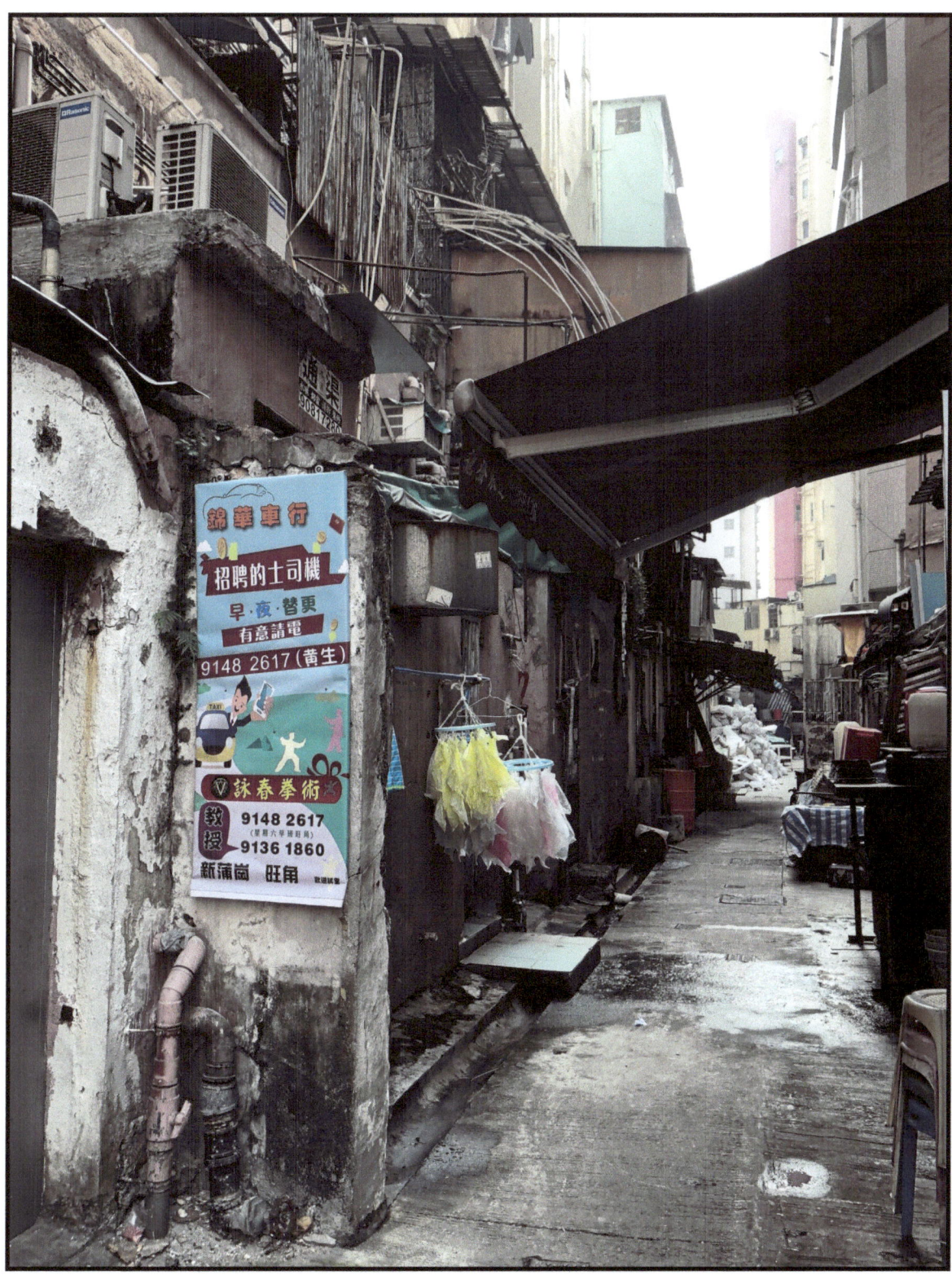

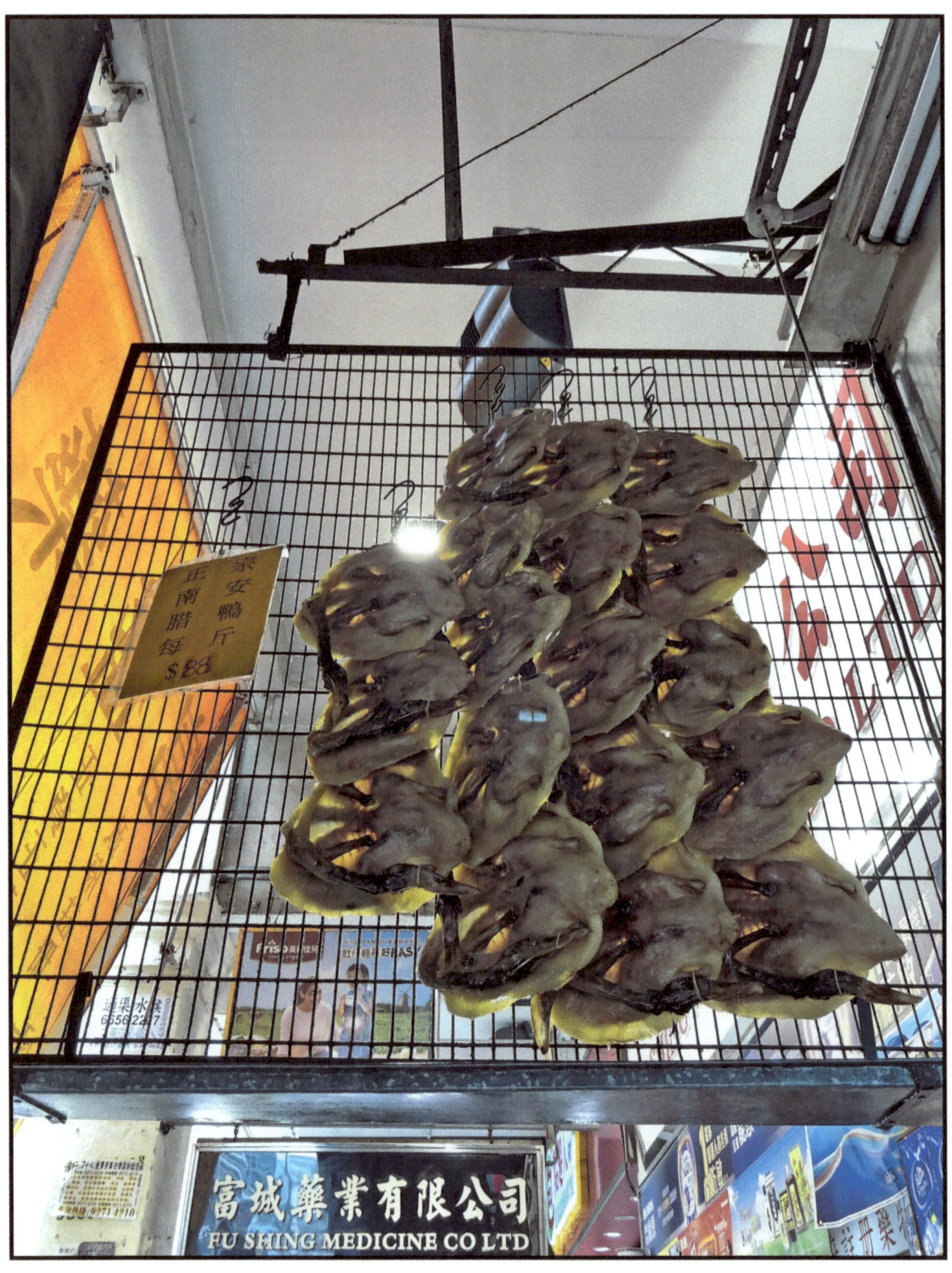

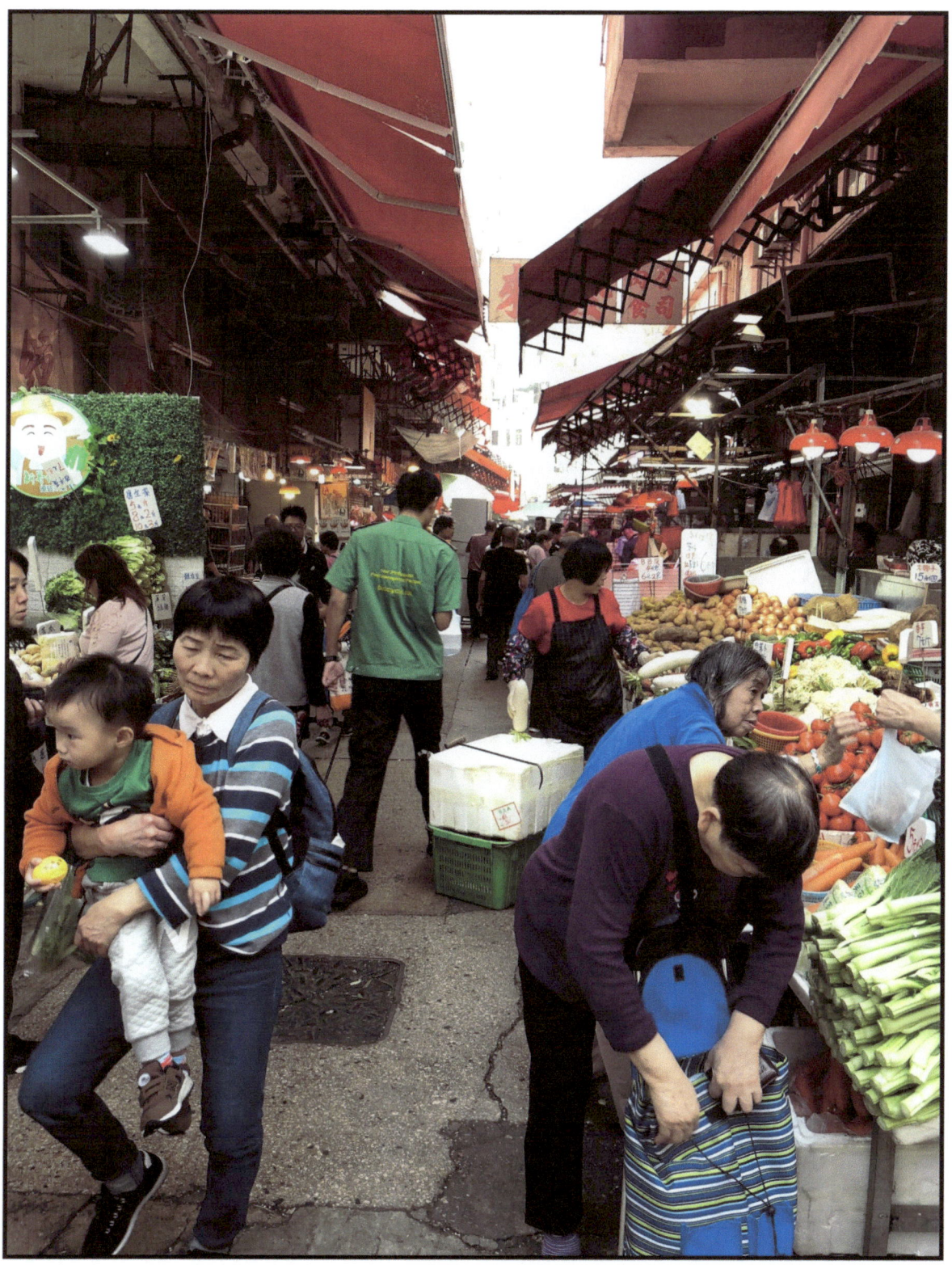

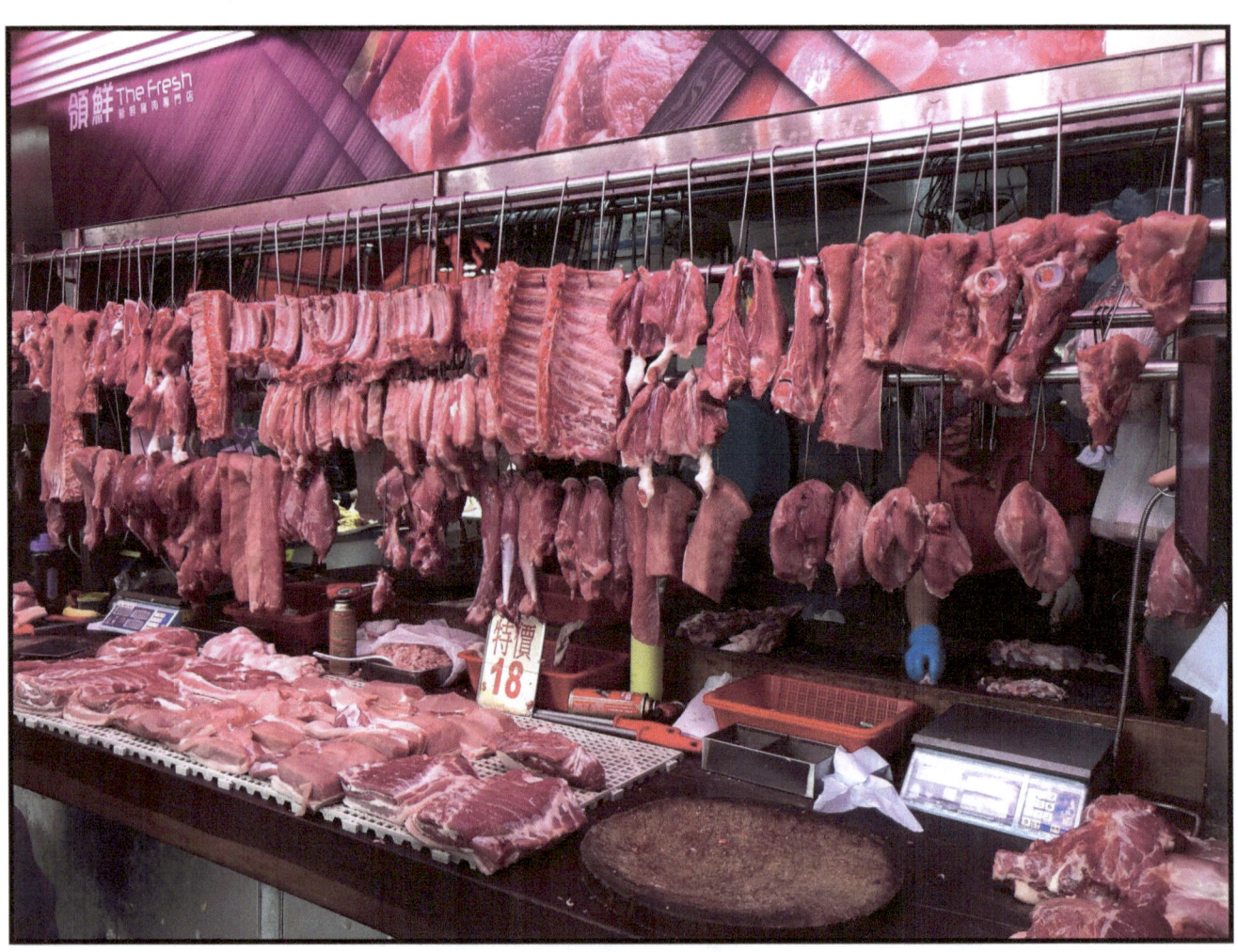

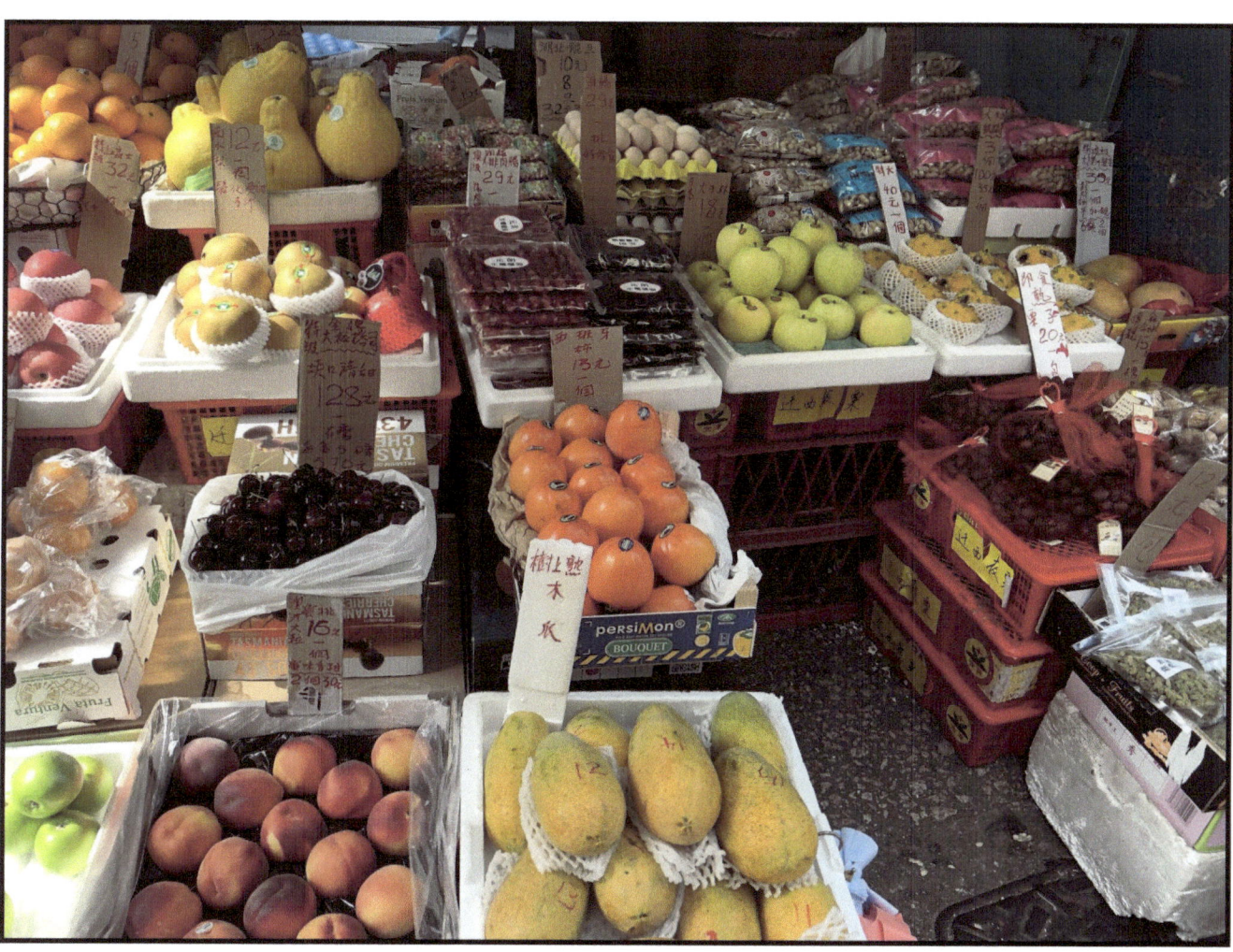

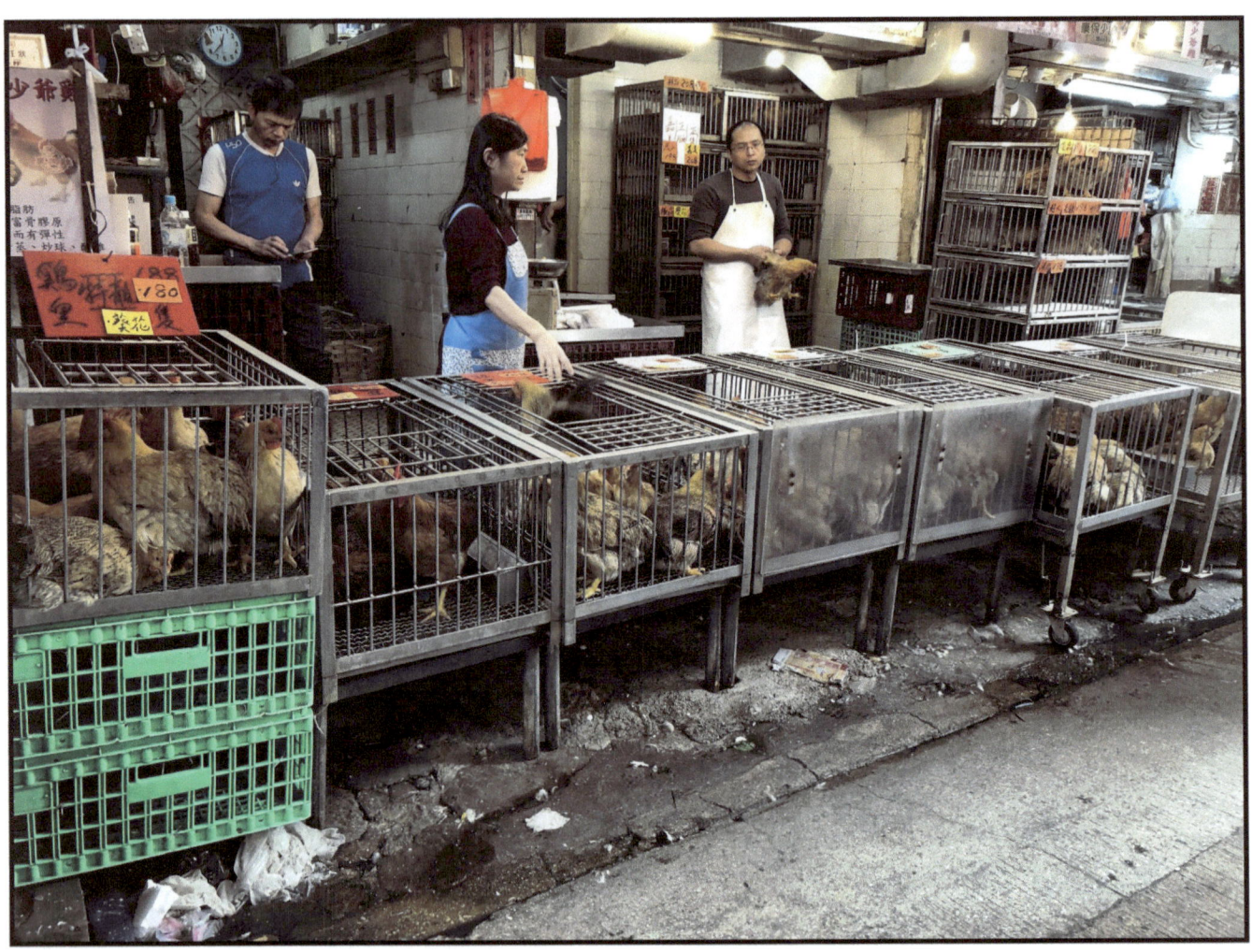

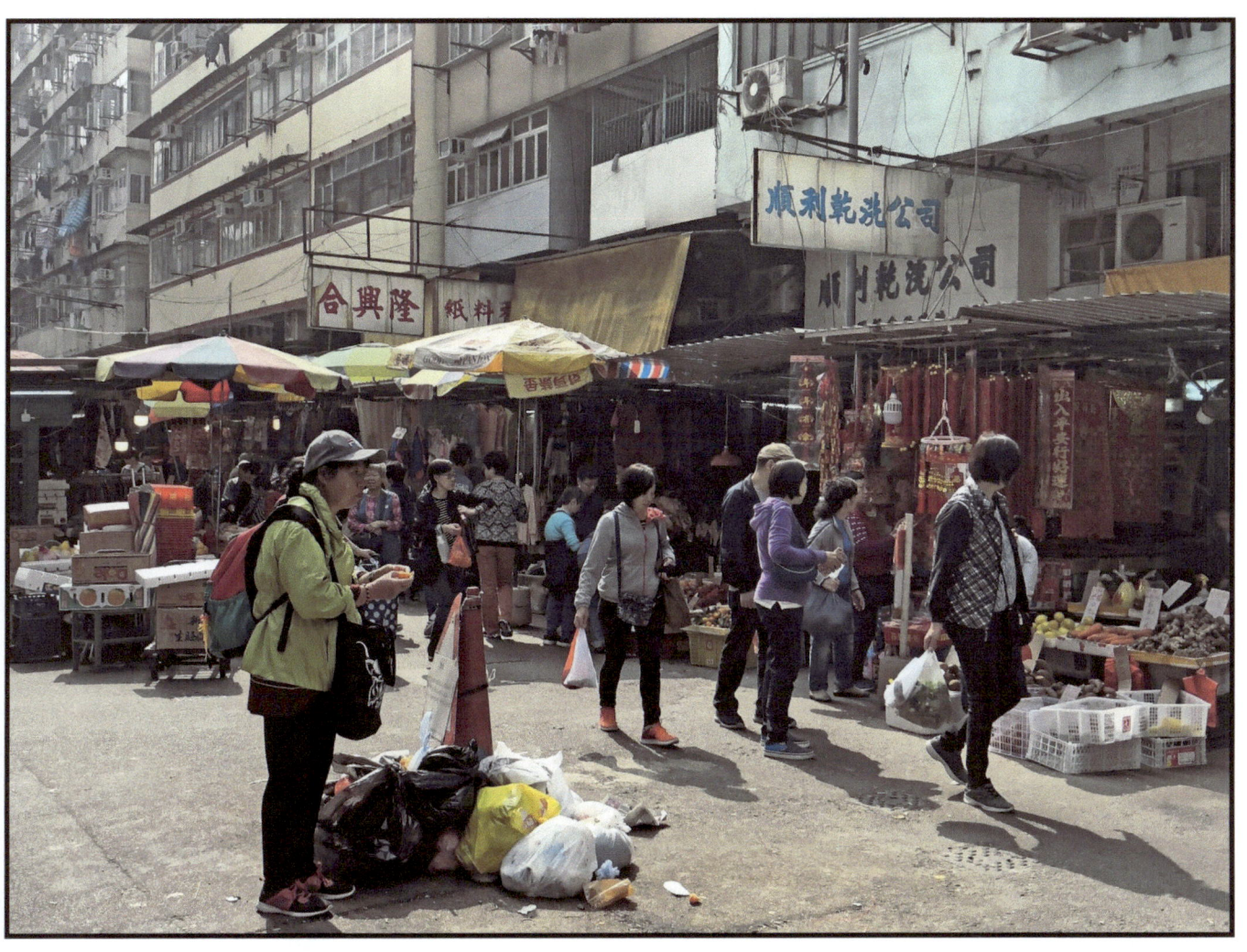

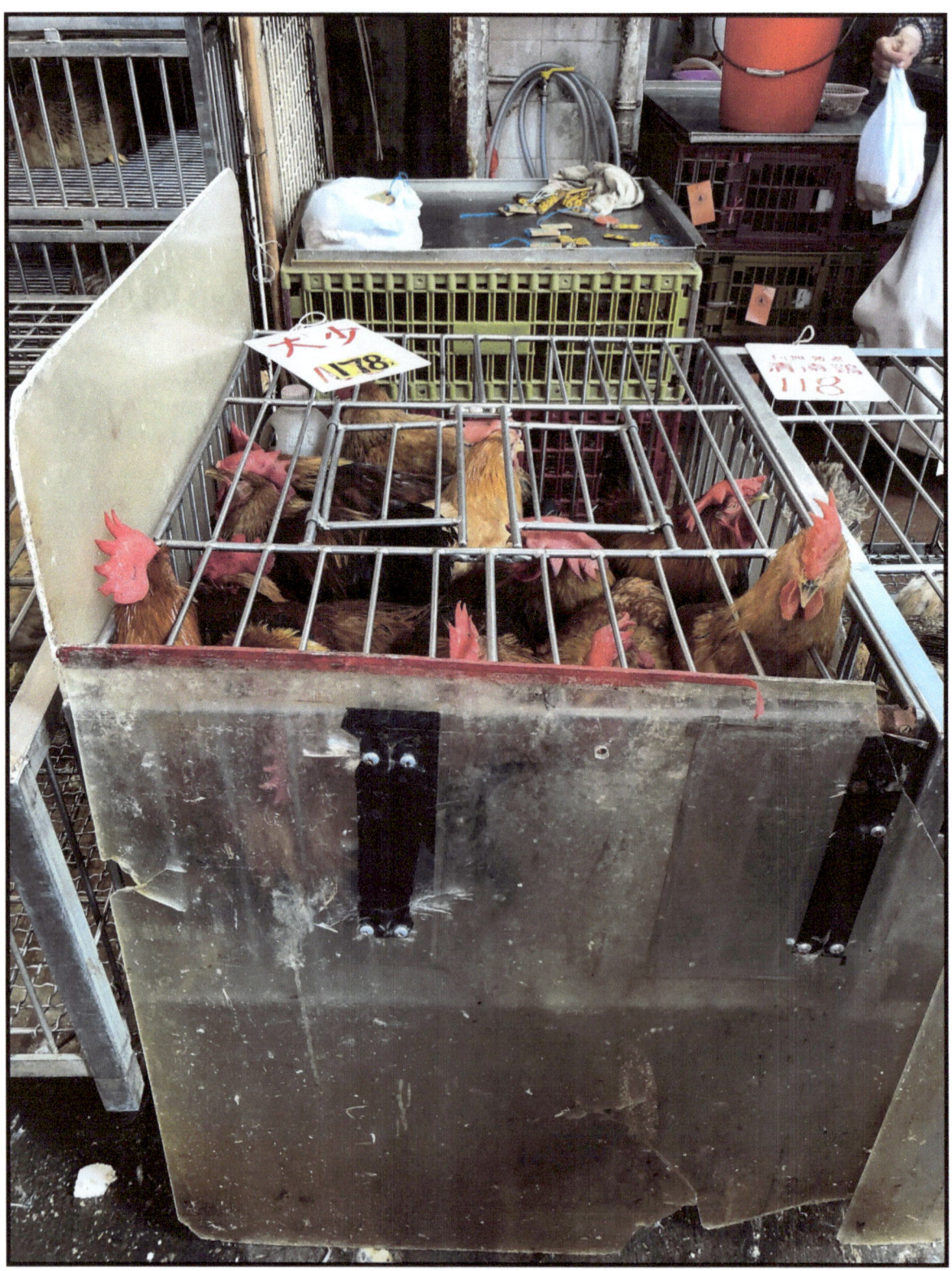

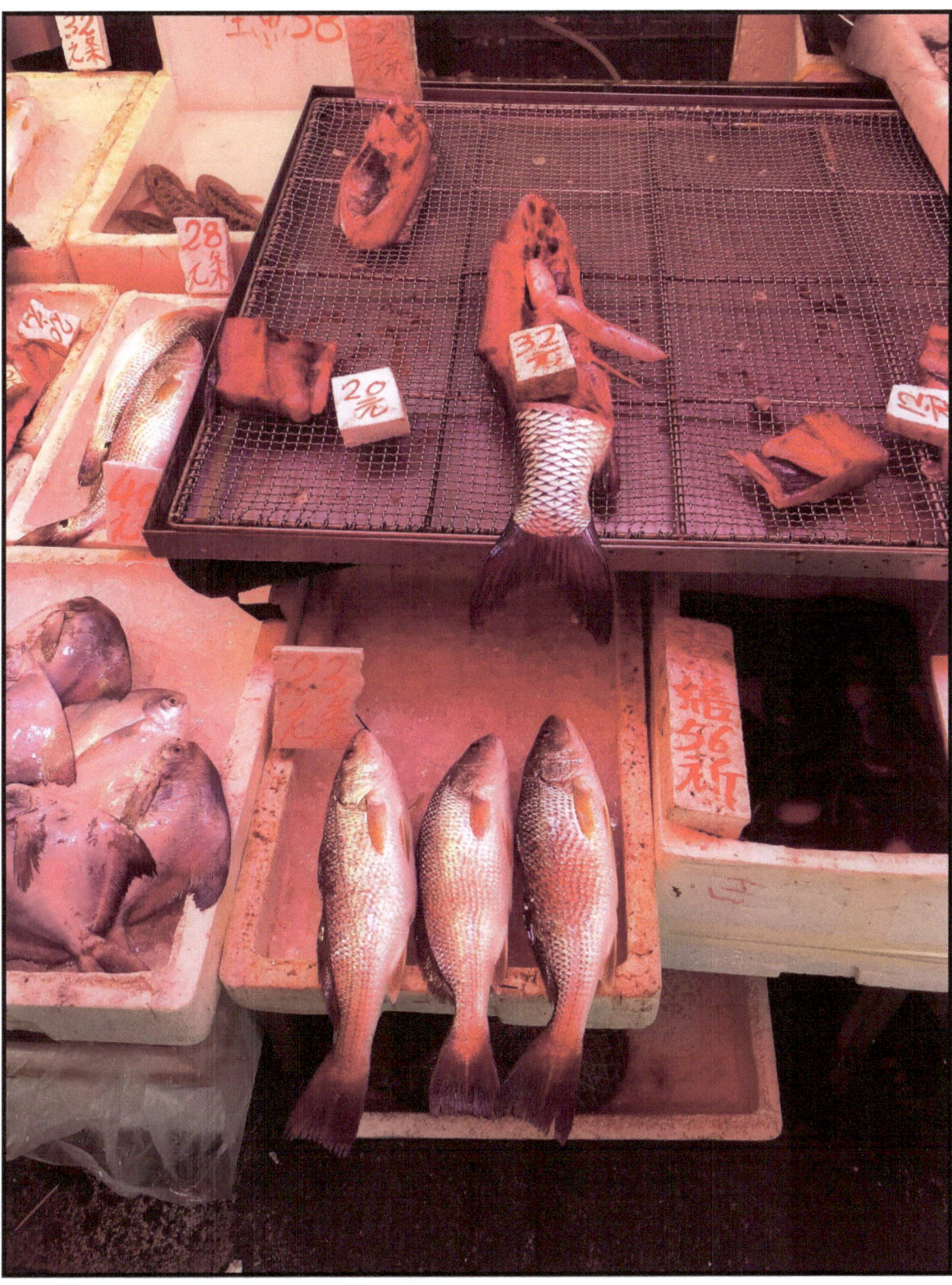

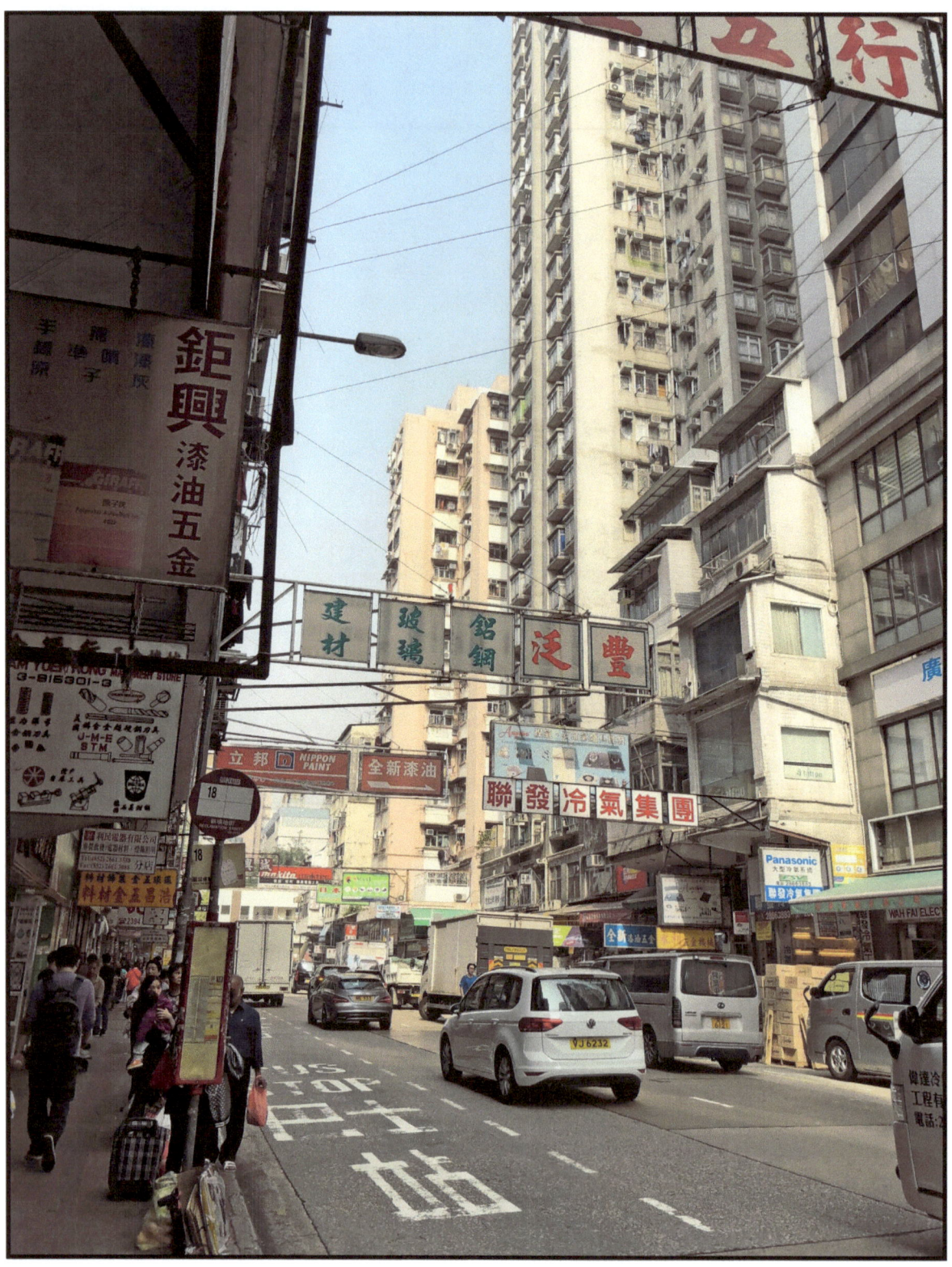

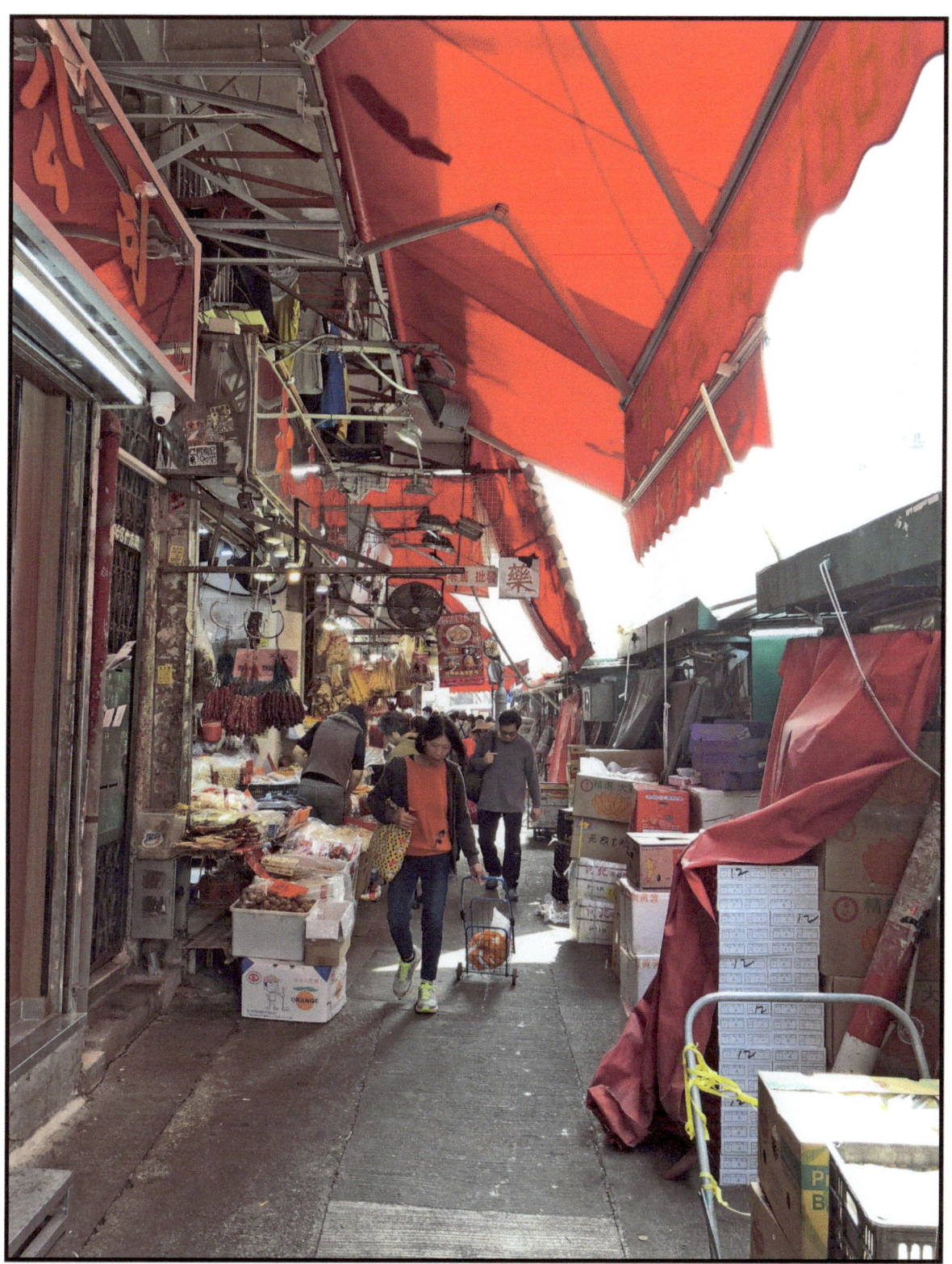

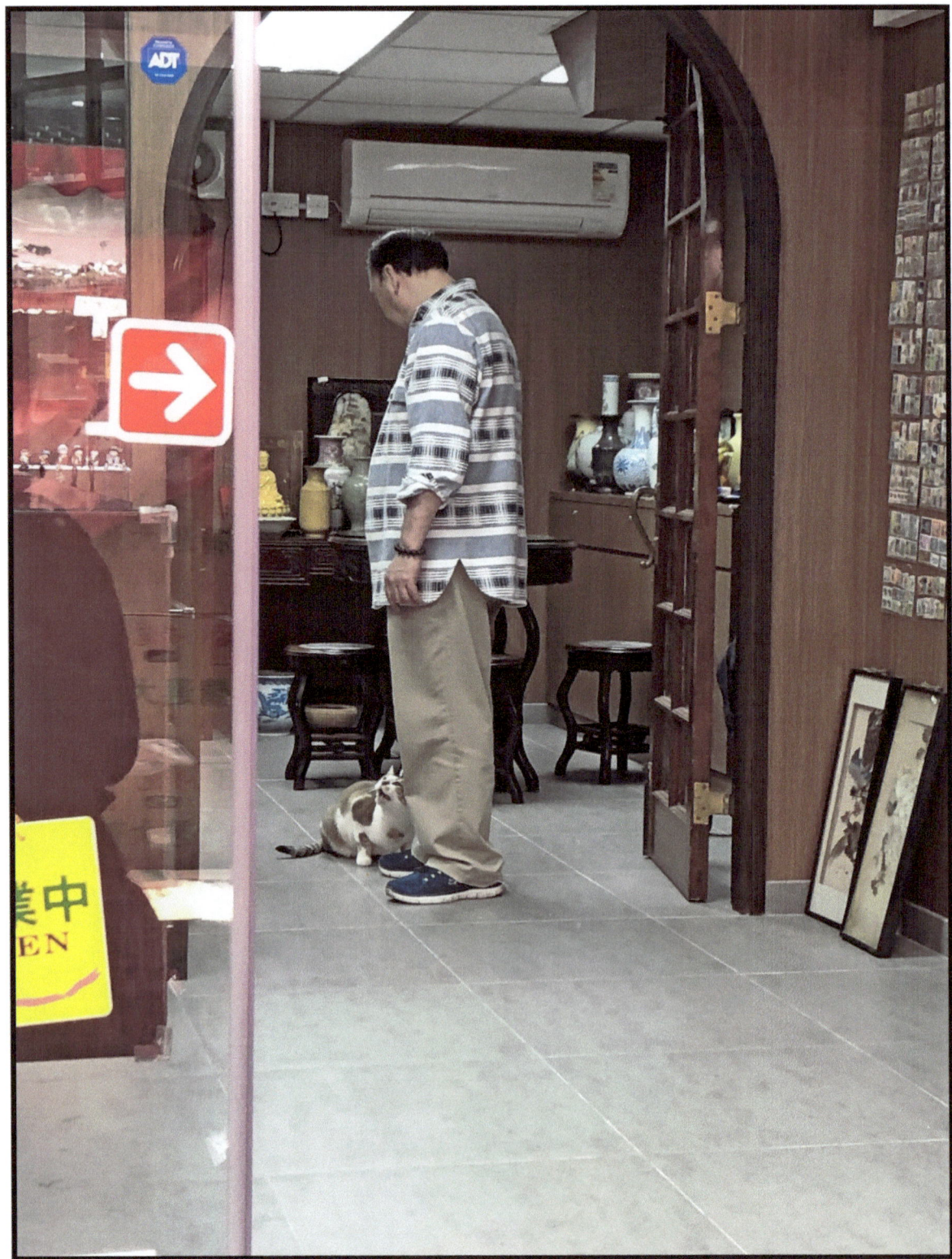

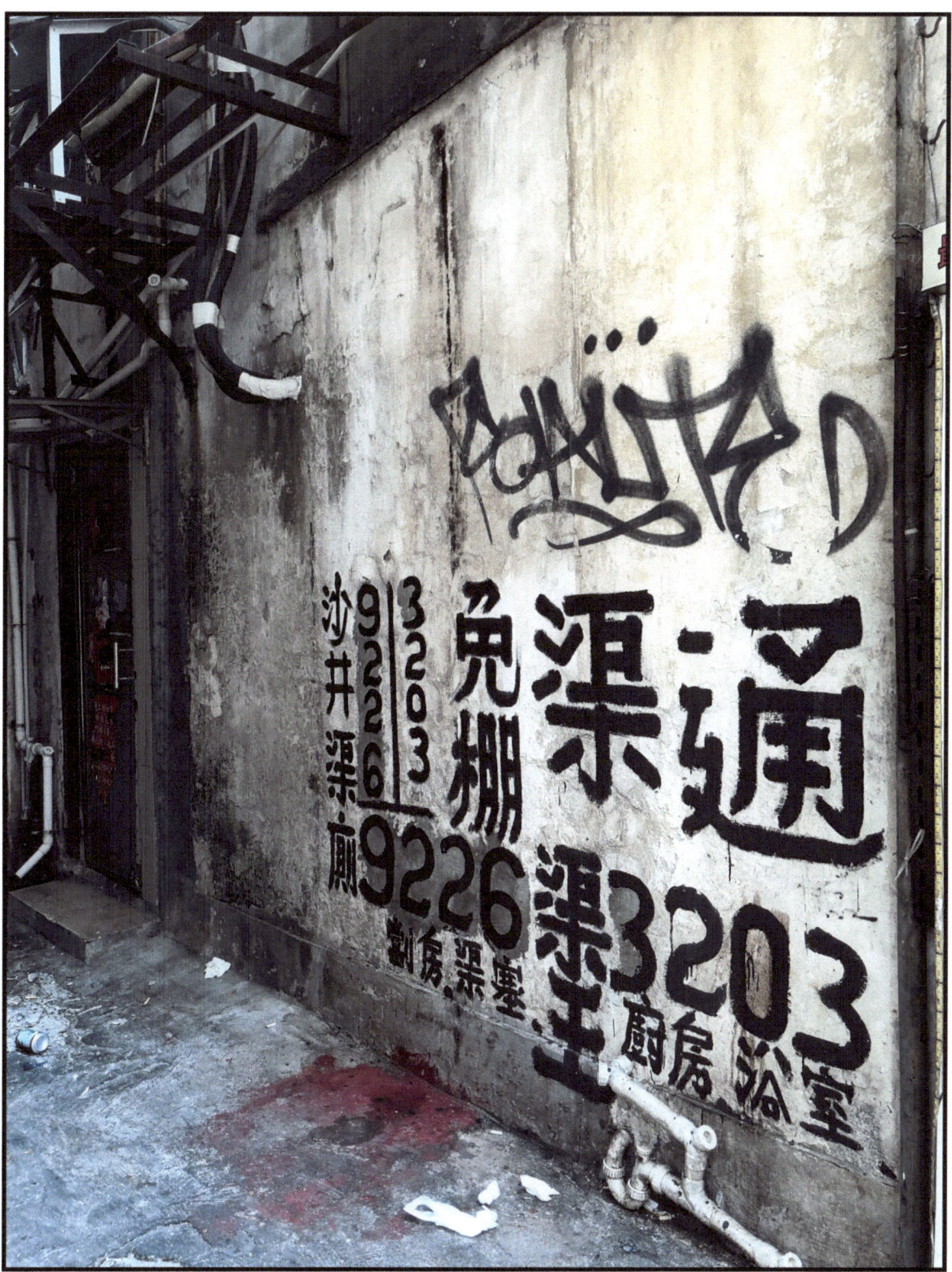

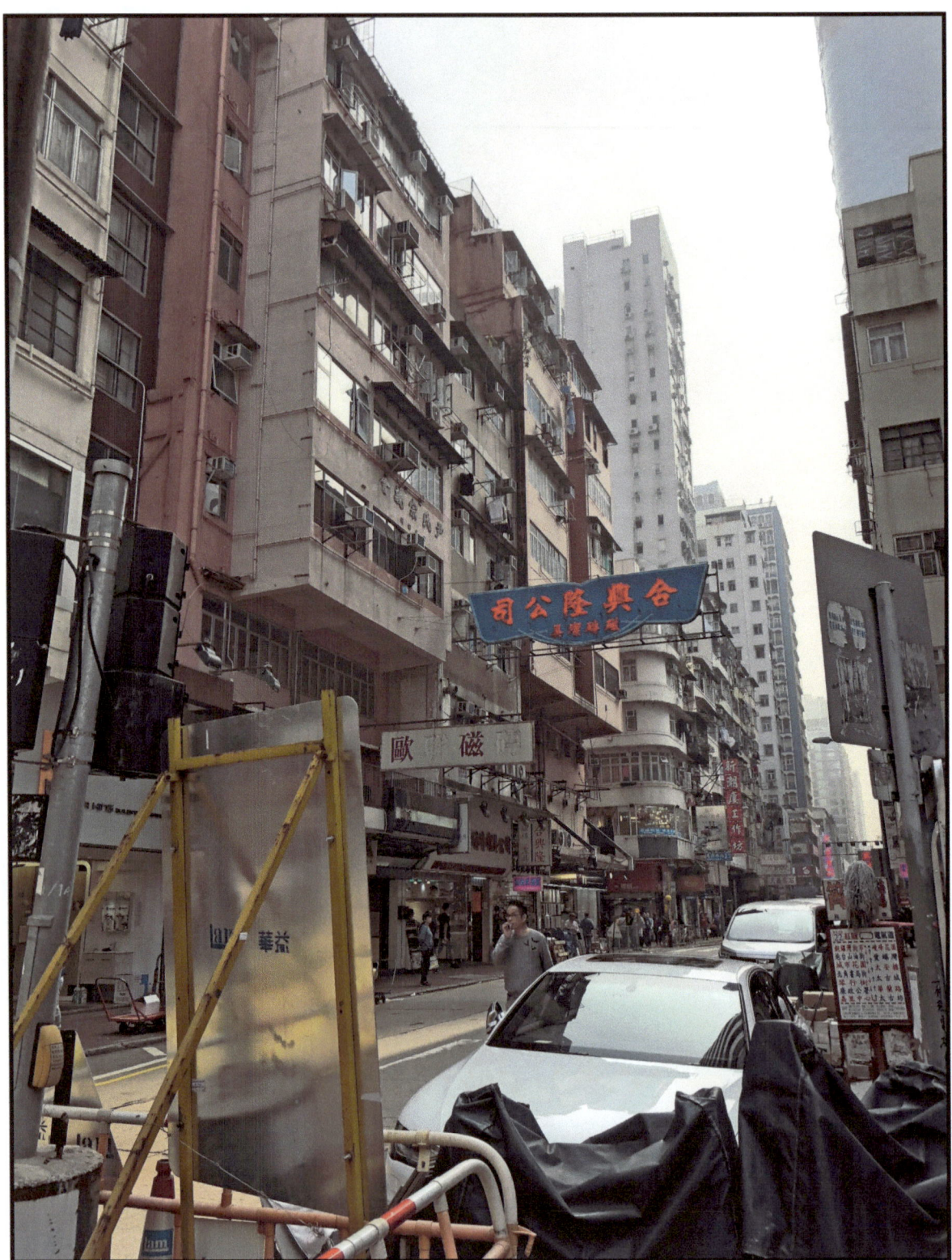

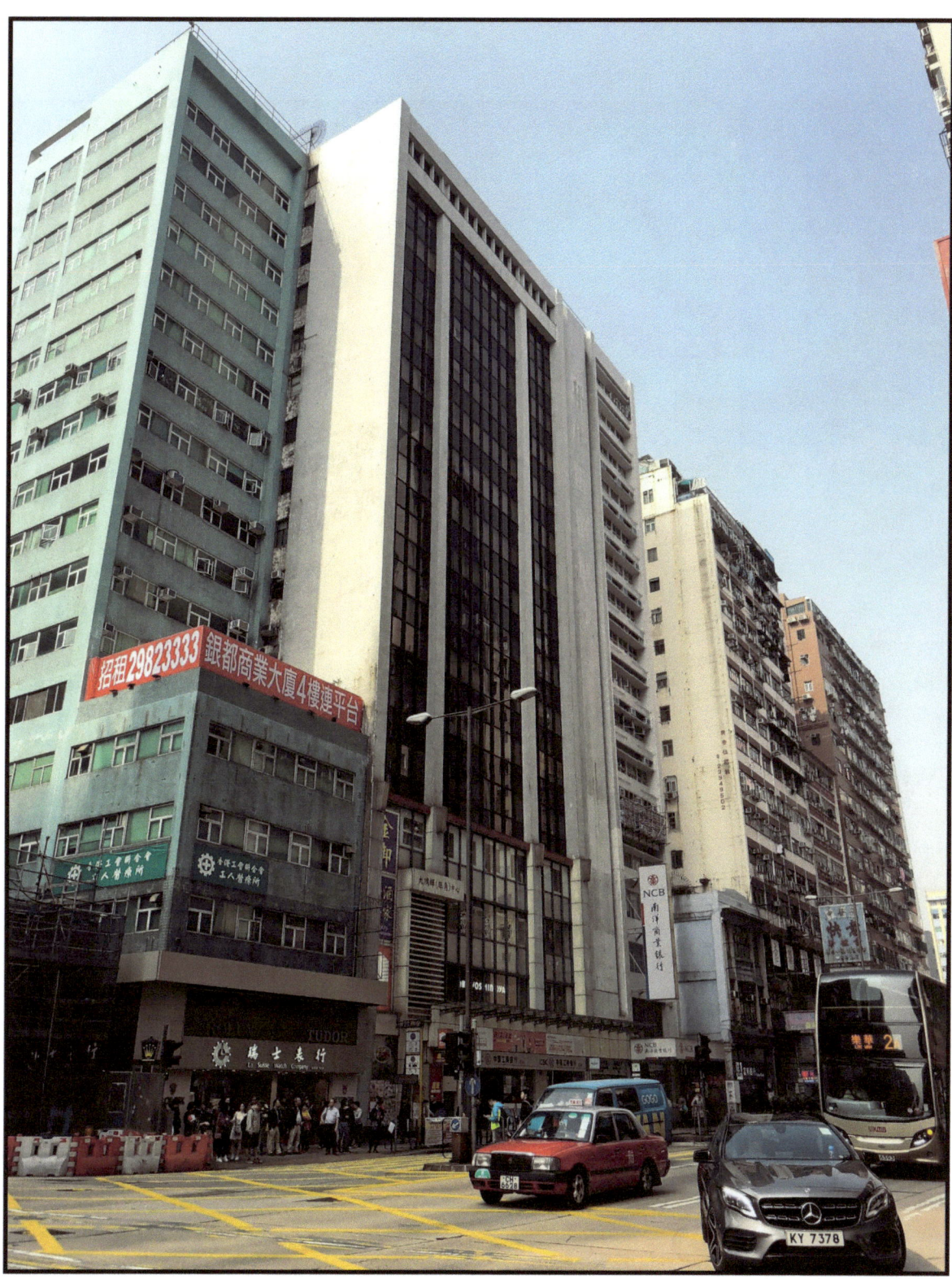

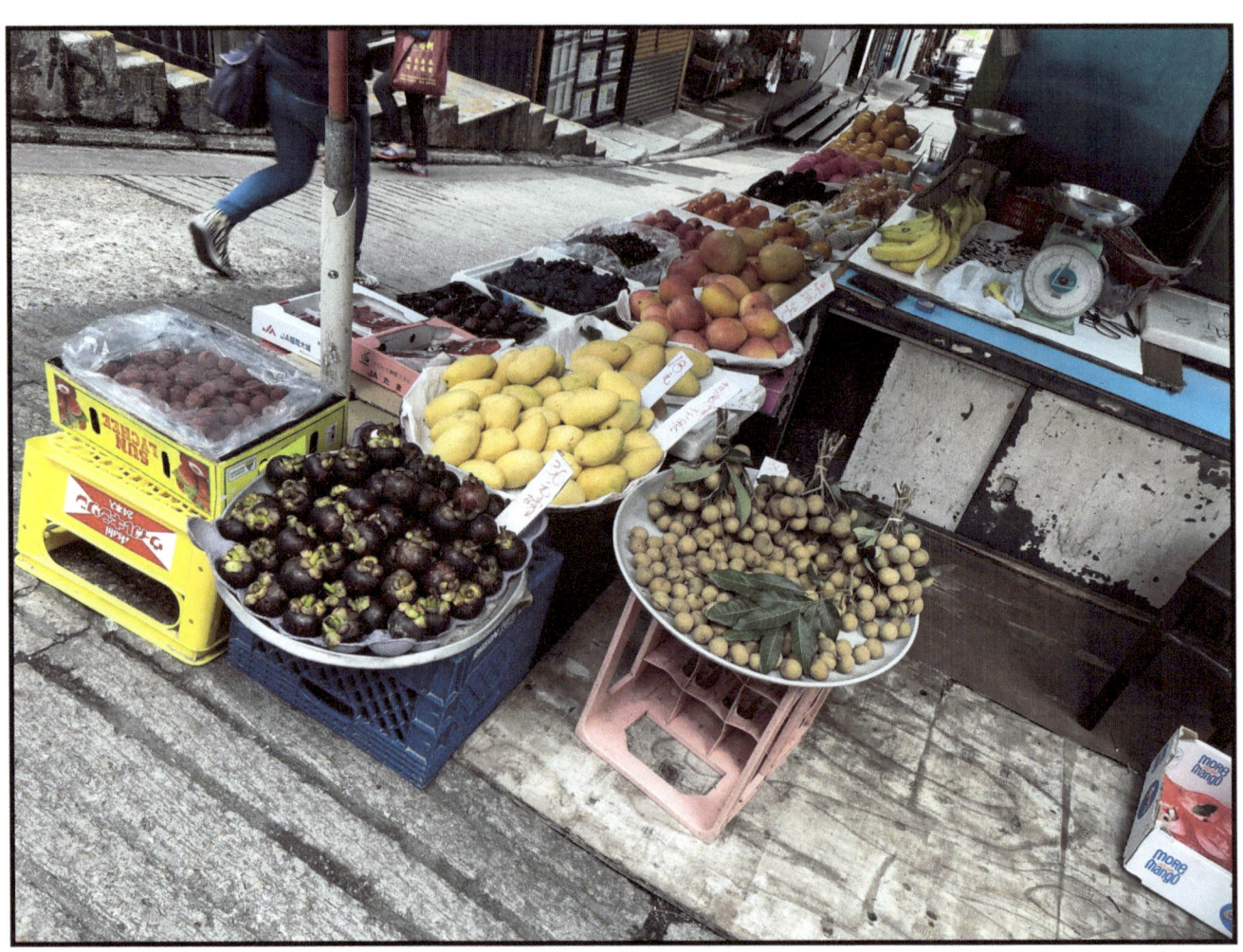

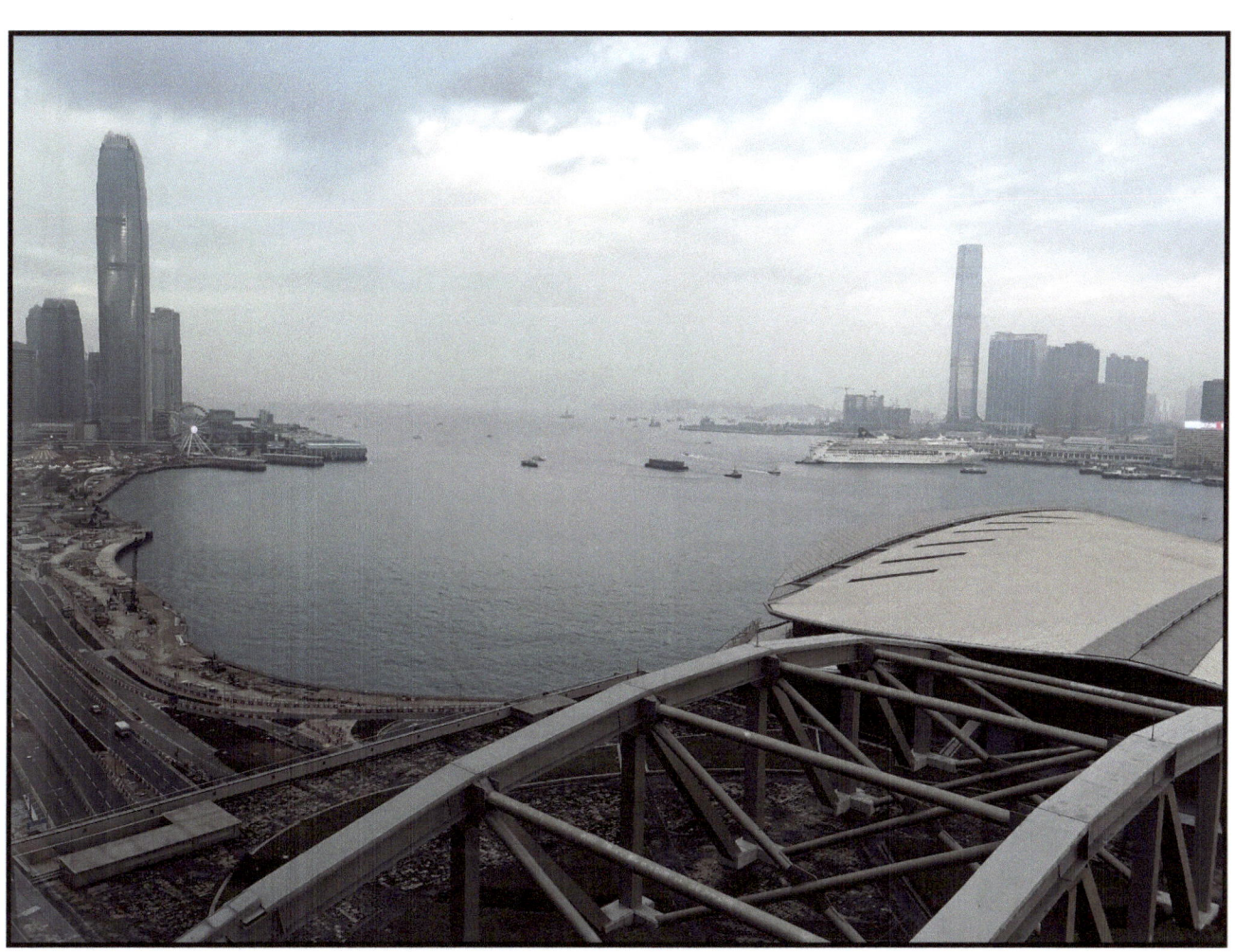

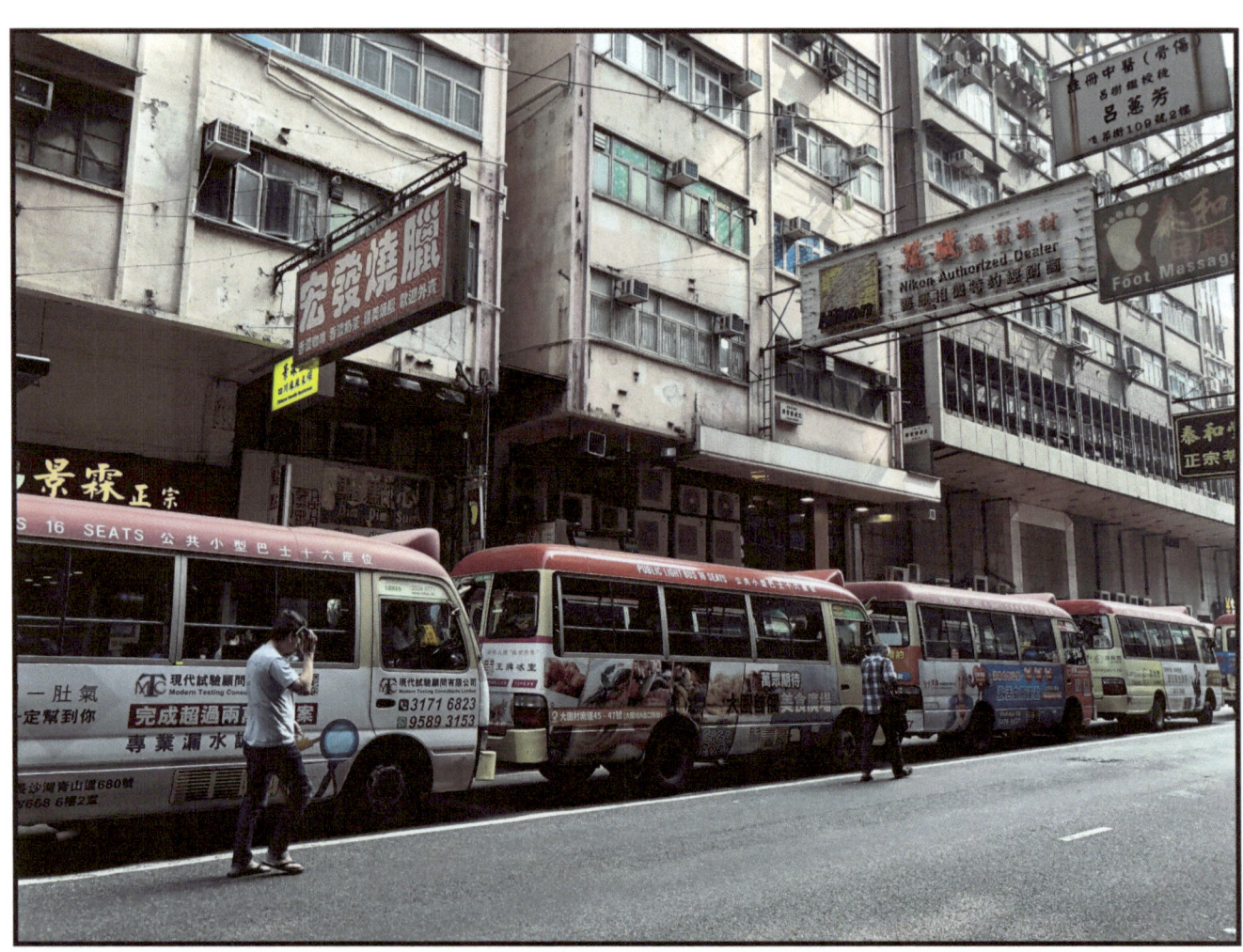

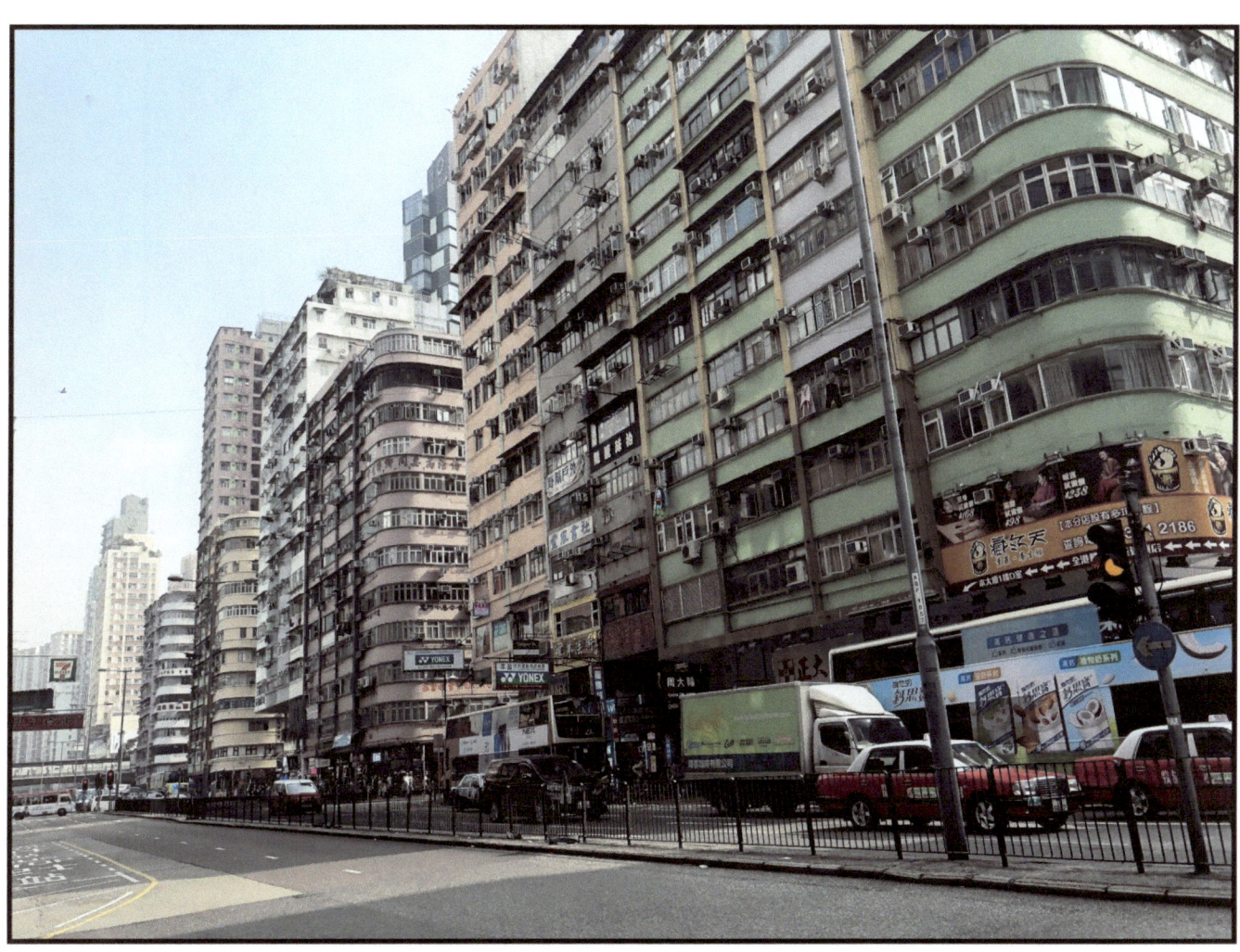

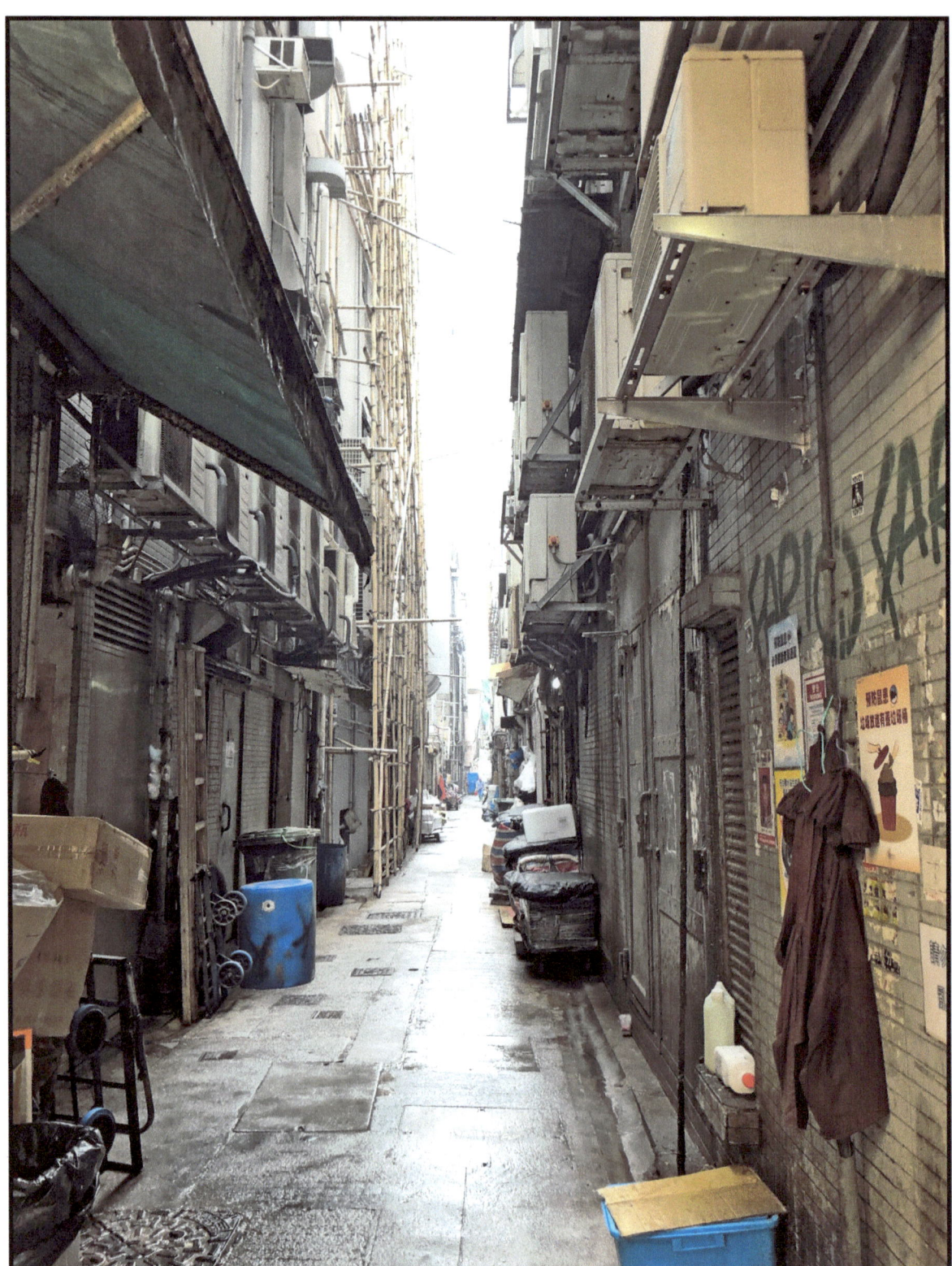

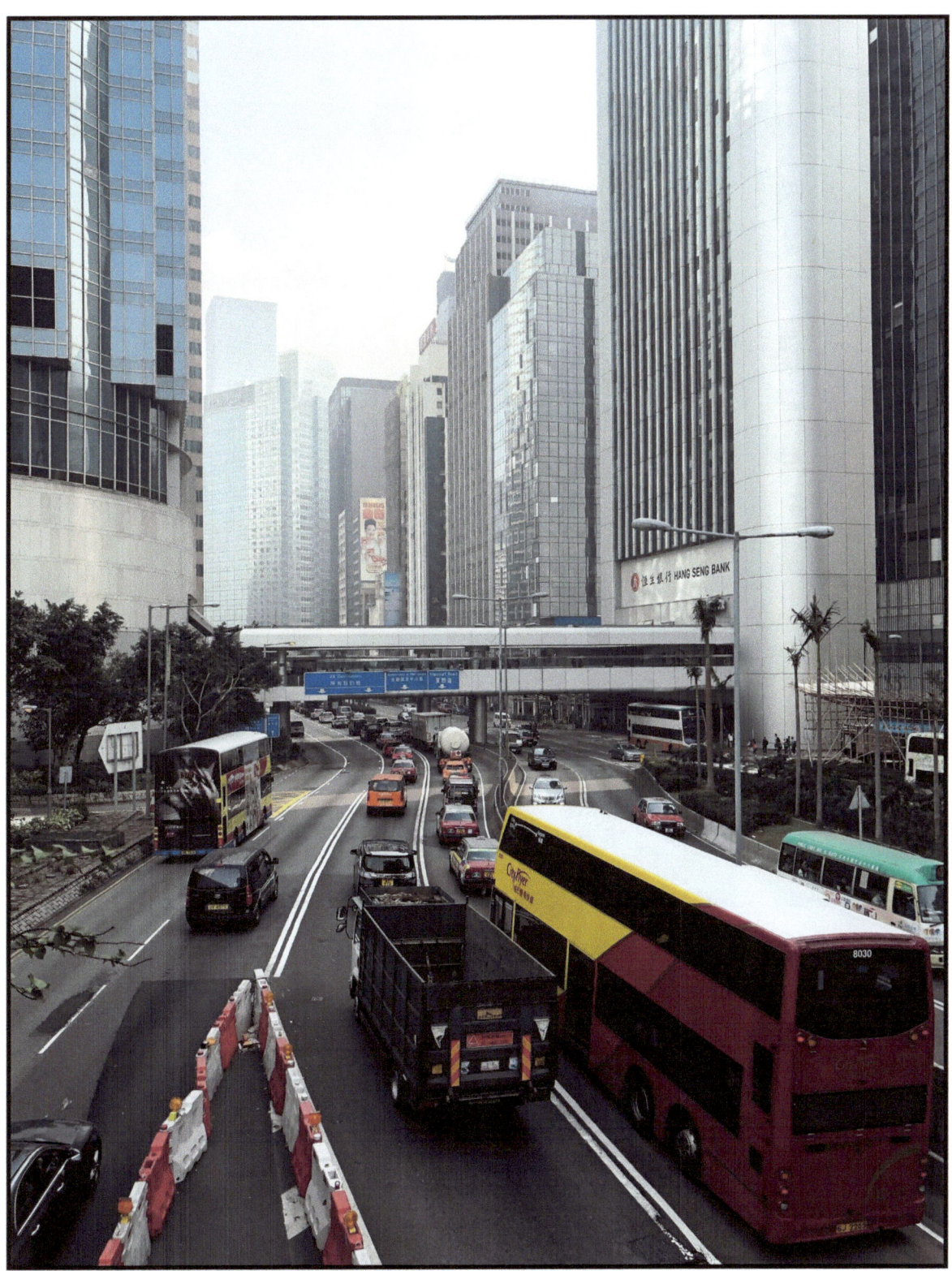

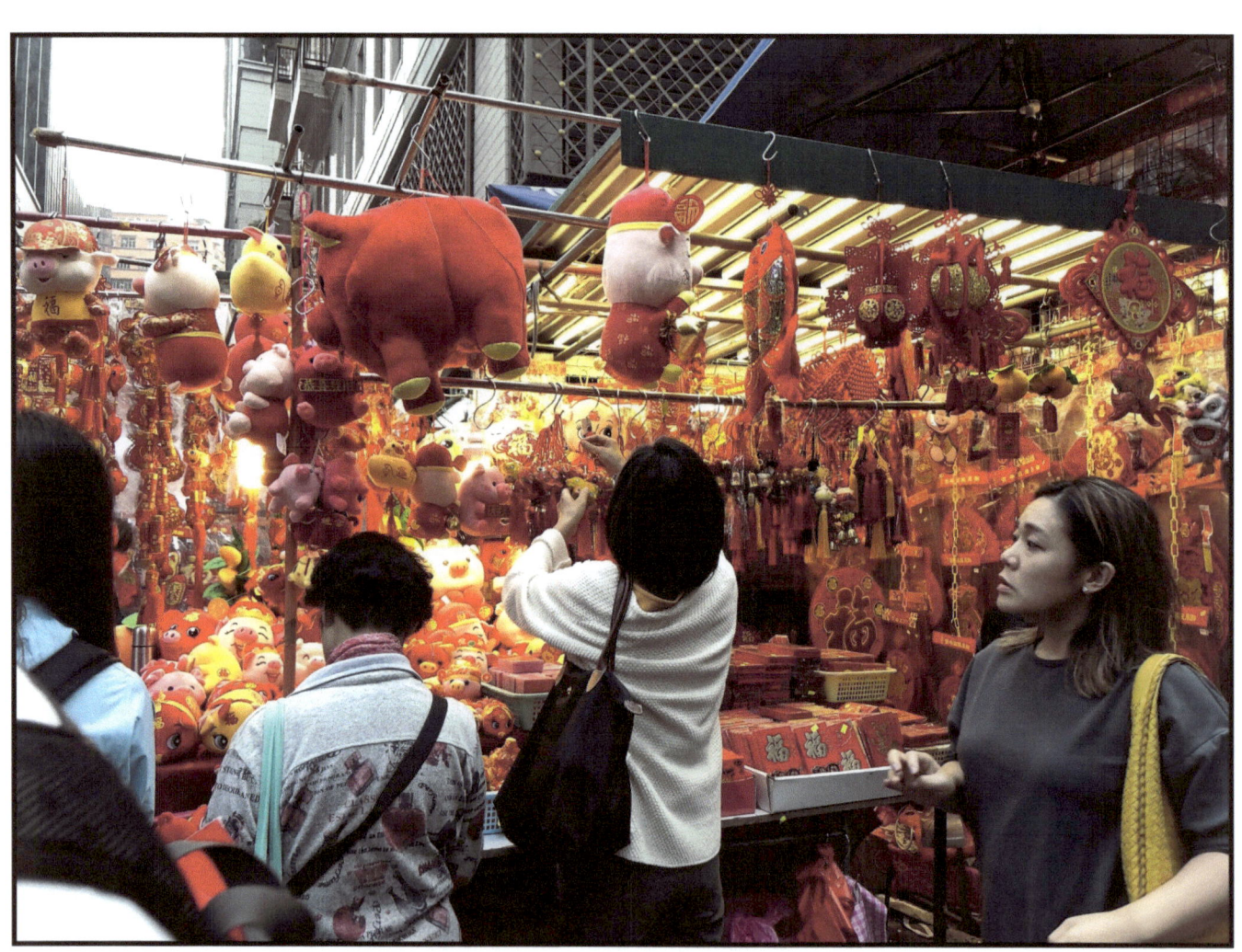

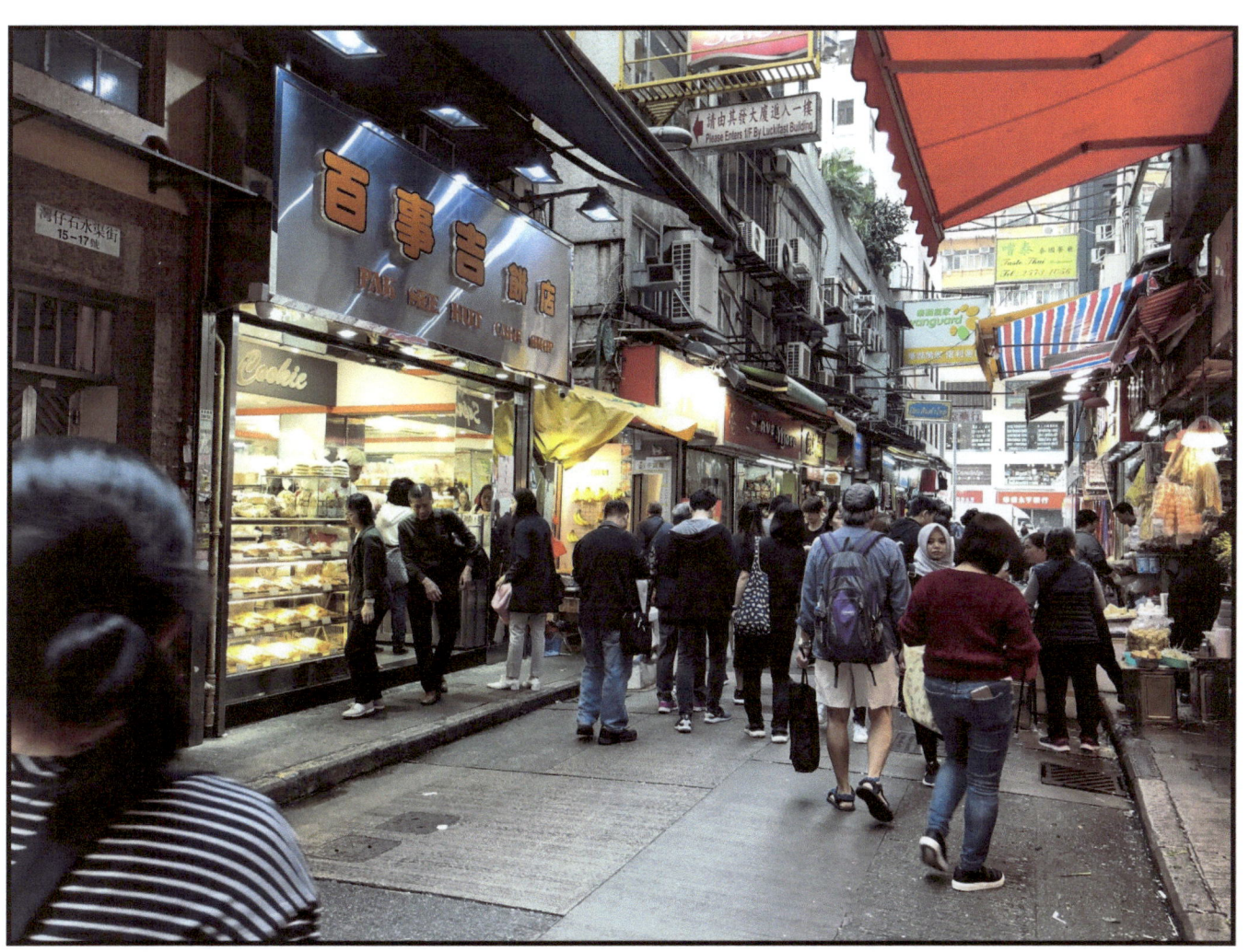

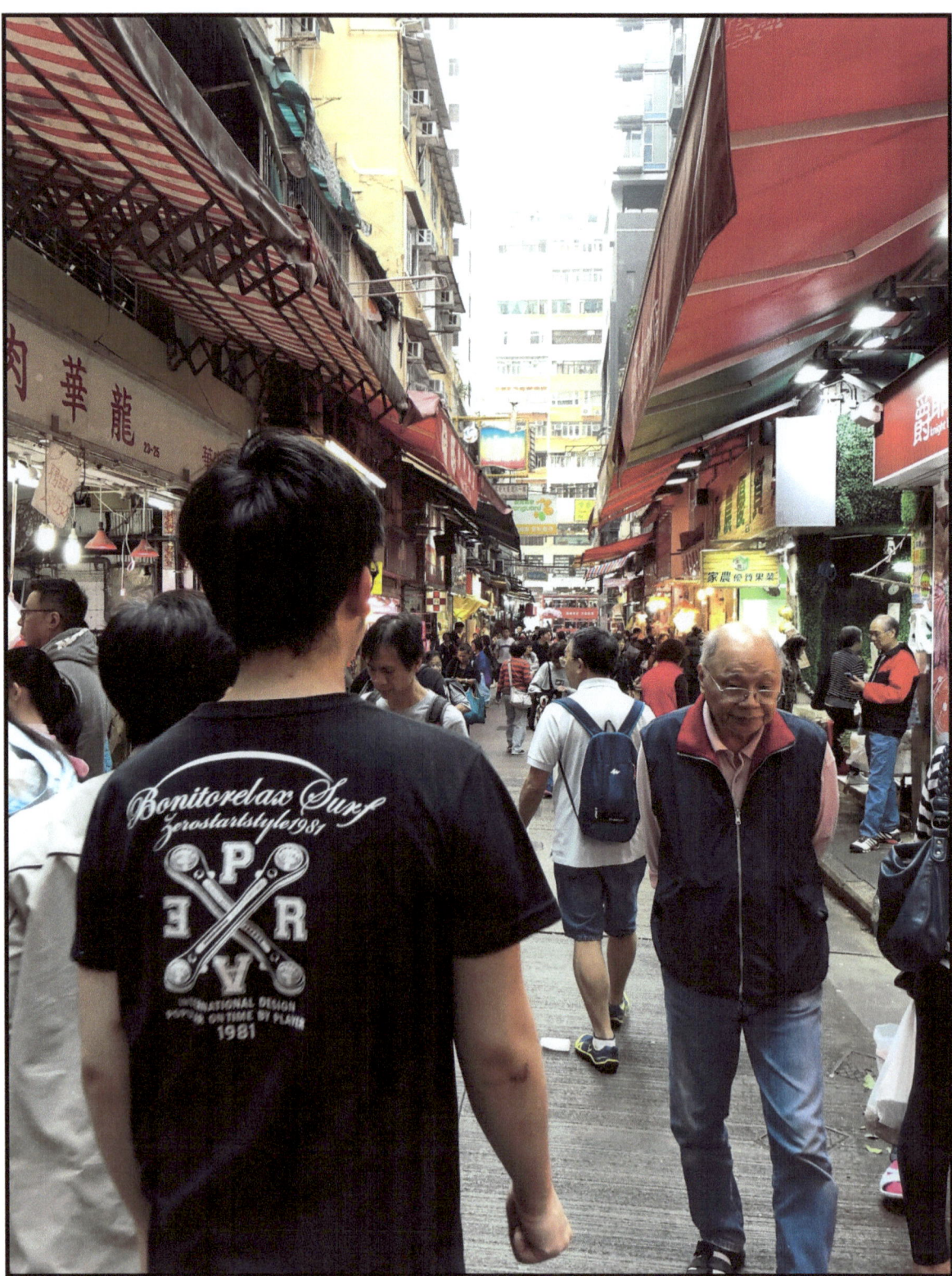

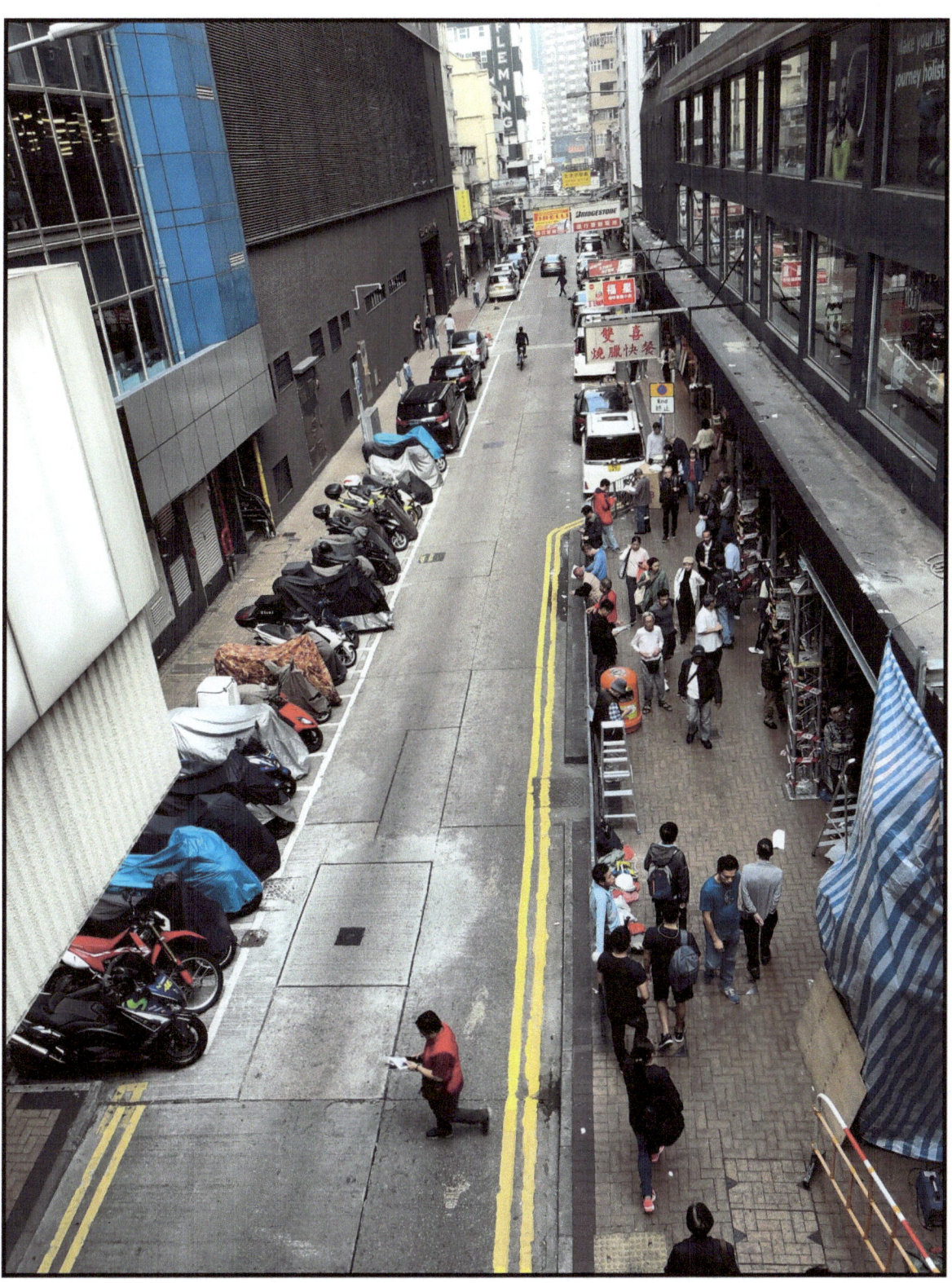

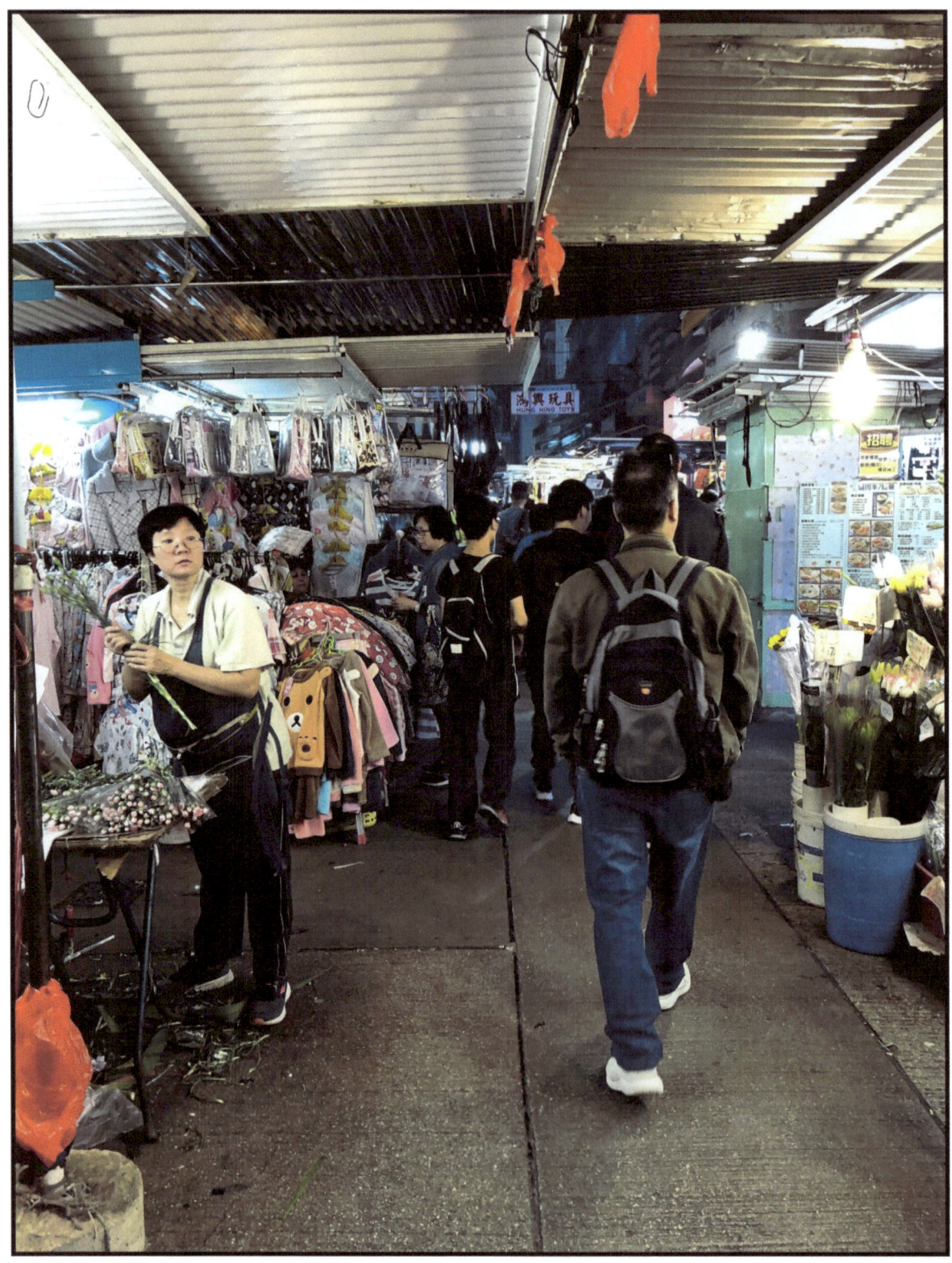

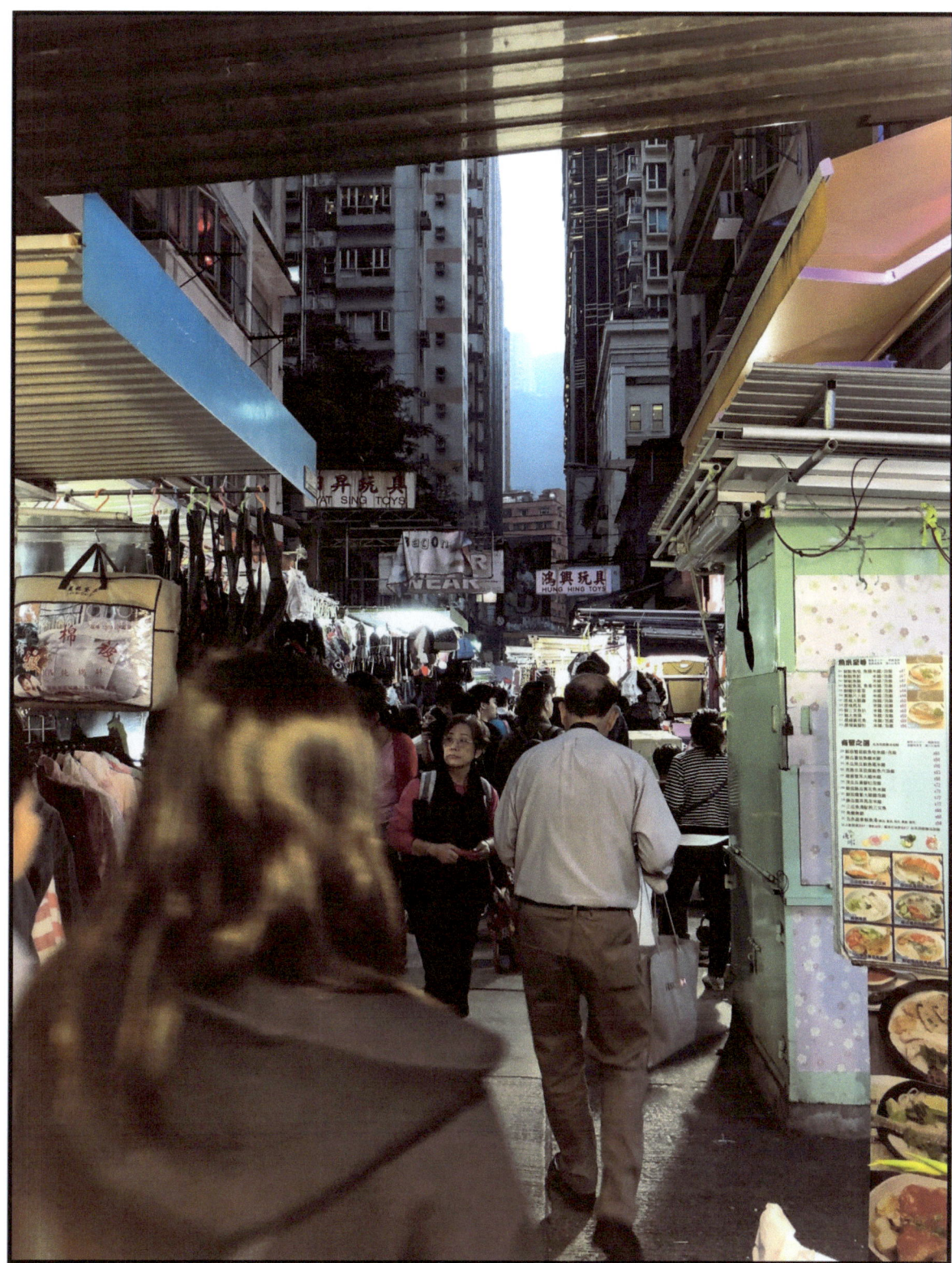

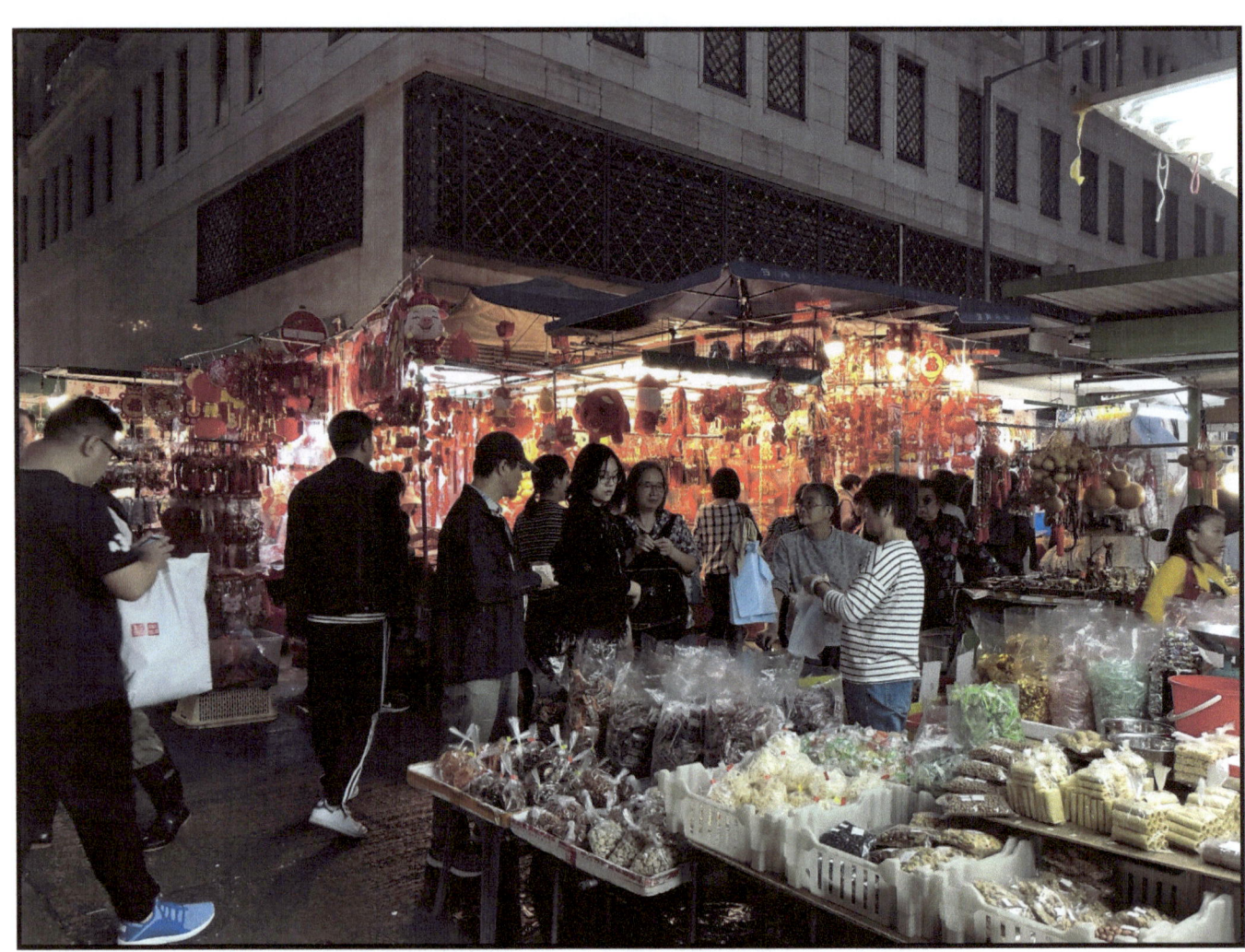

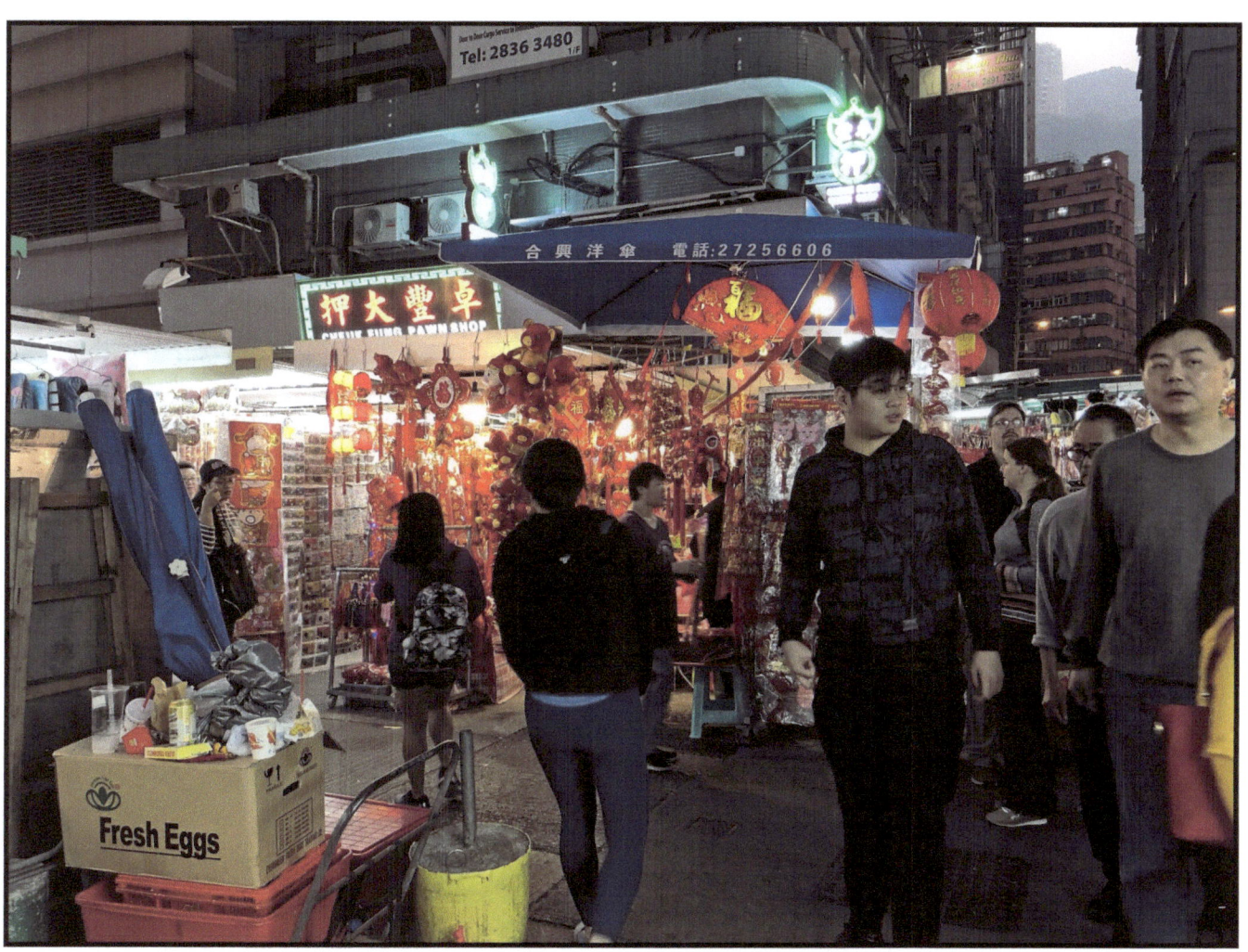

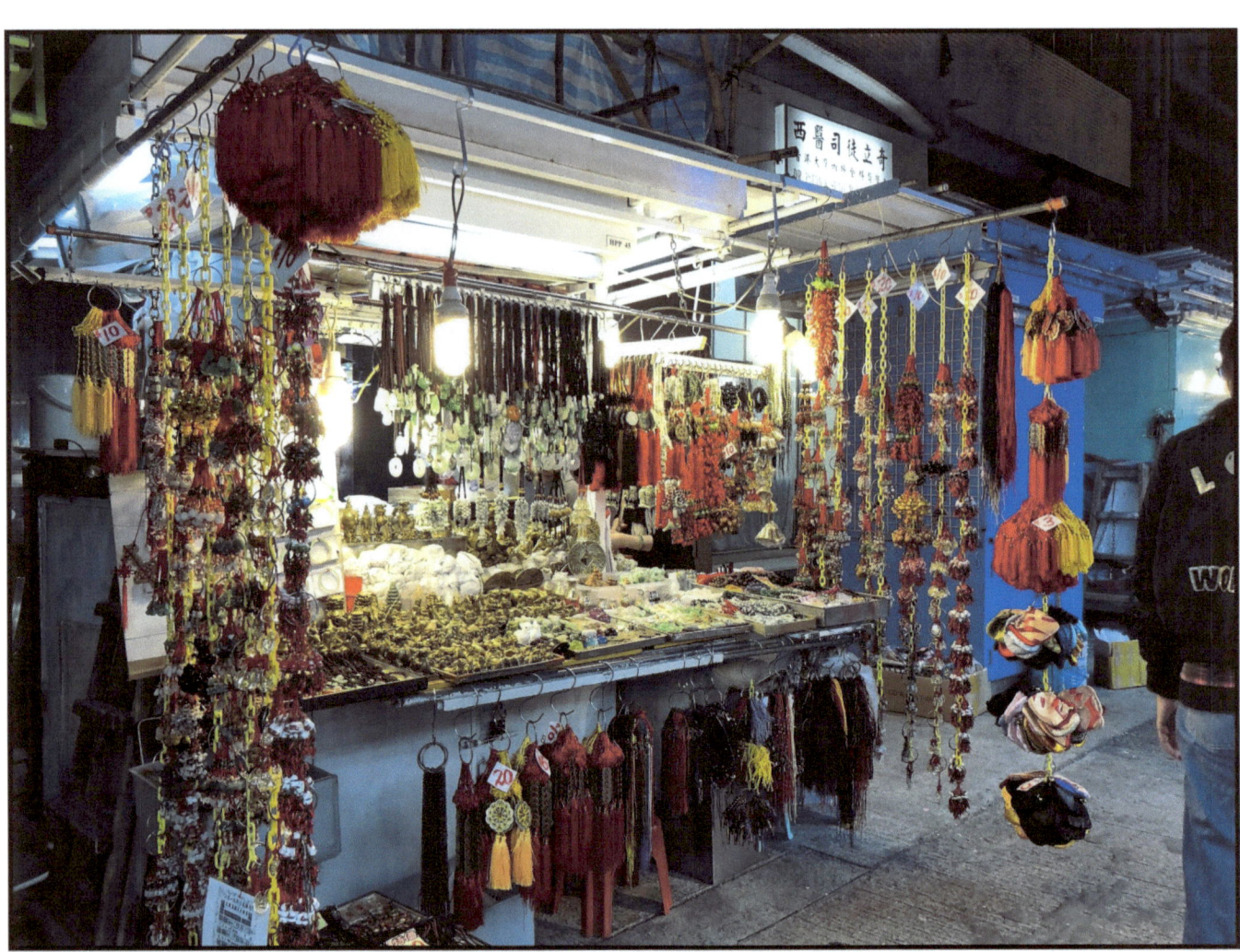

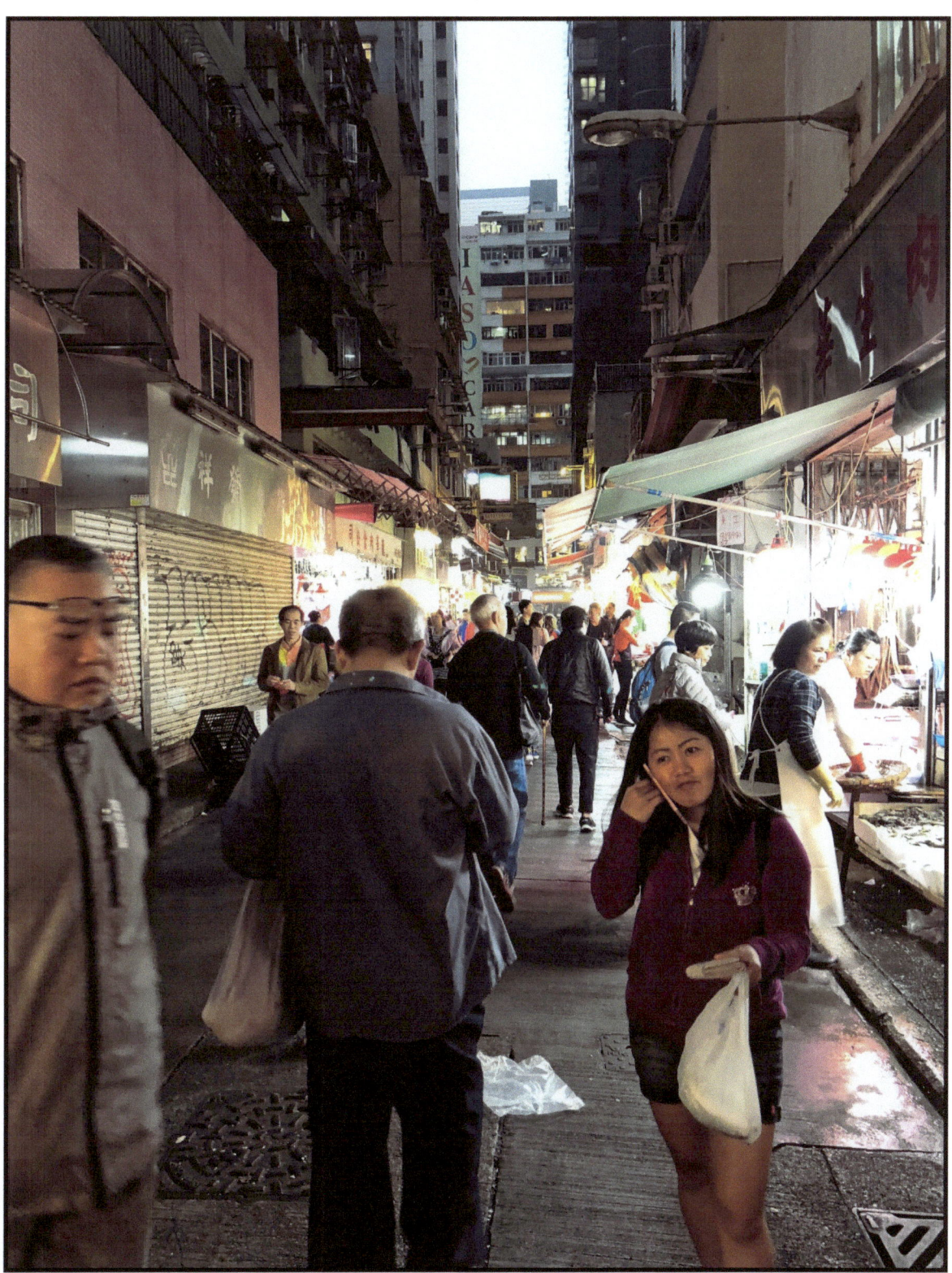

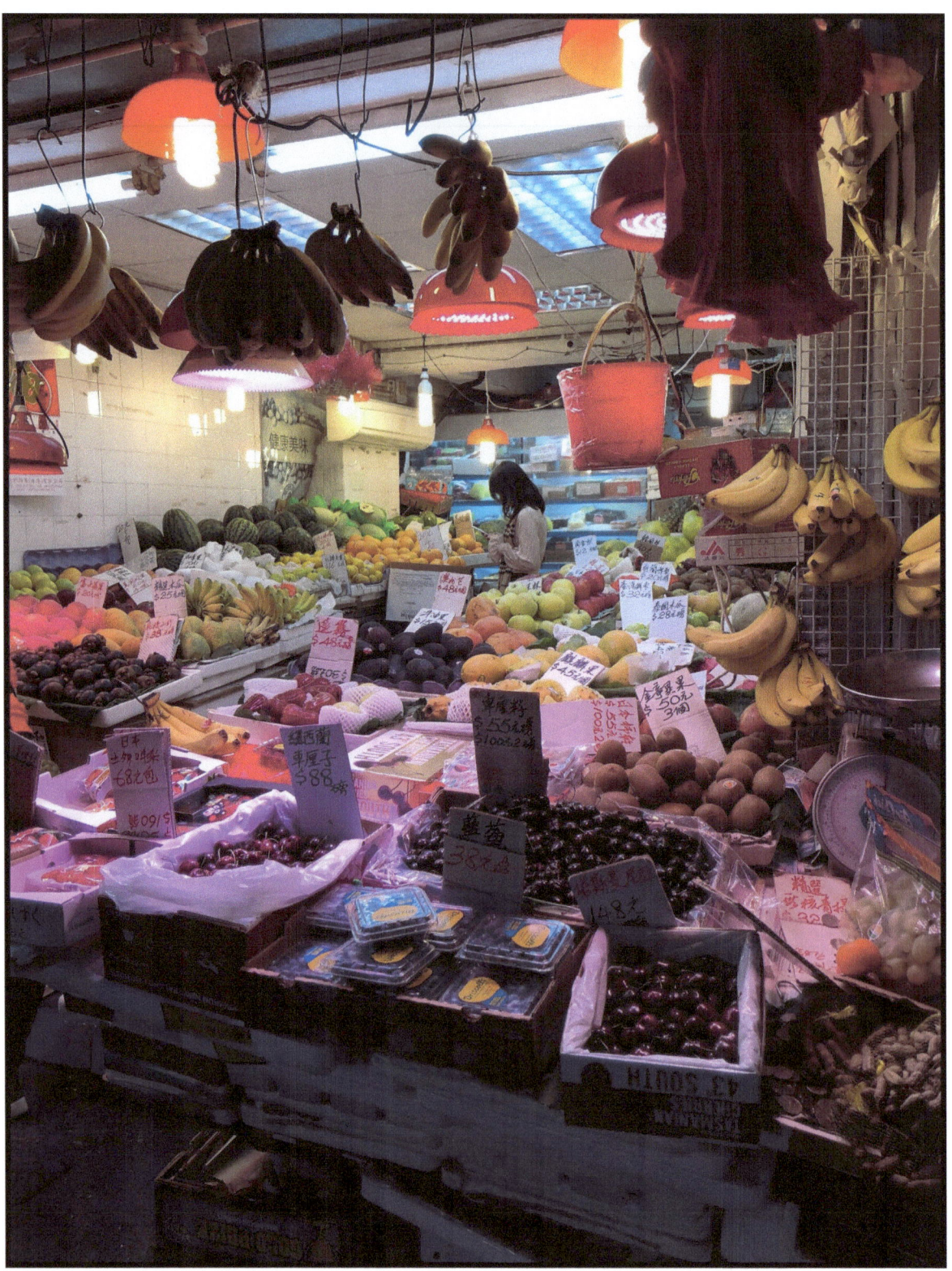

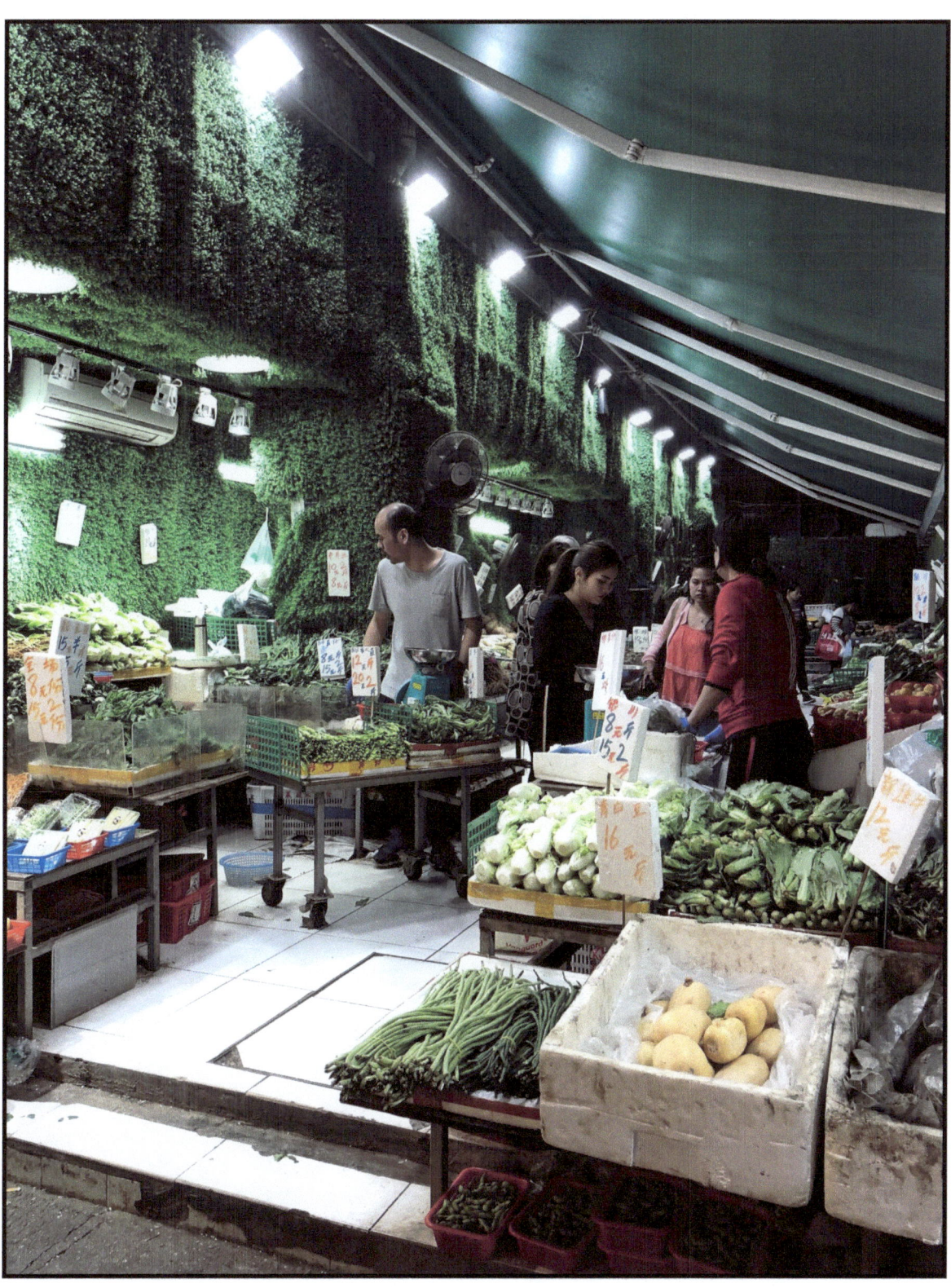

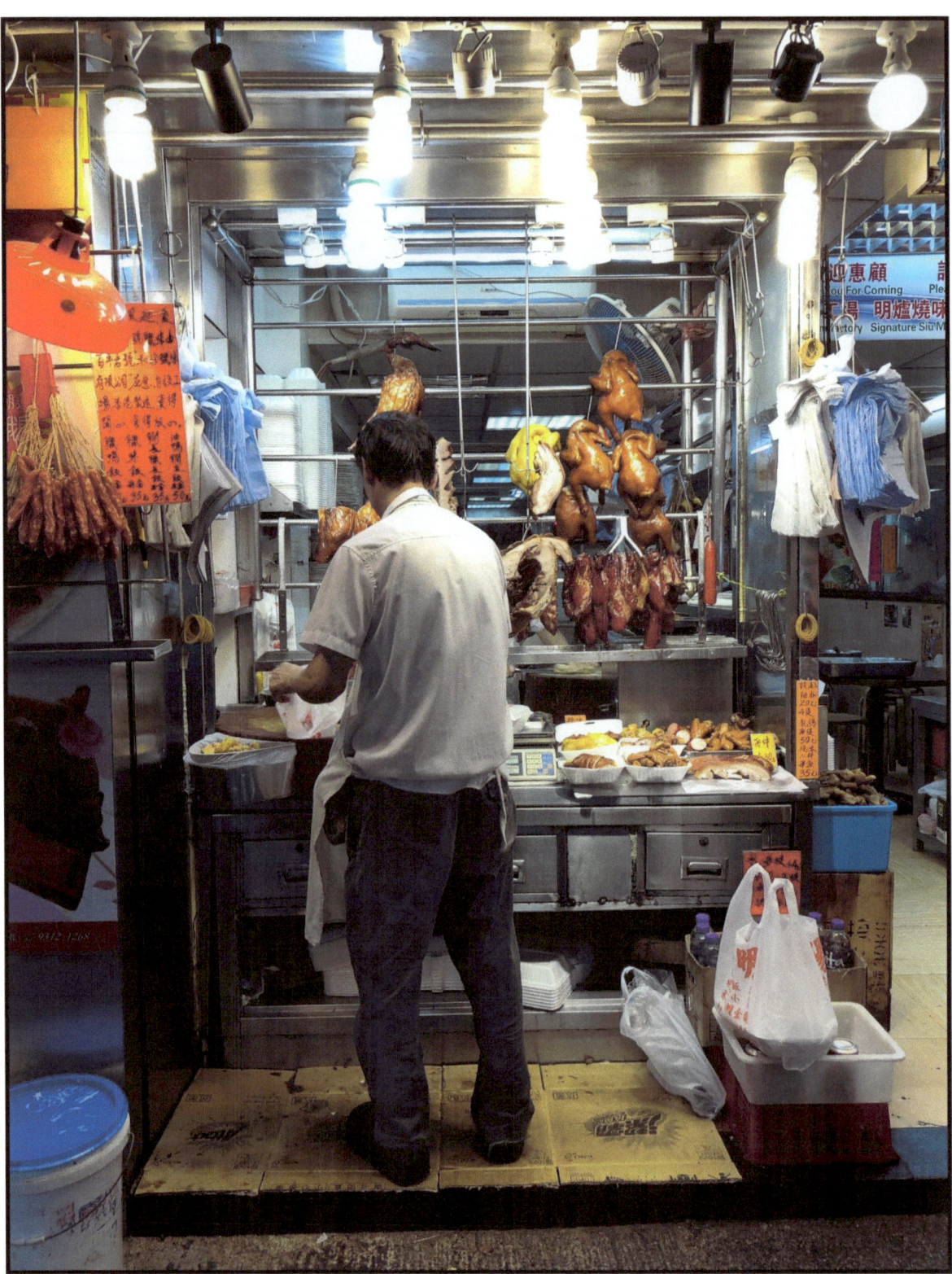

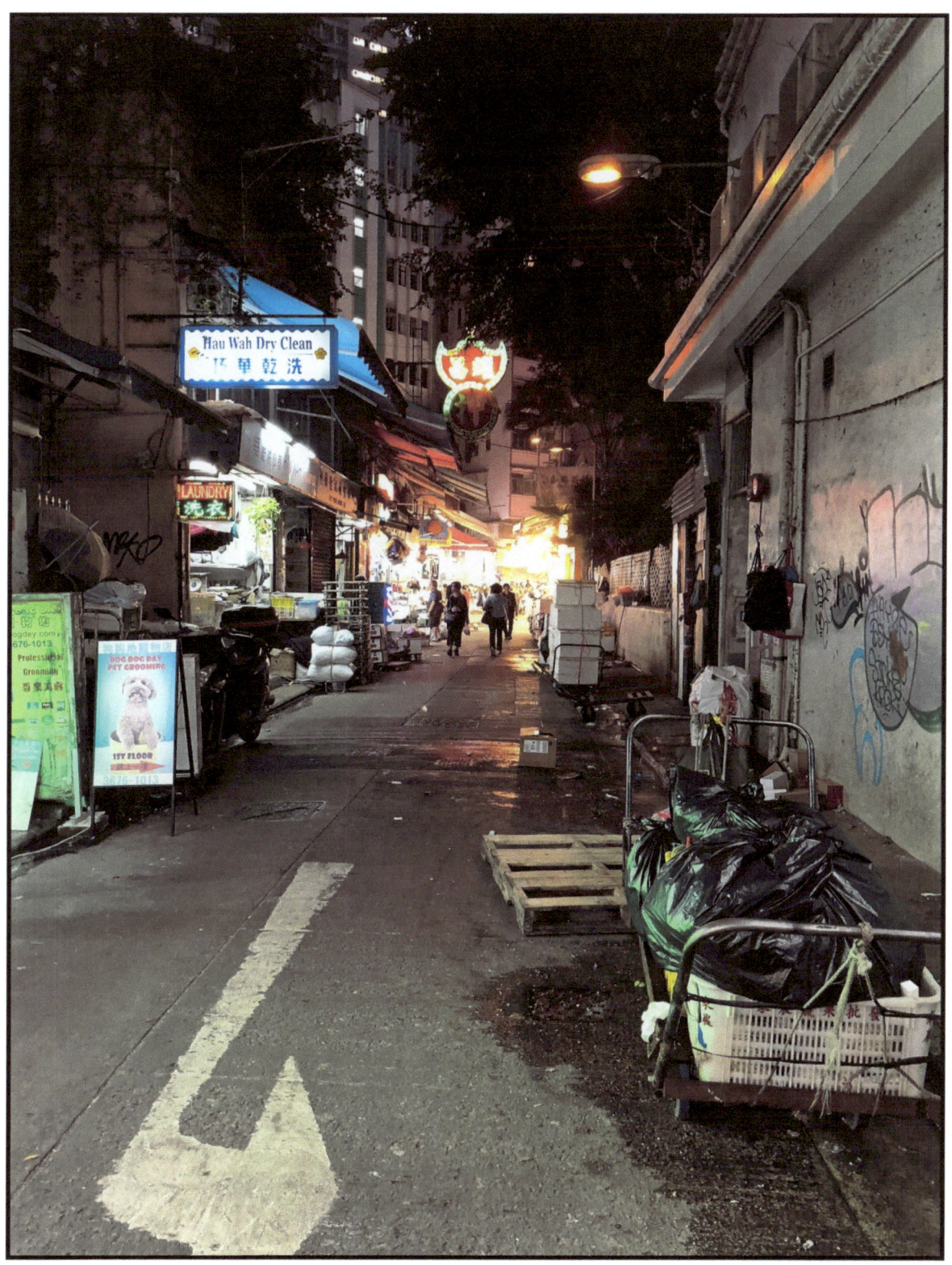

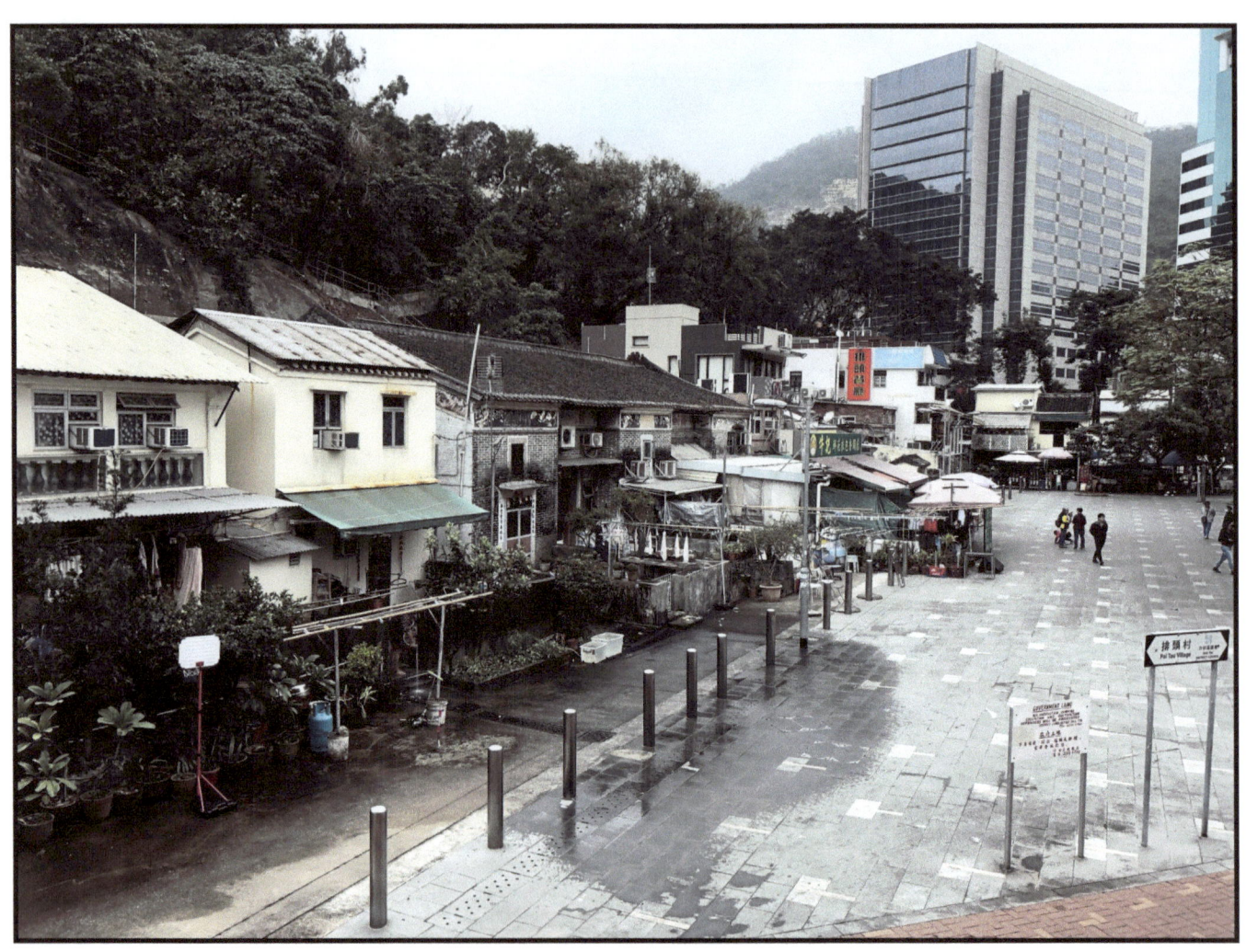

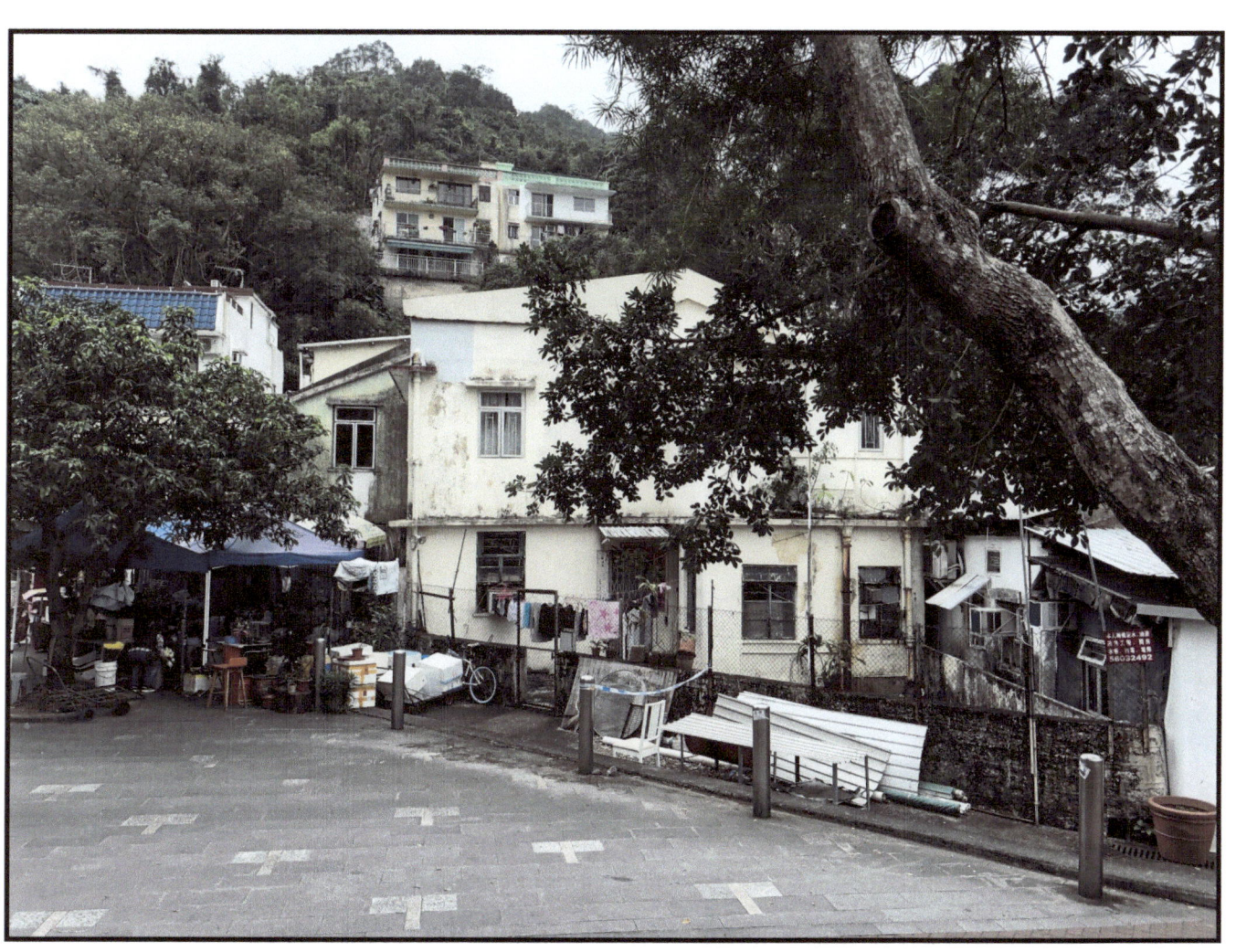

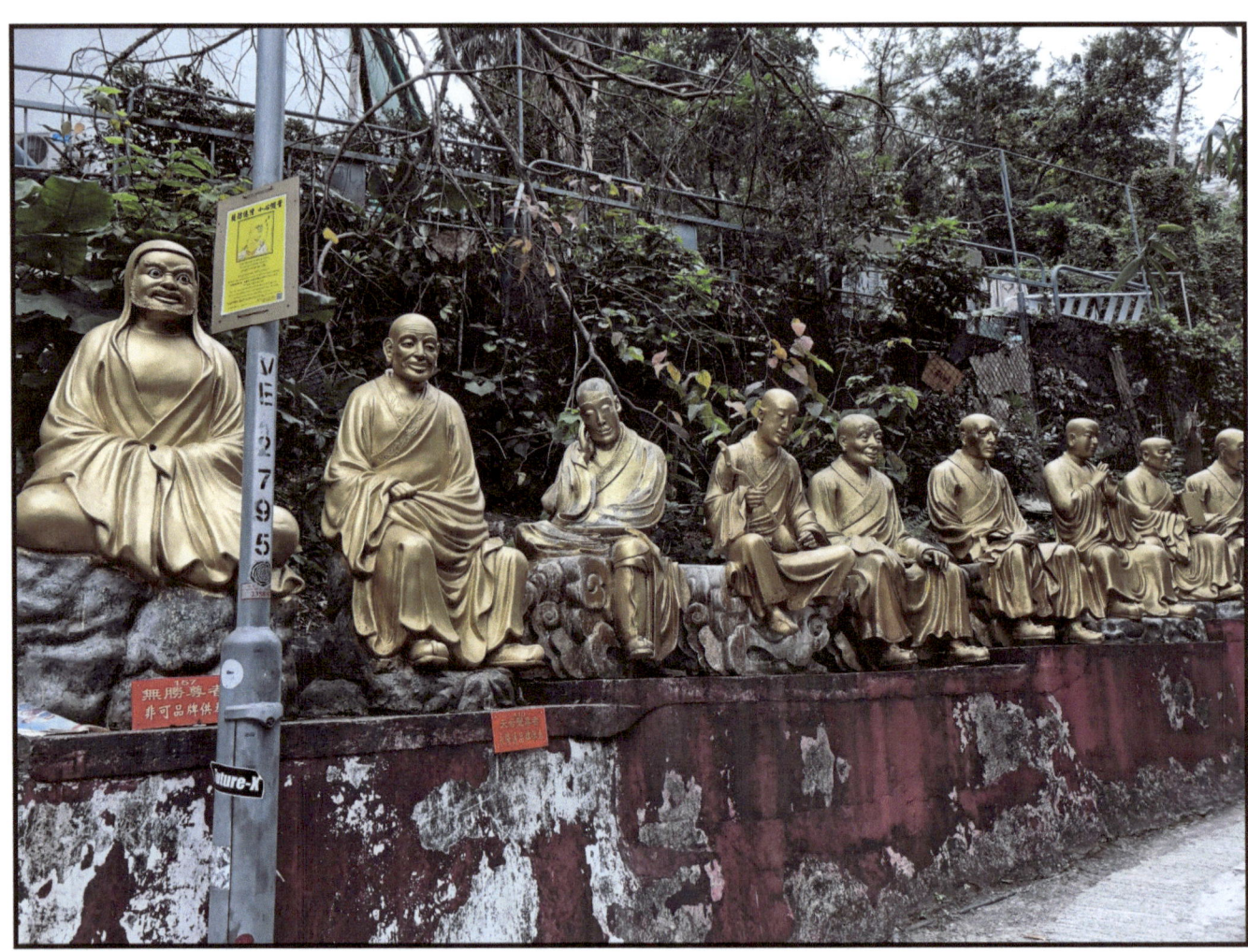

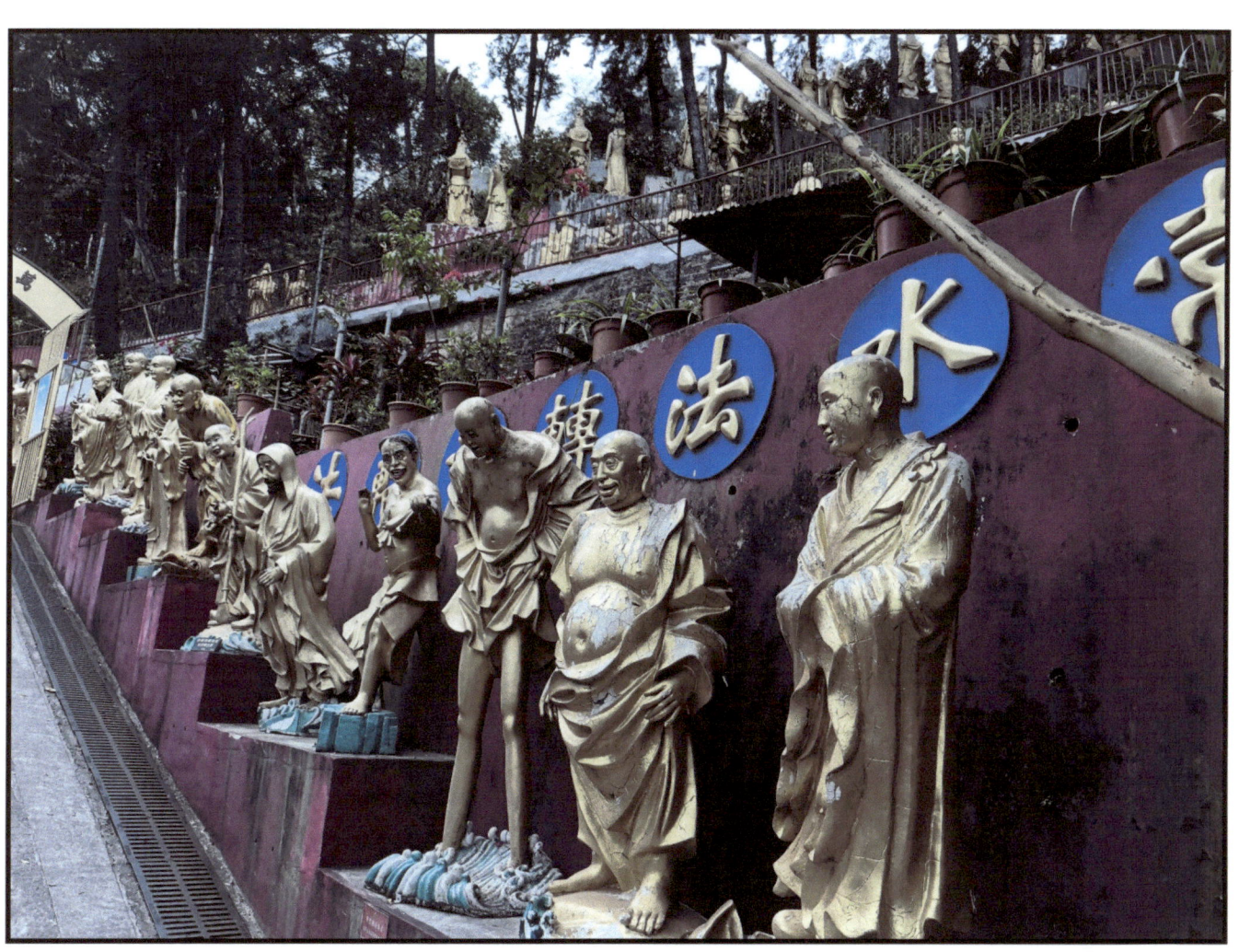

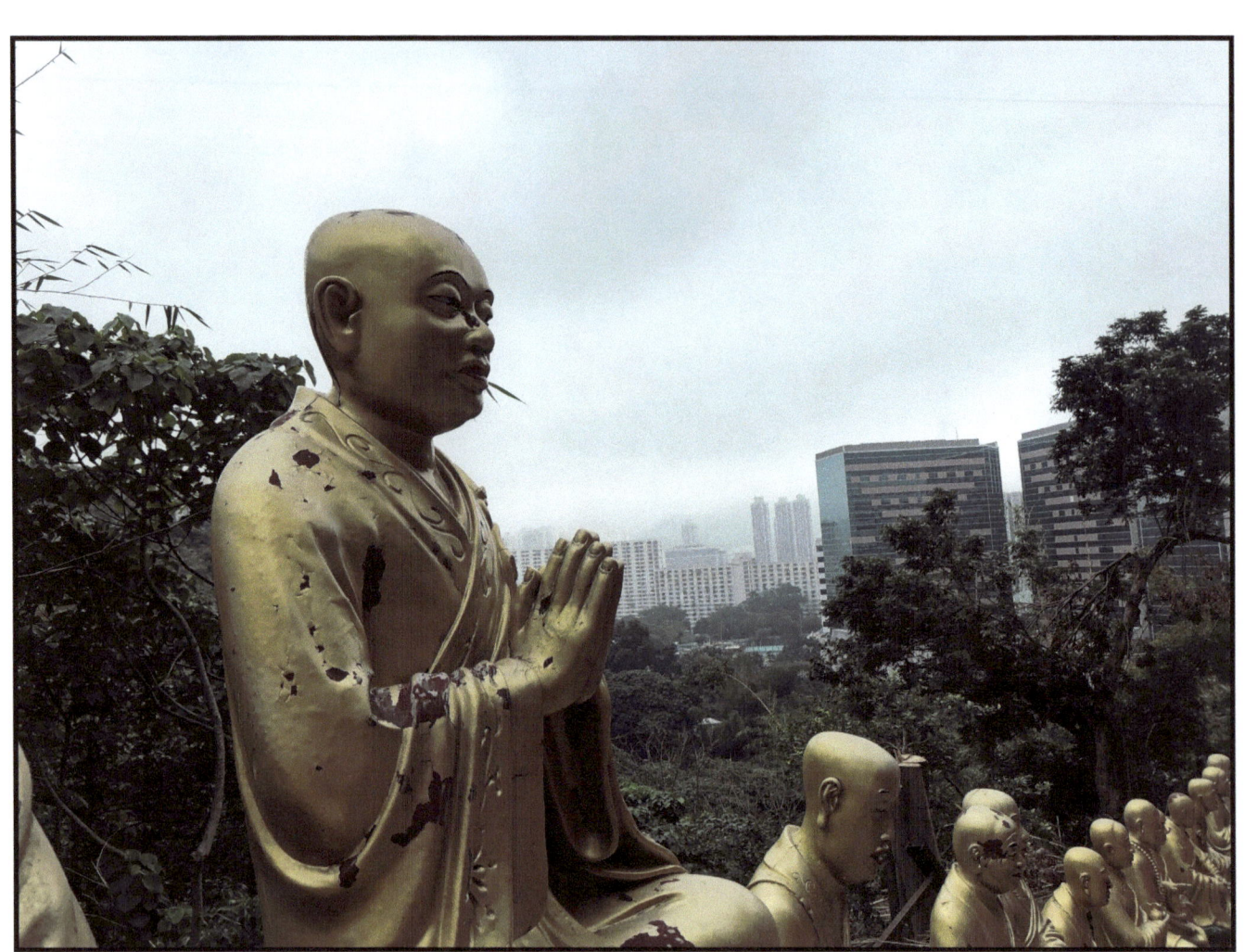

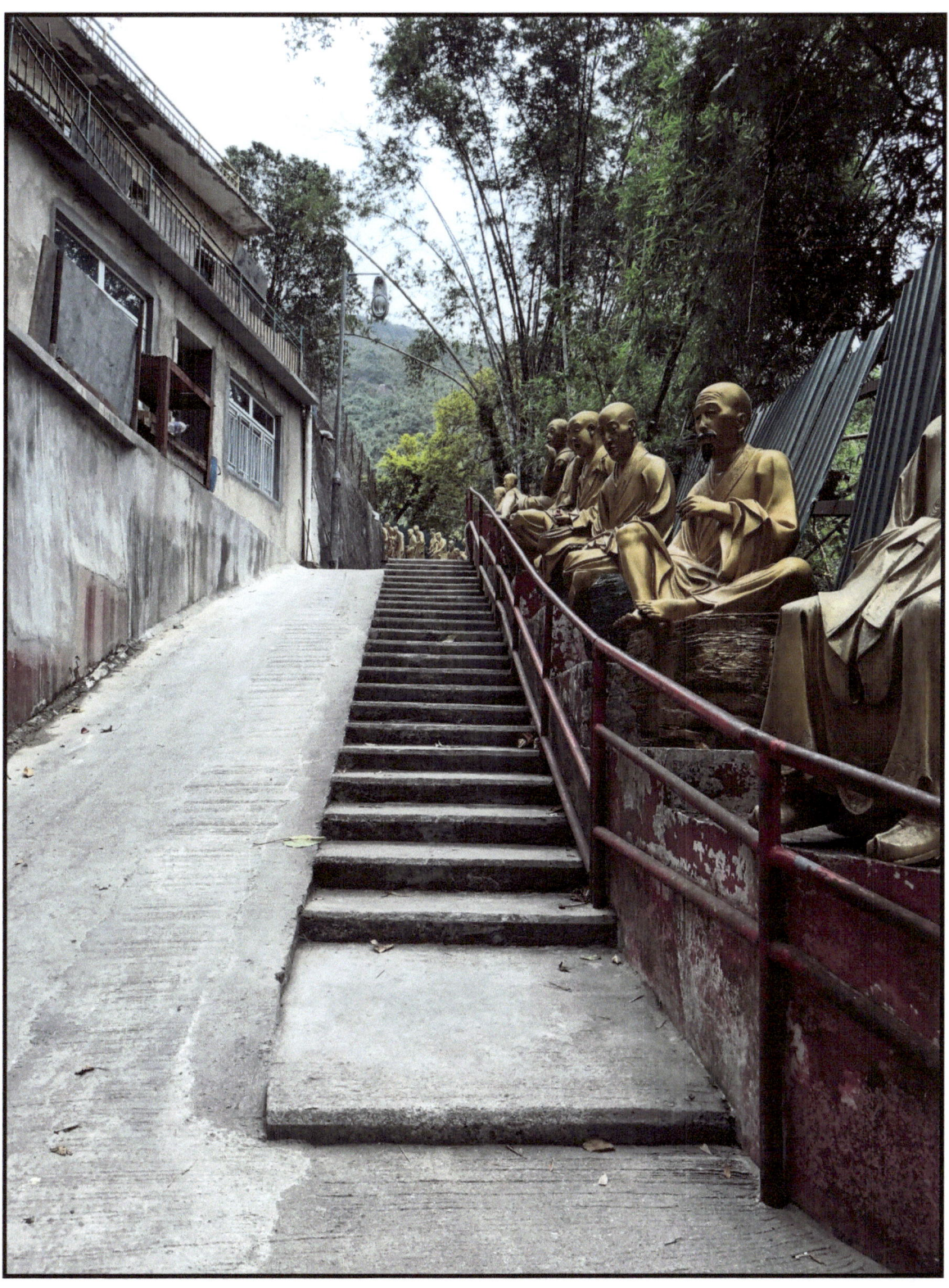

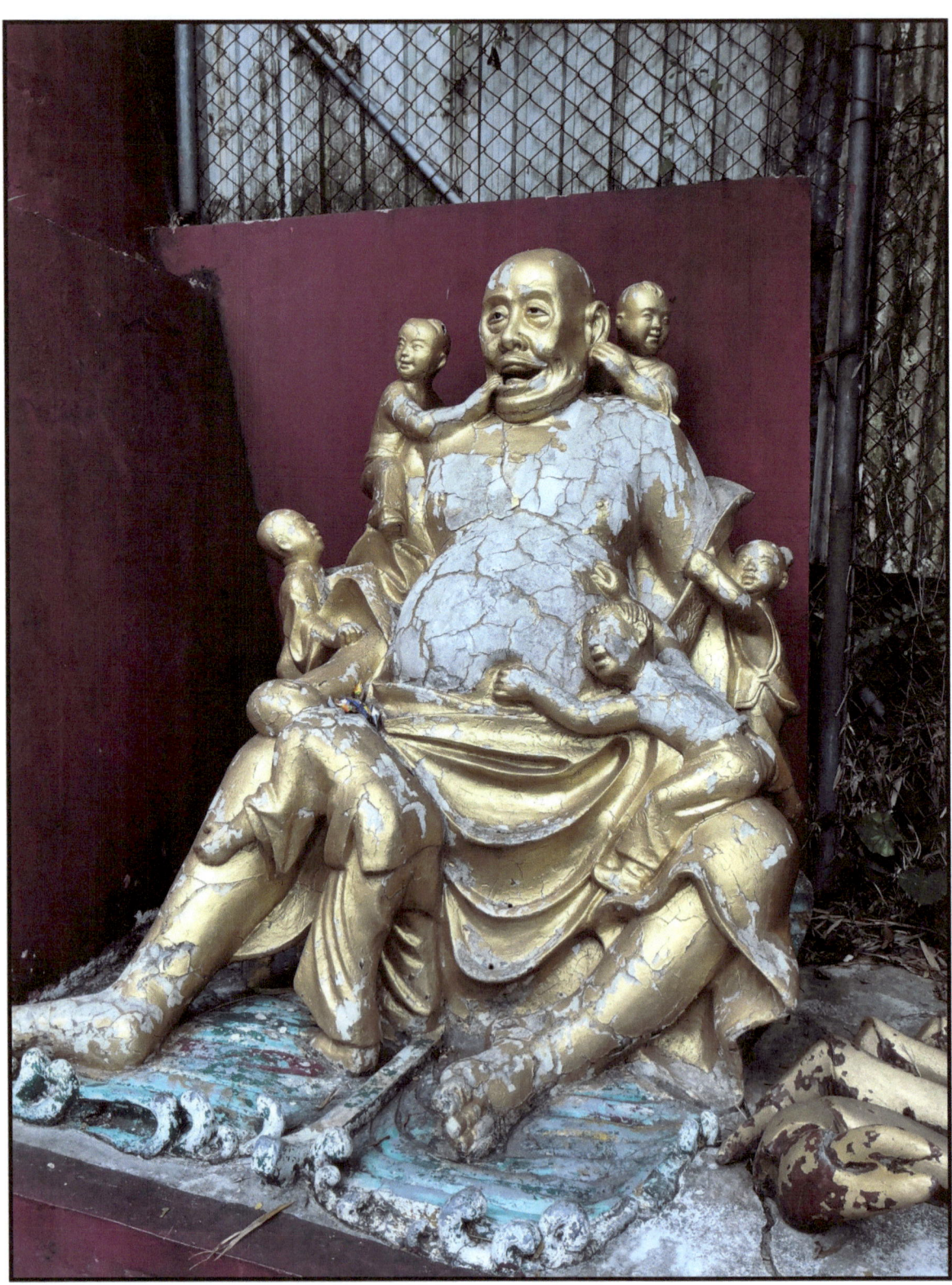

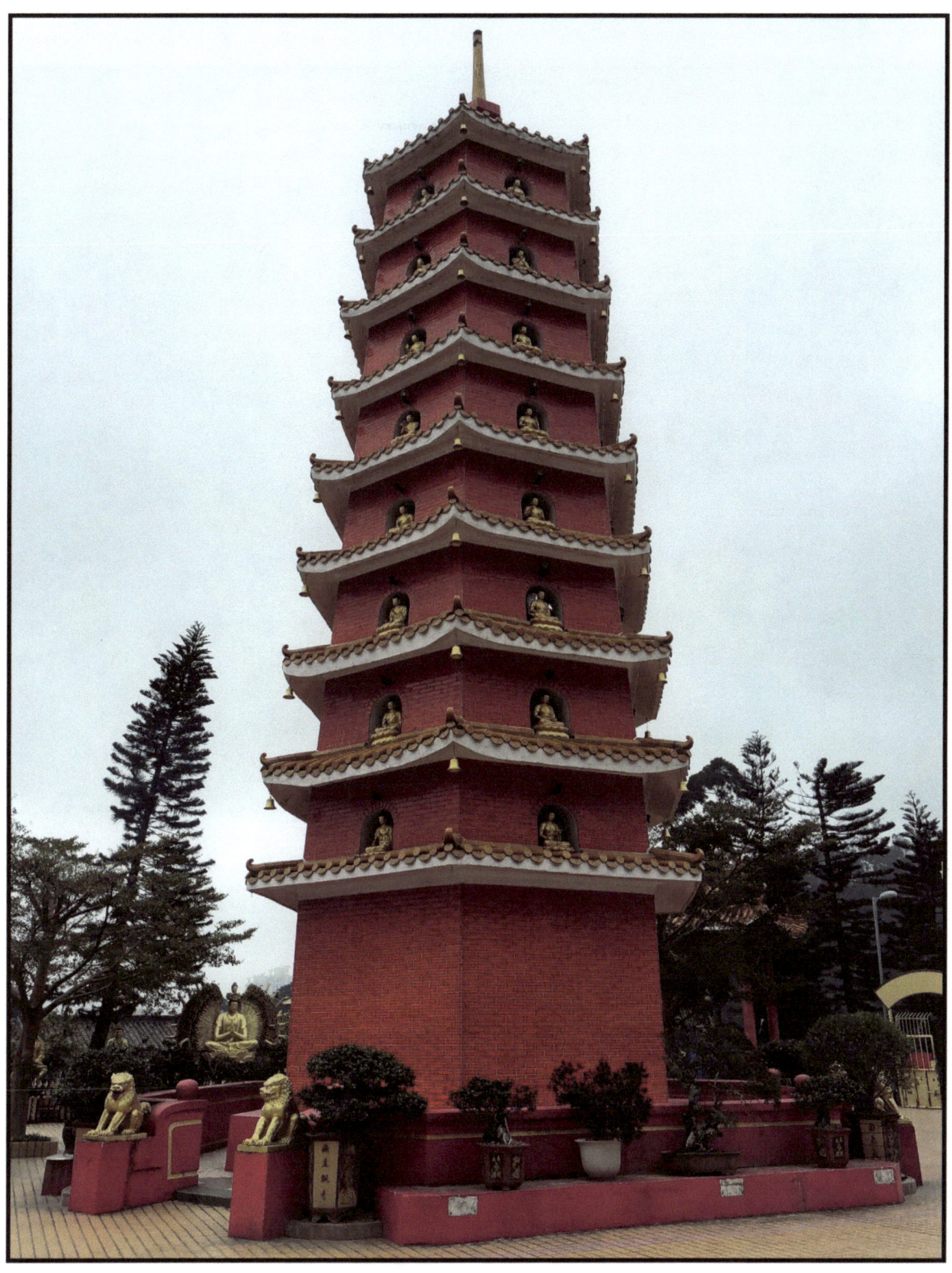

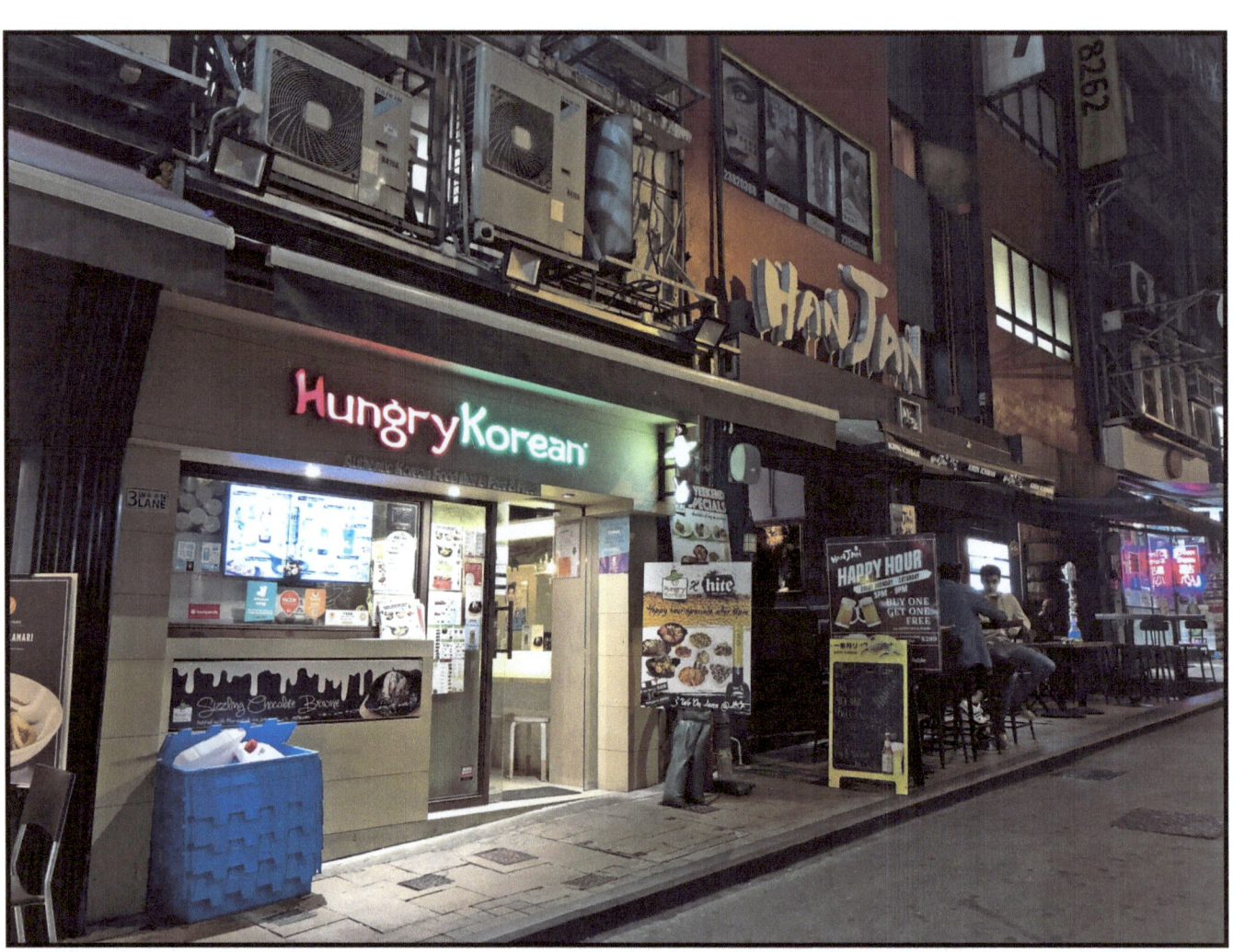

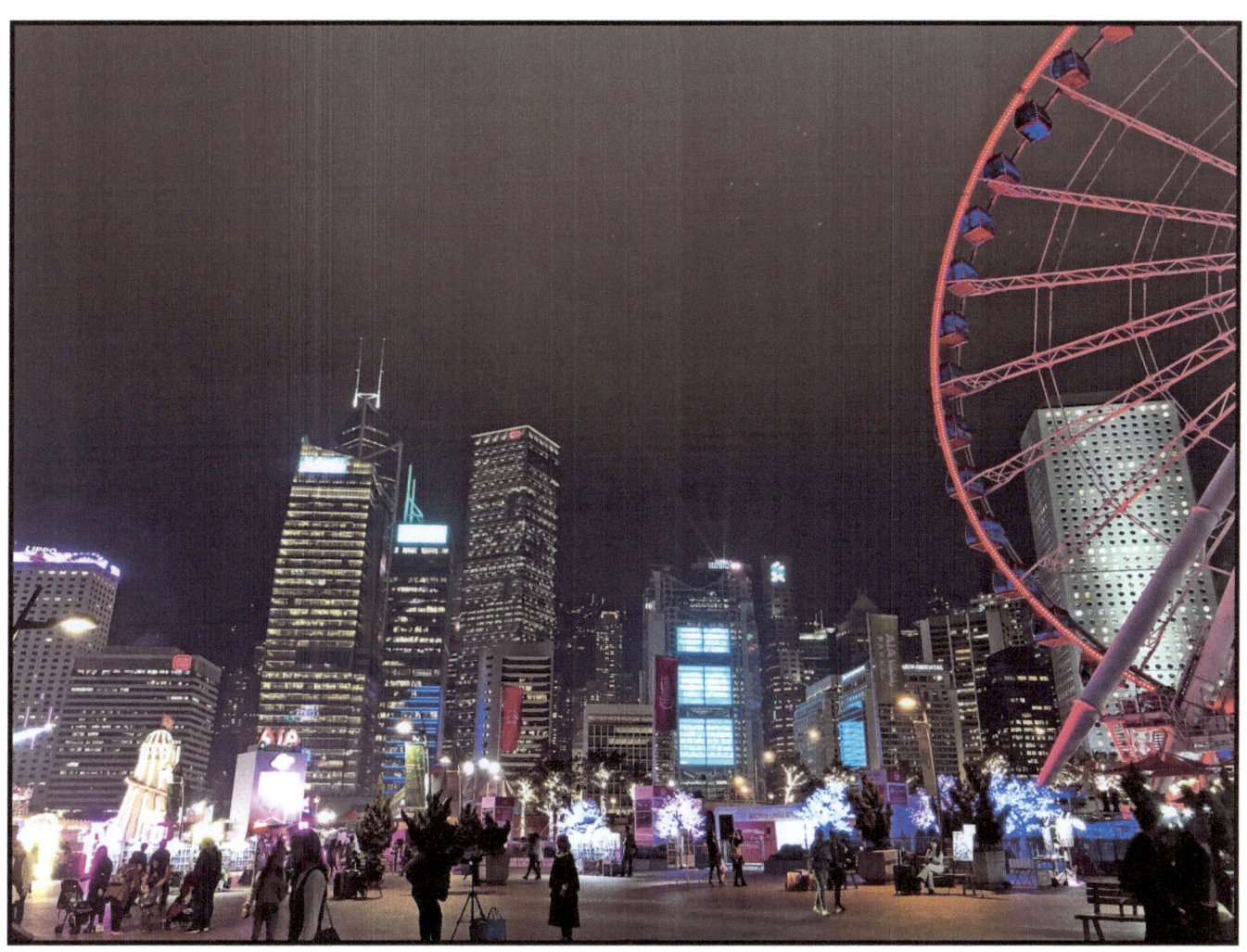

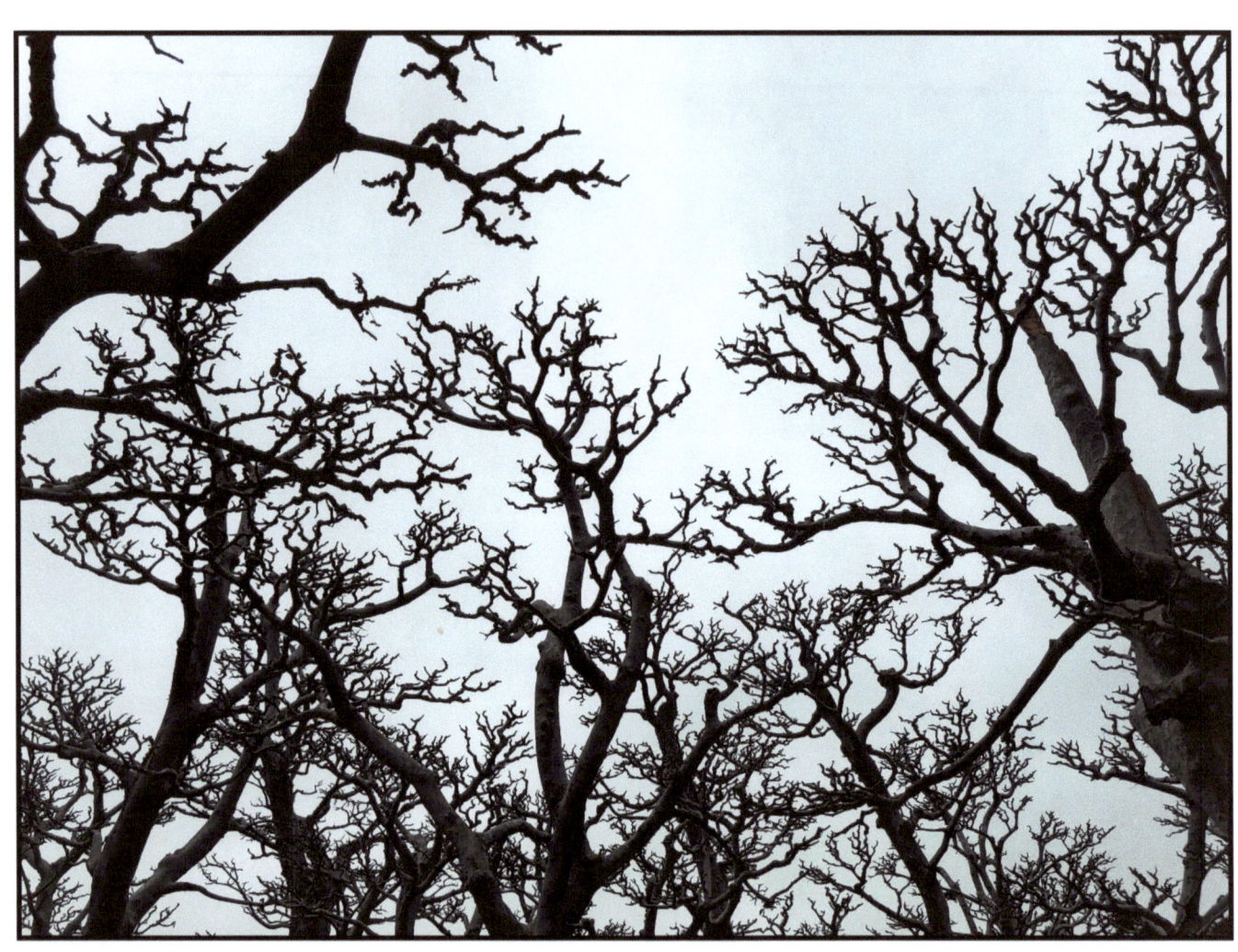

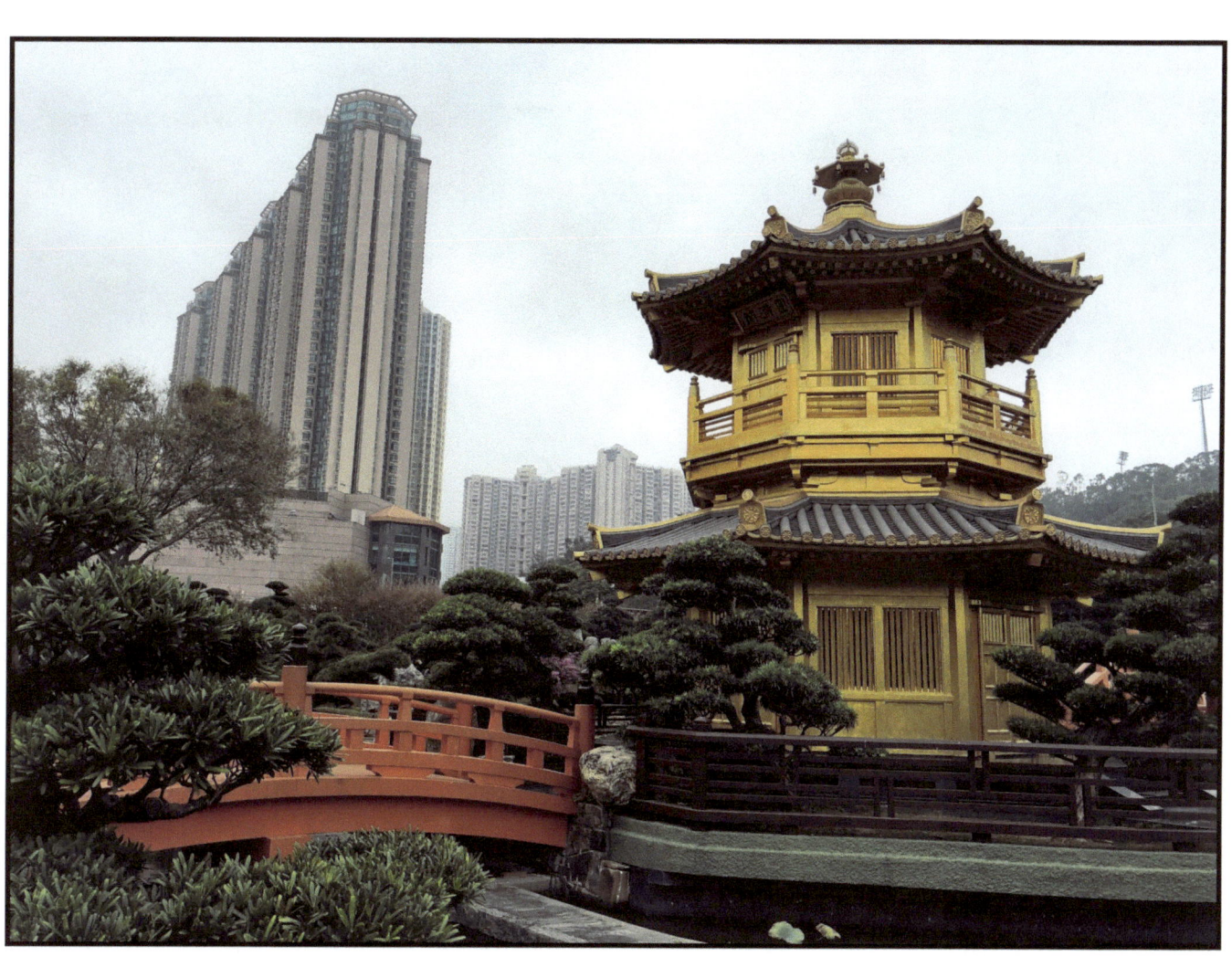

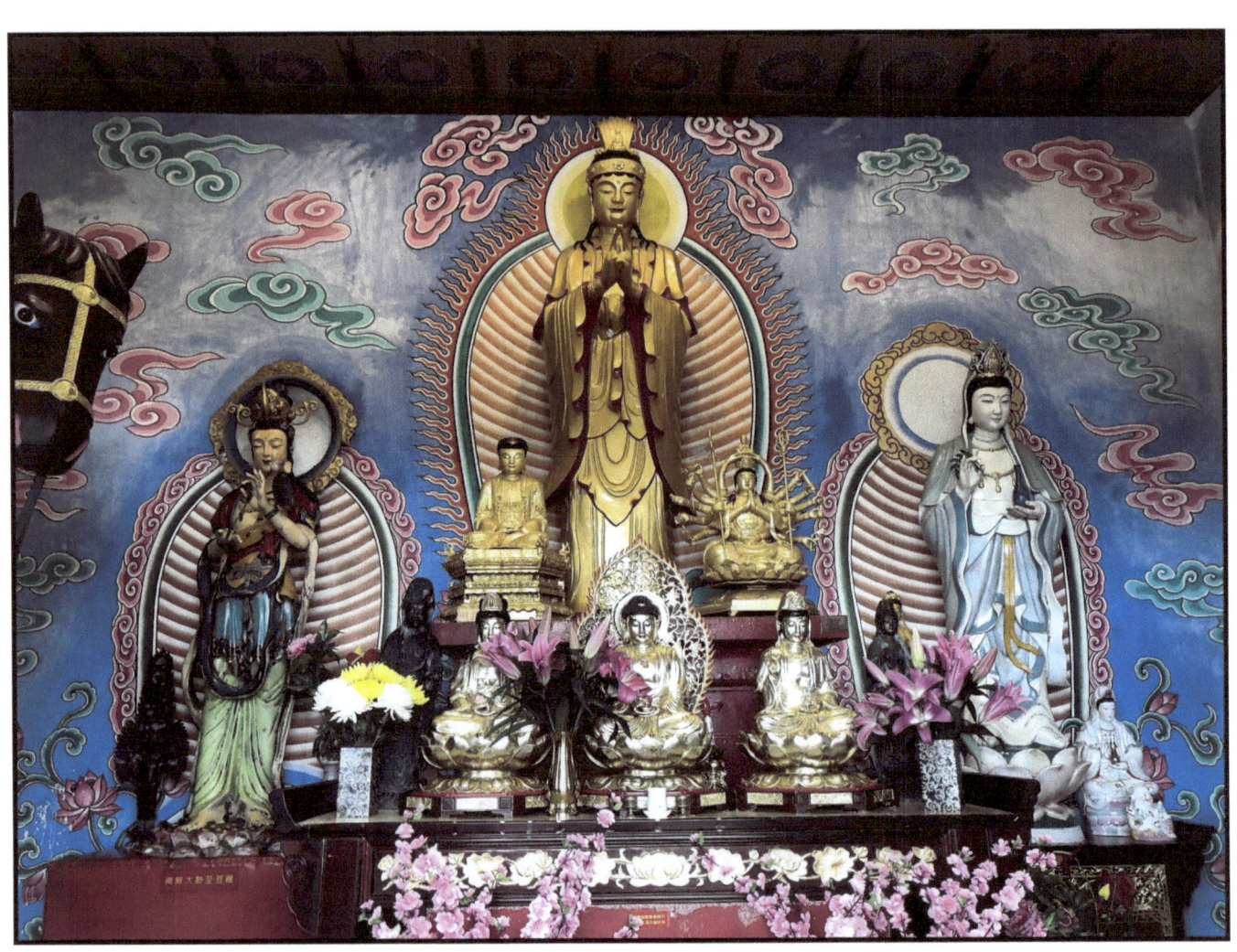

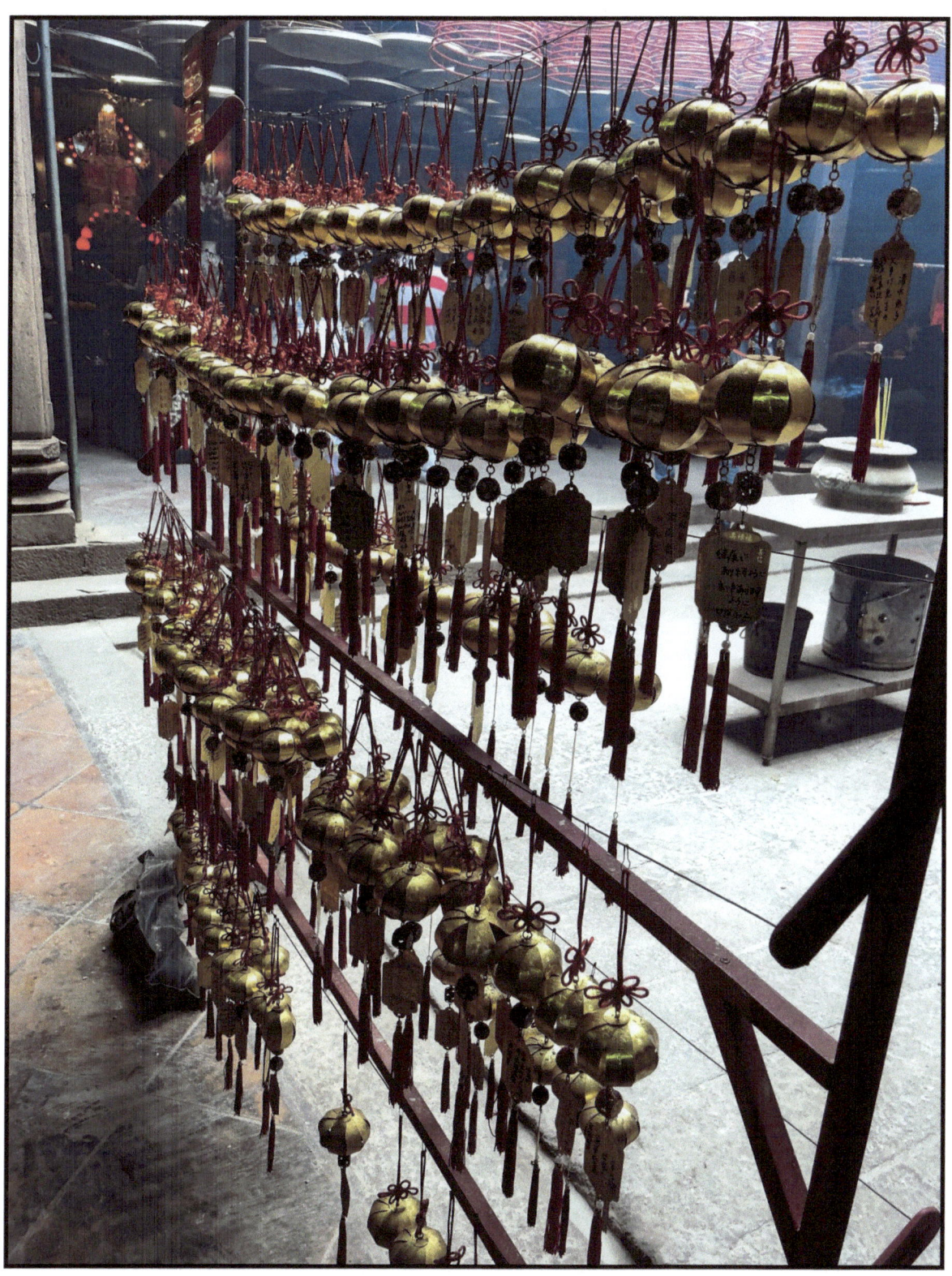

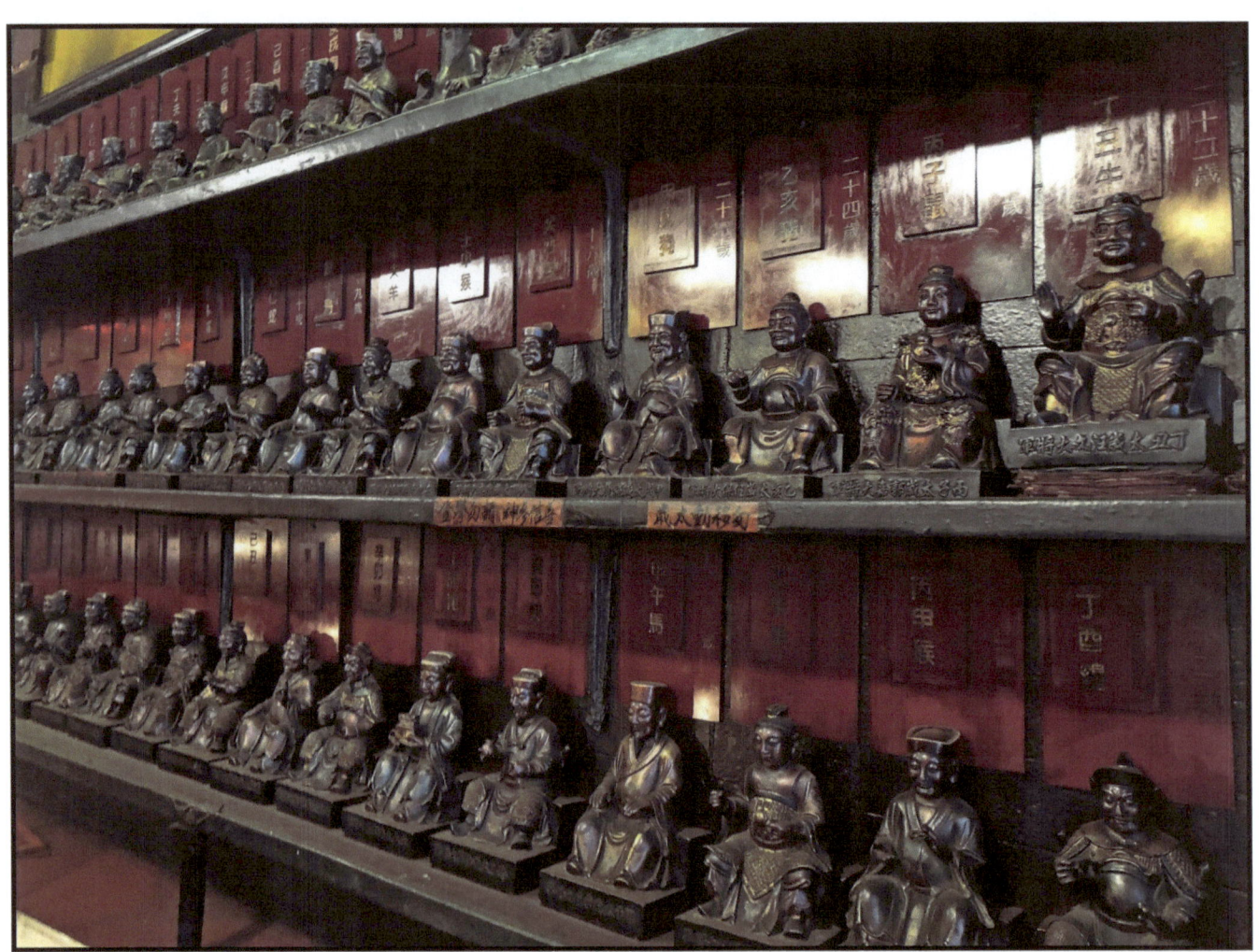

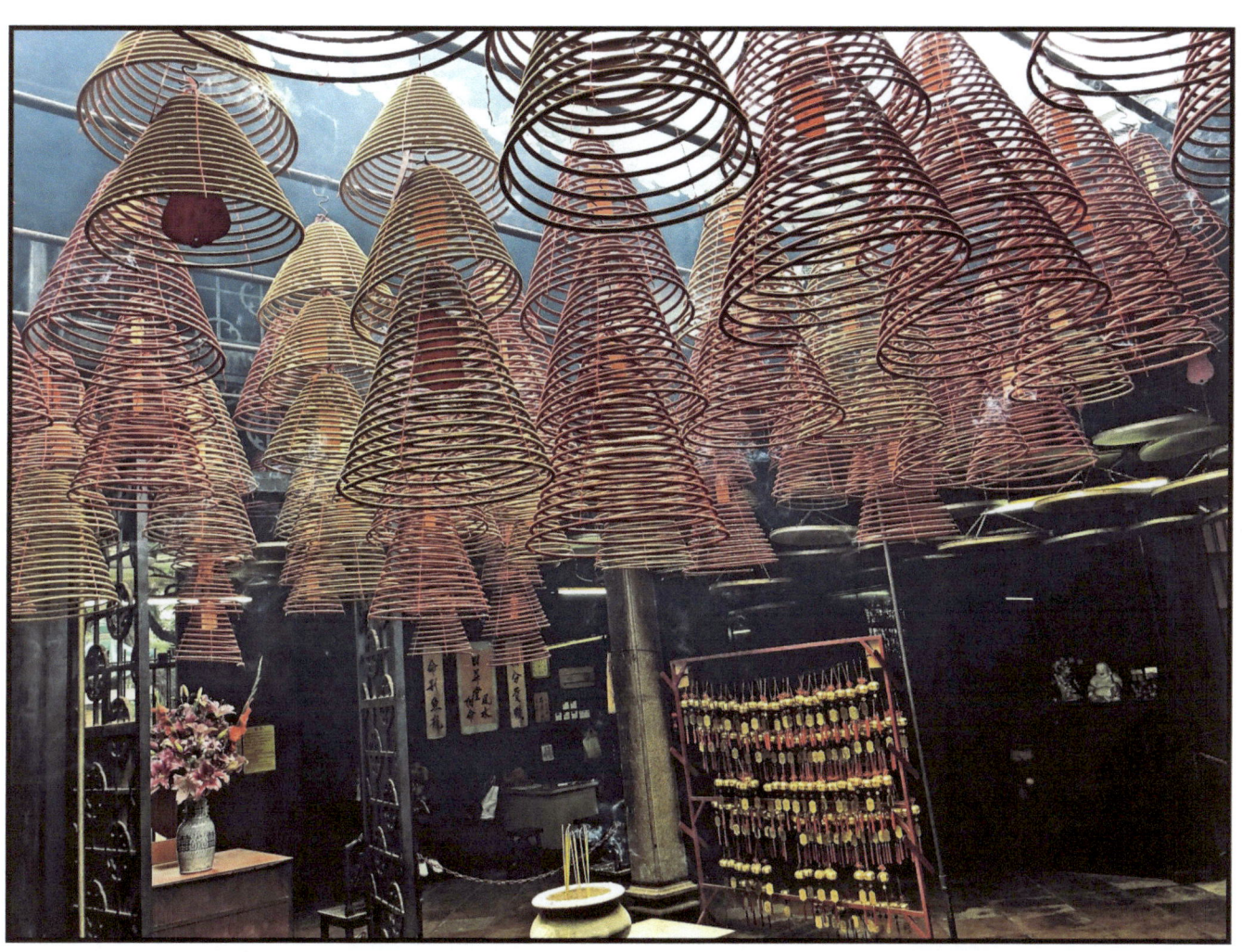

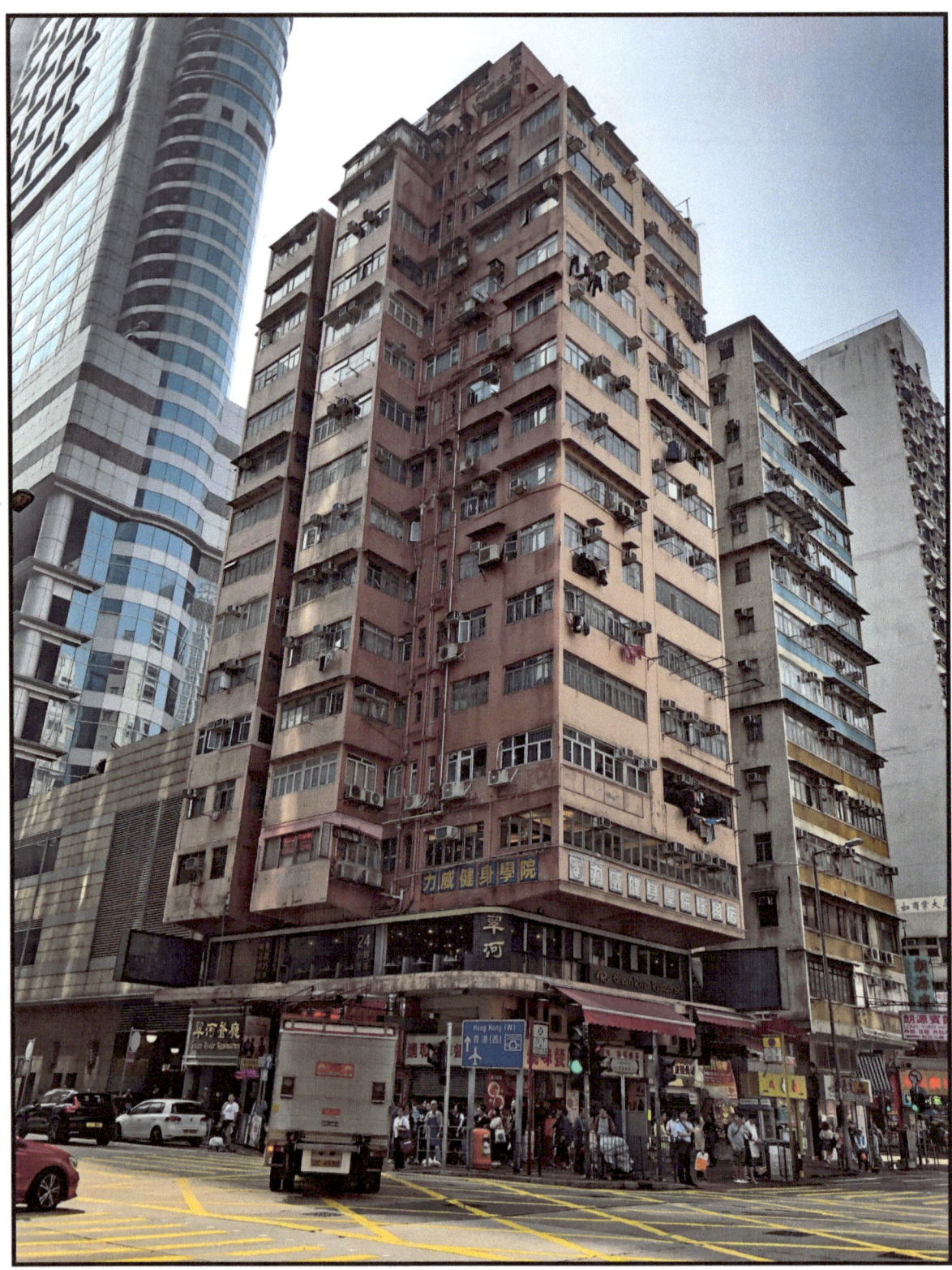

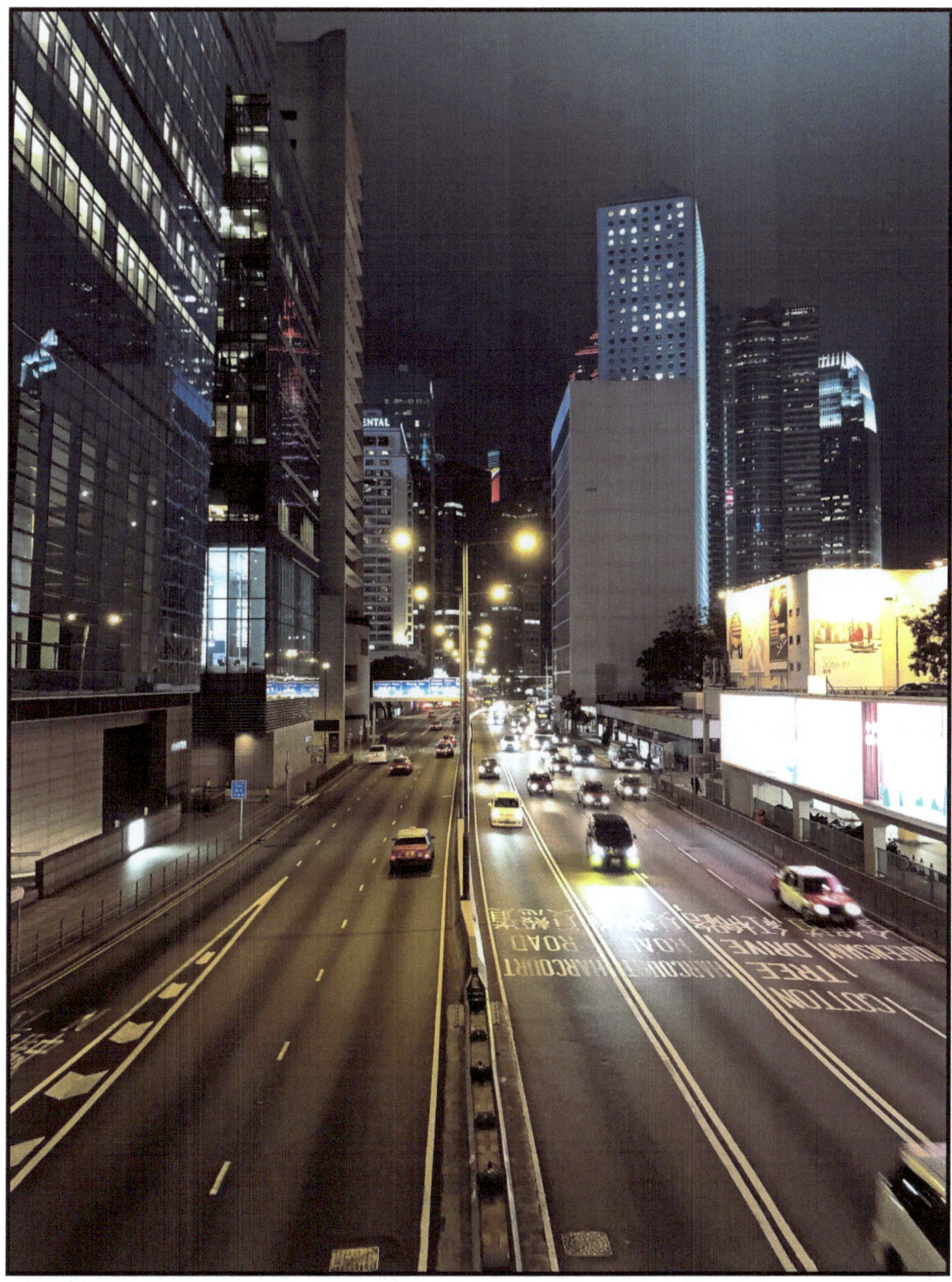

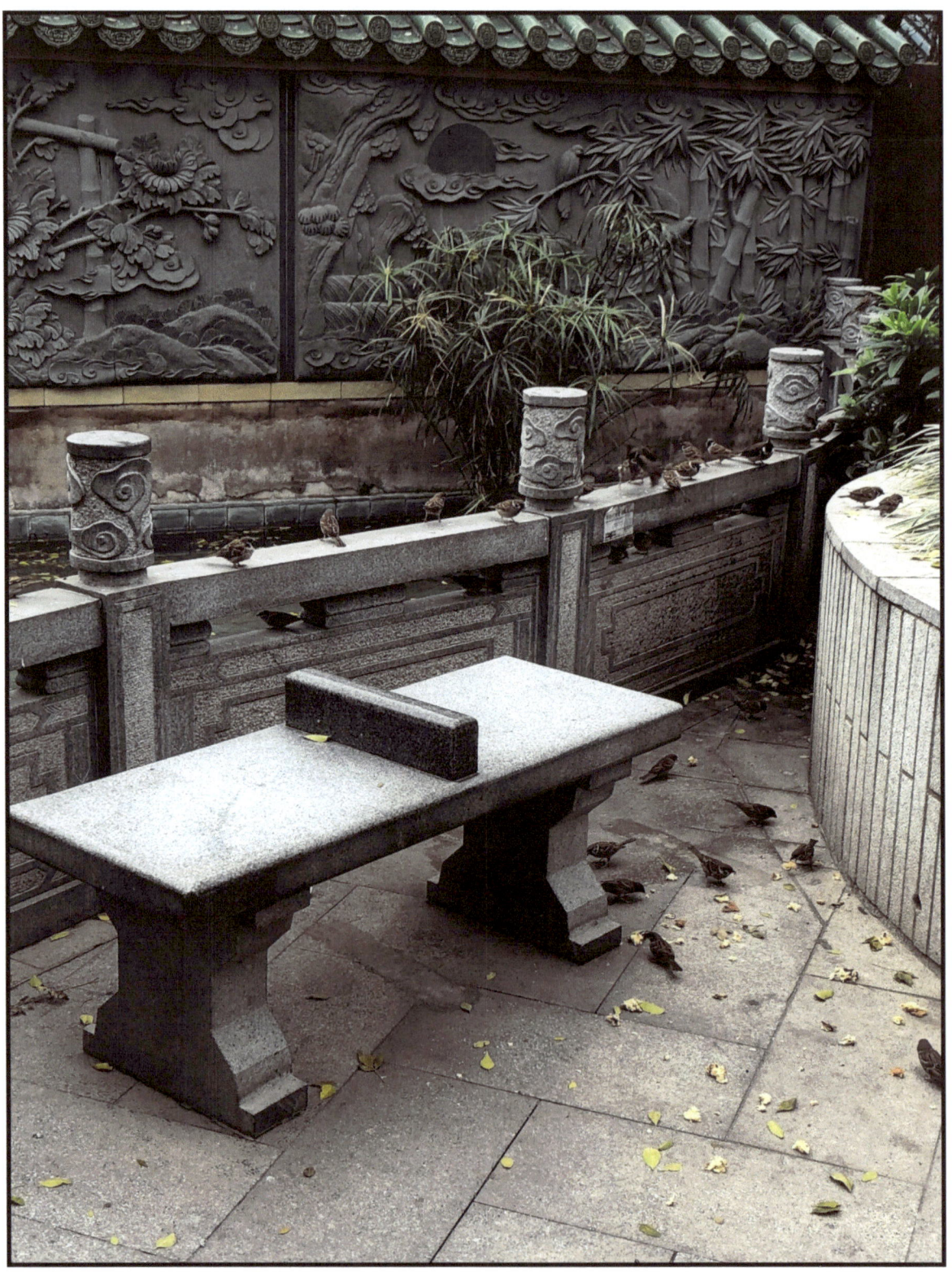

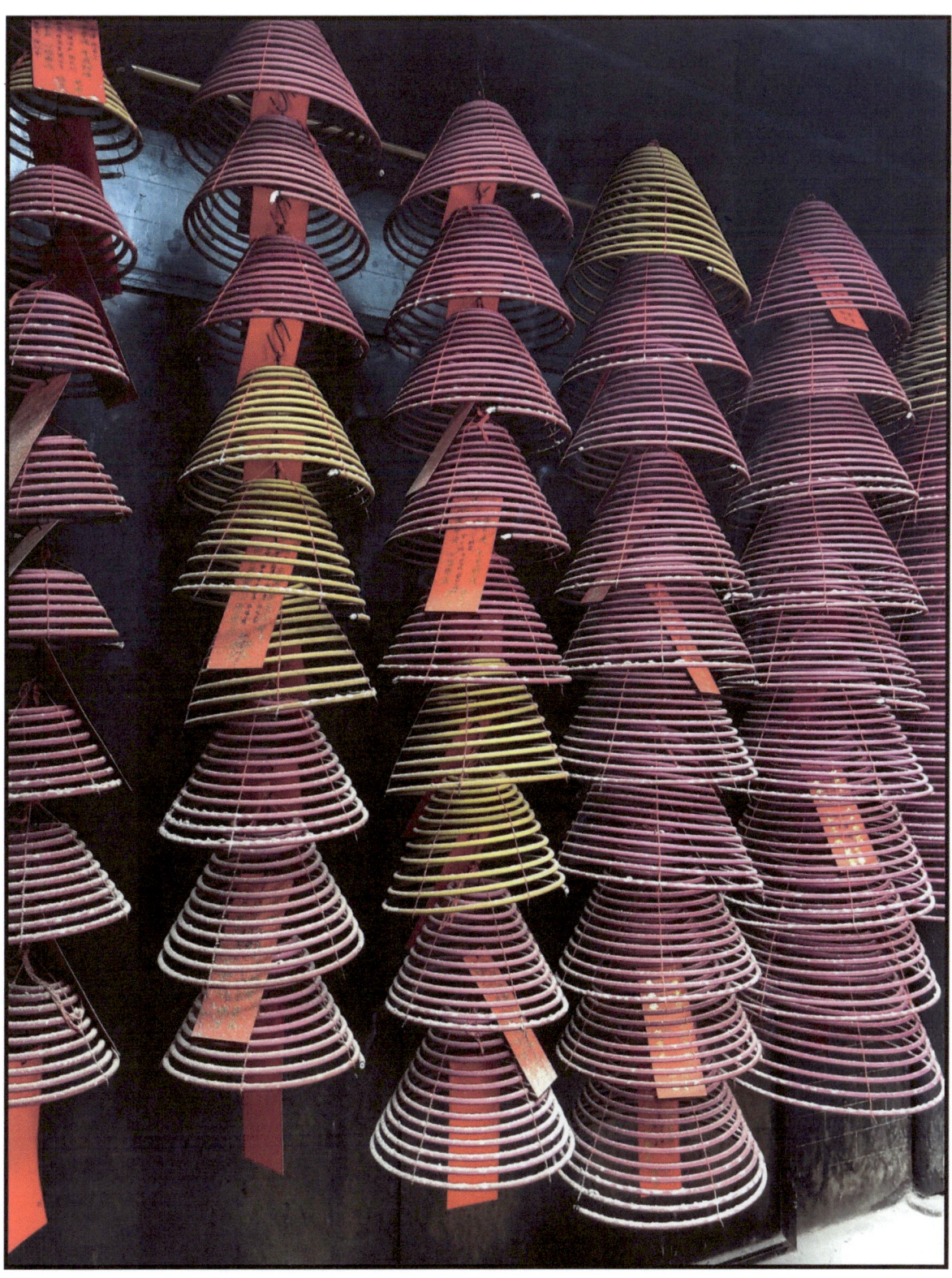

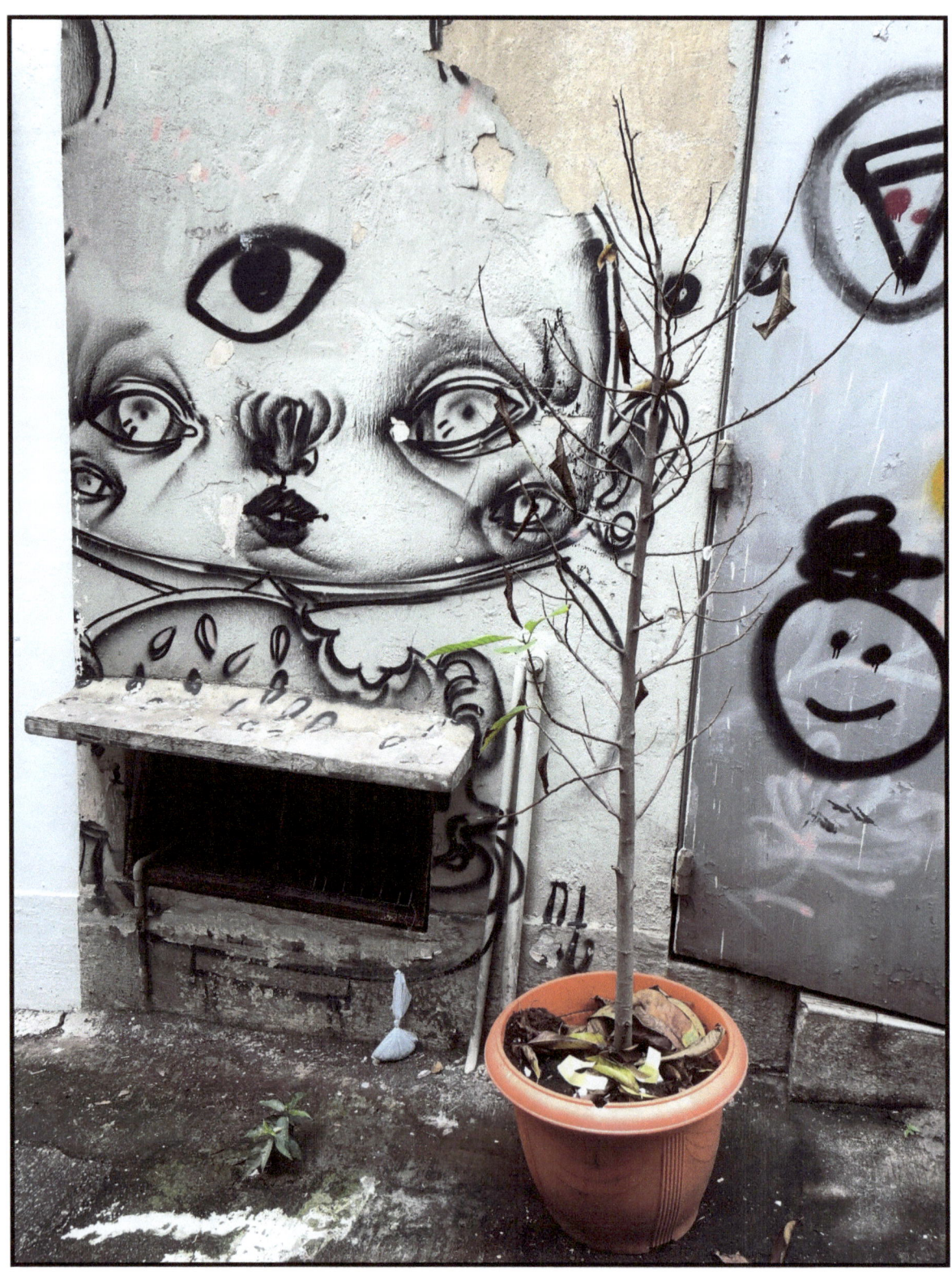

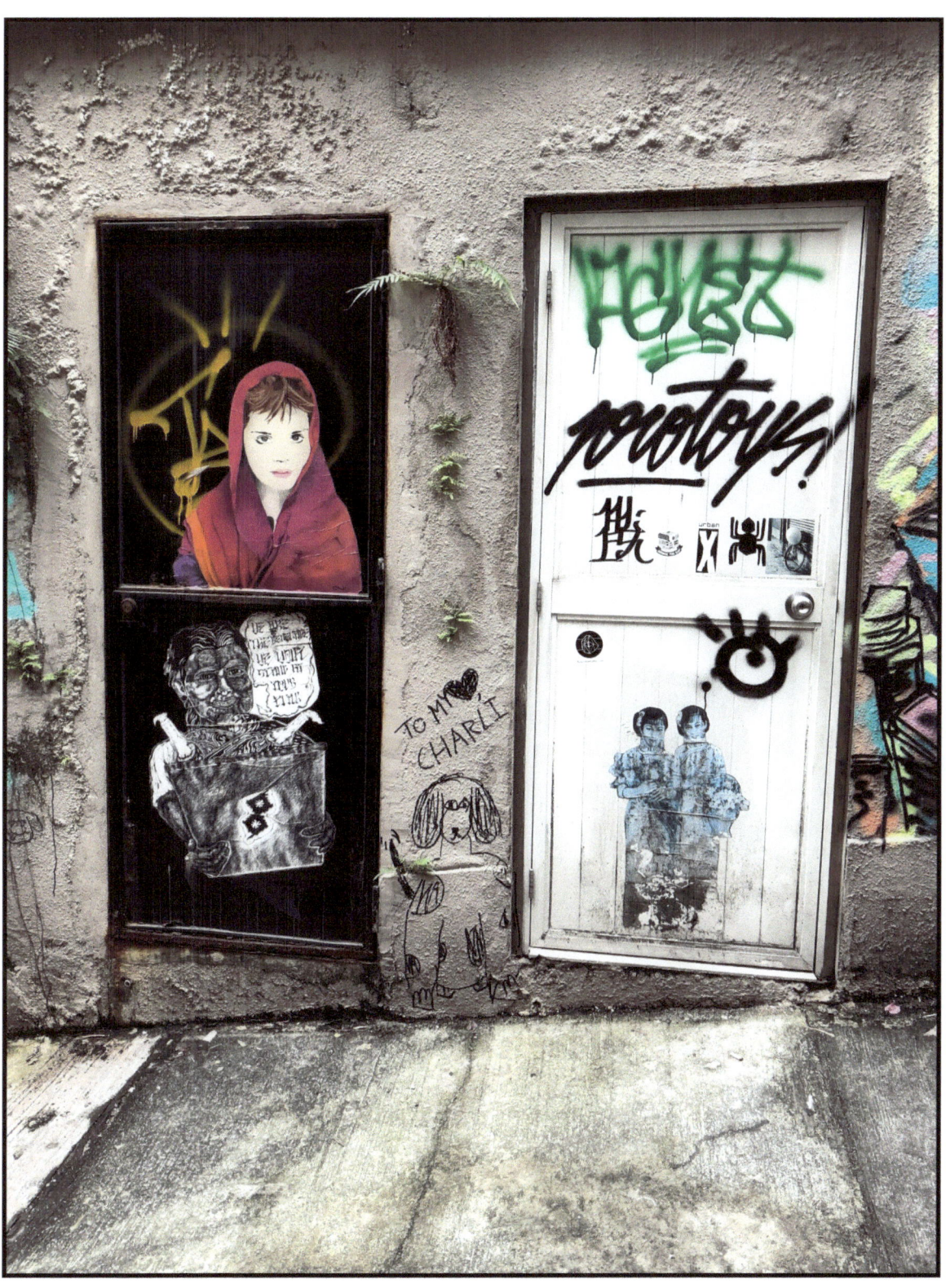

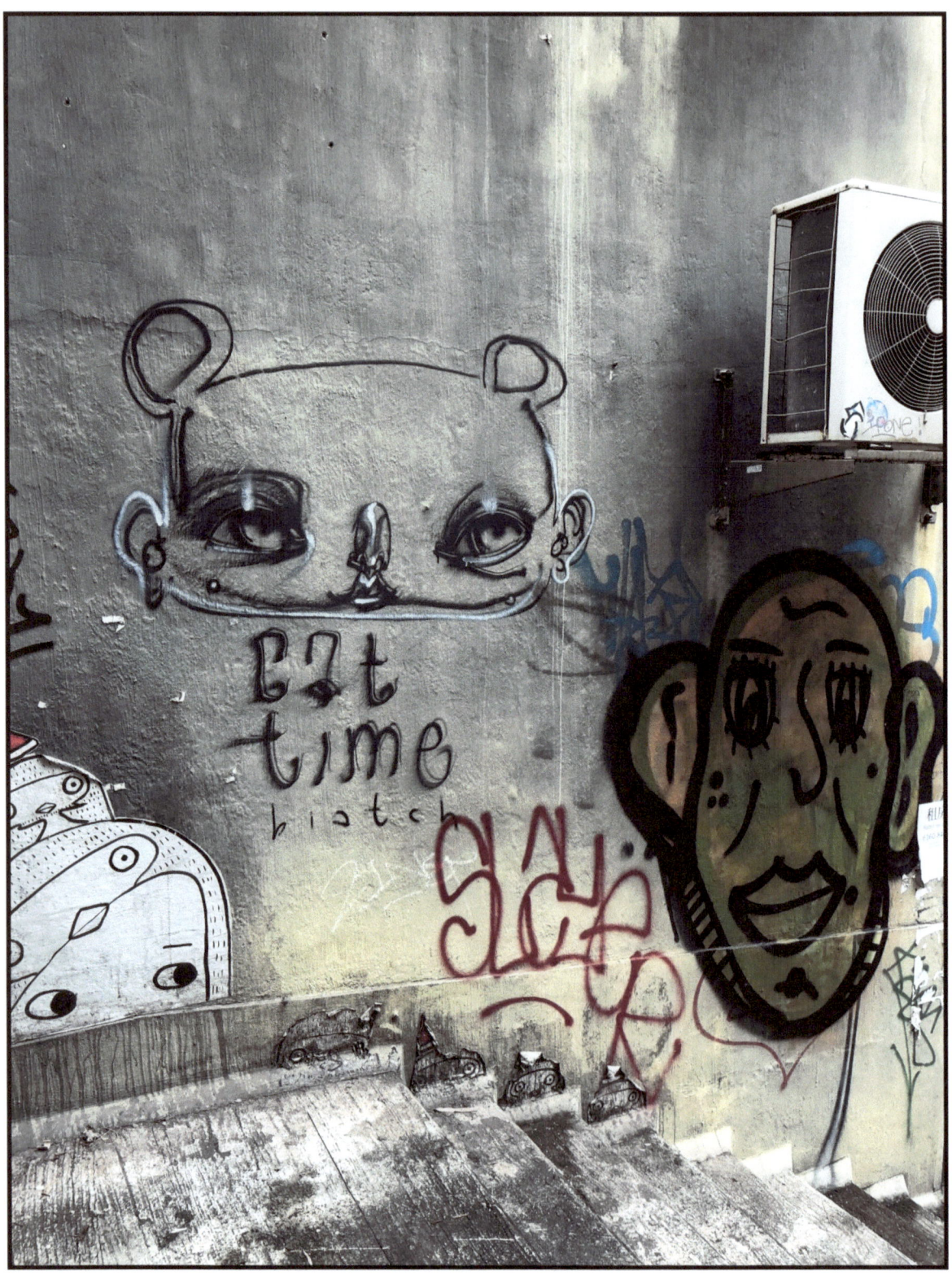

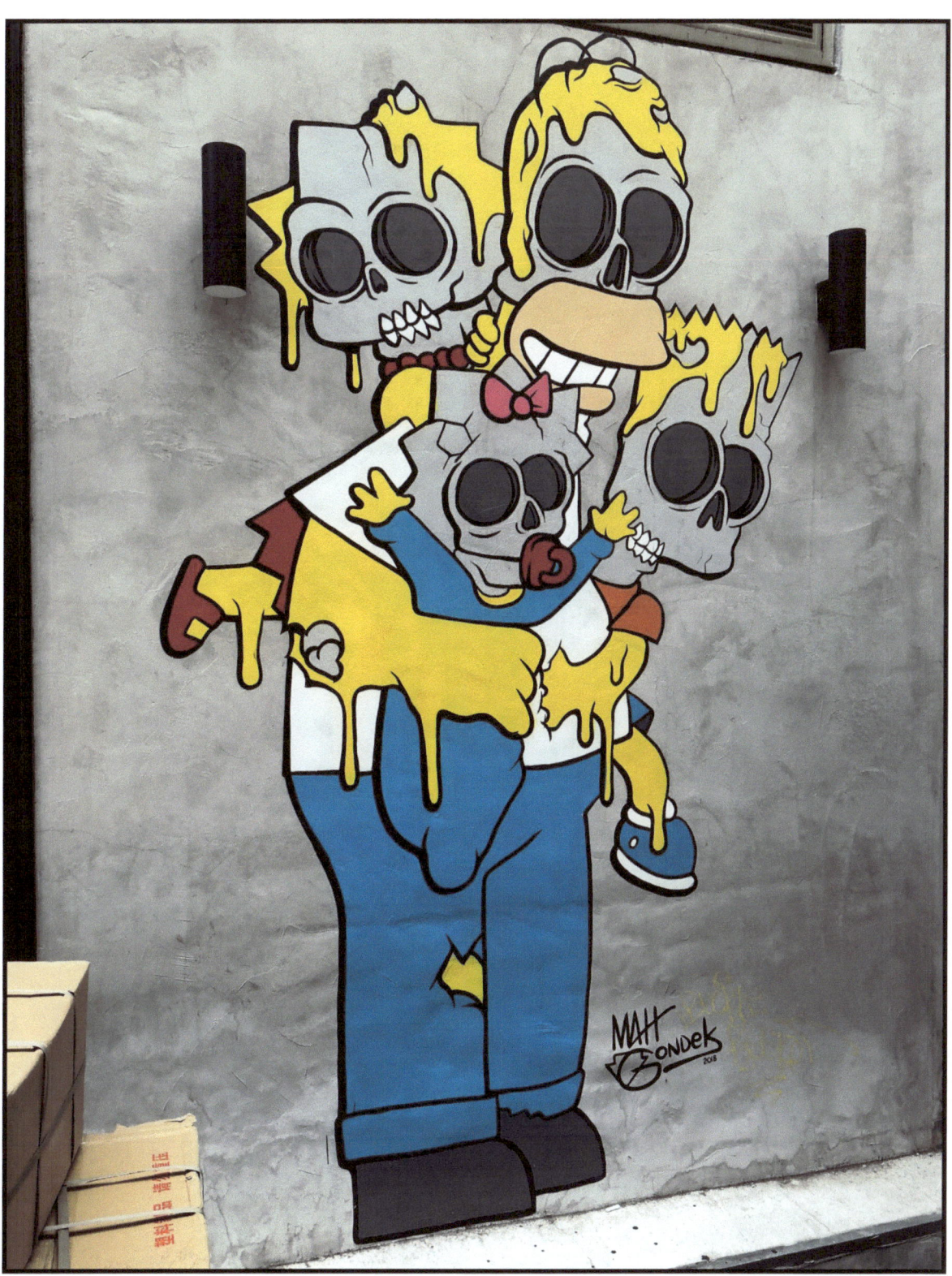

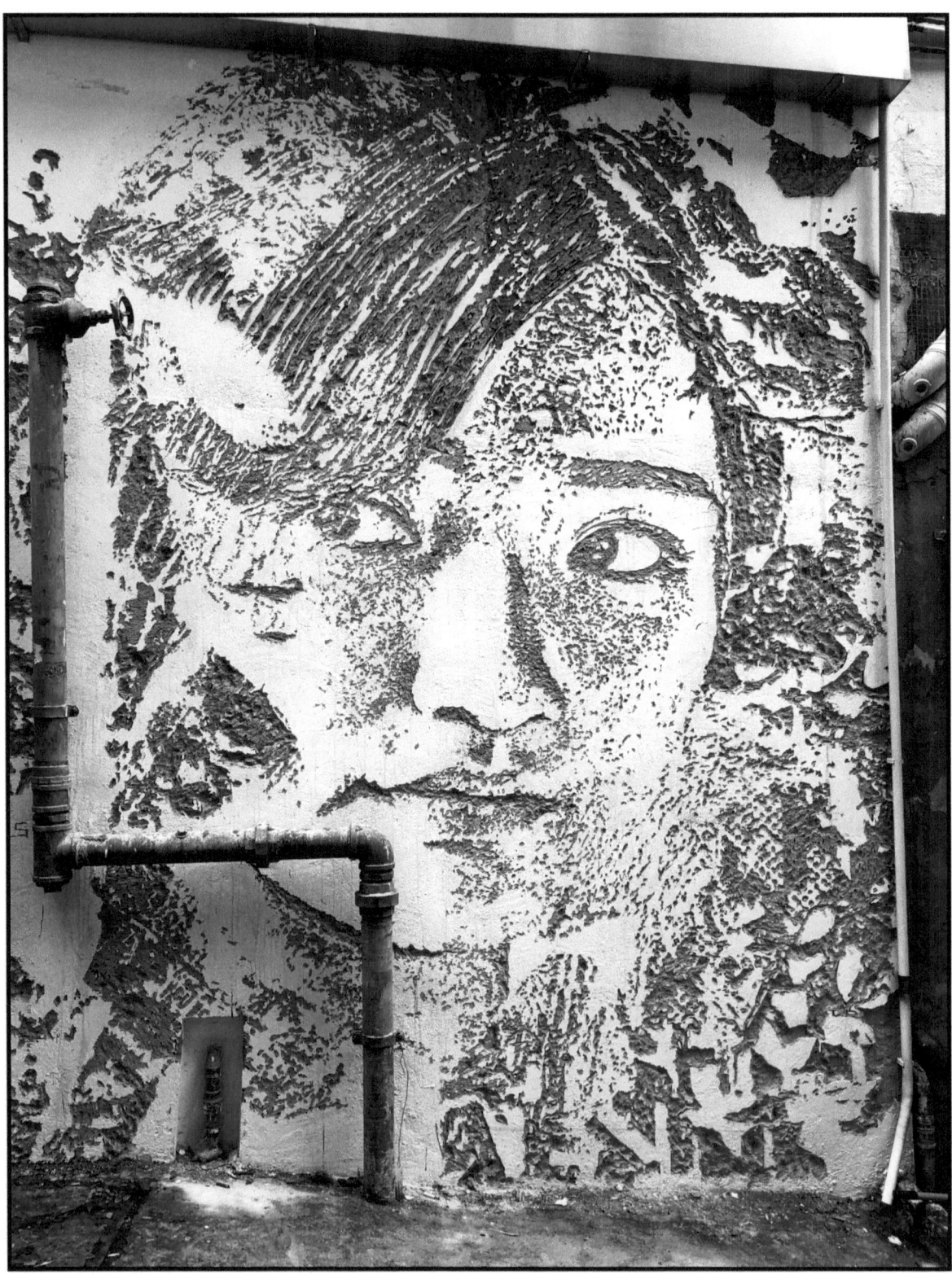

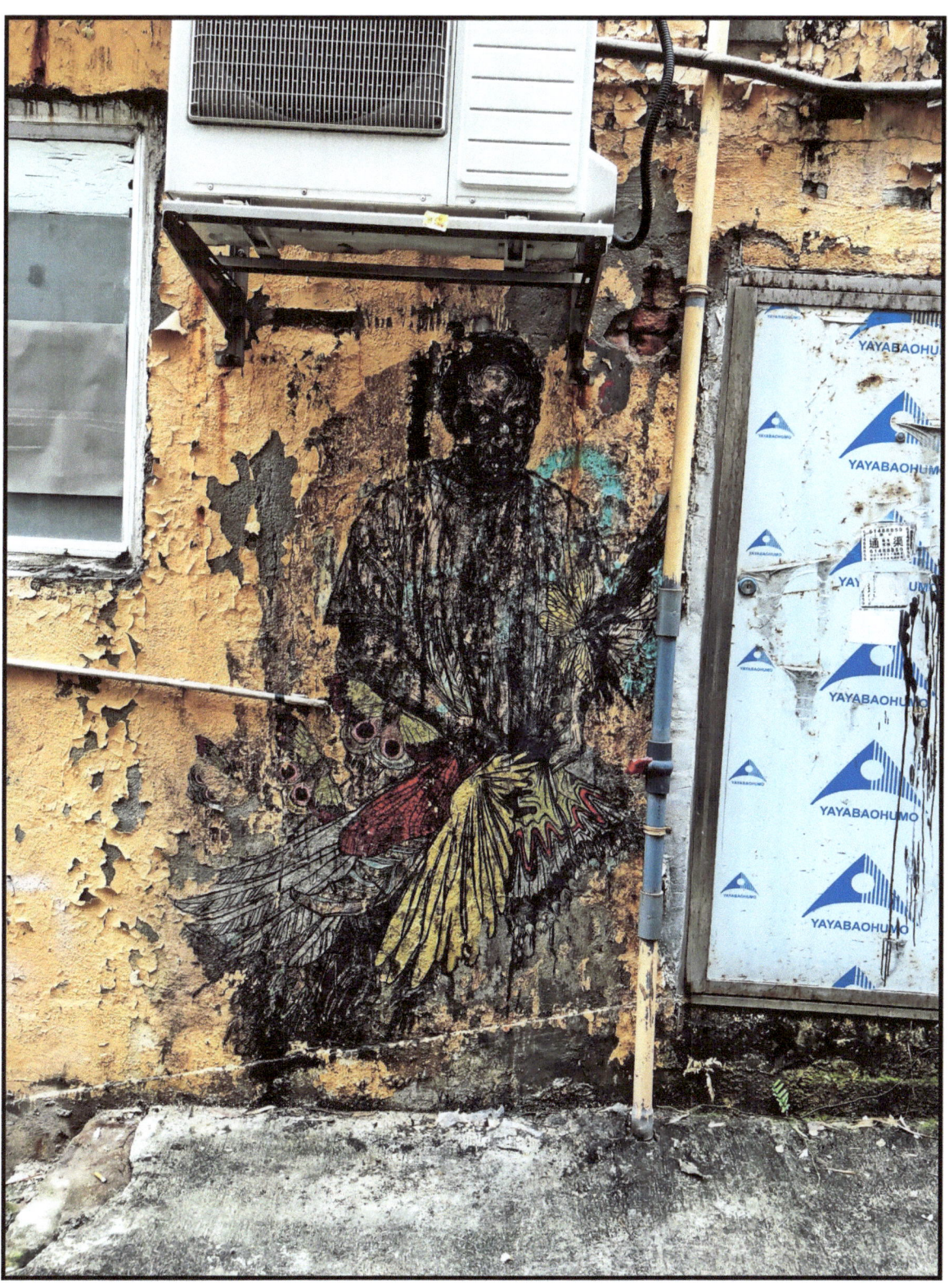

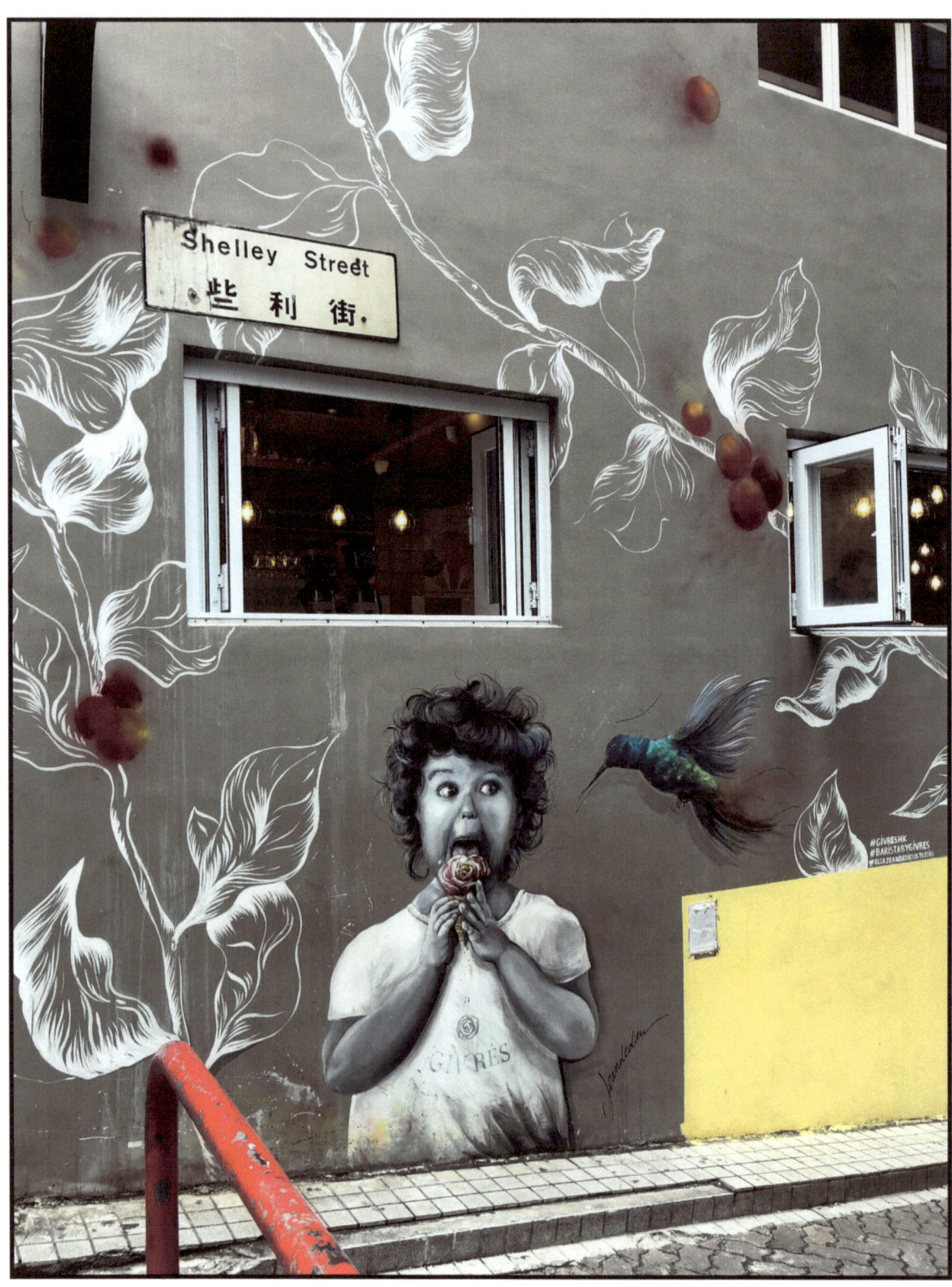

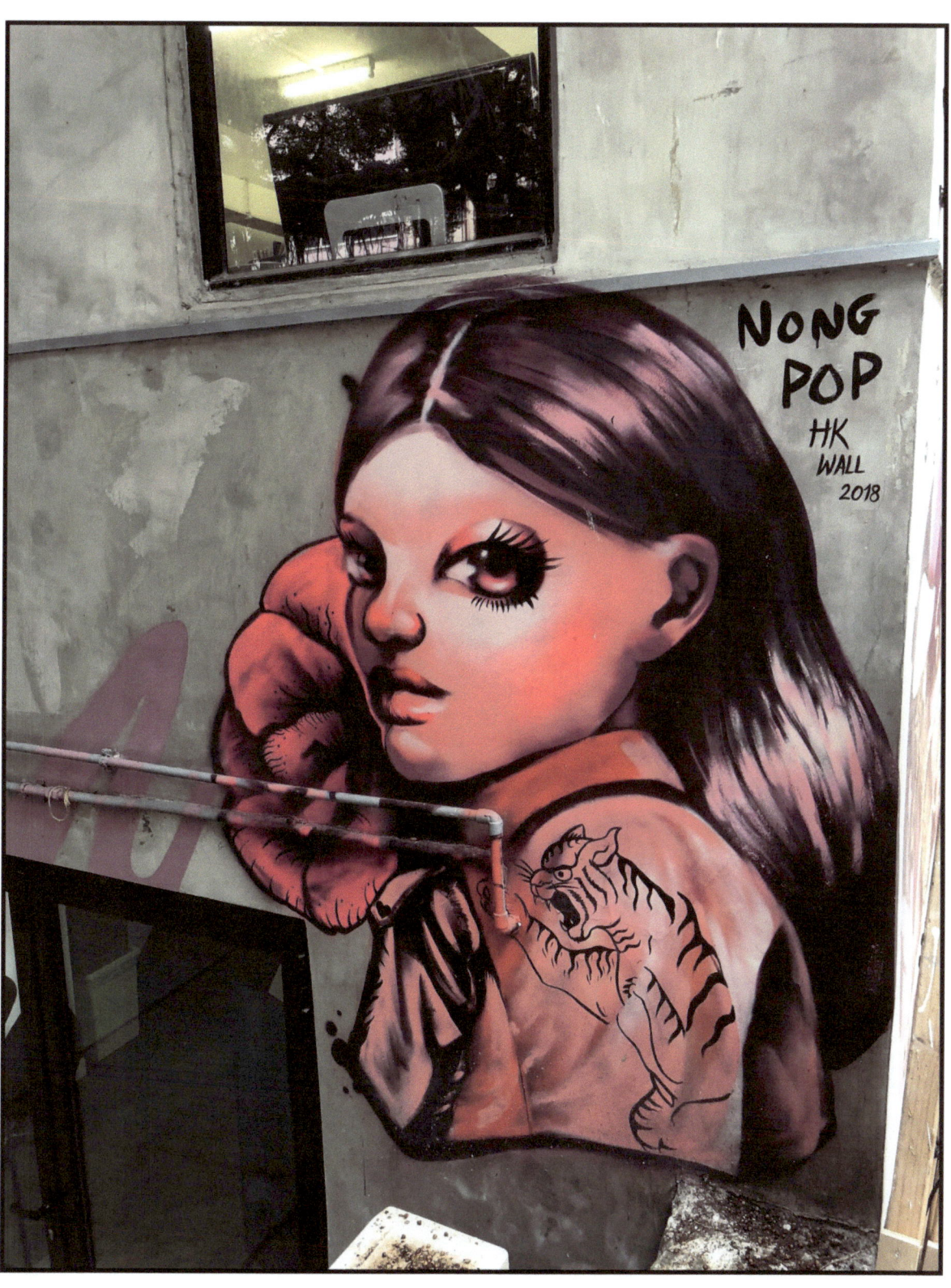

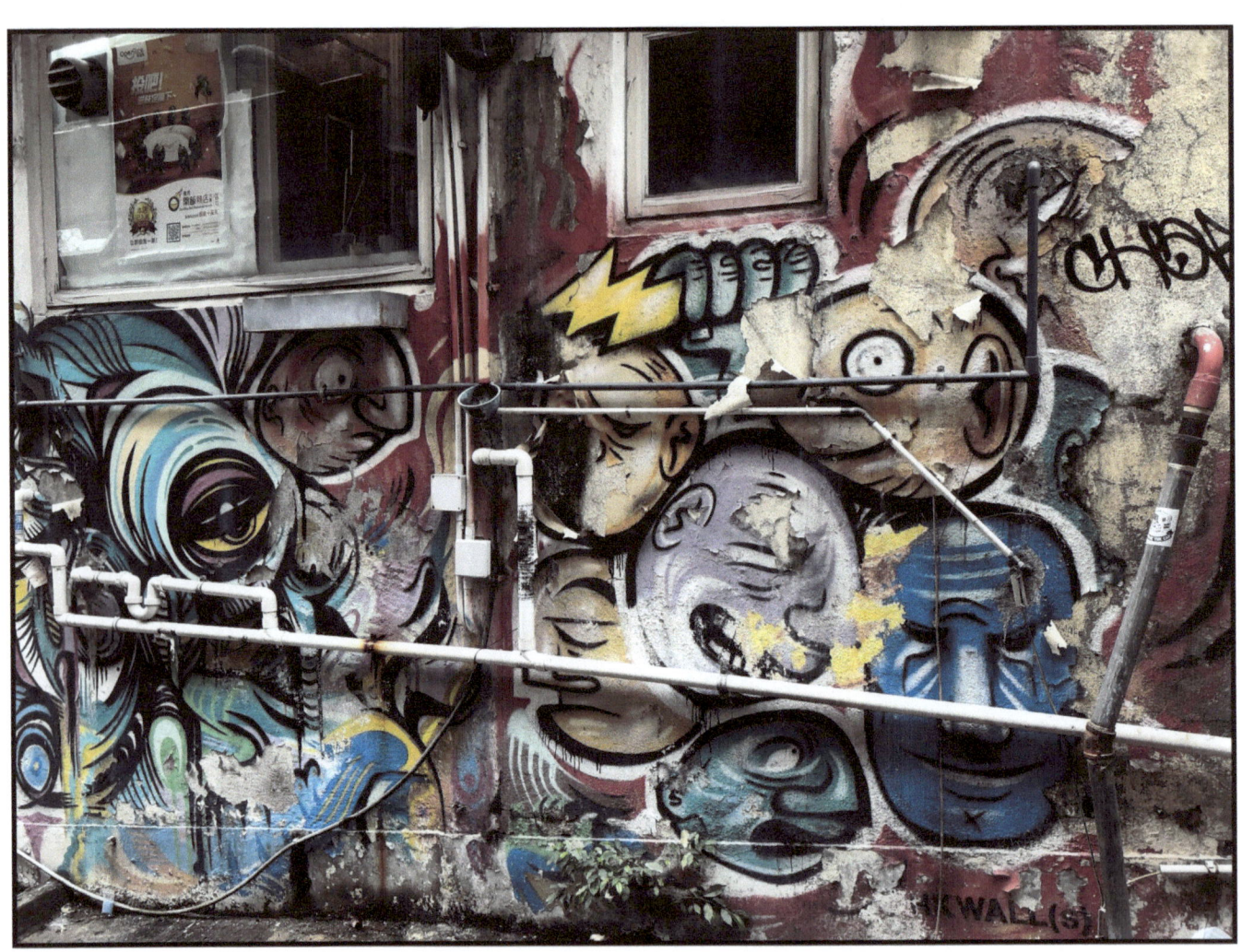

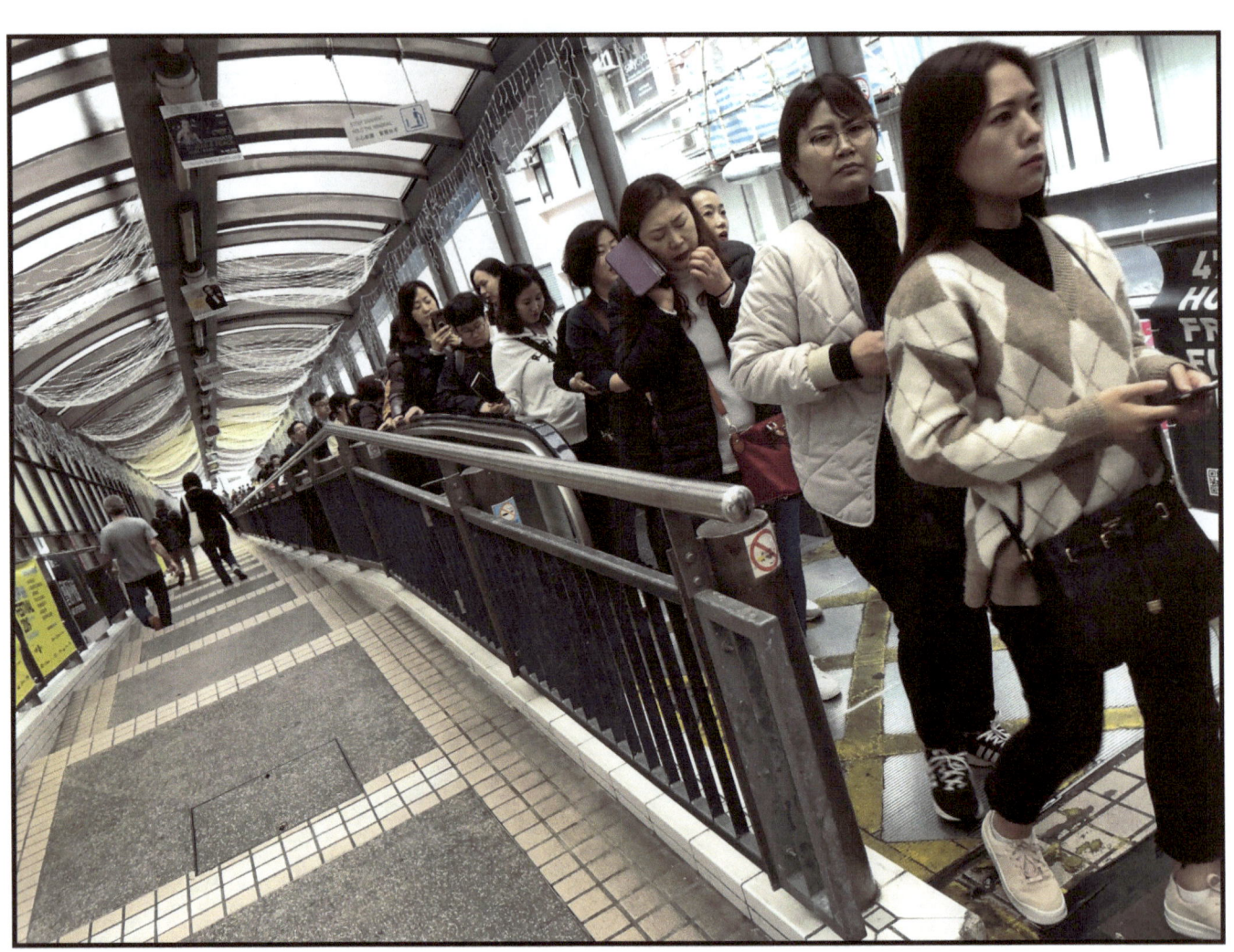

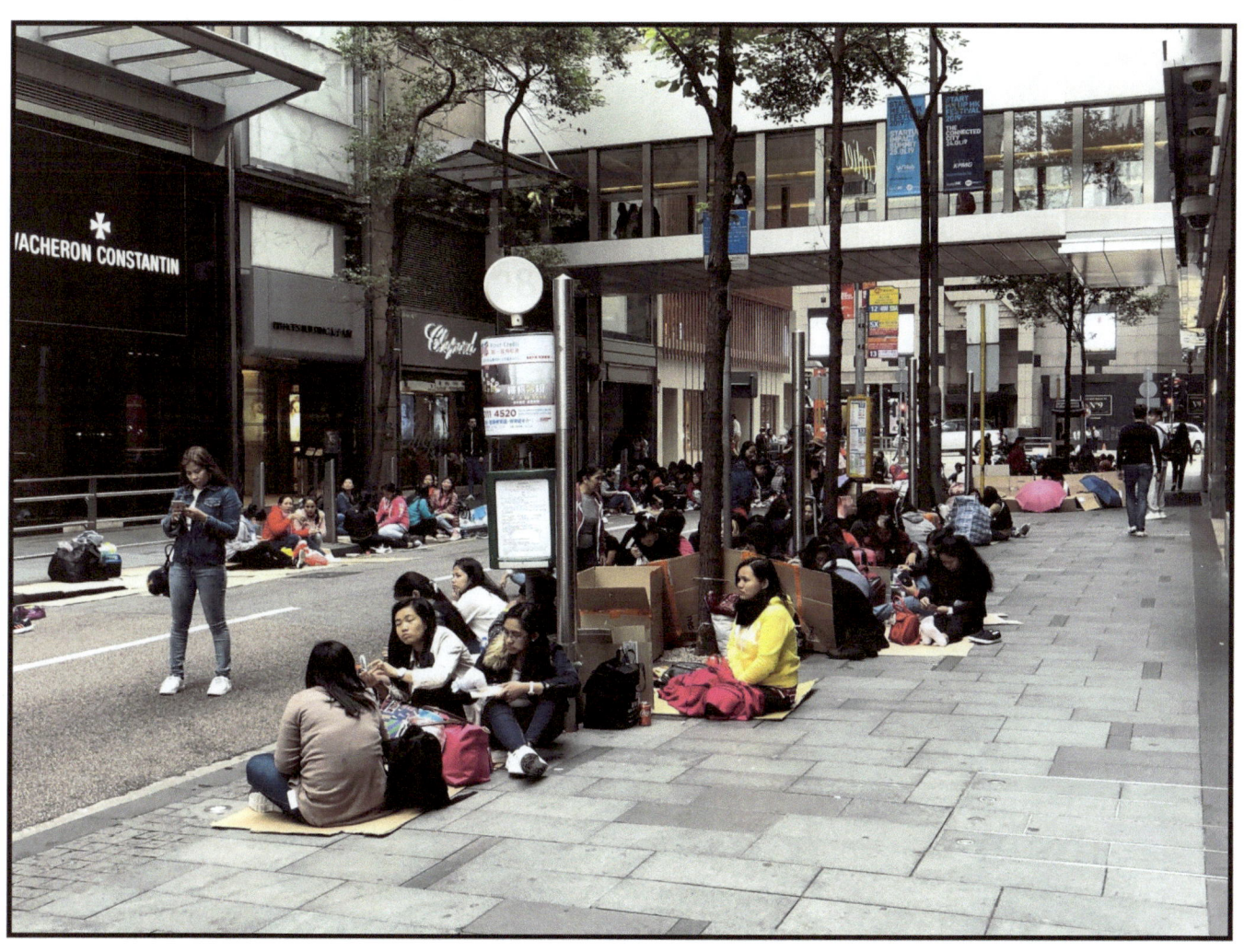

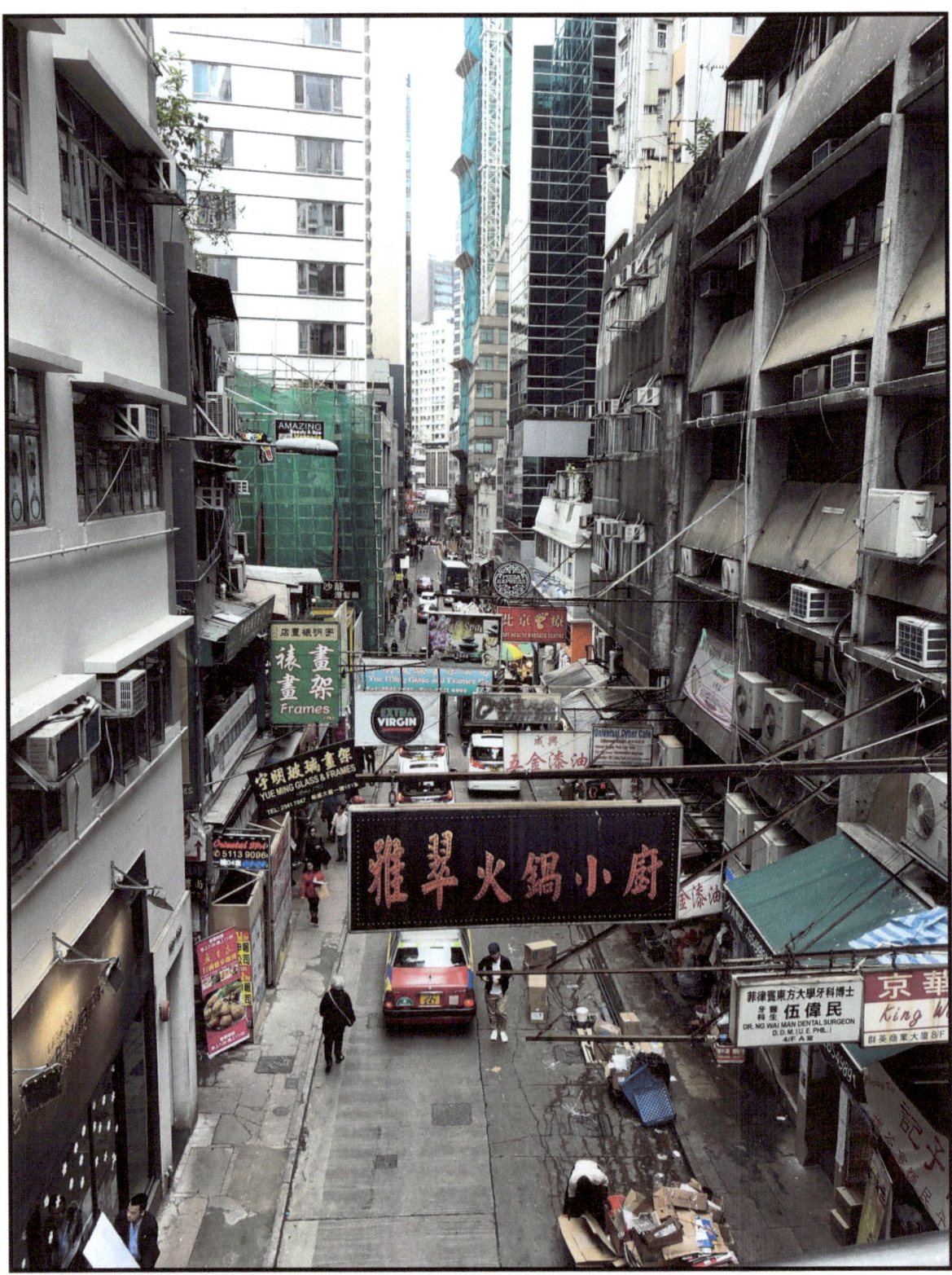

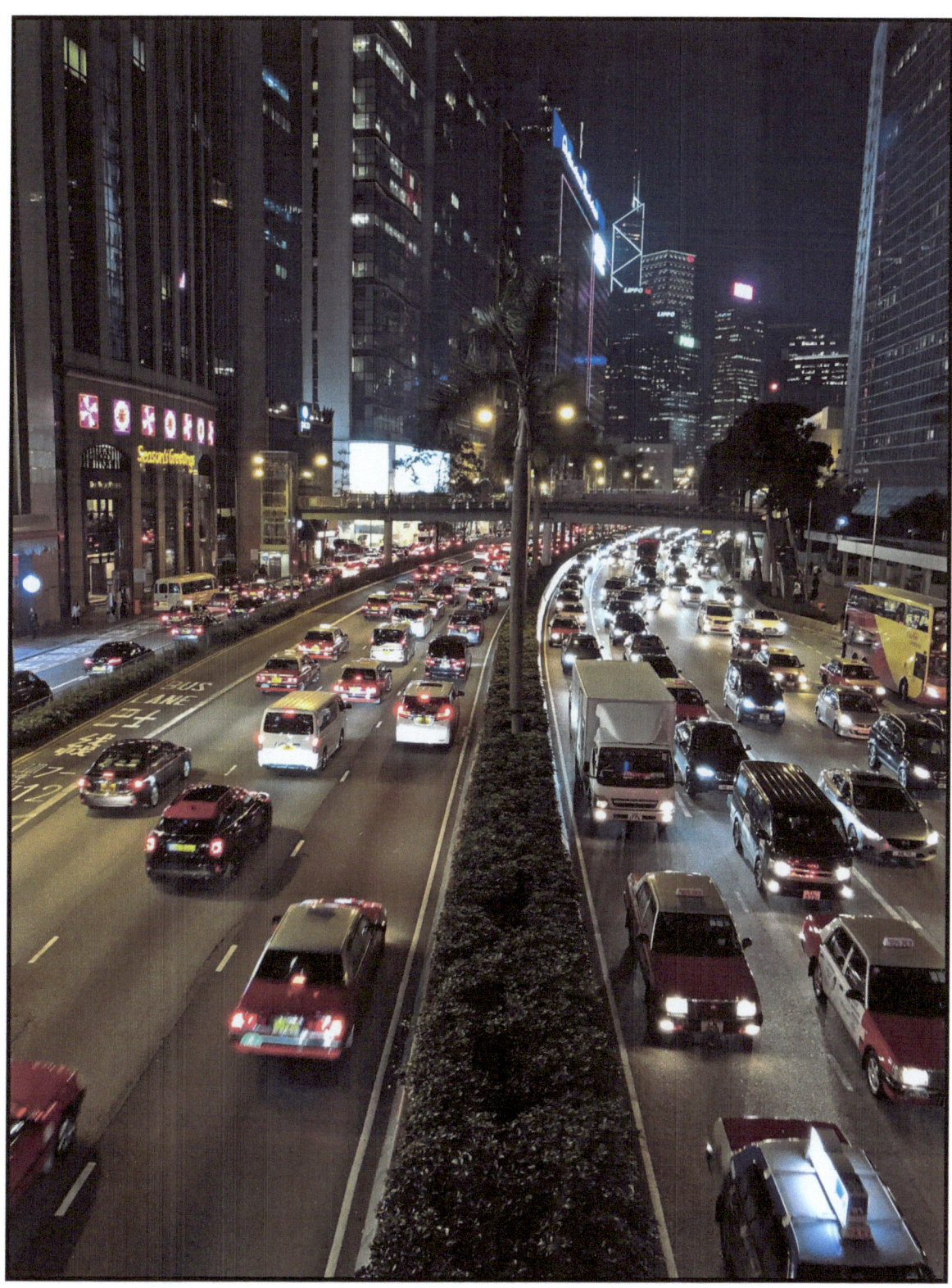

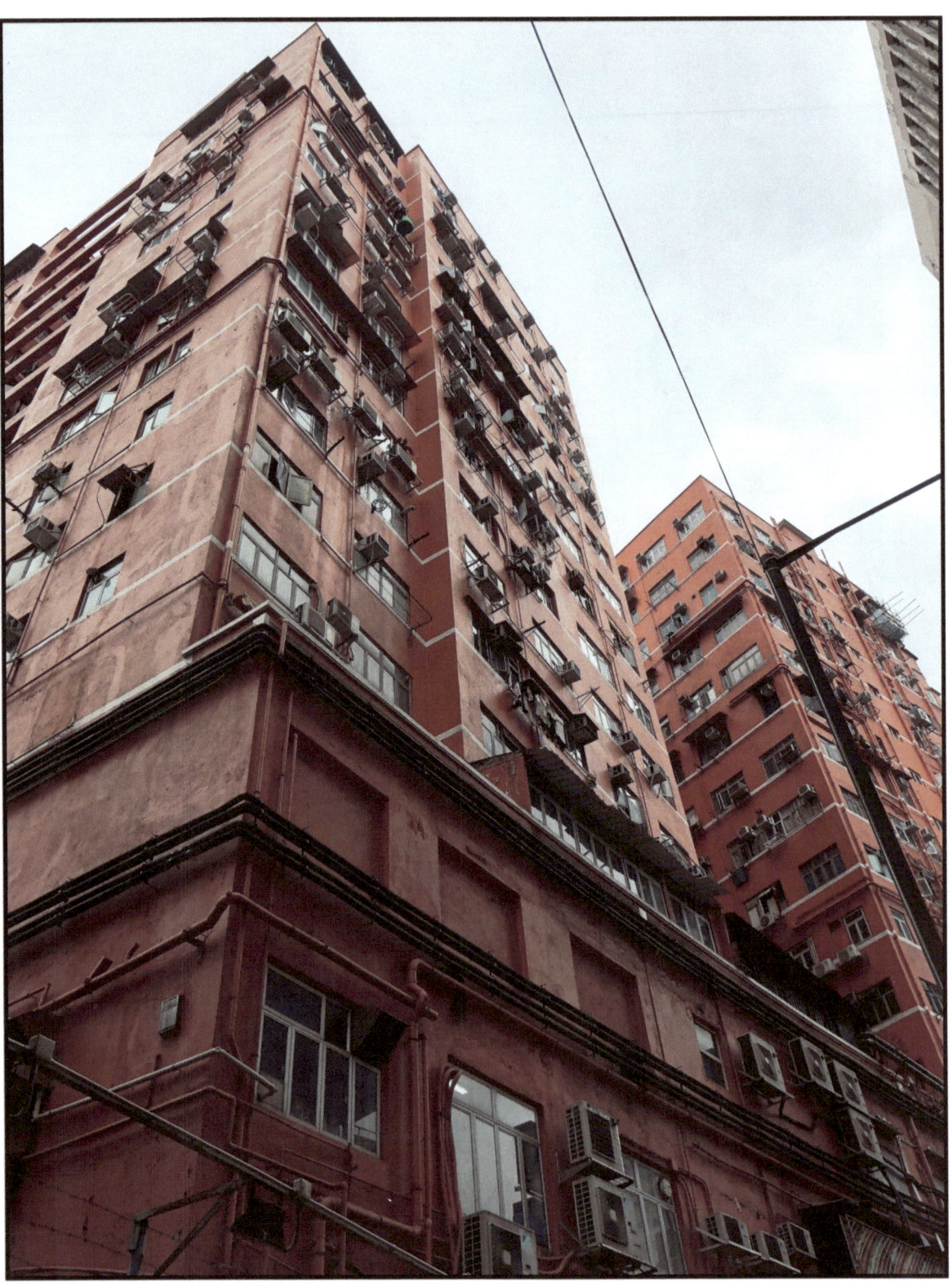

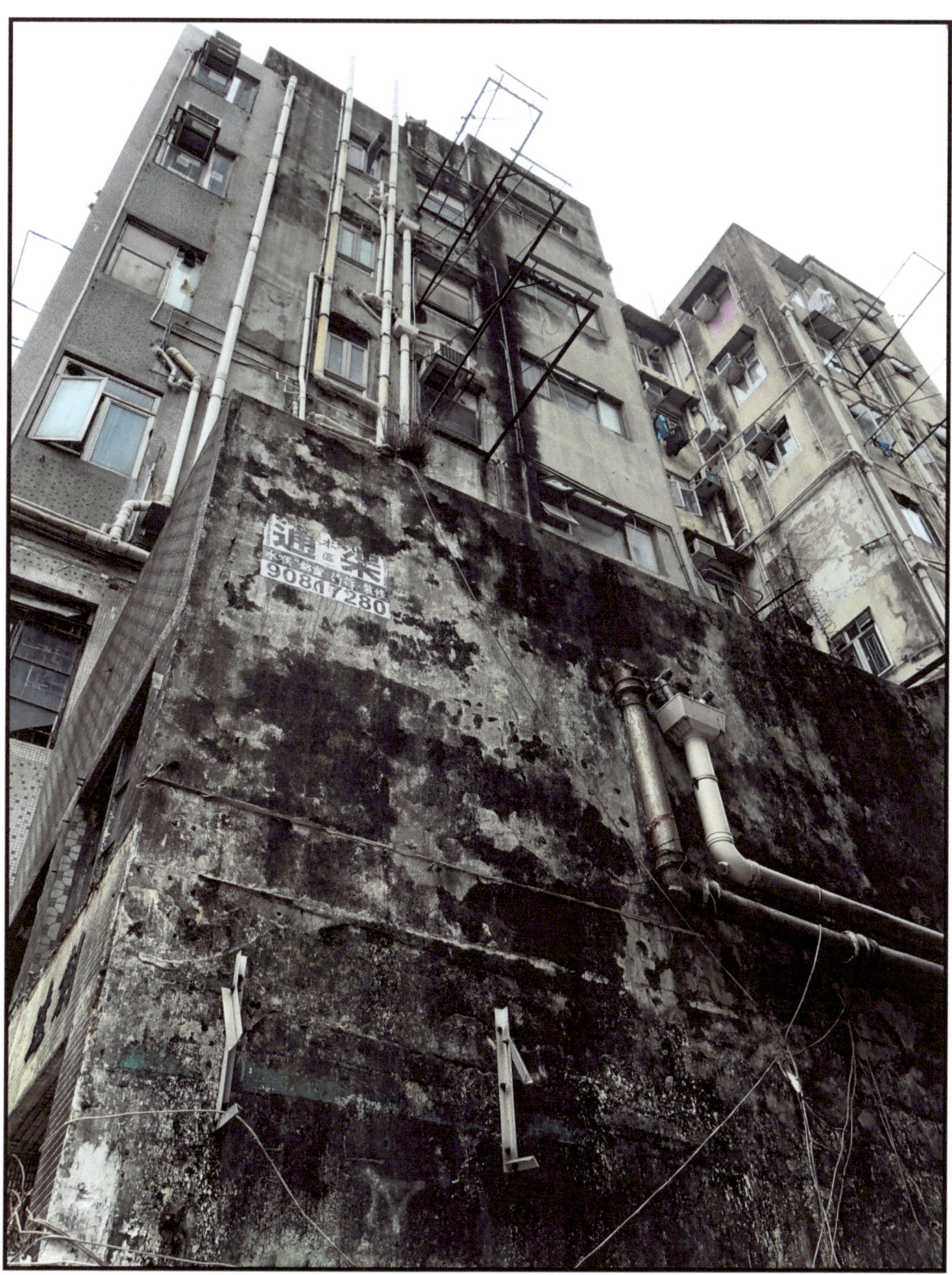

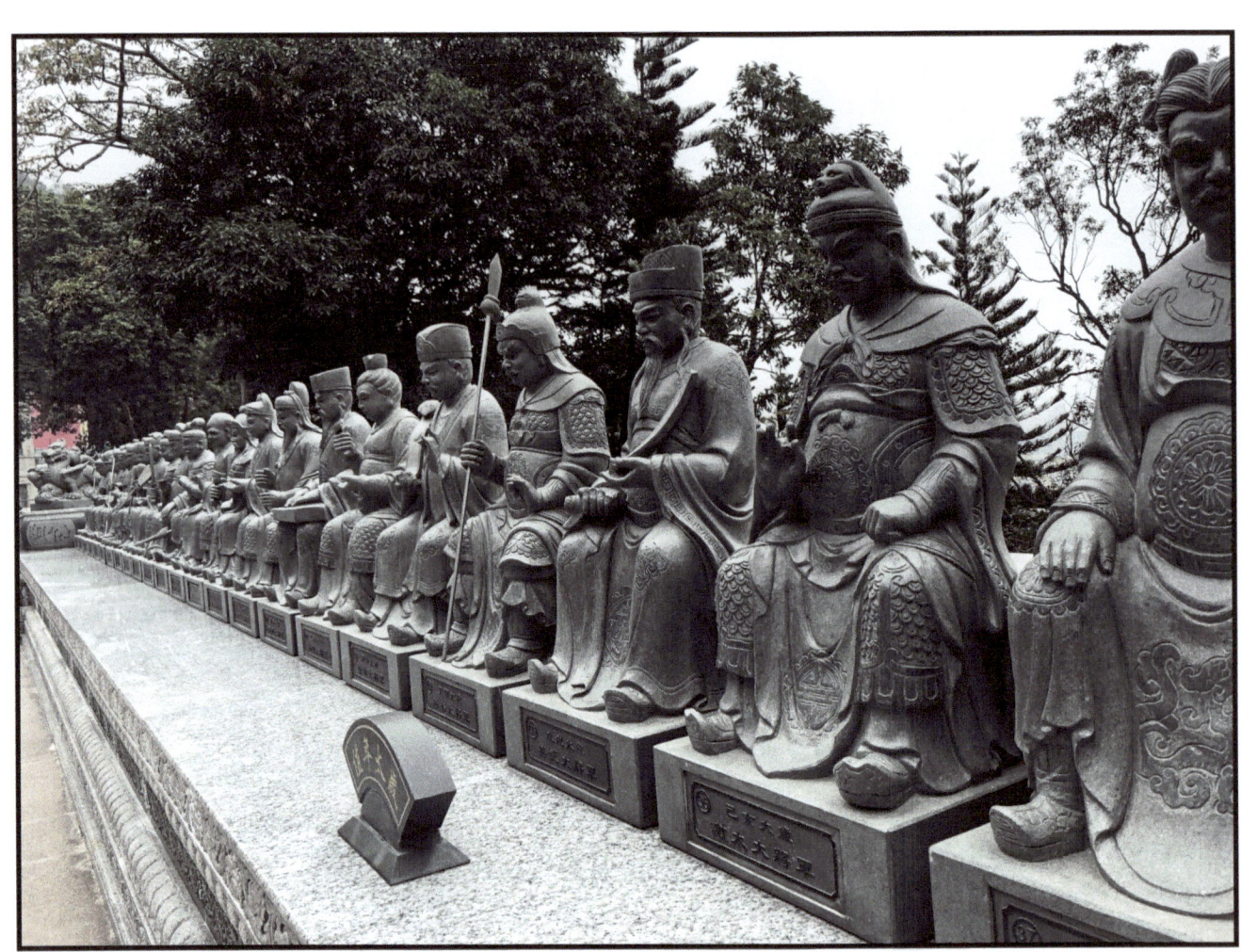

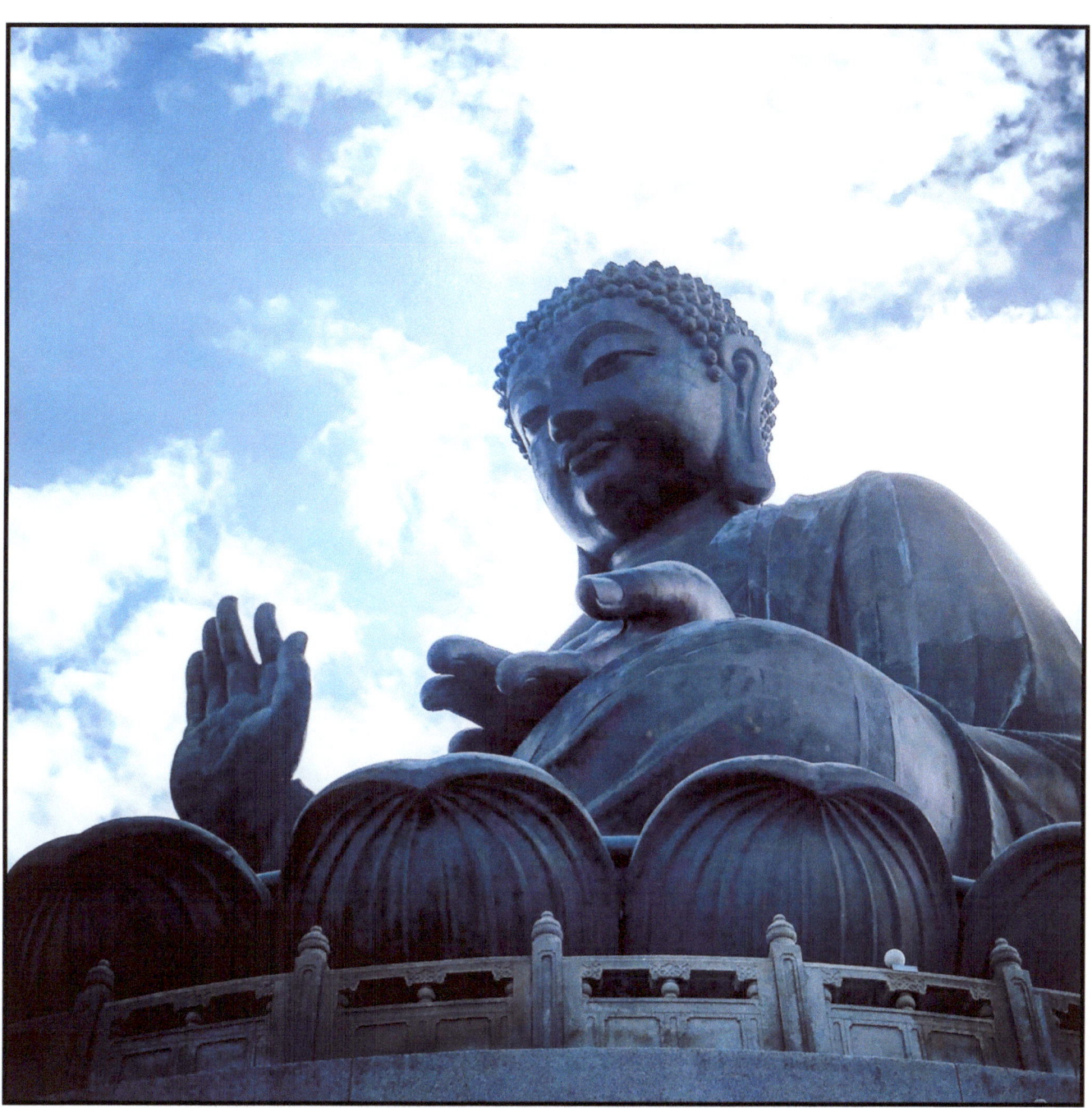

www.ingramcontent.com/pod-product-compliance
Lightning Source LLC
Chambersburg PA
CBHW051145220526
45473CB00003B/661